How Psychotherapi

How Psychotherapists Live is a landmark study of thousands of mental health practitioners worldwide. It significantly advances our understanding of psychotherapists and counselors by focusing on their individual qualities and lives, revealing the many ways they differ as persons and how those differences shape their experiences of therapeutic work.

Topics include the therapist's personal self, private life, individual beliefs, quality of life, childhood family experiences, and personal psychotherapy. Based on thirty years of research, the book is written to interest clinical practitioners while also providing researchers with a rich array of data.

Clinical psychologists, psychiatrists, clinical social workers, and counselors can easily compare their own experiences with the thousands of therapists in the study by reflecting on typologies constructed from research findings. The book will also be a valuable resource for researchers studying the sources of variation in therapists' effectiveness.

David E. Orlinsky, professor emeritus of Comparative Human Development at the University of Chicago, has made significant contributions to psychotherapy research for more than fifty years. He a founder of the international Society for Psychotherapy Research, is the author of many articles and books, and has received the International Sigmund Freud Award for Psychotherapy of the City of Vienna from the World Council for Psychotherapy, the Senior Research Career Award and the Lifetime Contribution Award of the Society for Psychotherapy Research, the Distinguished Psychologist Award of the American Psychological Association (Division 29), the Illinois Psychological Association Distinguished Contributions to the Profession of Psychology Award, and an honorary doctorate from the University of Oslo.

How Psychotherapists Live

The Personal Self and Private Life of
Professional Healers

David E. Orlinsky

Routledge
Taylor & Francis Group

NEW YORK AND LONDON

First published 2022
by Routledge
605 Third Avenue, New York, NY 10158

and by Routledge
2 Park Square, Milton Park, Abingdon, Oxon OX14 4RN

Routledge is an imprint of the Taylor & Francis Group, an informa business

Library of Congress Cataloging-in-Publication Data
A catalog record for this title has been requested

ISBN: 978-1-032-10878-0 (hbk)
ISBN: 978-1-032-10879-7 (pbk)
ISBN: 978-1-003-21757-2 (ebk)

DOI: 10.4324/9781003217572

Typeset in Bembo
by Taylor & Francis Books

This book is dedicated above all to my wife
Marcia Bourland
true love of my life, whose constant support made this
book possible;
and the deep-life ever-friends of my boyhood, youth,
maturity, and age
who shared, inspired, sustained:
Victor René Besso (1936–2021)
Kenneth Irwin Howard (1932–2000)
and Michael Helge Rønnestad

Contents

Figures

Acknowledgments

This book is based on research conducted by the Society for Psychotherapy Research (SPR) Collaborative Research Network'

Principals 2005–2020

David E. Orlinsky (University of Chicago, USA)
Michael Helge Rønnestad (University of Oslo, Norway)
Ulrike Willutzki (University of Witten/Herdecke, Germany)
Armin Hartmann (University of Freiburg, Germany)
Thomas Schröder (University of Nottingham, UK)
Margot J. Schofield (La Trobe University, Melbourne, Australia)

Main Co-workers 2005–2020

Poornima Bhola (National Institute of Mental Health and Neuro Sciences, Bangalore, India)
Gilles DeLisle (Université de Sherbrooke, Québec, Canada)
Erkki Heinonen (University of Oslo, Norway)
Shveta Kumaria (Smith College School of Social Work, Northampton, MA)
Helene A. Nissen-Lie (University of Oslo, Norway)
Hadas Wiseman (University of Haifa, Israel)

Preface

I was the first reader of this book, and indeed wrote it specifically to learn what it (or the data studied in it) would have to say. I also wrote it as a birthday present to myself, as a gift to my colleagues in psychotherapy research—especially longtime friends and co-workers in the SPR Collaborative Research Network[1]—and as a gift to psychotherapists everywhere (including the 12,000 who participated in our study) who consistently proved to be thoughtful, likeable, and fascinating persons.

My colleagues in the Collaborative Research Network (CRN) and I had been collecting personal information about psychotherapists in countries on every continent for three decades, using the quasi-interview style of quantitative survey instrument we had designed and called the Development of Psychotherapists Common Core Questionnaire (DPCCQ). However, till now we had mainly focused primarily on psychotherapists' *professional* activities, experiences and development (e.g., Orlinsky and Rønnestad, 2005). The rich data on psychotherapists as *persons* collected with the DPCCQ had been used so far largely to describe our research sample but was otherwise largely bypassed. Yet to me, data on psychotherapists as *persons* promised to be the most interesting of all, and my desire to know what would be found finally could no longer be denied.

After years when the work schedules, private lives, and health of colleagues made them unavailable, I realized as my 83rd birthday approached that if I really wanted to know what stories the personal data about therapists could tell, I would have to take the plunge and analyze, interpret, and present their personal data largely on my own. In the words of a wise historian, 'No one is going to write a book that will not interest some others; least of all to write a book that does not interest himself'(Taylor, 1961). Now as my 85th birthday passes, having abundantly satisfied my own curiosity, I am glad to share the results of this work with others whom I think will also be interested to know the results—fellow (and sister) psychotherapists and psychotherapy researchers.

Fortunately, I did not have to do this work entirely on my own. My close friends and longtime colleagues, Prof. Helge Rønnestad (University of Oslo) and Prof. Armin Hartmann (University of Freiburg), helpfully read and commented on most chapters of the book as my work on them progressed. Other close friends and colleagues, Prof. Ulrike Willutzki (Witten/Herdecke University), Prof. Thomas Schröder (Nottingham University), and Prof. Erkki Heinonen

(University of Oslo) read and commented on specific chapters. Prof. Heinonen also provided valuable bibliographic help.

In fact, this book could not have been written at all without the long-term contributions of these deeply valued friends, and others in the long list of contributors who since 1989 worked to design the DPCCQ, translate it into many languages, collect data among practicing psychotherapists in their own countries, and joined in one or another of many specific studies that have been published over the years. Their names and affiliations are listed both in the current volume and in its predecessor (Orlinsky and Rønnestad, 2005). In the present work, colleagues whose past collaborations are most relevant for each chapter are named after "with" in that chapter's author list. With the presumptuousness (or perhaps arrogance) of the very old, I have taken it to myself to be their spokesman; with the self-doubt (or perhaps humbleness) of the very old, I take full responsibility for the flaws and limitations of this work, and hope my colleagues see themselves only in its strengths.

Chicago, Illinois
July, 2021

Note

1 SPR is the acronym for the international Society for Psychotherapy Research; information about the organization can be found at www.psychotherapyresearch.org.

References

Orlinsky, D. E, and Rønnestad, M. H. (2005). *How psychotherapists develop: A study of therapeutic work and professional growth.* Washington, DC: American Psychological Association.

Taylor, A. J. P. (1961). *The origins of the Second World War.* Greenwich, CT: Fawcett Publications.

1 Psychotherapists as Persons

D. E. Orlinsky

"Psychotherapists Look Into the Mirror"[1]

How Psychotherapists Live is a study of psychotherapists living their lives away from the office, clinic, or hospital ward—focusing on therapists as persons "at home" in their own lives rather than as professionals at work. *How Psychotherapists Live* is an exploratory study, driven by curiosity to know more about who we psychotherapists are just as ourselves, a somewhat motley gathering of interesting individuals drawn to practice in a still multiform profession. This exploratory study was guided by a broad conceptual map in which details would be filled in as we progressed, rather than by a specific theory or set of hypotheses—and the ground explored was initially the shared experiences and reflections of a group of international colleagues with diverse therapeutic approaches asking how psychotherapists develop. In *How Psychotherapists Live*, that ground has expanded, after 30 years of asking questions, to include the experiences and reflections of approximately 12,000 therapist colleagues in countries around the world.

How Psychotherapists Live is a continuation and extension of the study of psychotherapists' work experiences and professional growth reported some time ago in *How Psychotherapists Develop* (Orlinsky & Rønnestad, 2005). Now, drawing on even more data, the book in hand adds a wider perspective, by focusing on the *personal* lives of psychotherapists—their self-experience, intimate relationships, belief-value patterns, and quality of life; and a deeper perspective, by exploring therapists' family backgrounds, formative childhood experiences, and their apparent effects on their current adult lives. The result is a collective family self-portrait of psychotherapists as they are, just as persons themselves on their own—not engaged in their professional work or clad in their occupational role.

Why Study Psychotherapists as Persons?

Purely in human terms, psychotherapy is an intensely interesting and often personally impactful experience, dealing as it does with personally traumatic events, enduring emotional conflicts, difficult intimate relationships, and challenging moral dilemmas of personal life.[2] Given the kind of work they do, it

DOI: 10.4324/9781003217572-1

follows that psychotherapists must also be *interesting* people. It must take a special kind of person to do such work, day after day as a lifetime career. Yet how are they special, if at all? What are they like as persons that enables them to do such challenging work? Are some kinds of persons better able than others to do this work? Is there a special psychotherapeutic talent? What kind or kinds of persons feel called to learn, practice, and tolerate the kind of work that psychotherapy entails.[3] What does a psychotherapeutic vocation require of those drawn to it?

Those questions broadly define the themes addressed in this book. The answers to be presented are based on a long-term large-scale study[4] of the characteristics and experiences of approximately 12,000 psychotherapists who were surveyed over a period of 30 years. These psychotherapists represent various professions, diverse theoretical orientations, and successive career levels. Yet although this group of persons is defined by their common professional practice, this book focuses primarily on what they are like as persons. It explores the personal selves and private lives of a large number of actually practicing therapists, systematically analyzing detailed empirical data that were provided voluntarily and anonymously by therapists about themselves.

Is This Book for You?

How Psychotherapists Live is addressed to everyone who may be interested in the kinds of people who become psychotherapists. Most narrowly, it is for fellow psychotherapist-researchers who are currently trying to understand what qualities enable some therapists to be successful with patients more than others (known as the "therapist effect"[5]). For these researchers, there are statistical analyses of many variables (sequestered at the book's end for the convenience of non-research readers); a review of other studies that used the *Development of Psychotherapists Common Core Questionnaire* (DPCCQ) as a research instrument in Chapter 11; and references in each chapter's notes to recent and relevant studies related to the topics covered in the book.

More broadly, *How Psychotherapists Live* should appeal to many of the same readers to whom the reviewer of *How Psychotherapists Develop* had recommended it (Kobos, 2005): "Practicing therapists will learn something about their own individual development and how they compare with others." "Researchers with an interest in personal and professional growth … will find much to stimulate their professional interests." "Teachers and supervisors of psychotherapists will be stimulated …." and "Students will know more about the stressful and healthy ways to cope with a demanding professional craft."

A Wavering Research Tradition

How Psychotherapists Live is the latest addition to a rather unsteady tradition of intermittent research on psychotherapists *per se*. The trickle of studies in this tradition was foreshadowed in an early and still valuable discussion of "The self-experience of the psychotherapist" (Wyatt, 1948). Three notable empirical studies appeared in the following decade, two focused on selection and training of therapists (Holt & Luborsky, 1958; Kelley & Fiske, 1951) and the other focused on the practical impact of psychotherapists' personal therapy or analysis (Strupp, 1955).

Next to no research on psychotherapists appeared in the 1960s—the one exception found being an article comparing psychotherapists and shamanic healers but also citing preliminary data from an ongoing study of the former (Henry, 1966). That ongoing study[6] resulted a few years later in the publication of two now-classic volumes: *The Fifth Profession: Becoming a Psychotherapist* (Henry, Sims & Spray, 1971) and *Public and Private Lives of Psychotherapists* (Henry, Sims & Spray, 1973). With a groundbreaking sample of more than 3,900 psychiatrists, psychoanalysts, clinical psychologists and clinical social workers located in New York City, Chicago and Los Angeles, the first volume argued persuasively that these four basically represented a single common ("fifth") profession of *Psychotherapist*. The practical possibilities of that idea were also discussed at the time by a number of leading thinkers (cf. Holt, 1971).[7]

However it was the second volume, *Public and Private Lives of Psychotherapists*, that has the greatest overlap with *How Psychotherapists Live*, and is most central to the tradition of research pursued fifty years later in the present book. Despite the accumulation of other valuable studies (e.g., Skovholt & Rønnestad, 1992), nothing of comparable scope can be cited until now. Two major advances of the present study can be claimed: the book in hand is based on about three times as many therapists as the earlier work, and the therapists in the present study are drawn from a wide range of countries—the USA, UK, Norway, Germany, Australia, Canada, Denmark, China, South Korea, and more—rather than just the USA. Also, while many similar aspects of therapists' lives are covered (to be noted where relevant), the conceptual perspectives differ. Henry and colleagues were social-and-personality psychologists and their main interest was the study of occupational groups (e.g., Henry, 1954), not professional and research psychotherapists (as are the contributors to this book), thus tending to ask different research questions.

Again there was a pause of nearly a decade before interest in studying psychotherapists was renewed. A chapter of research on the psychotherapist's experiences during psychotherapy sessions appeared (Orlinsky & Howard, 1977). Another study presented data on the personalities of effective psychotherapists (Dent & Furse, 1978). Soon thereafter, Norcross and Prochaska (1982, 1983) and Prochaska and Norcross (1983) launched a prodigious series of studies of clinical psychologists in the USA that has been intermittently updated in the 1980s (e.g., Norcross, Prochaska & Gallagher, 1989a; Norcross, Prochaska & Gallagher, 1989b; Norcross & Wogan, 1983), the 1990s (e.g., Norcross, Dryden & Brust, 1992; Norcross, Farber & Prochaska, 1993; Norcross, Karg & Prochaska, 1997a, 1997b), the 2000s (e.g., Norcross, Hedges & Castle, 2002; Norcross, Karpiak & Santoro, 2005), and the 2010s (e.g., Norcross & Karpiak, 2012; Norcross, Nolan, Kosman & Fernández-Alvarez, 2017).

The interest in psychotherapists has largely persisted since the 1980s, although research productivity was still intermittent. A well-received review of research and clinical discussion concerning *The Personal Life of the Psychotherapist* (Guy, 1989) stimulated interest within the profession, although (and perhaps because) it focused on "the impact of clinical practice on the therapist's intimate relationships and emotional well-being." Important studies of psychotherapists' experiences of satisfaction, stress and burnout began to appear (e.g., Deutsch, 1984; Farber, 1983; Farber & Heifetz, 1981; Guy, Poelstra & Stark, 1989). Another specific topic concerned the psychotherapist's personal psychotherapy (Deutsch, 1985; MacDevitt, 1987; McNamara, 1986; Norcross, Strausser & Missar, 1988; Pope & Tabachnik, 1994). Following on these a decade later, *The Psychotherapist's Own Psychotherapy* (Geller, Norcross & Orlinsky, 2005) presented a definitive volume of research, personal histories and essays.

This brief and necessarily selective sketch has been offered here to indicate the historical origins and context of research on psychotherapists, and breaks off around the time that the present study was launched. However, it is impossible to proceed without mention of another major research project that also began in the late 1980s: the landmark study by Skovholt and Rønnestad (1992) presented in *The Evolving Professional Self: Stages and Themes in Therapist and Counselor Development*—extended and updated two decades later (Rønnestad & Skovholt, 2013). Based on qualitative analyses of interviews with 100 Minnesota psychotherapists and counselors, divided in groups of 20 to reflect successive career cohorts, this study advanced a sophisticated theoretical model proposed by Rønnestad & Skovholt (1991). It was through learning about each other's ongoing studies that Orlinsky and Rønnestad became personally acquainted, and the latter also became a key member of the Society for Psychotherapy Research (SPR) Collaborative Research Network.

Clearly there must have been "something in the air" in the mid and late 1980s, some shift in the *zeitgeist* of psychotherapy, that made psychotherapists and their development more salient in the minds of researchers. Previously almost all scientific attention in the field had focused on therapeutic procedures, the "techniques" that therapists used (e.g., "interpretation" or "accurate empathy"), the processes that evolved in therapy from their use (e.g., "insight" or "self-acceptance"), and their impact on the patient's mental and emotional condition (i.e., "outcome"). In many ways this model still largely persists, based on the assumption (imported from biological medicine) that the "curative effect" of psychotherapy derives from effective treatment procedures correctly applied to specific disorders. In this highly sanitized "laboratory" model, physician-therapists are viewed as well-trained administrators of the therapeutic procedure, with all other personal and professional characteristics an irrelevance; and they are essentially interchangeable.[8]

The shift away from this concept of psychotherapy in the 1980s can be traced in large part to a dyadic view of psychotherapy as a working alliance between patient and psychotherapist, first formulated for researchers by Bordin (1979)[9] and made "operational" with research instruments designed by

Horvath (e.g., Horvath & Greenberg, 1986), Luborsky (e.g., Luborsky, Crits-Christoph, Alexander, et al., 1983) and Marmar and colleagues (e.g., Marmar, Horowitz, Weiss & Marziali, 1986). Research on the therapeutic alliance *per se* (bond, relationship, etc.) has continued unabated and with great success ever since (e.g., Norcross, 2002; Norcross & Wampold, 2019). But it also had the indirect consequence—important in the present context—of including the psychotherapist as a participant and partner in the alliance. The camel's nose had sneaked under the tent, and in the words of an old Arabian proverb: "If the *camel* once gets his *nose* in the *tent*, his body will soon follow." Conceptually, it was now easier for researchers to think of psychotherapists *per se* as active contributors to the process and outcome of psychotherapy—and, by extension, to be concerned with the processes and conditions of psychotherapists' development.

The SPR Collaborative Research Network Study of Psychotherapists

This general sense about psychotherapists was already afloat in the research culture when a number of international colleagues gathered at a meeting of the Society for Psychotherapy Research (SPR) in Bern Switzerland in the autumn of 1989. Discovering their shared interest in the development of psychotherapists—as researchers, trainers and clinical supervisors—these colleagues chose to form a Collaborative Research Network (CRN) within SPR (i.e., the SPR/CRN), and to join their individual resources to conduct an International Study of the Development of Psychotherapists (ISDP).[10] Having a common interest and our own computers, joining individual resources allowed the group to bypass the lengthy and often unsuccessful process of applying for research grants (Orlinsky, 1987).[11]

Our Research Instrument

As its first challenge, the new SPR/CRN team devoted the year and a half (from 1989 through 1990) to creating the initial version of the *Development of Psychotherapists Common Core Questionnaire* (DPCCQ) concurrently in English, French and German language versions with other translations in following years. Although modified and augmented over subsequent years, the initial version consisted of 392 items, mostly designed as quantitative structured-response scales or checklists, divided into ten sections covering diverse topics (see Orlinsky, Ambühl, Rønnestad, et al., 1999; Orlinsky & Rønnestad, 2005, Chapter 2).

The unusual length of the DPCCQ was determined partly by the need for a richly detailed description of the therapists who participated, as no universally accepted definition of who psychotherapists are could be found. The sets of DPCCQ items focusing primarily on therapists' occupational characteristics, work experiences and professional growth were previously analyzed and reported in *How Psychotherapists Develop* (Orlinsky & Rønnestad, 2005), and have been reanalyzed with a much larger sample as described in Chapter 10 of the present book. The present book, *How Psychotherapists Live*, explores the sets of DPCCQ items reflecting therapists' personal characteristics, qualities and life experiences. Specific items from those sets will be introduced as they are used in various chapters of this book.

Overall, the basic idea guiding construction of the DPCCQ was to make it resemble an interview between interested therapist-colleagues by asking all the questions for getting to know who our colleagues are that seemed relevant to those on our diverse team, and by avoiding the sort of items that seemed to us irrelevant, inane or inept, and that we ourselves would not want to answer.[12] The process required, and was in effect, an extended exercise in virtual empathy.

Data Collection

Data collection began in the spring of 1991, most fully at the annual *Lindauer Psychotherapie Wochen* (Lindau Psychotherapy Weeks), on the Bodensee (Lake Constance) island of Lindau, using the German language DPCCQ, where a sample of nearly 1,400 was gathered.[13] These were joined with smaller preliminary samples using the English language version collected in the UK and USA, and with the French language version in France and Belgium. In subsequent years, new colleagues from many countries volunteered to collect and share substantial "opportunity samples" of locally practicing psychotherapists. Without a workable definition of the population of psychotherapists at large, the only alternative was to collect a very large and diversified set of data from individuals in different countries who self-identified as psychotherapists so much that they volunteered to participate in this study by taking a lengthy questionnaire. A detailed description of the more than 12,000 psychotherapists worldwide who have participated in the SPR/CRN study to date is presented in Chapter 2, so that readers will have an opportunity to judge how typical they are of the therapists whom they know (or who they are).[14]

Data Analysis

The strategy of data analysis followed in *How Psychotherapists Live* is systematic, exploratory, and inductive. This involved three sequential levels of analysis. As a first step, the response distributions on the scales and checklists for *specific* questionnaire items were assessed in regard to central tendency (e.g., mean, median) and variability (e.g., range, standard deviation). Examples of individual items are questions about the therapist's age, gender, marital relationship status, ratings of self in close relationships as warm, reserved, forceful, etc.

A second step consisted of factor analyzing responses to the items *within sets of related questions* (typically by Principal Components method of extraction of factors plus Varimax rotation of those with eigenvalues ≥ 1), with assessment of the resulting dimensions for reliability (internal consistency) using Cronbach's alpha statistic. For example, ratings of all the varied single item scales with which therapists described themselves in their close relationships were analyzed resulting in a reduced number of reliable multiple-item scales (see Chapter 3).

A third step could then be taken to analyze the various sets of reliable, topically coherent *within-set* dimensions in relation to one another, which could involve analyses of association or correlations of dimensions *across-sets* to ask, for example, whether therapists' early family experiences appear to affect their current quality of life (see Chapter 8). Factor analyses of other *within-set* dimensions from different items sets could also be used to explore overall patterns of therapists' qualities ("second-level" factors) and types of therapists.

An effort has been made to rely primarily on simple and familiar statistical analyses: averages, percentages, and common measures of association like correlation coefficients (r) and Chi-square (χ^2). This discovery-oriented approach involved covering many professional and personal aspects of therapists' training, practice, lives and development, and allowed for panoramic *and* in-depth data analyses. While each of the many items represents a bit of information with its own potential interest, those specific items can be analyzed in relation to a lot of other information contained in the DPCCQ.

A Guide to the Organization of this Book

The organization implicit in the sequence of chapters is this. First (in Chapter 2) the 12,000 psychotherapists whose personal lives are explored in the book are introduced with regard to their professional characteristics—the reason they were invited to participate in the study—and with respect to their demographic characteristics (age, gender, nationality, etc.).

The next four chapters survey in turn the self-experience (Chapter 3), intimate relationships (Chapter 4), belief-value patterns (Chapter 5), and quality of life (Chapter 6) of therapists as adults. The first three topics respectively represent a phenomenological-psychodynamic perspective, a psycho-social perspective, and a psycho-cultural perspective based on the schema of "system" domains defined in the General Theory of Action (e.g., Parson & Shils, 1954). The last chapter in this set takes an integrative, overall view of the satisfactions and stresses that therapists experience in their personal lives as adults, exploring how well or poorly they feel their own lives are going.

To add depth to the understanding of psychotherapists as persons, the next two chapters open a temporal "fourth dimension" by exploring the past lives of psychotherapists. The first of these focuses on the families that psychotherapists grew up in, and their formative childhood experiences while growing up (Chapter 7). The next chapter reverses perspective by examining the apparent influence or impacts of those childhood experiences on their adult lives (Chapter 8).

Finally, two chapters in the last main section return to viewing psychotherapists as persons participating in psychotherapy: first, as patients themselves in their own personal therapy, working to overcome residual conflicts and deficits from childhood and prepare themselves for the extraordinary challenges of psychotherapeutic work (Chapter 9); second, at work in their role as psychotherapist, but now being able to look beyond the therapist role to see our therapists not as role-incumbents performing their role-function but *as persons with their own past and current lives*, experiencing themselves working for other persons who have come to seek their help (Chapter 10).

These chapters run in a course defined by two polarities: a Professional/ Personal cycle, leading from Professional through the Personal back to the Professional, enriched by insight from the explorations of the Personal; and within the Personal phase, a Present/Past cycle, leading from Present through the Past back to the Present, enriched by insight from explorations of the Past. The author isn't clever enough to have made that a conscious design; but after writing, editing, rewriting, and editing again, that was what had emerged—a welcome gift of the creative Preconscious.[15]

Two Last Words

First, an important word to readers about the research strategy underlying the book. This is a systematic exploratory study, inspired by experience-informed curiosity and a long-growing personal/professional desire to better know who psychotherapists are without specific hypotheses or particular psychotherapeutic theories. To conduct this exploration systematically, topics in successive chapters are analyzed both on their merit and with regard to the findings of preceding chapters, resulting in an evolving accumulation of information. If not recognized for what it is, this intentional strategy may create an impression of repetitiveness and irksome detail for some readers. The research journey is often a plodding one, but the journey's end can be one that enlightens.

Last, a final word to researchers: the familiar "research apparatus" that comprises the bulk of Methods and Results sections of journal articles have been placed at the end of the book. Chapter 11 discusses the *Development of Psychotherapists Common Core Questionnaire*—our main research instrument—in studies where it was combined with other instruments assessing process, outcome, and training to examine how the psychotherapist's perspective converges and diverges from other observational perspectives. And the Appendix, that not-so-vestigial organ, contains all of the statistical tables for data analyses referred to throughout the book.

Notes

1 Title of a book review of Orlinsky & Rønnestad, *How psychotherapists develop* by J. C. Kobos (2005).
2 Apparently it is so for psychotherapists as well as for the people they treat (e.g., Dryden & Spurling, 1991; Kahn & Fromm, 2001).
3 Regarding "the kind of work that psychotherapy entails" from the psychotherapist's perspective, see our previous book, *How psychotherapists develop* (Orlinsky & Rønnestad, 2005), which empirically defines two broad dimensions of therapist experience: *Healing Involvement* and *Stressful Involvement*. The former absorbs and

rewards the therapist in practice; the latter is what the therapist must learn to be able to tolerate. Also see Chapter 10 of this book.

4 The study was initially reviewed and approved by the Ethical Research Committee of the University of Chicago's Social Sciences Division.

5 See, for example, Baldwin & Imel (2013) and Johns, Barkham, Kellet & Saxon (2019).

6 A personal connection: years ago, when a clinical psychology intern at the Veterans Administration in Chicago, this writer became a subject in the study which perhaps established a preconscious interest in this topic that came to the fore again in 1989, after two decades of research focused on psychotherapeutic processes and outcomes rather than psychotherapists. The writer had also taken Prof. Henry's course on the Thematic Apperception Test while a graduate student at the University of Chicago, and as a young academic had been a colleague of John Sims teaching social sciences in the College (but with no reference to psychotherapy or psychotherapists in either case).

7 Sadly this very valid and empirically supported idea has seen no serious convergence of the four psychotherapeutic professions in the years since, but rather a further splintering of occupational identities (as detailed in Chapter 2).

8 Any 'effects" that might be attributable to individual differences—the physician's 'bedside manner" and its patient correlative, the "placebo effect"—are rigorously controlled, minimized, denied. Yet in the "real world" of medical treatment, the physician-therapist's "bedside manner"—conveying an attitude of attention, empathy, genuine caring—opens the patient to treatment, just as the relative absence evokes hesitancy and resistance. Often the impact is subtle, sometimes it is dramatic, but every patient has experienced this. The "placebo effect", the inclination of people who need and receive help to feel grateful and wish to please their benefactors, in fact has to be counted as a large part the "psychotherapeutic effect", recognized by Freud (1912a, 1912b) as a *(pre)conscious* "positive transference"—sadly too often confused with his concept of the *unconscious* "positive transference" (or "transference-love").

9 First presented as a paper at the annual meeting of the Society for Psychotherapy Research, Boston, June, 1975. The ground for this revolution in perspective had been prepared by earlier research in the Client-Centered tradition, which Bordin's work implicitly drew on and transformed (Orlinsky & Rønnestad, 2000). Rogers & Dymond's (1954) *Psychotherapy and personality change* deserves to be honored as our field's first major volume and fountainhead of empirical research. Rogers' (1957) formulation of therapist-offered conditions (empathy, positive regard, and genuineness) as the critical elements of psychotherapy led to a later perception of those conditions as *relationship* variables (e.g., Orlinsky & Howard, 1986).

10 To avoid future repetitions of cumbersome phrases, the following acronyms will be used throughout the book: *SPR* for the Society for Psychotherapy Research; *CRN* for the Collaborative Research Network; *ISDP* for the International Study of the Development of Psychotherapists; and *DPCCQ* for the *Development of Psychotherapists Common Core Questionnaire.*

11 A narrative describing the "Origins of the Society for Psychotherapy Research Collaborative Research Network Study" appears in Orlinsky and Rønnestad (2005, Appendix A). The initial group, in addition to myself, included (in alphabetical order): Nicoletta Aapro, M.D. (University of Geneva), Hansruedi Ambühl, Ph.D. (University of Bern), Jean-François Botermans, Ph.D. (University of Louvain), Christine Davidson, Ph.D. (Northwestern University Medical School), John Davis, Ph.D. (University of Warwick), Marcia Davis, Ph.D. (University of Warwick), Alice Dazord, M.D. (INSERM Lyon), Paul Gerin, M.D. (INSERM Lyon), Thomas Schröder, Ph.D. (University of Warwick), and Ulrike Willutzki, Ph.D. (Ruhr-University Bochum). The professions represented in this group included medicine, psychology, and social work.

12   All DPCCQs were collected anonymously in order to protect the personal identities of individual participants in the ISDP study, and to minimize social desirability bias.

13   This was arranged through the good offices of that master impresario of research, Prof. Horst Kächele (Ulm University), and organized with the warm support of Profs. Peter Buchheim and Manfred Cierpka who were that year's conference leaders. Hansruedi Ambühl and I served as data collectors, with the able assistance of Anna Buchheim.

14   Research-oriented readers will surely want to ask if our very large body of data is a representative sample of psychotherapists, so that generalizations can be confidently drawn—to which the honest reply is that the question can't be answered. That is because the concept of *psychotherapist* is a "fuzzy" construct whose borders are porous and whose boundaries are imprecise. Who is *in* and who is *out* isn't necessarily clear. Art therapists, music therapists, dance therapists; drug counselors, marital counselors, vocational counselors; psychoanalysts, behavioral modifiers, cognitive therapists, existential therapists, gestalt therapists, family therapists, personal coaches—the list of those with credible claims to practicing one or another form of psychotherapy goes on and on. The best alternative we have in a situation like this is to study a broad range of persons who identify themselves as "psychotherapists" and agreed to commit an hour or two of their valuable time (unpaid) to complete a lengthy survey titled the *Development of Psychotherapists Common Core Questionnaire*—and, in the process, to anonymously provide a great deal of information about themselves. This approach allows us to provide detailed depictions of what and how much therapists have in common, and how much and in what ways they differ. To apply the findings of this study to other therapists, the best alternative is to match descriptive data as closely as feasible to the specific groups of therapists in our study. This reflects the methodological principle *transferability* described by Lincoln and Guba (1985).

15   The author's thought here runs to the last line of John Donne's *The Canonization*: to "… beg from above/A pattern of your love!"

References

Baldwin, S., & Imel, Z. E. (2013). Therapist effects: Findings and methods. In M. J. Lambert (Ed.), *Bergin and Garfield's handbook of psychotherapy and behavior change* (6th ed.), New York, NY: Wiley, 258–297.

Bordin, E. (1979). The generalizability of the psychoanalytic concept of the working alliance. *Psychotherapy: Theory, Research and Practice*, 16(3), 252–260.

Dent, J. K., & Furse, G. A. (1978). *Dimensions of the psycho-social therapies as revealed by the personalities of effective therapists*. (DHEW Publication No. AD< 77–527). Washington, DC: US Government Printing Office.

Deutsch, C. J. (1984). Self-reported sources of stress among psychotherapists. *Professional Psychological: Research and Practice*, 15, 833–845.

Deutsch, C. J. (1985). A survey of therapists' personal problems and treatment. *Professional Psychological: Research and Practice*, 16, 305–315.

Dryden, W., & Spurling, L. (Eds.) (1991). *On becoming a psychotherapist*. London: Tavistock/Routledge.

Farber, B. A. (1983). The effects of psychotherapeutic practice on psychotherapists. *Psychotherapy: Theory, Research, and Practice*, 20, 174–182.

Farber, B. A., & Heifetz, L. J. (1981). The satisfactions and stresses of psychotherapeutic work: A factor analytic study. *Professional Psychology*, 12, 621–630.

Freud, S. (1912). The dynamics of the transference. In J. Strachey, Ed., *The standard edition of the complete psychological works of Sigmund Freud*, vol. XII, 97–108. London: Hogarth Press, 1958.

Freud, S. (1914). Observations on transference-love (Further recommendations on the technique of psychoanalysis III). In J. Strachey, Ed., *The standard edition of the complete psychological works of Sigmund Freud*, vol. XII, 157–171. London: Hogarth Press, 1958.

Geller, J. D., Norcross, J. C., & Orlinsky, D. E. (Eds.) (2005). *The psychotherapist's own psychotherapy: Patient and clinician perspectives*. New York: Oxford University Press.

Guy, J. D. (1989). *The personal life of the psychotherapist*. New York: Wiley.

Guy, J. D., Poelstra, G. P., & Stark, M. J. (1989). Personal distress and therapeutic effectiveness: National survey of psychologists practicing psychotherapy. *Professional Psychology*, 20, 48–50.

Henry, W. E. (1954). The business executive: A study of the psychodynamics of a social role. In H. Brad, Ed., *The study of personality: A book of readings*, 551–559. New York: Wiley.

Henry, W. E. (1966). Some observations on the lives of healers. *Human Development*, 9, 25–30.

Henry, W. E., Sims, J. H., & Spray, S. L. (1971). *The fifth profession: Becoming a psychotherapist*. San Francisco: Jossey-Bass.

Henry, W. E., Sims, J. H., & Spray, S. L. (1973). *Public and Private Lives of Psychotherapists*. San Francisco: Jossey-Bass.

Holt, R. R. (Ed.) (1971). *New horizon for psychotherapy: Autonomy as a profession*. New York: International Universities Press.

Holt, R. R., & Luborsky, L. (1958). *Personality patterns of psychiatrists* (2 vols.). New York: International Universities Press.

Horvath, A. O., & Greenberg, L. S. (1986). The development of the working alliance inventory. In L. S. Greenberg & W. M. Pinsof, Eds., *The psychotherapeutic process: A research handbook*, 529–556. New York: Guilford Press.

Johns, R. B., Barkham, M., Kellet, S., & Saxon, D. (2019). A systematic review of therapist effects: A critical update and refinement to Baldwin and Imel's (2013) review. *Clinical Psychology Review*, 67, 78–93.

Kahn, S., & Fromm, E. (Eds.) (2001). *Changes in the therapist*. Mahwah, NJ: Lawrence Erlbaum.

Kelley, F. L., & Fiske, D. W. (1951). *The prediction of performance in clinical psychology*. Ann Arbor, MI: University of Michigan Press.

Kobos, J. C. (2005). Therapists look into the mirror: A review of "How Psychotherapists Develop: A Study of Therapeutic Work and Professional Growth'. *PsycCRITIQUES*, 50 (29), issue 15 (no pagination specified).

Lincoln, Y. S., & Guba, E. G. (1985). *Naturalistic inquiry*. Newbury Park, CA: Sage.

Luborsky, L., Crits-Christoph, P., Alexander, L., Margolis, M., & Cohen, M. (1983). Two helping alliance methods for predicting outcomes of psychotherapy: A counting-signs vs. a global ratings method. *Journal of Nervous and Mental Diseases*, 171, 480–492.

Marmar, C. R., Horowitz, M. J., Weiss, D. S., & Marziali, E. (1986). The development of the Therapeutic Alliance Rating System. In L. S. Greenberg & W. M. Pinsof, Eds., *The psychotherapeutic process: A research handbook*, 367–390. New York: Guilford Press.

MacDevitt, J. W. (1987). Therapists' personal therapy and professional self-awareness. *Psychotherapy*, 24, 693–703.

McNamara, J. R. (1986). Personal therapy in the training of behavior therapists. *Psychotherapy*, 23, 370–374.

Norcross, J. C. (Ed.) (2002). *Psychotherapy relationships that work: Therapist contributions and responsiveness to patients*. New York: Oxford University Press.

Norcross, J. C., Dryden, W., & Brust, A. M. (1992). British clinical psychologists: II. Survey findings and American comparisons. *Clinical Psychology Forum*, 40, 25–29.

Norcross, J. C., Farber, J. A., & Prochaska, J. O. (1993). Psychologists conducting psychotherapy: New findings and historical comparisons on the Psychotherapy Division membership. *Psychotherapy*, 30, 692–697.

Norcross, J. C., Hedges, M., & Castle, P. H. (2002). Psychologists conducting psychotherapy in 2001: A study of the Division 29 membership. *Psychotherapy*, 39, 97–102.

Norcross, J. C., Karg, R., & Prochaska, J. O. (1997a). Clinical psychologists in the 1990s. I. *The Clinical Psychologist*, 50(2), 4–9.

Norcross, J. C., Karg, R., & Prochaska, J. O. (1997b). Clinical psychologists in the 1990s. II. *The Clinical Psychologist*, 50(3), 4–11.

Norcross, J. C., & Karpiak, C. P. (2012). Clinical psychologists in the 2010s: Fifty years of the APA Division of Clinical Psychology. *Clinical Psychology: Science and Practice*, 19 (1), 1–12.

Norcross, J. C., Karpiak, C. P., & Santoro, S. O. (2005). Clinical psychologists across the years: The Division of Clinical Psychology from 1960 to 2003. *Journal of Clinical Psychology*, 61, 1467–1483.

Norcross, J. C., & Lambert, M. J. (Eds.) (2019). *Psychotherapy relationships that work. Volume I: Evidence- based therapist contributions and responsiveness to patients.* New York: Oxford University Press.

Norcross, J. C., Nolan, B. M., Kosman, D. C., & Fernández-Alvarez, H. (2017). Redefining the future of SEPI: Member characteristics, integrative practices, and organizational satisfactions. *Journal of Psychotherapy Integration*, 27, 3–12.

Norcross, J. C., & Prochaska, J. O. (1982). A national survey of clinical psychologists: Characteristics and activities. *The Clinical Psychologist*, 35(2), 1–8.

Norcross, J. C., Prochaska, J. O., & Gallagher, K. M. (1989a). Clinical psychologists in the 1980s: I. Demographics, affiliations, and satisfactions. *The Clinical Psychologist*, 42, 29–39.

Norcross, J. C., Prochaska, J. O, & Gallagher, K. M. (1989b). Clinical psychologists in the 1980's: II. Theory, research, and practice. *The Clinical Psychologist*, 42, 45–53.

Norcross, J. C., Strausser, D. J., & Missar, C. D. (1988). The processes and outcomes of psychotherapists' personal treatment experiences. *Psychotherapy*, 25, 36–43.

Norcross, J. C., & Wampold, B. E. (Eds.) (2019). *Psychotherapy relationships that work. Volume II: Evidence-based therapist responsiveness.* New York: Oxford University Press.

Norcross, J. C., & Wogan, M. (1983). American psychotherapists of diverse persuasions: Characteristics, theories, practices, and clients. *Professional Psychology*, 14, 529–539.

Orlinsky, D. E. (1987). *How to do research on psychotherapy without a grant.* Ulm, Germany: PSZ-Verlag Ulm.

Orlinsky, D. E., Ambühl, H., Rønnestad, M. H., Davis, J. D., Gerin, P., Davis, M. L., et al. (1999). The development of psychotherapists: Concepts, questions, and methods of a collaborative international study. *Psychotherapy Research*, 9, 127–153.

Orlinsky, D. E., & Howard, K. I. (1977). The therapist's experience of psychotherapy. In A. E. Gurman & A. M. Razin (Eds.), *Effective psychotherapy: A handbook of research.* Oxford/New York: Pergamon Press, 566–589.

Orlinsky, D. E., & Howard, K. I. (1986). Process and outcome in psychotherapy. In S. L. Garfield & A. E. Bergin, Eds., *Handbook of psychotherapy and behavior change*, 3rd edition, 311–381. New York: Wiley.

Orlinsky, D. E., & Rønnestad, M. H. (2000). Ironies in the history of psychotherapy research: Rogers, Bordin, and the shape of things that came. *Journal of Clinical Psychology*, 56, 841–851.

Orlinsky, D. E., & Rønnestad, M. H. (2005). *How psychotherapists develop: A study of therapeutic work and professional growth.* Washington, DC: APA Books.

Parson, T., & Shils, E. A. (Eds.) (1954). *Toward a general theory of action.* Cambridge, MA: Harvard University Press.

Pope, K. S., & Tabachnik, B. G. (1994). Therapists as patients: A national survey of psychologists' experiences, problems, and beliefs. *Professional Psychology: Research and Practice,* 25, 247–258.

Prochaska, J. O., & Norcross J. C. (1983). Contemporary psychotherapists: A national survey of characteristics, practices, orientations, and attitudes. *Psychotherapy: Theory, Research, and Practice,* 20, 161–173.

Rogers, C. R. (1957). The necessary and sufficient conditions of therapeutic personality change. *Journal of Consulting Psychology,* 22, 95–103.

Rogers, C. R., & Dymond, R. F. (Eds.) (1954). *Psychotherapy and personality change.* Chicago: University of Chicago Press.

Rønnestad, M. H., & Skovholt, T. M. (1991). En modell for profesjonell utvikling og stagnasjon hos terapeuter og radgivere. *Tidsskrift for Norsk psykologofrening,* 28, 555–567. (A model of professional development and stagnation of therapists and counselors. *Journal of the Norwegian Psychological Association*).

Rønnestad, M. H., & Skovholt, T. M. (2013). *The developing practitioner: Growth and stagnation of therapists and counselors.* New York & London: Routledge.

Skovholt, T. M., & Rønnestad, M. H. (1992). *The evolving professional self: Stages and themes in therapist and counselor development.* New York: Wiley.

Strupp, H. H. (1955). The effect of the psychotherapist's personal analysis upon his techniques. *Journal of Consulting Psychology,* 19, 197–204.

Wyatt, F. (1948). The self-experience of the psychotherapist. *Journal of Consulting Psychology,* 12, 82–87.

2 Professional Psychotherapists

D. E. Orlinsky with M. H. Rønnestad, U. Willutzki, T. Schroder, E. Heinonen and M. J. Schofield

Who, then, are the participants in our study? This chapter presents some answers to that question by focusing successively on (1) professional characteristics, (2) basic biosocial qualities of age and gender, and (3) demographic attributes like national, social, and cultural backgrounds.[1] This detailed delineation of "external" characteristics provides a basis for comparison with other therapists and an essential "outer" framework within which to understand the "inner" qualities of psychotherapists as persons that is the main matter of our book.

Therapists' Professional Characteristics

Professional Disciplines

As has long been observed (e.g., Henry, Sims & Spray, 1972; Holt, 1971; Orlinsky, 2009) there is no single, inclusive and comprehensive *profession* of psychotherapy.[2] This differs markedly from other established professions such as medicine and law, engineering and accounting, nursing and ministry, and so on. Instead, psychotherapy is practiced as a sub-specialty within several different professions, each of which itself follows no single pattern of practice guided by a generally accepted theoretical framework. Thus our initial challenge in describing the people in this book is to trace the web of professions and theoretical approaches that jointly define "the psychotherapeutic professions"—and to extend that in terms of their successive career levels.

All of the 12,036 persons who thought it worth their time to complete the DPCCQ were asked "What is your professional identity? That is, how do you refer to yourself in professional contexts?" Their responses are summarized in Figure 2.1.

The largest group by far consisted of those who answered *Psychology* (n = 5,611, or 47% of the sample), followed at a distance by those who answered *Psychiatry* [3] (n = 2,235, or 19%) or *Counseling* (n = 2,193, or 18%). Smaller but still substantial groups identified professionally as *Social Workers* (n = 722, or 6%) or as *Nurses* (n = 226, or 2%), together with groups who identified solely as *Psychotherapists* or nonmedical Lay Psychoanalysts (together n = 661, or 5%), or as some *Other* [4] profession (n = 242, or 2%).

DOI: 10.4324/9781003217572-2

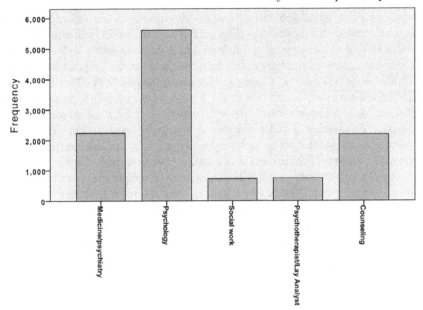

Figure 2.1 Psychotherapeutic Professions

Clearly, Social Workers and Counselors, who in some countries (like the USA) provide a very large proportion of therapeutic services, are substantially under-represented; and Psychiatrists may be as well, although in recent decades the profession of Psychiatry ceded psychotherapy as a treatment and specialized instead in pharmaceutical treatments (e.g., Luhrmann, 2000). However, if one disregards the relative proportions in our sample,[5] this list does illustrate the broad range of professions in which some subgroups of members engage in the practice of psychotherapy.

Theoretical Orientations

Perhaps even more than professional background, the therapist's theoretical approach to clinical practice is a decisive facet in defining a psychotherapist's identity,[6] and those theoretical approaches are also very diverse. In the clinical literature there appear to be literally hundreds of theoretical orientations, often closely related to one another, and with labels differing just by a word or two, sometimes prompted by therapists' desires to have their own "brand" in the marketplace.

However, using the concept of theoretical orientation in research requires some simplification and systemization. For example, the *Development of Psychotherapists Common Core Questionnaire* (DPCCQ) focused on broad families of distinctive therapeutic approaches rather than the many specific variants within each. To assess their theoretical approaches to practice, respondents were asked "How much is your current therapeutic approach guided by each of the following theoretical frameworks?" This question was followed by a set of six rating scales that allowed therapists to rate the relative influence on their current clinical practice of *Analytic/ Psychodynamic, Behavioral, Cognitive, Humanistic, Systemic* and *Other* orientations,[7] each rated separately from "Not at all" (0) to "Very greatly" (5). An advantage of this approach is the freedom it allows therapists to create their own nuanced theoretical orientation profiles within a systematic framework, also allowing researchers to use the ratings scales either separately as continuous measures or to construct categories of theoretical orientation based on their patterns.

Results of the scales ratings for the 11,700 therapists who provided usable data indicated that *Analytic/Psychodynamic* was the most popular influence (3.0 on a 0–5 scale), followed by *Humanistic* (rated 2.5) and *Cognitive* (rated 2.4).

But the diversity of theoretical orientations among therapists is better illustrated by the categories constructed from the ratings. The procedure for constructing categories involved defining ratings of 4 or 5 on each scale (i.e., a "great" or "very great" influence on current practice) as a *salient* influence, and then counting the number and content of salient orientations. Therapists might report having one, two, or even three or more *salient* orientations—or, if none of the scales were rated at 4 or 5, the category would be "no *salient* orientation".[8]

The results of this analysis identified a striking total of 33 different patterns or combinations as salient approaches to therapeutic practice reported by at least 5 therapists in our sample, and another 18 patterns with even fewer representatives. This probably gives a fairly realistic impression of the great diversity and individualization in theoretical orientations that characterize the field of psychotherapy. To simplify and summarize the picture, Figure 2.2 shows only the 10 main salient orientation patterns represented by 300 or more therapists.

Overall, two orientation patterns stood out as most numerous in our data: a mono-focal (i.e., one salient) *Analytic/Psychodynamic* orientation (*n* = 2,655, or 23% of the total), and a *"Broad-spectrum"* (i.e., three or more salient) integrative eclectic pattern (*n* = 2,000, or 17%)—together comprising 40% of the sample. Two smaller but still numerous orientation patterns were mono-focal *Humanistic* (*n* = 931, or 8%) and *Cognitive-Behavioral* [9] (*n* = 894, or 7.5%). The four patterns represent more than half (56%) of the total sample.

Surprisingly, the next largest group included *"theoretically uncommitted"* therapists who said they were influenced no more than moderately by any particular orientation (*n* = 810, or 7%). There was a group of bi-focal *Analytic/ Psychodynamic + Humanistic* therapists (*n* = 679, or 6%); another group of bi-focal *Cognitive-Behavioral + Humanistic* therapists (*n* = 357, or 3%); some mono-focal *Systemic* therapists (*n* = 347, or 3%); some bi-focal *Systemic + Humanistic* therapists (*n* = 332, almost 3%); and a miscellaneous group having some *"other orientation"* (*n* = 304, nearly 3%).[10]

The findings illustrate three facts. First: the range of types of salient theoretical orientation patterns is remarkably large. Second: in practice, therapists typically integrate multiple, even sometimes seemingly conflicting[11] therapeutic

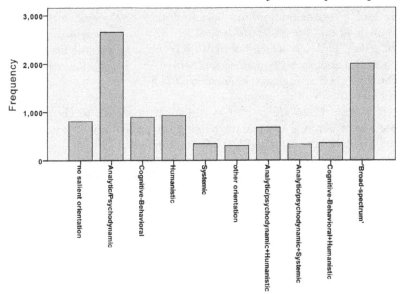

Figure 2.2 Salient Theoretical Orientations (N > 300)

approaches. Third: among the many who combine salient orientations, "Broad-spectrum" therapists are by far the most numerous, drawing heavily on three or more approaches to practice.

Profession and Theoretical Orientation

Therapists' professional backgrounds and theoretical approaches are both characterized by multiplicity and diversity, but the picture that emerges is further complicated by the fact that those professional characteristics are not fully independent of each other. One can find some therapists in every profession who say they are saliently influenced in practice by each of the main theoretical approaches, but there are clear differences in theoretical preference when comparing across professions (see Appendix Table 2.1).

Most of the Psychologists in our sample were divided between *Analytic/Psychodynamic* or *Analytic/Psychodynamic + Humanistic* (36%), *Broad-spectrum* (22%), and *Cognitive-Behavioral* or *C-B + Humanistic* (18%). Those together accounted for 76% in that profession. By contrast, a majority of the Psychiatrists were *Analytic/Psychodynamic* or *Analytic/Psychodynamic + Humanistic* (52%), and the next largest group (15%) had no salient orientation (i.e., was *theoretically uncommitted*). Only some were *Broad-spectrum* (12%), and even fewer were *Cognitive-Behavioral* or *Cognitive-Behavioral + Humanistic* (8%). Those orientations account for 87% of the psychiatrists.

The most popular orientations among Counselors were *Broad-spectrum* (28%), *Humanistic* (23%), and *Analytic/Psychodynamic* or *Analytic/Psychodynamic + Humanistic* (21%), accounting for 72% in the profession. *Broad-spectrum* was also the leading orientation among Social Workers (29%), and a slightly smaller group held an *Analytic/Psychodynamic* or *Analytic/Psychodynamic + Humanistic* orientation (26%). Notably, Social Workers were significantly more likely than other professions to be *Systemic* or *Systemic + Analytic/Psychodynamic* (19%), which may reflect a greater concern with families. Together these orientations represented 64% of the group.

The comparisons are at least as striking if one were to choose a therapist based on theoretical orientation rather than professional background. In our data, nearly three-quarters (71%) of the mono-focal *Cognitive-Behavioral* therapists were Psychologists—which more accurately reflects the prevalence of this orientation among professions. A mono-focal *Analytic/Psychodynamic* approach was strongly over-represented among the Psychiatrists (32% despite being only 21% of our total sample). Likewise, a mono-focal *Humanistic* approach was over-represented among Counsellors (43% despite being only19% of our whole sample). These results make quite clear that there is a real likelihood of experiencing a different form of psychotherapeutic treatment based on the professional background of the therapist one might choose.

Career Levels

Still another dimension on which therapists of all professions and orientations will differ is their career level, defined in our study as years of experience in therapeutic practice. Our therapists on average were quite highly experienced, with a mean of 12 years in practice (median = 10 years, SD = 9.2 years). In fact, however, they ranged from "novices" who had just started treating patients in the past year up to "seniors" who had been in clinical practice for 25 to 50 years or more.[12] For descriptive purposes, the therapeutic career can be divided into successive levels or cohorts, as in the following four broad categories.[13]

The least experienced group included those who had just begun to work with patients on up to those who had less than three years in practice, and were most likely in training at the time. These 1,542 *novice and apprentice* therapists comprised 14% of the sample.

A much larger group (*n* = 3,989, or 35%) consisted of *graduate and professionally established* practitioners who had worked therapeutically with patients from three to less than 10 years. Most of these would have completed their basic professional training and begun to practice in a regular clinical setting.

Another very large group in our sample (*n* = 3,570, or 31%) had practiced psychotherapy from 10 up to 20 years. These would meet Goldberg's (1992) criteria as *experienced or "seasoned"* therapists: "… we can operationally define the experienced therapist as someone who has had a serious commitment to being a practitioner for at least a decade" (p 2).

Finally, our sample includes a large group (*n* = 2,338, or 20%) of really *senior* therapists who had been in practice from 20 to 55 years. Compared to other career levels, they are most likely to have supervised a large number of other therapists[14] and to have been the personal therapists for other therapists.[15]

These large career cohorts allow for separate and comparative study of therapists in different career phases, both with regard to therapeutic work (e.g., the difficulties they experience in practice) and their professional growth (e.g., facilitative influences), which were the main focus of *How Psychotherapists Develop* (Orlinsky & Rønnestad, 2005). In *How Psychotherapists Live*, which focuses on therapists' personal experiences, interest turns instead to the highly correlated but not redundant variable of age ($r = .70$). Before proceeding though, it may be worth noting that clients who can only afford to seek therapy at training hospitals or clinics will have a good chance of receiving treatment from novice or apprentice therapists who, as students under supervision, have mainly their native therapeutic talent and enthusiasm to offer. Others who can may seek treatment from established, seasoned or senior therapists who, while also supervising apprentices, clearly possess more prestige and presumably are more skilled and resourceful.[16]

A Unifying Thread

The fact that psychotherapists vary so much in their professional identities, theoretical orientations, and across career levels, implies that to describe any particular psychotherapist minimally requires specification of all three components—profession, orientation, and career level. Yet given all the variations so far described, it is worth reflecting for a moment on what psychotherapists of all professions, orientations and career levels do actually have in common. The short answer to that question of course is that they all practice psychotherapy—but then the question becomes "What do all psychotherapies have in common?"

A good way to start answering this is to recall the fourfold definition of psychotherapy provided by Frank and Frank (1991, 39–43) excerpted as follows:

> In our view, all psychotherapies share at least four effective features:
>
> 1   An emotionally charged, confiding relationship with a helping person ... the therapeutic alliance is a necessary, and perhaps often sufficient, condition of improvement in any kind of therapy. ...
>
> 2   A healing setting ... [typically] a therapist's office, a hospital, or a clinic ... [within whose] protective walls patients know they can freely express feelings, dare to reveal aspects of themselves that they have concealed from others, and do whatever else the therapy prescribes. ...
>
> 3   A rationale, conceptual scheme, or myth that provides a plausible explanation for the patient's symptoms and prescribes a ritual or procedure for resolving them. ...
>
> 4   A ritual or procedure that requires active participation of both patient and therapist and that is believed by both to be the means of restoring the patient's health.

The first of their four criteria highlights the critical importance of the therapeutic relationship.[17] Every form of psychotherapy operates through the medium of an interpersonal relationship between patient and therapist[18] as that develops over time through a series of person-to-person encounters (or "therapy sessions"). What makes the relationship "therapeutic" is a consistently empathetic, discerning, and caring engagement of the therapist with the patient, matched by the patient's awareness of it and acceptance of its sincerity (or "genuineness"). All forms of psychotherapy—and, to the extent that they are effective, all psychotherapists—operate by establishing and sustaining a mutually meaningful relationship, rooted deeply in human species biology and culture. As infants we are born into a nexus of caring relationships and only survive in and thrive through them. As infants we are objectively helpless and are born pre-adapted only with the reflexes needed to establish an attachment to care-givers, and be able from the outset to communicate states of satisfaction and distress. All forms of psychotherapy "work" through relationships that reactivate and partially replicate—to the extent that they can—a deep nonverbal caring connection that is foundational to our human being.[19]

The second of the Franks' four criteria for all psychotherapies is a "healing" setting, typically a therapist's office, a hospital, or a clinic. Those settings are linked to the therapist's occupation in a recognized "health care" profession—medicine (specifically psychological medicine or psychiatry) as the first modern example,[20] as well as related professions that historically started as clinical adjuncts to psychiatry and became more or less independent, such as clinical psychology, clinical social work, psychiatric nursing, and more recently various forms of psychological counseling.[21] Although there are legal variations across different countries, only certified members of these professions (and their trainees) have a right to access and utilize these healing settings (as well as insurance reimbursement for their services).

The third and fourth of the Franks' criteria refer specifically to psychotherapists' theoretical orientations and approaches to practice, which are aspects of the therapist's clinical treatment model, the effective learning of which results in their being certified as professionally qualified. *Theoretical orientations* offer a conceptual scheme involving a model of personality (including a view of human vulnerability and human potential) which provides a *culturally plausible* (i.e., non-supernatural or "scientific") explanation for the patient's symptoms and suffering, and envisions paths of return to "normality" and "growth". Typically this is achieved by "diagnosing" the patient's symptoms and suffering as the results of one or another "underlying" disorder, which therapists' mastery of their theoretical concepts enables them to discern and communicate to patients—typically providing patients with relief from the anxiety of "not knowing what is wrong", together with the hope that what is wrong can be set right. This is key to counteracting the demoralized state that Frank (1974; Frank & Frank, 1991) described as characteristic of patients who come to therapy, and as the major function of psychotherapy in restoring patients' morale.[22]

Approaches to practice is the complementary aspect of the therapist's clinical model that defines the treatment method or "technical" procedures to be enacted by therapist and patient respectively as the means to restoring and enhancing the patient's wellbeing. These corresponding patient and therapist actions are highly varied, both between and within different treatment models, indeed sometimes "migrating" from one treatment model to another as therapists of different persuasions notice their utility and adapt them to their own schemas.

In sum, despite the clearly documented diversity of those who work as professional psychotherapists, the essential features of the work that therapists do effectively provides a coherent thread of unity.[23]

Personal Demographics

So far we have introduced our psychotherapists with reference to their distinguishing professional characteristics instead of the promised focus on their personal characteristics, but this was necessary to show the basis on which those persons have been selected. Professional background, theoretical approach, and career level are the defining criteria, but in themselves are just disembodied constructs. The next step in introducing our psychotherapists is to describe them in their human bodies as gendered individuals of various ages. The combination of age and gender may be taken as foundational to how individuals experience themselves and how they are viewed by others. That information also frames their life cycle status at the time they joined the study to report about themselves.

Age

In terms of longevity—and, by implication, life experience—most of the therapists in our sample were mature individuals, with an overall mean age of 45.1 years (median = 44.6) in a nearly normal age distribution, with the standard deviation of 11.5 years meaning that most therapists were between 33.5 and 56.5 of age. There appears to be a slight excess of therapists in their thirties, although the most numerous decade is that of therapists in their forties. The overall range extended from youngest at just over 21 to oldest at over 90. If age brings wisdom, it may be worth noting that a third of the therapists were 50 or older.

Gender

Traditionally in most cultures, the great majority of individuals are assigned to one or another of the two genders, male and female, and provided with ideal gender images of how they themselves should try to embody those ideals. So individuals came to know themselves and live their lives (more or less unquestioningly) as men and women. Even allowing for historical change in the contents, contrasts and values assigned to them— and for individual differences in erotic orientation—the cultural binaries of male and female have functioned as broadly influential foundations of personhood. (No disrespect towards persons who reject cis-gender categories and prefer variant or ambiguous identities is intended or implied.) However, when asked on the DPCCQ to indicate their gender, only 135 (1.1%) of 12,036 therapists failed to reply. For the other 99% these categories appeared to suffice, and to define the data that we have to report.[24] These show there were nearly twice as many women than men in our sample: 7,533 (63.3%) women vs. 4,363 (36.7%) men.[25]

Age and Gender Combined

Therapist groups defined by the combination of age and gender are shown in Figure 2.3, where one sees a roughly parallel distribution of age among men as among women. The smallest group overall is that of younger men in their twenties to mid-thirties, comprising under 7% of the total sample as compared to women of the same ages at nearly 15%.

It has often been observed in recent decades that the psychotherapeutic professions have become "feminized", in the sense that more women have been entering these fields than in the past. This impression is certainly supported by our results for the overall sample (63% women) as well as the youngest age group (71% women).

Generation

A more accurate comparison would be based on the therapists' historical birth year cohort or "generation", which shows there was a majority (53%) of men among therapists born in the period 1907–1936 (see Appendix Table 2.2). After this, the proportion of male therapists (as reflected in our sample) declined consistently over time to a mere 27% of those born 1967–1990. Among those born between 1937 and 1946, who came of age in the immediate post-war era, women already constituted a substantial majority (60%)—a majority that increased slowly to 64% women for those born 1957–1966, and nearly three-quarters (73%) among those born 1967–1990.

This significant shift from male to female predominance over successive generations was seen when the analyses were repeated separately for the profession of Psychology, which changed from 58% male among the oldest to 75% female among the youngest; and in Psychiatry, which declined progressively from 70% male among the oldest to only 52% male in the youngest cohort—still majority male, but 18% less so (see Appendix Table 2.3). By contrast, Counselors remained predominantly female (at about 80%) across successive birth cohorts; and unsurprisingly, a consistent prevalence of women was also found among Social Workers.[26]

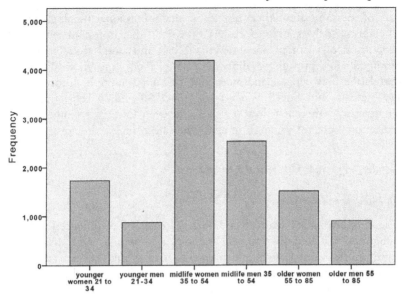

Figure 2.3 Psychotherapists by Age and Gender

Gender, Age and Profession

Although women outnumber men by a 2:1 ratio in our total sample, the facts noted above also reflect a differential presence of men and women in various psychotherapeutic professions (see Appendix Table 2.4). Men were a majority (59%) only among medical doctors (Psychiatrists and medical psychotherapists). The predominance of women in the other professional subgroups ranges from 63% among Psychologists to 71% of Lay Therapists/Analysts, 77% of Social Workers, and 79% of Counselors. (These were not based on representative samples of those professions but correspond reasonably well with informal impressions of those fields.)

Although the average mean age of our therapists in the sample was 45 years, a statistically significant difference was observed between two professional subgroups (see Appendix Table 2.5, left sector). Psychologists, Psychiatrists, and Social Workers averaged very close to 44 years with no significant differences between them, but Counselors and Lay Therapists/Analysts were significantly older, each with a mean age of 49 years. More interestingly, these seem to reflect differences in the average age at which therapists in the different professions began to practice (see Appendix Table 2.5, right sector). Psychologists started youngest on average at 31 years; Psychiatrists and Social Workers started on average when about 33 years old; Lay Therapists/Analysts started even later at around age 37; and the oldest were Counselors, who on average were just over 39 when starting to practice (presumably as supervised trainees). Apparently Psychologists, Psychiatrists and Social Workers begin to treat patients as part of, or soon after, their university and professional training, whereas Lay Therapists/Analysts and especially Counselors (the profession with the highest proportion of women) often may have had and raised children first, or have retrained after pursuing a different career. Reflecting these differences, the correlation between age and practice duration was quite high for Psychologists, Psychiatrists, and Social Workers (r =.79, .80 and.73 respectively); for Lay Therapists/Analysts it is low (r =.63) and even lower for Counselors (r =.52) indicating a greater variation in ages when becoming a therapist.

Gender, Age and Theoretical Orientation

Orientation and Gender

The proportions of women and men in each of the theoretical orientation categories matched that for the sample as a whole, with two exceptions. Significantly more Humanistic therapists than would be expected by chance (70%) were women; and among Cognitive-Behavioral therapists, although more women were present, significantly more than expected by chance (43%) of men were Cognitive-Behavioral (see Appendix Table 2.6). One wonders how much this may echo cultural stereotypes by viewing Humanistic therapists as "feminine" (i.e., focused on relationships and feelings) and Cognitive-Behavioral therapists as "masculine" (i.e., focused on ideas and actions). Still, as if to counter these stereotypes, one notes that 30% of Humanistic therapists were men and 57% of the Cognitive-Behavioral were women.

Orientation and Age

Significant differences in average age were also observed among the six main theoretical orientation categories. The two youngest groups consisted of the theoretically "uncommitted" with no salient orientation (at least as yet), and the Cognitive-Behavioral therapists—both significantly younger than those in other orientations (see Appendix Table 2.7). The oldest groups were saliently Humanistic, Analytic/Psychodynamic and Broad Spectrum integrative therapists. Those who combined Analytic/Psychodynamic + Humanistic orientations comprised a middle group, significantly younger than Humanistic and significantly older than Cognitive-Behavioral or "uncommitted" therapists. This snapshot of age differences reflects the period during which data for the study were collected but doesn't show trends over time. Nevertheless it is plausible to envision both a career progression in which younger therapists become committed to an orientation as they develop, and a trend over time in which Cognitive-Behavioral therapists become a progressively larger presence in the psychotherapy field.

To sum up this shift in focus from their professional characteristics to the men and women who actually work as psychotherapists, it is clear in our sample that a substantial majority of therapists in all professions other than psychiatry are women; that the field of professional psychotherapy has become progressively represented by women, even among psychiatrists; that therapists tend to enter their professions and start to practice at different ages and with varied life experience, some directly from school and others later on after pursuing other goals; and finally, that overall most (80%) of therapists in our sample were mature individuals between 30 and 60 years old, although given the size of our sample there were plenty of younger and older therapists too.

Social Demographics

Age and gender are the minimal biosocial *human* characteristics that differentiate individuals as persons, but of course psychotherapists are more than just men and women of a certain age. They live and work in different countries whose internal social and cultural systems must affect them. We need to locate them in those contexts as well.

Nationality

Our sample of therapists contains individuals from 43 separate countries representing every continent except Antarctica (see Appendix Table 2.8). Of those, five countries had more than a thousand therapists each—Norway (n = 1,678), USA (n = 1,207), Germany (n = 1,175), UK (n = 1,108), and Australia (n = 1,004). These likely are among the largest therapist samples (if not the largest) collected in those countries. More moderate but still meaningful groups of therapists were from Canada (*n* = 600), Denmark (*n* = 540), Portugal (*n* = 416), New Zealand (*n* = 331), Switzerland (*n* = 306), Austria (*n* = 234), and Israel (*n* = 205). Moreover, a substantial number of therapists were recruited from culturally different countries in Asia (*n* =539 in South Korea, *n* =509 in China, and *n* =277 in India). Finally, small groups were also included from countries in Latin America (*n* = 346), Eastern Europe (*n* = 205), the Middle East (*n* = 100) and Africa (*n* = 41).

Although the proportion of therapists from different countries in our sample probably corresponds only roughly at best with the worldwide distribution of professional psychotherapists, the fact remains that the sample is remarkably diverse in nationalities and includes relatively large numbers of therapists from countries where psychotherapists have not been studied before.[27]

Nationality, Profession and Gender

The different psychotherapeutic professions are not equally represented in all of these countries. Most of the 5,611 Psychologists in our sample were from Norway (21%), the USA (13%), Denmark (9%), Germany (8%), Canada (6%), Portugal (6%), Switzerland (4%) and other West European countries (9%). By contrast, the 2,235 Psychiatrists and medically trained therapists were mainly from three countries: Germany (27%), South Korea (16%), Norway (15%), along with a few other West European countries (12%). Counselors were the other large group in our sample, and of 2,193 most were from the UK (32%), Australia (29%) and New Zealand (6%), and China (12%).

Proportions of women and men also varied across nationalities. Men were a majority (65%) only in South Korea, where most (70%) of our therapists were Psychiatrists. By contrast, women predominated in Australia (77%), the UK (75%), and China (75%), but majorities of the therapists from Australia, the UK and China were Counselors (71%, 65% and 54% respectively).[28] Thus there tends to be a three-way confound between therapeutic profession, therapist gender, and nationality—which may partially reflect an actual state of affairs but which also will need to be kept in mind when interpreting results.

Social Marginality vs. Social Mainstream

In their groundbreaking study of nearly 4,000 psychotherapists in three American cities, Henry, Sims and Spray (1971) noted the role of social and cultural marginality in the recruitment and careers of psychotherapists. Focusing on private practice as the most desired form of practice among established therapists, they observed (p. 4) that: "Careers terminating in the private practice of psychotherapy are populated, to a very great extent, by practitioners ... [who] ... come from a highly circumscribed sector of the social world, representing a special combination of social marginality in ethnic, religious, political, and social-class terms." It is worth asking whether these observations on psychotherapists still apply more than a generation later and in a broadly international context. Minority status and immigrant status are two indicators of therapists' social marginality for which we have data.

Minority Status

In the DPCCQ, therapists were asked: "In the country where you live, would you be considered a member of a social, cultural or ethnic minority?" If they answered yes, they were then asked to specify their minority.[29] Only 12% said they would be viewed as a member of minority group while 88% indicate that they were majority or mainstream persons in the country where they lived. This clearly runs against the observation of Henry and his colleagues, whose therapists were from New York City, Chicago, and Los Angeles.

However, the percentages of minority membership in our large international sample did vary a lot from country to country—and the USA had by far the highest proportion (29%) of minorities among the main countries. The only comparable rates of minority status were among therapists in New Zealand (23%), Canada (19%), the UK (19%), and India (17%). Several countries had the lowest rates of minority status (i.e., were socially most homogeneous): South Korea (2%), Portugal (3%), Germany (4%), Norway (5%), Denmark (6%), Austria (6%), and China (6%). Thus perhaps there is still some support for the observations of Henry, Sims and Spray (1971) on social marginality among therapists in the USA, but also evidence that this is not typical of therapists in many other countries.

Immigrant Status

A question about whether they were natives of the country where they lived and worked or were immigrants who had been born elsewhere was also included in versions of the DPCCQ given to about two-thirds of our therapists (*n* = 8,415). Only 13% said they had immigrated to their present country, while a large majority (87%) indicated they were native-born. Here again the rates varied considerably between countries. The highest percentages of therapists with immigrant status were Australia (36%), Switzerland (26%) and Israel (25%).[30] The lowest rates of therapist immigration were in South Korea (1%), China (3%), and India (4%). The rate for the USA was 11%, which closely matches the rate of foreign-born found by Henry, Sims and Spray (1971) for clinical psychologists and social workers in their study of American therapists.[31]

Cultural Marginality

Another aspect of marginality that may apply to psychotherapists, at least in some countries, concerns the extent to which they are culturally secular rather than religiously oriented persons, as they are often thought to be. Qualified support for this view is provided by data from the 4,128 therapists who responded to a question about their current affiliation in the DPCCQ version they were given. Of those, by far the largest single group (49%) indicated they had no current religious affiliation, confirming the popular impression—but that still leaves a majority (51%) who said they personally identified with one or another religious community (Appendix Table 2.9).[32] Overall, the most populous groups were Protestant Christian denominations (21%) and Roman Catholic and Orthodox communions (10%)—thus close to one-third of the total sample identified as Christian. Smaller groups included therapists who identified as Jewish (5%), Buddhist (5%), Muslim (1%), other Asian religion (1%), and "mixed or other" (8%).

The psychotherapists in our sample vary greatly from country to country in the extent of their secularity. Among the countries for which data on approximately 300 or more therapists were available, the most secular in terms of lacking a religious affiliation were New Zealand, Denmark, Canada, and the UK (68%, 63%, 62% and 59% respectively); and the least secular in terms of having a religious affiliation were Australia and the USA (31% and 41% respectively). However, whether a therapist's secular or religious identity counts as cultural marginality depends on the rates of religious affiliation in their respective countries.[33]

Outer Characteristics versus Inner Experiences

This chapter has focused mainly on the outer characteristics of psychotherapists as professionals, both to introduce the therapists and as a framework for the chapters to come which will deal at length and in detail with their personal experiences and private lives. Although there are some undeniable areas of commonality—for example, the large proportion of therapists who are women, who belong to the social mainstream in their countries, whose cultural orientations are largely secular, and above all whose work involves person-to-person relationships with patients—perhaps the main impression about professional psychotherapists in this chapter is their diversity. They are diverse in their professional backgrounds, theoretical approaches, nationalities, social and cultural characteristics. Having described many of these outer similarities and differences, the following chapters will concentrate on their inner worlds—how they experience their personal selves, their private lives, their beliefs and values, their quality of life, their memories of childhood, their emotional struggles and own personal therapy. How the diversity of their outer characteristics is reflected in their inner experiences, and how their personal selves and private lives relate to their experiences in therapeutic work, are also topics of this book. Hopefully, by its end, readers will have gained a richer knowledge and understanding of psychotherapists—inside and out.

Notes

1 The data that are analyzed in this and subsequent chapters were collected by many members of the SPR Collaborative Research Network whose contributions are gratefully acknowledged here (in the order of sample size, down to N ≥ 100): in Norway (M. H. Rønnestad, A. Von de Lippe, S. Lorentzen); in the USA (D. E. Orlinsky, J. C. Norcross, L. E. Beutler, T. Northcutt, L. Knobloch-Fedders, M. Silverman); in Germany (M. Cierpka, P. Buchheim, U. Willutzki, J. Meyerberg, H. Kächele); in the UK (T. Schroder, J. Davis, M. Davis, S. Wheeler); in Australia (M. J. Schofield, J. Grant); in Canada (G. DeLisle, S. Toukmanian, S. Grafanaki); in Denmark (E. F. Jørgensen, C. H. Jacobsen); in Portugal (S. Arriaga, A. Branco Vasco); in South Korea (S. H. Bae, E. Joo); in China (Li Yawen, Chen Xiangyi, Yang Yunping); in New Zealand (N. Kazantzis); in Switzerland (H. Ambühl, N. Aapro); in India (P. Bhola, S. Kumaria); in Austria (A. Leireiter); in Israel (H. Wiseman, G. Shefler); in the Republic of Ireland (L. Timulak, C. Hickey, A. Davis); in Spain (I. Caro Gabalda, A. Avila Espada); in Chile (L. Moncada); in Mexico (M. Taragona); in Belgium (J-F. Botermans); in France (P. Gerin, A. Dazord); in Sweden (D. Stiwne); in Malaysia (Ng Wai Sheng); in Greece (G. Lampropoulos); in Russia (K. Kalmykova).

2 With an exception in recent years in Austria, where laws have been passed defining a unified profession of "psychotherapy", and a more recent partial exception in the Canadian province of Québec.

3 In Germany, this includes the separate specialty of "medical psychotherapist".

4 This included occupational therapists, music therapists, hypnotherapists, psychotherapeutically trained religious ministers, and some who just checked "Other" without further indication.

5 The disproportionate representation of professions is due in part to the fact that most colleagues who helped to collect data for our study as members of the Society

for Psychotherapy Research Collaborative Research Network were psychologists themselves, whose contacts were largely within their own profession.

6 In many European countries (unlike North America) training and certification in one or another theoretical approach, at an institute following university-based professional qualification, often constitutes *the* critical defining factor of a therapist's identity.

7 The separate scales for Behavioral and Cognitive were averaged to create a *Cognitive-Behavioral* scale.

8 Therapists having one salient orientation will be referred to as "mono-focal", two salient orientations as "bi-focal", and three or more salient orientations as "Broad-spectrum" integrative and eclectic, while those with no salient orientation can be viewed as "theoretically uncommitted".

9 Although separate Behavioral and Cognitive scales were presented in the DPCCQ, the joint pattern is commonly viewed as a single orientation. In recognition of this, as well as the fact that separate cognitive and behavioral orientations also exist, the data were combined into three mutually exclusive categories: mono-focal *Cognitive-Behavioral*, having both salient or at least one salient and the other rated "moderate" (3 on 0–5); mono-focal *Cognitive*, with Cognitive salient and Behavioral less than moderate (n=180 or 1.5%); mono-focal *Behavioral*, with Behavioral salient and Cognitive less than moderate (n=51 or < 1%).

10 It is interesting to note that all three bi-focal patterns consisted of a salient *Humanistic* orientation plus one other, and this was repeated as well in two smaller groups: *Humanistic + Other* orientation (289) and *Humanistic + Systemic* orientation (273—another 5% of the sample). Moreover, four-fifths of the "*Broad-spectrum*" therapists (1,692) included *Humanistic* as a salient orientation, suggesting how readily it can be combined with others. About as many bi-focal or broad-spectrum therapists combined a salient *Humanistic* orientation as reported having a single or mono-focal *Humanistic*—together, making *Humanistic* and *Analytic/psychodynamic* approaches about equal as leading orientations among our therapists.

11 Some 222 therapists reported combining a salient *Analytic/psychodynamic* with a salient *Cognitive-Behavioral* orientation, which would strike many others in the field as basically incompatible.

12 Although career level in principle is independent of profession, small but statistically significant differences occurred in our sample between Psychologists (M = 13.2 years), Psychiatrists (M = 11 years), and Counselors (M = 10 years).

13 In some subsequent analyses a similar but more differentiated six-category scheme may be used.

14 χ^2 = 3628, *df* = 18, *p* =.000.

15 χ^2 = 2812, *df* = 18, *p* =.000.

16 Whether in fact this happens, and for which therapists, was recently examined in a longitudinal study by Goldberg, Rousmaniere, Miller et al. (2016).

17 For example, see the compilations of research evidence edited by Norcross and Lambert (2019) and Norcross and Wampold (2019).

18 This is implicit even in the extreme example of computer based therapy, since the algorithm directing the computer's response had to have been designed either by a therapist or a therapeutically very well-informed code writer.

19 The adaptive strategy progressively elaborated by the hominids that became homo sapiens and its evolutionary close relatives favored adaptation through intelligence and real-time cognitive processing relying on symbolic processes, which required sizeable complex brain and heads large enough to contain them, but still small enough to pass through the birth canal without frequent damage to itself or its mother. The solution to this challenge has been birth of a basically helpless premature offspring that continues in fetal development for a long period postpartum, during which the individual depended on the nurturance, protection and guidance

of groups of adult caregivers. This forms the oldest, deepest layer of experience within each individual; and although moderated and modulated as children become adults, it remains dependent on cohesive adult relationships in a culturally meaningful community, and can be a source not only of developmental vulnerabilities but also of healing relationships that encourage "creative and reparative regression".

20 Establishment of medicine/psychiatry as the first modern "mental health" profession was described by Abbott (1988) as a wresting of "jurisdiction" over "troubled souls" from the traditional domain of religious ministers by medical doctors as proponents of a scientific worldview. The long "premodern" history of clerical pastoral care was described by Clebsch and Jaekle (1964).

21 Counseling also has a major historical root in education, as most recognizable in college or university "counseling centers"—a familiar locale that should be included in the Franks' list of healing settings.

22 The greatly undervalued concept of *morale* has both psychological and social relevance, as was richly explored in works by the great French sociologist Emile Durkheim (e.g., Durkheim, 1899/1951, 1915/1965). Morale is familiar in a military context as "unit cohesion", in an athletic context as "team spirit", and in a religious context as "enthusiasm". But morale is also a pervasive aspect of society at large; psychologically it is a source of optimism, energy and perseverance in the daily lives of individuals.

23 This is further explored theoretically in Orlinsky (2017).

24 In a currently ongoing and closely related study of psychotherapy trainees (N=1,354 at present), a third option (Other) was given along with Male and Female: 1,143 checked "Female", 210 checked "Male", and 1 checked "Other".

25 This disproportion between men and women would almost certainly have appeared greater yet if our sample adequately represented Social Work and Counseling professions.

26 Not shown in Appendix Table 2.3 due to the relatively small sample size for this profession.

27 Studies of psychotherapist populations in specific countries vary greatly and typically focus on one or another of the psychotherapy disciplines, but interested readers can explore the following: for *China*—Hou & Zhang (2007), and Huang (2015); for *Denmark*—Jacobsen, Nielsen & Orlinsky (2013); for *Germany, Austria and Switzerland*—Willutzki, Orlinsky, Cierpka, Ambühl, Laireiter & Meyerberg (2005); for *New Zealand*—Calvert, Kazantzis, Merrick Orlinsky, Ronan & Staniforth (2007), Kazantzis & Deane (1998), Kazantzis, Calvert, Orlinsky, Rooke, Ronan & Merrick (2009), Kazantzis, Calvert, Orlinsky, Rooke, Ronan & Merrick (2010), as well as Kazantzis, Calvert, Orlinsky, Merrick, Ronan & Munro (2009); for *South Korea*— Bae, Joo, & Orlinsky (2003), Bae & Orlinsky (2006), and Joo, Bae & Orlinsky (2005); for the *United Kingdom*—Norcross, Dryden & Brust (1992a), Norcross, Dryden & Brust (1992b), and Norcross, Dryden & DeMichele (1992); for the USA—Norcross, Farber & Prochaska (1993), Norcross, Karg & Prochaska (1997a), Norcross, Karg & Prochaska (1997b), and Norcross & Rogan (2013).

28 Exceptions included Denmark and Portugal, most of whose therapists were women (75% and 72% respectively) but most of whom were Psychologists by profession (92% and 78% respectively).

29 Only 36% (*n* = 490) of those who said they would be viewed as minorities specified what they were: 31% religious minorities; 24% sexual minorities; 23% racial/ethnic minorities; 9% immigrant minorities; 1% physical disability minorities; and 12% "other".

30 Full data on countries of origin are only available for Australia, which received emigrants from an amazing 57 different countries: the UK (44%), New Zealand (10%); South Africa (6%); and 4% each from the USA, Netherlands, and Germany. Limited data for Switzerland lists emigrants from 10 countries, mainly Germany (56%), France (12%), and Italy (12%). Very limited data for Israel lists emigrants

from 16 countries: USA (27%), Russia (12%), Romania (12%), and 9% each from Canada and Poland. Limitations on data are due to omission of relevant questions from some versions of the DPCCQ.

31 One of the rare studies of therapists' immigrant status is Kissil, Davey & Davey (2013).
32 Chapter 5 of this book deals with the topic more extensively.
33 In the context of the USA, two older studies may still be relevant: Henry, Sims & Spray (1971), and Marx & Spray (1972).

References

Abbott, A. (1988). *The system of professions: An essay on the division of expert labor.* Chicago: University of Chicago Press.

Bae, S., Joo, E., & Orlinsky, D.E. (2003). Psychotherapists in South Korea: Professional and practice characteristics. *Psychotherapy: Theory, Research, Practice, and Training,* 40, 302–316.

Bae, S. H., & Orlinsky, D. E. (2006). Gender, marital status, and age in the professional development of psychotherapists in Korea. *Asian Journal of Women's Studies,* 12, 36–62.

Calvert, S. J., Kazantzis, N., Merrick, P. L., Orlinsky, D. E., Ronan, K. R., & Staniforth, B. (2007). Professional development of New Zealand social workers who engage in psychotherapy: Perceptions and activities. *Social Work Review,* 19, 16–31.

Clebsch, W. A., & Jaekle, C. R. (1964). *Pastoral care in historical perspective: An essay with exhibits.* New York: Harper Torchbook.

Durkheim, E. (1899/1951). *Suicide: A study in sociology.* Glencoe, IL: Free Press.

Durkheim, E. (1915/1965). *The elementary forms of the religious life.* New York: Free Press.

Frank, J. D. (1974). Psychotherapy: The restoration of morale. *American Journal of Psychotherapy,* 131, 271–274.

Frank, J. D., & Frank, J. B. (1991). *Persuasion and healing: A comparative study of psychotherapy,* 3rd ed. Baltimore, MD: Johns Hopkins University Press.

Goldberg, C. (1992). *The seasoned psychotherapist: Triumph over adversity.* New York: Norton.

Goldberg, S. B., Rousmaniere, T., Miller, S. D., Whipple, J., Nielsen, S. L., Hoyt, W. T., & Wampold, B. E. (2016). Do psychotherapists improve with time and experience? A longitudinal analysis of outcomes in a clinical setting. *Journal of Counseling Psychology,* 63, 1–11.

Henry, W. E., Sims, J. H., & Spray, S. L. (1971). *The fifth profession: Becoming a psychotherapist* [Chapter 2, "Cultural origins and the marginal perspective"; Chapter 3, "Social Class Origins And Career Mobility" (pp. 9–44)]. San Francisco, CA: Jossey-Bass.

Holt, R. R. (Ed.) (1971). *New horizon for psychotherapy: Autonomy as a profession.* New York: International Universities Press.

Hou, Z-J., & Zhang, N. (2007). Counseling psychology in China. *Applied Psychology: An International Review,* 56(1), 33–50.

Huang, H-Y. (2015). From psychotherapy to psycho-boom: A historical overview of psychotherapy in China. *Psychoanalysis and Psychotherapy in China,* 1, 1–30.

Jacobsen, C. H., Nielsen, J., & Orlinsky, D. E. (2013). Danish psychologists as psychotherapists: Professional, demographic and personal characteristics, and change in theoretical orientations. *Nordic Psychology,* 64(3), 22–35.

Joo, E., Bae, S. H., & Orlinsky, D. E. (2005). Korean psychotherapists' self-report on strengths and limitations in practice: An exploratory qualitative study. *Korean Social Science Journal,* 32, 71–89.

Kazantzis, N., Calvert, S. J., Orlinsky, D. E., Rooke, S., Ronan, K., & Merrick, P. (2009). Activities influencing the professional development of New Zealand counsellors across their careers. *New Zealand Journal of Counselling,* 29, 73–92.

Kazantzis, N., Calvert, S. J., Orlinsky, D. E., Merrick, P. L., Ronan, K. R. & Munro, M. (2009). Perceived professional development in psychological therapies: Comparing New Zealand, Canadian and US psychologists. *The Bulletin*, 36–47.

Kazantzis, N., Calvert, S. J., Orlinsky, D. E., Rooke, S., Ronan, K., & Merrick, P. (2010). Professional development perceptions and activities of psychiatrists and mental health nurses in New Zealand. *The New Zealand Medical Journal*, 123, 24–34.

Kazantzis, N., & Deane, F. P. (1998). Theoretical orientations of New Zealand psychologists: An international comparison. *Journal of Psychotherapy Integration* 8, 97–113.

Kissil, K., Davey, M., & Davey, A. (2013). Therapists in a foreign land: Acculturation, language proficiency and counseling self-efficacy among foreign-born therapists practicing in the United States. *International Journal of Advances in Counselling*, 35, 216–223.

Luhrmann, T. M. (2000). *Of two minds: The growing disorder in American psychiatry.* New York: Knopf.

Marx, J. H., & Spray, S. L. (1972). "Birds of a Feather": Social-class status and religio-cultural value homophily in the mental health field. *Journal of Health and Social Behavior*, 13, 413–428.

Norcross, J. C., Dryden, W., & Brust, A. M. (1992a). British clinical psychologists: I. A national survey of the BPS Clinical Division. *Clinical Psychology Forum*, 40, 19–24.

Norcross, J. C., Dryden, W., & Brust, A. M. (1992b). British clinical psychologists: II. Survey findings and American comparisons. *Clinical Psychology Forum*, 40, 25–29.

Norcross, J. C., Dryden, W., & DeMichele, J. T. (1992). British clinical psychologists and personal therapy: What's good for the goose? *Clinical Psychology Forum*, 44, 29–33.

Norcross, J. C., Farber, J. A., & Prochaska, J. O. (1993). Psychologists conducting psychotherapy: New findings and historical comparisons on the Psychotherapy Division membership. *Psychotherapy*, 30, 692–697.

Norcross, J. C., Karg, R., & Prochaska, J. O. (1997a). Clinical psychologists in the 1990s. I. *The Clinical Psychologist*, 50(2), 4–9.

Norcross, J. C., Karg, R., & Prochaska, J. O. (1997b). Clinical psychologists in the 1990s. II. *The Clinical Psychologist*, 50(3), 4–11.

Norcross, J. C., & Lambert, M. J. (Eds.) (2019). *Psychotherapy relationships that work. Volume I: Evidence- based therapist contributions and responsiveness to patients.* New York: Oxford University Press.

Norcross, J. C., & Rogan, J. D. (2013). Psychologists conducting psychotherapy in 2012: Current practices and historical trends among Division 29 members. *Psychotherapy*, 50, 490–495.

Norcross, J. C., & Wampold, B. E. (Eds.) (2019). *Psychotherapy relationships that work. Volume II: Evidence-based therapist responsiveness.* New York: Oxford University Press.

Orlinsky, D. E. (2009). Research on psychotherapy and the psychotherapeutic profession(s): A brief introduction. *European Journal of Psychotherapy and Counselling*, 11, 183–190.

Orlinsky, D. E. (2017). Unity and diversity among psychotherapies. In A. J. Consoli, L. E. Beutler, & B. Bongar, Eds., *Comprehensive textbook of psychotherapy: Theory and practice*, 11–30. New York: Oxford University Press.

Willutzki, U., Orlinsky, D., Cierpka, M., Ambühl, H., Laireiter, A.-R., Meyerberg, J. (2005). WIR: Daten uber uns. Psychotherapeuten in Deutschland, Österreich und der Schweiz. [WE: Data about us. Psychotherapists in Germany, Austria and Switzerland.] In O. F. Kernberg, B. Dulz, & J. Eckert, *WIR: Psychotherapists* (pp. 26–38). Stuttgart, Germany: Schattauer.

3 Personal Self

D. E. Orlinsky with M. H. Rønnestad, A. Hartmann,
E. Heinonen and U. Willutzki

In this chapter[1] the perspective shifts from an external view of psychotherapists' professional and demographic characteristics to the internal view that psychotherapists have of themselves, as promised in ending the previous chapter. Probably nothing is more "internal" to what individuals experience than their own *personal self*—as true for psychotherapists as for others.[2]

A Concept of Personal Self

Personal self can be defined briefly for our purpose[3] as one's sense of identity and agency as a participant in close personal relationships. *Identity* is simply one's sense of "who I am" and "what I'm like" in a particular social setting and relationship. *Agency* similarly is one's sense of "what I can do" and "how I do it". *Close personal relationships* include the emotionally compelling involvements with significant others to whom one feels meaningfully connected. These typically include childhood family members (e.g., parents, siblings, and "favorite" others), adult family members (partners, children, and "connected" others), and other loved ones ("best" friends, romantic interests, "old" comrades, helpers and supporters). *Personal self* is grounded in one's experiences in close relationships, and is expressed through one's actions in those relationships. In so far as they typically occur "at home" and in similarly private places, one's *personal self* can be thought of as one's "home self" or "private self".

Similarly, the self-experiences that therapists have in their professional work relationships, especially vis-à-vis clients, can be described as the therapist's "work self" or professional self. Maintaining an appropriate distance between one's professional self and one's personal self is regarded as essential for psychotherapists, as much or even more so than it is for other professions and service occupations. On one hand, the therapists need to shield patients from their own private interests and concerns; yet at the same time, some congruence or integration of the therapist's private self and work self is probably what makes therapists empathetic and allows them to respond not routinely but rather to "be spontaneous and alive in the work of psychotherapy".[4]

Taking the view that self-experience is socially embedded (e.g., Goffman, 1959; Mead, 1967; Sullivan, 1953) allows recognition of other aspects of self

DOI: 10.4324/9781003217572-3

which become salient in other social contexts. For the dedicated athlete who regularly engages in team play or individual competition, one could speak of an "athlete self". For the individual devoted to national service or to charitable works, one could speak of a "patriot self" and a "humanitarian self", each rooted in a distinctive set of social settings and relationships. These socially grounded self-components and others like them reflect the multifaceted richness and complexity of individual personality.

The totality of self experience is a complex organization of multiple component "selves", evolving over the course of life (e.g., Erikson, 1959; McCall & Simmons, 1978). This is no "multiple personality disorder", a pathological condition of separated and disconnected selves. Indeed the healthy personality might be described as a "multiple personality order"—a differentiated, flexibly integrated system composed of psychologically active[5] interpersonal facets of self or role-identities.[6]

The *personal self*, as defined above, has a developmental primacy and central place in this. During one's early years, most relationships involve family members and "familiar" others in the family's orbit, so inevitably one's first self-experience is a *personal self*. Other self-aspects or personas become differentiated from this but remain linked to it as the child's world expands with new social roles and relationships. The *personal self* becomes over time just one part of the whole, activated and experienced mainly in the context of close personal relationships, but these earlier connections keep *personal self* a core part of one's total identity; and, together with one's bodily sensations and body-image, a major thread of continuity in self-experience.[7]

A Measure of Personal Self

Turning from the theoretical to the practical: measures of both the therapist's *personal self* and *professional self* were included in well-separated parts of the *Development of Psychotherapists Common Core Questionnaire* (DPCCQ). Both measures were informed by the view just presented of self-aspects or role-identities as situationally activated, experienced and expressed in specific social settings and relationships.

The measures each consisted of 28 self-descriptive adjectives as possible responses to this question for *personal self*: "How would you describe yourself (e.g., as you are in your close personal relationships?" For the *professional self* the question was: "How would you describe yourself as a therapist—your actual style or manner with clients."[8] Each adjective was followed by a 4-point scale (0 = Not at all, 1 = Some, 2 = Much, 3 = Very much). The adjectives used to represent the therapist's *personal self* were selected to reflect both their characteristic *interpersonal style* and *individual temperament*.

Interpersonal Style

The view of interpersonal style, and the particular adjectives selected, were based on the long familiar "circumplex" model of interpersonal behavior introduced by Leary (1957) and elaborated by Carson (1969). The model posits two basic bipolar dimensions of social interactions: social cohesion or *Affiliation* (affirmation vs. negation) and social control or *Influence* (assertion vs. passivity). All interactive behaviors vary in the degree to which the participants express Affiliation and exert Influence with respect to one another. These dimensions generate a circular field, as illustrated in Figure 3.1.

Affiliation is represented on the horizontal axis and reflects variation between affirmation–acceptance–approach on the right, through a neutral point, to negation–rejection–distance on the left. The "approach" or *affirming* pole is expressed through warm, caring, friendly social behavior; the "distant" or *negating* pole is expressed through cold, critical, rejecting social behavior. The mid-point represents a relatively impersonal, disinterested or indifferent behavioral attitude.

Influence is represented on the vertical axis and reflects variation between assertive–authoritative–directive action on the top, through a neutral point, to passive–receptive–permissive behavior at the bottom. The mid-point represents a relatively collaborative, cooperative or mutual mode of behavior.

In this model, two orthogonal bipolar dimensions are differentiated into quadrants representing meaningful combinations or blends. The combination of assertive and affirming social behavior is *Protective* action. The contrasting quadrant defines social behavior that is both assertive and negating, reflected in

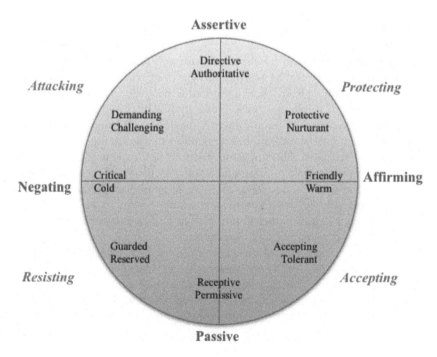

Figure 3.1 Interpersonal Circumplex: Dimensions and Adjectives

various forms of *Attack*. In the quadrant where the negativity and passivity combine, behavior is reflected in modes of *Resistant* or defensive behavior expressed by being guarded and reserved. Completing the circle, passively affirming social behavior manifests in diverse forms of harmony, agreement and *Acceptance*.

By selecting two approximately synonymous adjectives to represent each octant of the circumplex, 16 conceptually grounded rating scales were created. To allow for meaningful comparisons of personal self and professional self, the same 16 adjective scales were used in both contexts. Moreover, in selecting adjectives it was obviously important to be sure they could be appropriately used to describe behaviors likely to occur in close personal relationships *and* in therapeutic relationships. As both personal and therapeutic relationships normally entail Affirming behavior, that task required particular attention selecting adjectives for the Negating pole of the circumplex.

Individual Temperament

Affiliation and control are aspects of relationship rooted directly in the process of social interaction, variously modulated in different settings and relationships. Individual temperament is another source of influence modulating the quality of participation and self-experience in relationships. It reflects recognizable individual differences in the characteristic behavioral styles of the participants themselves, typically expressed *across* varied situations like a personal "signature" or musical leitmotif—as when one is tempted to say "Oh, that's just like Jack" (or "just like Jill"). The concept of temperament is familiar both in casual observation and in psychological research (e.g., Buss & Plomin, 1984; Halverson, Kohnstamm & Martin, 1994). It refers to persistent behavioral traits that may be "inborn" (i.e., inherited genetically or induced by the fetal environment), or result from early "formative" childhood learning.

In thinking about the temperamental qualities of relating that might enter self-experience in relationships, one dimension that stood out was the *expressive amplitude* of behavior. This appeared variously as "expansive" and "open" at one extreme, in contrast to "restrained" and "focused" on the other: fireworks vs. candlelight, force vs. finesse; quaffing vs. sipping; blaring vs. muted; rampant vs. contained; and so on. Expressive amplitude seems to be recognizable in several domains of psychological functioning, representing the response phases of thought, feeling, action, and expectation.

To delineate temperament aspects in the DPCCQ, adjectives were selected to reflect degrees of *expansiveness/openness* vs. *restrictedness/focus* in those different areas of psychological functioning, as illustrated in Figure 3.2.

Contrasting cognitive-ideational styles were conceived as *intuitive* (open) and *skeptical* (restrained). Affective-emotive "expansive" terms were *demonstrative, energetic, intense*; and "restricted" styles are *quiet, private, subtle*. Open intentional-enactive styles are *energetic* and *pragmatic*; focused enactive-intention styles are *determined* and *organized*. Finally, an expansive effect in expectancy is

Domain of Functioning	Expressive Amplitude	
	Expansive-Open	Restrained-Focused
Cognitive-Ideational	*Intuitive*	*Skeptical*
Affect-Emotive	*Demonstrative*	*Private*
	Energetic	*Quiet*
	Intense	*Subtle*
Intentional-Enactive	*Energetic*	*Determined*
	Pragmatic	*Organized*
Effect Expectancy	*Optimistic*	*Fatalistic*

Figure 3.2 Temperament: Facets and Adjectives

optimistic; a restrained outcome-expectation is *fatalistic*. These temperament style adjectives were presented along with those based on the interpersonal circumplex in sections of the DPCCQ where therapists were asked to describe themselves. Each adjective was rated on a 4-point scale as: 0 = Not at all, 1 = Some, 2 = Much, 3 = Very much. (The "Personal Self" scales are presented at chapter's end for the reader's use as a source of self-reflection.)

Personal Self Qualities

Common Qualities of Therapists' Personal Self

What are the most and least common aspects of psychotherapists' *personal self*? And in what ways do therapists differ most from one another. To simplify answering these questions, the 4-point ratings of the adjective were condensed into "high" (Much or Very much) vs. "low" (Some or Not at all) and the percentages of high and low were counted for each (see Appendix Table 3.1).

Given the focus on close personal relationships, it isn't surprising that the most common interpersonal circumplex-based qualities of *personal self* were being *warm* and *friendly* (rated "high" by 94% of more than 11,000 therapists). In addition, being *tolerant, accepting, nurturing* and *receptive* rated "high" as qualities of *personal self* by 80% to 90% of therapists. By contrast, being *cold* in close relationships was the least characteristic quality of therapists' *personal self* (rated "low" by 94% of all therapists).

The most common temperament-related qualities of *personal self* that were rated "high" were being *intuitive* and *optimistic* (84% on both), and the least characteristic were being *fatalistic* and *skeptical* (89% and 75% rated "low" respectively). The high rating of *intuitive* and relatively low rating of *skeptical* suggests a primarily affective rather than rational mode of involvement. The high rating of *optimistic* and very low rating of *fatalistic* suggests these relationships are expected to reward and satisfy.

Undoubtedly psychotherapists are like most people when at home in the circle of their close friends and family—warm, caring, tolerant, expansive and open. It is impossible to know if they are distinctively so without comparing therapists with groups in other fields (e.g., engineers, or artists).[9] Yet, comparison with other groups may be beside the point. As the core experience of *personal self*, it provides a firm foundation for the kind of professional work that psychotherapists are called to do outside their circle of close friends and family.

In other respects, therapists differed considerably among themselves. Interpersonally, about half (53%) rated themselves "high" on *permissive* with the rest (44%) "low". Similarly, by temperament basically half were "high" on *quiet* or on *demonstrative* (50% and 49% respectively) while the other half were "low". Variability in other respects was shown in that 75% to 25% of the therapists rated themselves as "high" on how much they are *protective, challenging, directive, demanding, authoritative, critical, reserved* and *guarded*.[10] Similarly, from 76% to 45% of the therapists also rated themselves as "high" on how *energetic, pragmatic, determined, organized, intense, private* and *subtle* they are. There was clearly a broad range of individual difference in *personal self*, over and around the core experience of self in close personal relations as loving, expansive and open.

Personal Self Dimensions

The individual differences among therapists can be examined more meaningfully through the use of exploratory factor analysis, which probes the correlations between adjective scales to determine their fewer underlying dimensions.[11] Once internally coherent or reliable dimensions are found, the adjective scales that correlate most strongly with each can be combined to make a smaller set of more robust measures. This procedure successfully identified four dimensions of individual difference in therapists' experiences of *personal self* (see Appendix Tables 3.2 and 3.3).[12] Each dimension is a continuum along which therapists have varying scores as relatively high, medium or low. Although each dimension has its own name and characteristic, different regions of each will be named to suggest how qualitative differences can arise from quantitative variation—just as changing colors are seen at different wavelengths of light.[13]

Genial/Caring

The first dimension clearly mirrored one of the circumplex axes illustrated in Figure 3.1. The Affirming pole of the horizontal (Affiliation) axis defined a dimension appropriately labelled Genial/Caring, reflecting the combined effect of being *warm*, *friendly, nurturant, tolerant, receptive* and *accepting*. It measures what might be called *self-bestowal*—a readiness to give of one's attention, concern, companionship, good cheer, and helpfulness to others. It may be viewed as a propensity to return bene- volence in reciprocity (see Gouldner, 1960) for benevolence received from others in the past, a generalization of gratitude (e.g., for one's parents' care) that is too large in scope to be repaid directly (Simmel, 1950). Different degrees of self-bestowal in the personal self of therapists are shown in Figure 3.3.

First, at its highest level, Genial/Caring reflects a degree of self-bestowal well described as *devoted*, which one would likely be with one's children and spouse, best- friend or lover. About one-third (32%) of therapists experienced their *personal self* as devoted. Second, a lower but still strong degree of self-bestowal was reported by about half (49%) of therapists. This more moderate level could be described as *affec- tionate* (e.g., with a friend or sibling). Third, a more modest level yet of Genial/Caring characterized a fifth (19%) of the therapists—cool selves who typically experienced themselves in close relationships as no more than *sympathetic* (averaging between "Some" to less than "Much" on Genial/Caring). Finally, almost none (0.3%) of the psychotherapists scored below this level, in the uncaring or *indifferent* range—as would be expected, and one hopes would be found, in a close personal relationship.

Forceful/Exacting

The Assertive pole on the vertical (Control) axis of the circumplex basically defined the second dimension, although with some tilt towards the Negating

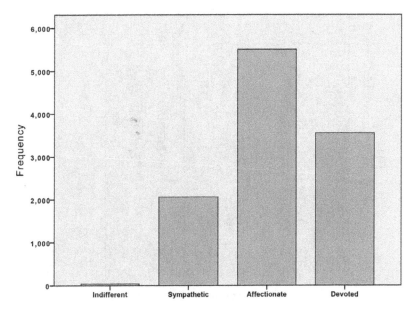

Figure 3.3 Levels of Genial/Caring (Self-Bestowal)

pole of Affiliation. This dimension was called Forceful/Exacting because it showed the extent to which therapists inclined to be *directive, demanding, authoritative, critical* and *challenging* in close personal relationships. Scores on the Forceful/Exacting dimension can be viewed as reflecting individual differences in *self-assertion*, with varying levels and proportions among therapists shown in Figure 3.4.

Scores at the highest levels on Forceful/Exacting reflect an experience of one's typical behavior in close relationships as *directive*; that is, as persons who prefer to take charge and be the dominant partner in relationships, exert pressure on others to meet their expectations, and who may act in an authoritarian or confronting manner. Characteristically, only a few (10%) of the therapists feel themselves to be at this extreme (i.e., self-described as more than "Much"). Even more (17%) were in the lowest range of scores, seeming to be shy and *retiring* in their close relationships. Most therapists by far were somewhere in the middle on this dimension: 38% were *collaborative*, being moderately assertive but able to share control in their relationships, and almost as many (36%) saw themselves as just "somewhat" Forceful with intimates and more likely than not to be *accommodating*.

Reclusive/Remote

A third dimension of self-experience combined some interpersonal adjective scales with others from the realm of temperament. The interpersonal adjectives

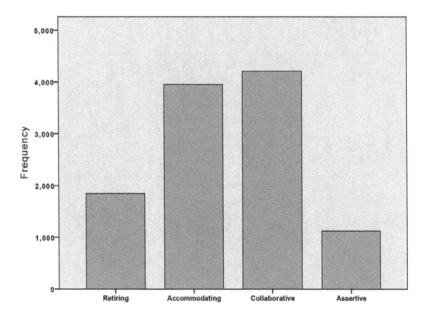

Figure 3.4 Levels of Forceful/Exacting (Self-Assertion)

were *reserved, guarded,* and *cold* from the Passive/Negating (lower left) quadrant of the circumplex. The temperament adjectives were *skeptical, private* and *subtle.* This combination of qualities was labelled Reclusive/Remote and was interpreted as a tendency to be *self-protective* in close relationships. Figure 3.5 describes four levels of self-protectiveness and the proportions of therapists at each level.

The relatively small proportion (6%) of therapists at the highest level of self-protectiveness (who rated themselves on Reclusive/Remote as more than "Much") would be well described as *wary*—even in close relationships. The other 94% divided evenly between the other three levels: 32% as typically but not excessively self-protective, or *circumspect* (i.e., "Some" but not more than "Much" on Reclusive/Remote); 32% as barely or "Somewhat" self-protective in close relationships, and thus designated as *approachable*; and 30% not even "Somewhat" Reclusive/Remote, but instead experiencing themselves as *trusting* in close relationships.

Ardent/Expressive

The fourth dimension of *personal self* was defined by the temperament adjectives *intense, energetic, intuitive, demonstrative* and *determined.* It was labeled Ardent/Expressive, and was understood as reflecting the relative amplitude of a therapist's *self-expression,* ranging from reticent and restrained to vivid and dramatic. Figure 3.6 illustrates varying levels on the Ardent/Expressive dimension of therapists' self-experience.

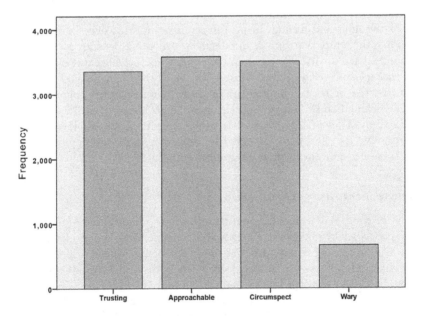

Figure 3.5 Levels of Reclusive/Remote (Self-Protection)

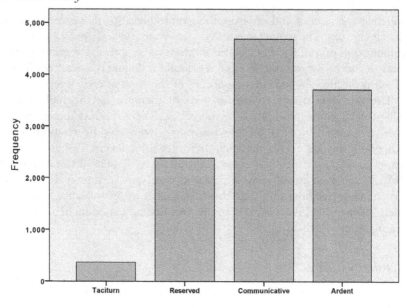

Figure 3.6 Levels of Ardent/Expressive (Self-Expression)

A third (33%) of our therapists described themselves as highly Ardent/ Expressive (i.e., more than "Much") or as *ardent* in their close relationships. They see themselves as forthright, intense, demonstrative individuals, and might be seen by others as candid, outspoken people who generally let you know their thoughts and feelings in no uncertain terms. However, a plurality (42%) among therapists were more moderately Ardent/Expressive (i.e., more than "Somewhat" up to "Much"), and appeared openly self-expressive or *communicative* in close relationships. Most of the rest (21%) experienced themselves as understated or *reserved* individuals—persons whose partners might need to be quite attuned and sensitive to them in order to know what they thought and felt. Only a few (3%) of the therapists were at the lowest level of Ardent/ Expressive (i.e., less than "Somewhat" self-expressive), and could be described *as taciturn* or reticent in their close relationships.

Interrelations Among Dimensions

The method of Varimax factor rotation used to identify these four dimensions of *personal self* heightens their statistical independence, but a moderate degree of correlation among dimensions was observed. Being Ardent/Expressive in close intimate relations was positively correlated both with Genial/Caring ($r = .34$) and Forceful/Exacting ($r = .37$)—even though Genial/Caring and Forceful/ Exacting trends were themselves somewhat negatively correlated to each other (see Appendix Table 3.3). Perhaps the Ardent/Expressive temperament dimension is best understood as amplifying or attenuating the other dimensions. When combined at high levels with Genial/Caring, the effect could be one of passion, yearning or devotion. When combined at high levels with Force-ful/Exacting, the effect would be a person who is overbearing, aggressive, and dictatorial, resembling the so-called "Type A personality". When combined at high levels with Reclusive/Remote, the effect would be one of personal mistrust, suspicion and insularity.

Other small but significant correlations were observed between the *personal self* dimensions.

Genial/Caring tended to be negatively associated with Reclusive/Remote ($r = -.18$), although the level of correlation suggests they are incompatible mainly at extreme levels. Being moderately Reclusive/Remote may be compatible with being Genial/Caring (e.g., as in being a shy but caring person). On the other hand, Forceful/Exacting tended to be positively associated with Reclusive/Remote ($r = .27$). A possible interpretation is that the self-assertive quality of Forceful/Exacting may in some cases reflect a defensive stance against an underlying discomfort with intimacy. That is, for some persons acting "tough" may be less threatening than feeling insecure.

Personal Self Profiles

The fact that four relatively independent dimensions of *personal self* were found logically implies that describing the self-experience of individual therapists should require specifying an individual's score on each of the four dimensions. Each therapist would have an individual profile based on a panel of the four scores. It is tempting to pursue that level of description, but unfortunately if each dimension is viewed as a continuum there would be a very large number of possible scores on each, and an even larger number of combinations among the four dimensions whose specific meaning would be hard to grasp and whose practical value would be questionable. One advantage of treating each dimension as having four meaningfully distinct levels is reducing the number of possible scores for each profile to 16, which in practice can be reduced to 14 given that virtually no therapists were *indifferent* on Genial/Caring and very few were *reticent* on Ardent/Expressive. Although this must remain a task for future research, the possible results can be illustrated here regarding the 10 most and 10 least frequent *personal self* profiles found in our data, where the 10 most common include a third (34%) of all therapists and the 10 least common are just 1% (see Appendix Table 3.4).

Comparing the most and least common profiles, one difference that stands out is the fact therapists characteristically viewed themselves as *collaborative* on the Forceful/Exacting dimension in seven of the 10 common profiles, and *assertive* in only one—in contrast to the 10 least common profiles, where *assertive* appeared six times and *collaborative* appeared only once. This suggests that therapists tend to approach close relationships as equal partners rather than as leaders or followers.

An equally striking difference was found on the Ardent/Dramatic dimension, where being open or *communicative* was in eight of the 10 most common therapists' profiles, and was absent from all of the 10 least common profiles. The latter were split between extremes of being not self-expressive or *reserved* (six of 10), and being very self-expressive, or *ardent* (four of 10). One could imagine that neither *reserved* nor *ardent* styles of self-expression would be helpful if also occurring in therapeutic relationships.

Similarly, on the Reclusive/Remote dimension, being *circumspect* (i.e., somewhat cautious or prudent) typified six of the 10 most common, which does suggest that therapists may carry some of their professional restraint into their personal life. On the other hand, being *wary* (i.e., highly cautious or avoidant) in close relationships was atypical for therapists, found only once among the 10 most common profiles but in five of the 10 least common therapist profiles.

Therapist Characteristics and Personal Self

Since varying scores on the four dimensions reflect individual differences in *personal self* among therapists, it is worth asking whether any of their "external" characteristics are related to those differences. The most public yet immediately personal of any individual's characteristics are their gender and age. The most distinctive of therapists' occupational characteristics are their professional background and approach to practice. How much, if at all, is the therapist's *personal self* influenced by or associated with these characteristics?

Gender

How much if at all do male and female therapists, viewed as men and women, differ in how they experience their selves in close personal relationships? A comparison of the mean scores of men and women on the four dimensions showed small but statistically significant differences in three (see Appendix Table 3.5). On average, women more than men experienced themselves as Genial/Caring (self-bestowing) and as Ardent/Expressive (self-expressive), whereas men more than women experienced themselves as Reclusive/Remote (self-protective). Interestingly, women and men therapists were equally Forceful/Exacting (self-assertive) in close relationships.

Comparing different levels on the four dimensions showed more nuanced differences (see Appendix Table 3.6). On Genial/Caring, women were significantly more likely to feel *devoted* (35% vs. 27%) while men were more likely to be *sympathetic* (23% vs. 16%). On Ardent/Expressive, women were more likely to be *ardent* (38% vs. 26%) and men were more likely to be reserved (28% vs 18%). On Reclusive/Remote, women tended to be more *trusting* (33% vs. 25%) while men tended to be a little more *circumspect* (35% vs 30%).

Cultural gender patterns were consistent for our sample of therapists in some but not all dimensions of *personal self*. Women on average were personally more self-bestowing and self-expressive than men, and men in general tended to be more self-protective than women. However, there was little difference between the sexes in regard to being self-assertive: women who are professional psychotherapists were equally if not slightly more self-assertive in close relationships than were men. However, the differences were not large, and both men and women were represented in every category.

Age

There were also small but statistically significant correlations of therapist age with the four dimensions of *personal self* (see Table 3.7). Linear trends showed Genial/Caring *increasing* with age, especially among men, and showed Forceful/ Exacting and Reclusive/Remote *decreasing* with age. There was also a tendency for Older men, but not women, to be more self-expressive. These results may reflect a modest degree of "mellowing" with age. However, the increase with age was clearly stronger for men in being Genial/Caring ($r = .18$ vs. $r = .08$) and Ardent/Expressive ($r = .09$ vs. $r = .02$). Men appear to become more self-bestowing and self-expressive with age, perhaps because they experience lower levels on both when young.

The inflection points in these age-related changes are suggested by comparing Younger (age 21–34), Midlife (age 35–54), and Older (age 55–85) therapists (see Table 3.8). There is a progressive increase from Younger to Midlife to Older with respect to Genial/Caring, and a progressive decrease with respect to Reclusive/Remote. However, the lessening of Forceful/Exacting only occurs with the transition from Midlife to Older age group, and the heightening of Ardent/Expressive seems to occur gradually with only the Younger and Older therapists having distinct levels (probably because it is mainly male therapists who reflected this change).

Gender and Age Combined

A combined analysis of age and gender provides a more refined view of where the differences in personal self are most significant (see Appendix Table 3.9). This was done by checking the observed incidence of women and men of different age groups against what would be expected by chance over the four levels previously described for each of the four dimensions.

With respect to Genial/Caring, Younger men (21–34) and Midlife men (35–54) were significantly more likely than chance to be *sympathetic* and less likely than chance to be *devoted*. Older women and men (55–85) were both more likely to be *devoted*. Still, by far the largest proportion of both male and female therapists in all age groups (about 50%) experienced a moderately high or *affectionate* level of Genial/Caring.

With respect to Forceful/Exacting, Younger women (21–34) were more likely to be *assertive* and less likely to be *accommodating*. Midlife women (35–54) were also more likely to be *assertive*, and less likely to be *retiring* and *collaborative*.

By contrast, Older women (55–85) were more *accommodating* and *retiring* and less *collaborative* or *assertive*. The trends for male therapists mirrored those for females although somewhat less dramatically. Older men and women were the least self-assertive of all.

With respect to Reclusive/Remote, Younger and Midlife men were significantly more likely than their female counterparts to be *circumspect*, and less likely to be *trusting* in close relationships. Older women were significantly more likely to be *trusting* and less likely to be *circumspect* or *wary*.

Finally, with respect to Ardent/Expressive, Younger men (21–34) were not only the most self-protective group but also personally the least self-expressive in close relationships, tending to experience themselves as reserved or *reticent* and not as *ardent*. Midlife men (35–54) were also more reserved and less *ardent*. By contrast, both Midlife and Older women were more likely to be *ardent* in self-expression. In every age group, women therapists experienced themselves as more self-expressive in close relationships than did men.

In sum, age and gender appeared to be statistically significant but relatively minor influences or nuances in how therapists experience themselves in their close personal relationships.[14]

Professional Characteristics

The next question concerns whether and how the therapist's *personal self* might be differentially related to occupational characteristics like their professional background and theoretical orientation.

Professional Discipline

Because of the significant differences in personal self between male and female therapists noted above, and because Chapter 2 showed the incidence of gender to vary between professions, the relationships of *personal self* and profession are examined separately for men and women (see Appendix Table 3.10).[15]

In regard to Genial/Caring, both male and female Counselors had the highest scores and Psychiatrists of both genders were significantly lower than those in other professions (though still in the *affectionate* range).

In regard to Forceful/Exacting, both male and female Psychologists were the most self-assertive in close personal relationships, and Counselors were significantly less so than other therapists.

In regard to Reclusive/Remote, men and women Psychiatrists were most self-protective in close relationships; among women therapists, Social Workers and Counselors were least self-protective; and among male therapists, Psychiatrists were more self-protective and Counselors and Psychologists were the least.

In regard to Ardent/Expressive, among female therapists Psychiatrists were the least and Lay Therapist/Analysts were the most self-expressive. Among male therapists, Psychiatrists and Psychologists were the least self-expressive and Lay Therapist/Analysts were again the most.

Overall, there were some notable differences in *personal self* between professions. Psychiatrists of both genders were personally the least self-bestowing, least self-expressive, and most self-protective. This evokes an image that is consistent with a professional "medical" manner of detachment and objectivity. On the other hand, Counselors of both genders were the most self-bestowing, least self-assertive, among the least self-protective, and among the most self-expressive. This profile evokes an image that is consistent with a professional manner of warmth, openness and involvement. Finally, Psychologists of both genders were the most self-assertive in close personal relationships, as well as moderately high in self-bestowal and fairly low in self-expressiveness. The image evoked by this profile is consistent with an "expert" professional manner that is active and directive but also warm if understated.

Of course, these average differences between groups do not apply to all individuals in each profession. There is always overlap between groups at the individual level, and one may certainly meet therapists who differ from the typical professional patterns. Still, given the differences that were observed, it is interesting to ask whether individuals with different personal qualities are drawn to training in different psychotherapeutic professions, or whether they also (or otherwise) tend to be shaped as persons over time by the characteristics of their profession. Answers about the direction of influence require longitudinal research that follows practitioners from entry level training to subsequent career levels.[16]

Theoretical Approach

The relation of therapists' *personal self* qualities to their theoretical orientations is another topic that has interested researchers, and the evidence to date[17] suggests a statistically significant but relatively small degree of convergence between those variables. For the present chapter, correlations between theoretical orientation and the four dimensions of therapists' *personal self* for total sample will be reported as the gender differences in results were very slight (see Appendix Table 3.11).

Genial/Caring

Genial/Caring was the only dimension that consistently (although modestly) correlated with theoretical approach. The more committed therapists were to any theoretical orientation except Analytic/Psychodynamic, the higher their scores were on Genial/Caring (ranging from r =.10 to r =.17). It isn't clear why this might be, or why this dimension was neutral (i.e., uncorrelated) with Analytic/Psychodynamic.

Forceful/Exacting

Variations in this dimension were unrelated to therapists' theoretical orientations.

Reclusive/Remote

Some very small but statistically significant correlations were found among male therapists. These were negative for Cognitive-Behavioral, Humanistic, Systemic and Broad Spectrum therapists, indicating a tendency to be less self-protective in close personal relationships, but were positive for Analytic/Psychodynamic psychotherapists. A similar pattern but of even weaker correlations appeared for women.

Ardent/Expressive

Finally, it appeared that Broad-Spectrum therapists in particular tended to be somewhat more self-expressive in close personal relationships than did therapists of other orientations, although with similar smaller trends among Humanistic and Systemic therapists.

Overall, the associations between therapists' theoretical orientations and the qualities of *personal self* were relatively weak. There was a slight differentiation between therapists espousing Analytic/Psychodynamic versus other orientations, more or less matching the image of the psychoanalyst as an impassive observer behind the couch and out of the patient's view. However, for the most part it is clear that therapists with varied *personal self* profiles may be found among therapists of all theoretical persuasions.

In Sum

Just as Chapter 2 explored the outwardly apparent characteristics of professional psychotherapists, this chapter dove directly into one of their most inward characteristics by presenting data reflecting the therapists' *personal self*.

Concepts reflecting interactive behavior in social relationships (the interpersonal circumplex) and temperamental traits across varied situations (response amplitude) were introduced as the basis for constructing item–scales used in the DPCCQ to assess the therapists' *personal self*. Interpersonal scales were generated from the interplay of Affiliation (affirming vs. negating) and Control (assertive vs. passive). Temperament scales were chosen to reflect expansion vs. restriction of responsiveness in several domains of psychological functioning. On the interpersonal scales, therapists typically described themselves in close relationships as *friendly, warm, tolerant, accepting* and *nurturant*, and rarely as *cold* or *guarded*. On the temperament scales, therapists commonly described themselves as *optimistic, intuitive, energetic*, and rarely as *fatalistic* or *skeptical*.

Exploratory factor analyses of the self-descriptive adjective scales revealed four relatively independent and meaningful dimensions that could be reliably used in subsequent analyses as multi-item factor scales. The factor scales reflecting interpersonal dimensions of *personal self* were *Genial/Caring* (self-bestowal), *Forceful/Exacting* (self-assertion), and *Reclusive/Remote* (self-protection). The factor scale based on temperament was *Ardent/Expressive* (self-expression), interpreted as amplifying or softening the manner in which interpersonal dimensions are expressed.

Four levels of intensity were described for each of the four dimensions. For *Genial/Caring* (self-bestowal), these ranged from most to least intense as being *devoted, affectionate, sympathetic,* or *indifferent.* For *Forceful/Exacting* (self-assertion), these appeared from most to least intense as *directive, collaborative, accommodating,* or *retiring.* For *Reclusive/Remote* (self-protection), the range from most to least intense was described as *wary, circumspect, approachable,* or *trusting.* Levels of being *Ardent/Expressive* (self-expression) were distinguished from most to least intense as *ardent, communicative, reserved,* or *reticent.*

Next, the interrelations of *personal self* with other therapist characteristics were examined. With respect to age and gender, women and Older therapists were significantly more likely than men or Younger therapists to be *Genial/ Caring* and *Ardent/Expressive,* and significantly less likely than men and Older therapists to be *Reclusive/Remote.* Contrary to gender stereotypes, female therapists were equally if not slightly more *Forceful/Exacting* in close personal relationships than the male therapists. Interactions of age and gender suggested the potential vulnerability of Younger men and the greater need of male therapists for personal development in order to achieve the level, as Older men, that approximated those shown by women in all age groups.

Comparison of therapists of different professional backgrounds, separately for women and men, revealed significant and largely consistent differences. In close personal relationships, Psychiatrists of both genders as a group (although not all individuals) were less Genial/Caring, less Ardent/Expressive, and more Reclusive/ Remote. Counselors of both genders as a group were more Genial/Caring, less Forceful/Exacting, and less Reclusive/Remote. Psychologists of both genders as a group were more Forceful/Exacting but moderate on the other dimensions. By contrast, only slight differences between therapists' theoretical orientations were observed, although those seemed meaningful.

The study of psychotherapists in this chapter focused on the self-experience in close personal relationships. For readers who would like to compare their own scores on the four dimensions with therapists in our sample, the relevant DPCCQ scales and a scoring guide are provided here below. The next chapter explores those close personal relationships more directly by examining their variations in therapists' private lives.

Personal Self Rating Scales

How would you describe yourself (e.g., as you are in your close personal relationships)?

		Not at all	Some	Much	Very much
1.	Accepting	0	1	2	3
2.	Authoritative	0	1	2	3
3.	Challenging	0	1	2	3
4.	Cold	0	1	2	3

Personal Self Rating Scales

How would you describe yourself (e.g., as you are in your close personal relationships)?

		Not at all	Some	Much	Very much
5.	Critical	0	1	2	3
6.	Demanding	0	1	2	3
7.	Demonstrative	0	1	2	3
8.	Determined	0	1	2	3
9.	Directive	0	1	2	3
10.	Energetic	0	1	2	3
11.	Friendly	0	1	2	3
12.	Guarded	0	1	2	3
13.	Intense	0	1	2	3
14.	Intuitive	0	1	2	3
15.	Nurturing	0	1	2	3
16.	Optimistic	0	1	2	3
17.	Organized	0	1	2	3
18.	Permissive	0	1	2	3
19.	Pragmatic	0	1	2	3
20.	Private	0	1	2	3
21.	Protective	0	1	2	3
22.	Quiet	0	1	2	3
23.	Receptive	0	1	2	3
24.	Reserved	0	1	2	3
25.	Skeptical	0	1	2	3
26.	Subtle	0	1	2	3
27.	Tolerant	0	1	2	3
28.	Warm	0	1	2	3

Personal Self Dimension-Algorithms

Genial/Caring   accepting + friendly + nurturing+ optimistic + tolerant + warm

Forceful/Exacting   authoritative + critical + challenging + demanding + directive

Reclusive/Remote   guarded + private + reserved + skeptical

Ardent/Expressive   demonstrative + determined + energetic + intense + intuitive

To compute each dimension, add the scores for each 0–3 adjective scale, then divide by the number of adjective scales for that dimension.

Notes

1 This chapter is a much expanded version of Orlinsky, Rønnestad, Hartmann et al. (2019).

2 The psychotherapist's personality has long been a topic of interest for researchers, generating a variety of studies that readers might like to compare, such as: Arthur (2000); Burkhard, Böbel, Hagl, Richter & Kazén (2017); Delgadillo, Branson, Kellett, Myles-Hooton, Hardy & Shafran (2020); Dent (1978); Heinonen & Nissen-Lie (2020); Heinonen & Orlinsky (2013); Henry, Schacht & Strupp (1990); Hersoug (2004); Hersoug, Høglend, Havik, von der Lippe & Monsen (2009); Ogunfowora & Drapeau (2008); Orlinsky, Willutzki, Meyerberg, Cierpka, Buchheim & Ambühl (1996); Scandell, Wlazelek & Scandell (1997); Topolinski & Hertel (2007).

3 The purpose at hand being to define "personal self" as a working concept accessible to empirical study. There are many conceptual and philosophical aspects to the idea of self whose discussion here would only divert and detract from the purpose at hand.

4 Eckler-Hart, 1987, p. 684; see also Rønnestad & Skovholt, 2013; Skovholt & Rønnestad, 1995.

5 Psychologically "active" in the sense of cognitive structures (sensorimotor, imaginal, or ideational) that are affectively charged and accordingly motivated (e.g., by desire to approach, by anger to attack, by fear to avoid or withdraw).

6 The opposite view of personality broken down in a state of pathology was presented by Freud (1923) in terms of conflict between bodily drives, dictates of conscience, and the frustrations of social reality—a view that he corrected for psychological normal functioning in his next, unfortunately much less often read, published book (Freud, 1926).

7 Readers who relish poetry might enjoy reflecting on the famous lines from Shakespeare's *Midsummer Night's Dream*: "…As imagination bodies forth the forms of things unknown, the poet's pen turns them to shapes and gives to airy nothing a local habitation and a name." If individuals are poets who must imagine their selves, then bodily experience is the "local habitation", identified socially and reflexively with the "name" parents give at birth to one's personal self—and without which, later self-aspects and personas would remain "airy nothings".

8 Details of the scales and results for the therapist's professional self were initially reported in Chapter 4 of Orlinsky & Rønnestad (2005).

9 Several studies have compared practicing psychotherapists and trainees with other professions or groups in the general population: Burkhard, Böbel, Hagl, Richter & Kazén (2017); Burton & Topham (1997); Fincke, Moller & Taubner (2015); Radeke & Mahoney (2000); Wolfer, Visla, Held, Hilpert & Fluckiger (2020).

10 Behind the veil of anonymity provided by the DPCCQ, a substantial number of therapists were willing to portray themselves in a somewhat negative light, which suggests a reassuring level of candidness.

11 Technical details of the factor analysis are presented in Orlinsky et al. (2019); the internal coherence or reliability of dimensions was assessed using Cronbach's alpha, with $\alpha \geq .7$ viewed as satisfactory.

12 A fifth dimension defined by the temperament adjectives *organized, pragmatic* and *optimistic* suggested a trait that could be called Practical/Businesslike, ranging from being scattered, diffuse and disorganized to highly focused and task-oriented; but with only three items a scale based on this dimension did not reach an acceptable level of reliability.

13 Four regions are named on each dimension but continuous scores on each dimension will be used in subsequent data analyses to prevent unnecessary loss of information.

14 Age and gender can be considered "influences" even though correlations do not establish causality, because it isn't possible that age or gender are influenced by the qualities of one's *personal self*.

15 In this case, it is possible that *personal self* might influence therapists' selection of their profession and/or their orientation, and that experiences in their profession or theoretical orientation might shape or reinforce some characteristics of their *personal self*.

16 A large-scale longitudinal study of psychotherapy trainees now underway may provide relevant data in a collaborative project of the SPR Interest Section on Therapist Training and Development (Orlinsky, Strauss, Rønnestad et al., 2015).

17 See Heinonen & Orlinsky (2013) and Orlinsky, Rønnestad, Hartmann, Heinonen & Willutzki (2019) for reviews of prior research and alternative methods of data analysis.

References

Arthur, A. R. (2000). The personality and cognitive-epistemological traits of cognitive-behavioural and psychoanalytic psychotherapists. *British Journal of Medical. Psychology*, 73, 243–257.

Burkhard, P., Böbel, E., Hagl, M., Richter, M., & Kazén, M. (2017). Personality styles of German-speaking psychotherapists differ from a norm, and male psychotherapists differ from their female colleagues. *Frontiers in Psychology*, 8, Article 840.

Burton, M., & Topham, D. (1997). Early loss experiences in psychotherapists, Church of England clergy, patients assessed for psychotherapy, and scientists and engineers. *Psychotherapy Research*, 7(3), 275–300.

Buss, A. H., & Plomin, R. (1984). *Temperament: Early developing personality traits.* Hillsdale, NJ: Erlbaum.

Carson, R. C. (1969). *Interaction concepts of personality.* Chicago: Aldine.

Delgadillo, J., Branson, A., Kellett, S., Myles-Hooton, P., Hardy, G. E., & Shafran, R. (2020). Therapists personality traits as predictors of psychological treatment outcomes. *Psychotherapy Research*, 30, 857–870.

Dent, J. K. (1978). *Exploring the psycho-social therapies through the personalities of effective therapists.* Rockville, MD: National Institute of Mental Health.

Eckler-Hart, A. H. (1987). True and false self in the development of the psychotherapist. *Psychotherapy: Theory, Research, Practice, Training*, 24, 683–692.

Erikson, E. H. (1959). *Identity and the life cycle: Selected papers.* New York: International Universities Press.

Fincke, J. L., Moller, H., & Taubner, S. (2015). Does interpersonal behavior of psychotherapy trainees differ in private and professional relationships? *Frontiers in Psychology*, 6, Article 765.

Freud, S. (1923). The ego and the id. In J. Strachey & A. Freud, Eds., *The complete psychological works of Sigmund Freud*, Vol. XIX, 3–66. London: Hogarth Press.

Freud, S. (1926). Inhibitions, symptoms, and anxiety. In J. Strachey & A. Freud, Eds., *The complete psychological works of Sigmund Freud*, Vol. XX, 77–174. London: Hogarth Press.

Goffman, E. (1959). *The presentation of self in everyday life.* Garden City, NY: Doubleday.

Gouldner, A. W. (1960). The norm of reciprocity: A preliminary statement. *American Sociological Review*, 25, 161–178.

Halverson, C. F., Jr., Kohnstamm, G. A., & Martin, R. P. (Eds.). (1994). *The developing structure of temperament and personality from infancy to adulthood.* Lawrence Erlbaum Associates, Inc.

Heinonen, E., & Nissen-Lie, H. A. (2020). The professional and personal characteristics of effective psychotherapists: A systematic review. *Psychotherapy Research*, 30, 417–432.

Heinonen, E., & Orlinsky, D. E. (2013). Psychotherapists' personal identities, theoretical orientations, and professional relationships: Elective affinity and role adjustment as modes of congruence. *Psychotherapy Research*, 23, 718–731.

Henry, W. E., Schacht, T. E., & Strupp, H. H. (1990). Patient and therapist introject, interpersonal process, and differential psychotherapy outcome. *Journal of Consulting and Clinical Psychology*, 58, 768–774.

Hersoug, A. G. (2004). Assessment of therapists' and patients' personality: Relationship to therapeutic technique and outcome in brief dynamic psychotherapy. *Journal of Personality Assessment*, 83, 191–200.

Hersoug, A. G., Høglend, P., Havik, O., von der Lippe, A., & Monsen, J. (2009). Therapist characteristics influencing the quality of alliance in long-term psychotherapy. *Clinical Psychology & Psychotherapy*, 16, 100–110.

Leary, T. (1957). *Interpersonal diagnosis of behavior.* New York: Ronald Press.

McCall, G. C., & Simmons, (1978). *Interactions and identities: An examination of human associations in everyday life* (revised ed.). New York: Free Press.

Mead, G. (1967). *Mind, self and society: From the standpoint of a social behaviorist.* (C. W. Morris, Ed.). Chicago: University of Chicago Press.

Ogunfowora, B., & Drapeau, M. (2008). A study of the relationship between personality traits and theoretical orientation preferences. *Counseling and Psychotherapy. Research*, 8, 151–159.

Orlinsky, D. E., & Rønnestad, M. H. (2005). *How psychotherapists develop: A study of therapeutic work and professional growth.* Washington, DC: American Psychological Association.

Orlinsky, D. E., Rønnestad, M. H., Hartmann, A., Heinonen, E., & Willutzki, U. (2019). The personal self of psychotherapists: Dimensions, correlates, and relations with clients. *Journal of Clinical Psychology*, 76, 461–475.

Orlinsky, D. E., Strauss, B., Rønnestad, M. H., Hill, C., Castonguay, L., Willutzki, U., Taubner, S., & Carlsson, J. (2015). A collaborative study of development in psychotherapy trainees. *Psychotherapy Bulletin*, 50, 21–25.

Orlinsky, D. E., Willutzki, U., Meyerberg, J., Cierpka, M., Buchheim, P., & Ambühl, H. (1996). Die Qualität der therapeutischen Beziehung: Entsprechen gemeinsame Faktoren in der Psychotherapie gemeinsamen Charakteristika von PsychotherapeutInnen? [Qualities of the psychotherapeutic relationship: Do common factors in psychotherapy reflect common characteristics of psychotherapists?] *Psychotherapie, Psychosomatik, medizinische Psychologie*, 46, 102–110.

Radeke, J. T., & Mahoney, M. J. (2000). Comparing the personal lives of psychotherapists and research psychologists. *Professional Psychology: Research and Practice*, 31, 82–84.

Rønnestad, M. H., & Skovholt, T. M. (2013). *The developing practitioner: Growth and stagnation of therapists and counselors.* New York & London: Routledge.

Scandell, D. J., Wlazelek, B. G., & Scandell, R. S. (1997). Personality of the therapist and theoretical orientation. *Irish Journal of Psychology*, 18, 413–418.

Simmel, G. (1950). Faithfulness and gratitude. In K. H. Wolff, Ed., *The sociology of Georg Simmel*, 379–395. Glencoe, IL: Free Press.

Skovholt, T. M., & Rønnestad, M. H. (1995). *The evolving professional self: Stages and themes in therapist and counselor development.* Chichester, UK: Wiley.

Sullivan, H. S. (1953). *The interpersonal theory of psychiatry.* New York: Norton.

Topolinski, S., & Hertel, G. (2007). The role of personality in psychotherapists' careers: Relationships between personality traits, therapeutic schools, and job satisfaction. *Psychotherapy Research*, 17, 378–390.

Wolfer, C., Visla, A., Held, J., Hilpert, P., & Fluckiger, C. (2021). Assessing inter-personal skills-a comparison of trainee therapists' and students' interpersonal skills assessed with two established assessments for interpersonal skills. *Clinical Psychology & Psychotherapy*, 28, 226–232.

4 Private Life

D. E. Orlinsky with M. J. Schofield, H. Wiseman and M. H. Rønnestad

Personal Relationships and Private Life

The concept of *personal self* was defined in the last chapter as self-experience in close personal relationships, with emphasis on the qualities and dimensions of therapists' self-experience. This chapter focuses on the close personal relationships that earlier were viewed as the contexts of *personal-self*. For most persons, those close personal relationships are nested mainly in the realm of private life.[1]

Private life is the realm in which most of the emotionally significant aspects of personality are manifested. The core relationships of private life typically are those of family life, intimate friendships, and (when aroused) romantic life.[2] Other aspects of private life include "home life" (centered on one's residence) which may be solo or shared, and may or may not coincide with family life; and, for individuals so involved, centered on the social contexts of religious, civic, cultural, avocational, or sport-based recreational life.[3]

Psychotherapists spend much of their working time delving into and dealing with the private lives of their clients; but of course, like the people who come to them for help, and others, psychotherapists have their own private lives. When their day's work is done, therapists leave their offices and clinics and, like other people, go home to the close relationships in their own private lives.

To collect as "background data", the earliest version of the *Development of Psychotherapists Common Core Questionnaire* (DPCCQ) asked only for the kind of personal information that is considered "demographic" or population-descriptive. This included nationality, gender and age—as previously reported—and "civil" or marital relationship status. As research interest in personal information grew over time, other questions were added: parental status, religious background and affiliation, quality of life, economic background, and attachment pattern. The present chapter focuses on close relationships in the therapist's current private life—marital/relationship status, parental status, and the intersections of those with gender and age, dimensions of *personal self*, and attachment patterns. Religious background and affiliation, current quality of life, and family backgrounds are dealt with in later chapters.

DOI: 10.4324/9781003217572-4

Family Relations

Like others in society, some therapists are "single", or married, or divorced; and among those, some do or do not have children. The various configurations of those alternative states largely define the core nexus of one's private life.[4] Therapists' marital and parental status are first analyzed separately, and then jointly with respect to the private life patterns they form. (The data for both marital and parental status are shown in Appendix Table 4.2).[5]

Marital Status

When therapists were asked "What is your current marital status?" three-fifths (59%, *n* = 6,698) reported being married, or remarried if a previous relationship had been dissolved.[6] An additional 12% indicated that, although not married, they were in fact living with a partner. Counting both together as "partnered", nearly three-fourths (71%) of the therapists surveyed had a committed adult intimate relationship[7] at the center of their private lives.

By contrast, about one in six (17%) of the therapists were single, and another small group (10%) were currently separated or divorced. Thus just over a fourth (27%) of the therapists could be considered voluntarily "unpartnered" and presumably not currently living in an intimate adult relationship.[8] There were also a very small number of widowed persons (1%), and a small number of others who answered by choosing "Other" (1%), some of whom specified "religiously celibate".

Parental Status

Another core emotional bond that decisively structures one's private life is the presence or absence of a relationship with children. Questions about the presence of children in therapists' lives were added to the DPCCQ after roughly half the current sample had been collected so that the amount of parental status data is about half the total who reported their marital relationship status.[9] Of therapists who received these questions, a large majority (70%, *n* = 4196) said they had children, while 30% (nearly half of whom were single) had none.

In fact, most of the therapists who were parents had several children: over a quarter (28%, *n* = 1,612) had two and 25% (*n* = 1,424) had three or more children. This reflects a certain "density" of family relationships for the majority of therapists who had to deal with multiple children, and whose children had siblings as well as parents. Only 18% (*n* = 1,031) had just one child. Of course, allowance has to be made for the fact that it takes time to have a child, and even more time to have several children—as indicated by the substantial correlation (*r* = .45) between number of children and therapist age.

Private Life Patterns

The relationships implied by the intersection of marital and parental status suggests the basic configuration of a person's private life situation. The range of private life relationship patterns among the therapists in our sample is shown in Figure 4.1 (excluding the very small number of those who were widowed or of "other" marital status).

By far the most common configuration overall was being married with children. This very large subgroup (52%, n = 2,883) represented the modal pattern of private life. Therapists with live-in partners and children comprised the most similar family units (6% overall, n = 343), adding to the majority. Together, as examples of domestic patterns, they might present a reassuring image of "normal" family life to clients. By contrast, the 10% of therapists who were currently divorced or separated reflect a disruption in therapists' own private lives—one that might seem a failure, but might also have provided a constructive solution of domestic difficulties, and become a source of empathy for their clients' own struggles.

The second largest group of therapists (14%, n = 791) were single and childless. As will be seen, nearly half (49%) of those were younger therapists less than 35 years old. Older therapists who were single and without children had, themselves, no direct experience of adult family life. Although they might be living perfectly satisfying lives, a question might also arise about their ability to empathize deeply with patients whose problems center in complex family relationships.

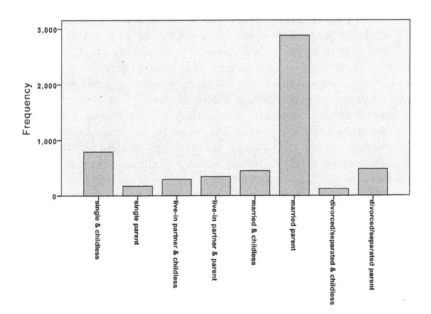

Figure 4.1 Family Configurations (Marital x Parental Status)

Private Life Patterns by Age and Gender

Parental status was substantially correlated with age, as was being married also, but to a lesser degree. Given the inevitably age-related nature of those variables, a fair understanding of private life patterns requires that they be contextualized by age, and likely by gender as well.

Age

To examine the association of private life patterns and age beyond those overall correlations, the distribution of patterns was computed separately for three age groups: Younger adults aged 21–34, Midlife adults aged 35–54, and Older adults aged 55–85. (Comparisons for the total sample are shown in Appendix Table 4.3.)

Younger therapists were divided mainly into those who were single and childless (42%) and those who were already married (38%). Younger married therapists included some who had children and others not (respectively, 21% and 17%). The only other private life pattern with a moderate proportion (14%) of Younger therapists were those living with a partner, mostly without children (12%). Combining those who were married with those living with a partner, a majority (52%) of the Younger therapists were in committed adult intimate relationships, but only a fourth (27%) of Younger therapists had become parents. Very few (3%) had become separated or divorced.

Midlife therapists were mostly married and parents (57%), with no other private life pattern even close. Of the rest, 8% were married but childless, 12% lived with a partner, 11% had separated or divorced, and 13% remained single. The combined proportion of those in a committed adult intimate relationship was 76%, half again more than among Younger therapists. Likewise 74% of Midlife therapists had become parents. Thus most Midlife therapists had begun building their own families. On the other hand, the proportion who were divorced or separated had increased from less than 3% to 11%.

Older therapists showed a continuation of the trends observed in the Younger and Midlife age groups. They were predominantly married (65%) or living with a partner (10%), and even more had children (85%). There were even fewer singles (10%), mostly without children (7%) but more Older therapists had gotten divorced or separated (15%) and most of the latter did have children (14%), reflecting a minority that had experienced family disruption. Obviously growing older allows more time for normatively scheduled changes in life situation to occur.

Gender

Comparison of male and female therapists regarding their private life relationship patterns showed only a few specific significant differences, even though statistically significant overall (see Appendix Table 4.4). A higher proportion of men than women (60% vs. 49%) were married and parents. By contrast, a small but significantly higher proportion of women than men (10% vs. 6%) were divorced or separated parents. Slightly but significantly more women than men (4% vs. 2%) were single parents. These differences suggest that women more than men may encounter a potentially disruptive strain between their professional and conjugal roles.

Age and Gender

Comparing private life patterns across therapist groups defined jointly by age and gender shows that significant gender differences only emerge across successive age groups (see Appendix Table 4.5). No statistically significant differences between men and women were found among Younger therapists. However, among those in Midlife, 62% of the men but only 55% of the women therapists were married and parents. Among Older therapists that discrepancy was even greater, with 70% of men as compared with 56% of women being married parents. Moreover, only among Older therapists was there a significant difference between women and men in being divorced or separated and a parent (17% of women vs. 8% of men). This is a further reflection of the personal burden experienced in private life by some female therapists.

Private Life Patterns by Profession and Orientation

Are differences among therapists in terms of occupational characteristics reflected in their private life patterns? Do therapists' differences in professional background or theoretical orientation appear related to how they live as persons? Given the demonstrated effects of age and gender on adult relationship and parental statuses, and gender differences between professions and orientations noted in Chapter 2, answering these questions about profession and orientation will also need to account for those personal factors.

Professional Discipline

Marital Status

Marital status rates differed significantly between therapeutic professions (shown in the upper tier of Appendix Table 4.6). Although a majority in each profession were currently married, that was significantly more likely the case for Psychiatrists (69%) and Counselors (64%) than for Psychologists (57%) and Social Workers (54%). Psychologists were significantly more likely than average to be either single (19%) or living with a partner (15%), and Social Workers were also more likely than average to be single (22%). Psychiatrists were least likely to be divorced or separated (7%), especially as compared to Lay Therapists/Analysts (15%).

The patterns were basically similar when computed separately for men and women, except that the larger number of women made the result statistically significant (see middle and lower tiers of Appendix Table 4.6). Psychiatrists were significantly more often married, both among men (74%) and women (62%). Psychologists were significantly more likely than chance to be living with a partner, both among men (14%) and women (15%); female Psychologists were also significantly more likely to be single (21%) and less likely to be married (52%). The women who were Counselors were significantly more likely than chance to be married (63%). The men who were Lay Therapists/Analysts were significantly more likely to be living with a partner (22%).

A somewhat clearer view of differences between professions in marital status is gained when analyses are carried out separately by age group (as in Appendix Table 4.7). Among the Younger Therapists, only a majority (54%) of the Psychiatrists were married, while a majority (52%) of the Social Workers were single. Psychologists were significantly underrepresented among the married but overrepresented among those living with a partner. Psychiatrists were still significantly more often married among the Midlife and Older therapists (74% and 78% respectively). Among the Midlife therapists, Psychologists and Lay Therapists/Analysts were both significantly less likely to be married and more likely to be living with a partner.

If marriage can be said at least partially to represent a conservative social and economic condition of life, then Psychiatrists as a group seem most committed to a socially conventional lifestyle. The fact that they were also least likely to be living with a partner unmarried, and less likely to be separated or divorced, reinforces this impression. Possibly their background and training in the medical profession tends to foster a degree of social conservatism, and their typically stronger economic position may provide more stable support for their private lives.

Parental Status

As well as having married, a substantial majority (71%) of therapists in all professional groups were parents (see Appendix Table 4.8)—but Psychologists were significantly less likely to be parents (66%), just as they were less likely to be married. On the other hand Counselors, who were the second most married group, were significantly more likely to be parents (76%). Separate analyses by gender (Appendix Table 4.9a) showed that the significantly lower proportion of parents was found mainly for female Psychologists (62% vs. a high of 76% for Counselors); and when analyzing separately by age group (Appendix Table 4.9b), the significantly lower proportion of parents was found mainly for Younger Psychologists (21% of Psychologists vs. 42% of Counselors and Psychiatrists). Evidently the prospect of parenthood is most challenging for Younger female Psychologists, possibly due to the fact that the extensive training they are engaged in typically requires a lengthy research project as well as clinical practice.

No significant differences between professions were observed among Midlife and Older therapists of both genders.

Theoretical Orientation

Private life patterns varied far less among therapists of different theoretical orientations (see Appendix Tables 4.10a and 4.10b). No significant associations were found for parental status, and only one significant difference was found for marital status: saliently Cognitive-Behavioral therapists were somewhat less likely to be separated or divorced (6% vs. the sample total of 10%).

Private Life Patterns and Personal Self

It is plausible to suppose that individuals with different *personal self* characteristics might either seek out, or naturally gravitate towards, situations in private life that are comfortable for them and provide opportunities for self-realization. It is also plausible to suppose that different private life situations might be conducive to, or become reflected in, the individuals' *personal self*. Being on one's own as a single person or having an intimate partner should make a difference, as should having to care for children versus having no dependents. As a first approach to exploring this question, the scores made by therapists on each dimension of *personal self* were compared. Since gender was found to be significantly associated with these dimensions in Chapter 3, analyses were conducted separately for the men and women. (See Appendix Table 4.11 for marital status and Table 4.12 for parental status.)

On *Genial/Caring*, single therapists appeared to be significantly less self-bestowing than divorced or separated therapists, with cohabiting and married therapists in between.[10] That was true for men and women, although only women but not the men who were parents were significantly more Genial/Caring.

On *Forceful/Exacting*, cohabiting and married women were significantly more self-assertive than divorced or separated women, but no differences were found for men and no differences in parental status were found for both men and women.

On *Reclusive/Remote*, single therapists of both genders appeared to be significantly more self-protective than all other groups, and this was also the case for therapists without children. Analysis by levels of Reclusive/Remote showed that therapists who were single and childless, compared to the total sample, were significantly less trusting (23% vs. 32%), and significantly more circumspect (38% vs. 29%) and even more wary (9% vs. 5%) in close relationships.[11] The results were basically the same when analyses for marital status were conducted separately for men and women (Appendix Table 4.14), and for parental status (Appendix Table 4.15) were also significant for women but not for men . When conducted separately by age group, the same findings appeared among Younger and Midlife therapists but only partially among Older therapists (Table 4.16).

On *Ardent/Expressive*, divorced or separated women therapists were significantly more self-expressive than those who were single or cohabiting, and among the men divorced or separated therapists were significantly more self-expressive than all others. No significant association with parental status was found for this dimension.

Overall, the single and childless private life pattern was associated with significantly lower scores on Genial/Caring (being less self-bestowing) and significantly higher scores on Reclusive/Remote (being more self-protective). In order not to take these findings about childless singles out of context, two important facts must be remembered. First, a majority were in the *trusting* and *approachable* range on Reclusive/Remote, making half of therapists in this private life pattern indistinguishable from those in other life situations. Simply being single and childless is not in itself "diagnostic" of high levels of self-protectiveness, and ought not be viewed as "damaging" information about therapists as individuals. Second, for many therapists the single and childless private life pattern is a transitional lifecycle state, as it is for people generally. Being single and childless was the norm among Younger therapists—at 42%, including twice as many people as the next largest group (see top tier in Appendix Table 4.5). Among Midlife therapists, the proportion of therapists in the childless single private life pattern was only 10%, and among Older therapists only 7% were childless and single. With these cautions in mind, the statistical association of self-protectiveness with the single childless private life pattern is striking. Logically the next question is whether a Reclusive/Remote person chooses or gravitates toward a single and childless private life, or if having a relatively isolated private life pattern tends to accentuate and embed that trait of *personal self*—or, if both may happen in varying degrees. The cross-sectional design of the present study does not permit a direct answer. However, additional information on attachment patterns was collected about a number of therapists that might give an indirect answer.

Private Life, Personal Self, and Adult Attachment

The additional information came from use of a popular brief version of the *Experiences in Close Relationship Scale* (ECRS)[12] to the DPCCQ. This instrument is grounded in the well-known theory of interpersonal attachment and attachment behavior formulated by John Bowlby (1969) in his classic volumes, *Attachment and Loss* and subsequently elaborated through studies by Ainsworth (e.g. Ainsworth, Blehar, Waters, & Wall, 1978), Main (e.g., Main, Kaplan & Cassidy, 1985) and others. This theory posits two broad types of children's attachment to their caregivers as emotionally secure or insecure, and distinguishes several types of insecure attachment. The theory was later extended from childhood to adult behavior in close relationships. The ECRS is a 12-item instrument which initially focused on romantic relationships with scales assessing two insecure attachment dimensions: Anxious and Avoidant. Anxious attachment reflects an eager but insecure desire for closeness to others; Avoidant attachment reflects a fearful retreat from closeness with others. Low scores on both scales indicate relatively secure attachment behavior.[13]

A version of the ECRS that specified "close personal relationships" instead of "romantic" relationships as the target behavior was included in recent editions of the DPCCQ[14]—with the result that adult attachment has been assessed for about 10% of our therapists. An exploratory factor analysis of 1,223 therapists with ECRS-12 data yielded three dimensions, the two most robust being readily identified as Anxious Attachment and Avoidant Attachment (see Appendix Table 4.17). Reliable scales based on the dimensions were then used to explore this subjective aspect of therapists' private life patterns and *personal self*.

Private Life

Scores on Anxious Attachment and Avoidant Attachment were analyzed in relation to *marital status* separately for male and female psychotherapists (shown in top tier of Appendix Table 4.18). Single women were significantly higher than married women on both Anxious Attachment and Avoidant Attachment, and single men were significantly higher than married men on Avoidant Attachment— although married men and married women had the lowest scores of all, and thus were the most secure group with respect to attachment behavior.

With respect to therapists' *parental status* (shown in bottom tier of Appendix Table 4.18) childless women therapists were significantly higher on both Anxious Attachment and Avoidant Attachment than women with two or more children. However, differences for men were either nonsignificant or just marginally significant—suggesting that the psychological impact of parental status is likely greater for mothers than for fathers.

Separate analyses of attachment by therapist age groups focused on Midlife and Older therapists since the number of Younger therapists who were parents was small. With respect to *marital status*, both Midlife and Older therapists who were single were significantly higher in Avoidant Attachment than those who were married (see top tier of Appendix Table 4.19), and together with divorced or separated therapists tended to be higher on Anxious Attachment too. Differences were not so clear cut with respect to *parental status*: only Avoidant Attachment was significant for Midlife therapists, with childless therapists significantly higher than parents of 3+ children; and for Older therapists, no specific groups were significantly differentiated as higher or lower. In these analyses, single therapists and to some extent childless therapists were assessed as showing less secure attachment behavior, and married therapists as most securely attached. When the number of children are counted, therapists (especially mothers) with several children appear to have the lowest levels of both Anxious Attachment and Avoidant Attachment, implying that as a group they have the most secure attachment patterns among our therapists.[15]

Generally, Avoidant attachment more than Anxious Attachment was a differential factor in regard to both components of therapists' private life patterns— relationship status and parental status—and was at its highest level among those whose private life seemed less deeply immersed in family relations.

Personal Self

The links between attachment and dimensions of *personal self* were even more striking, both in the total sample, and separately for men and women and different age groups (see Appendix Table 4.20).

Avoidant Attachment was strongly and *positively* correlated with being Reclusive/Remote ($r =.42$) for all therapists, as well as for both genders and all age groups. The correlation was consistently high but strongest for Younger therapists ($r =.48$) and for men ($r =.47$). Therapists high on Avoidant Attachment are strongly predisposed to be self-protective.

Avoidant Attachment was also significantly and *negatively* correlated with Genial/Caring. The overall value was $r = -.34$, but again it tended to be higher for Younger therapists ($r = -.39$) and for men ($r = -.41$). High Avoidant Attachment strongly counteracts the therapist's inclination to be self-bestowing.

By comparison, Anxious Attachment was not as strongly associated with *personal self*. It was *positively* but moderately correlated with Reclusive/Remote ($r =.21$) and Forceful/Exacting ($r =.19$), reflecting a tendency for Anxious Attachment to foster both self-protection and self-assertion. Anxious Attachment was also moderately *negatively* correlated with Genial/Caring ($r = -.19$) suggesting that self-bestowal is associated with secure attachment behavior.

In Sum

In their private lives, a great majority of the therapists studied were married, and a great majority of those with available data had families (i.e., were married and had children). This is the normative group in our sample, especially among Midlife and Older therapists of all professional backgrounds. None of the therapists in other private life patterns had comparable numbers. Thus the private lives of psychotherapists appear to be organized much the same as other persons in society, and as in others' lives to some extent reflect the practical circumstances that bring people together or keep them apart. However, the data analyzed in this chapter clearly establish a meaningful role for psychological factors that both shape and are shaped by a person's private life situation—one's *personal self* and the attachment patterns, developed in childhood, that may influence it. Those themes are examined further in Chapter 7 on therapists' family backgrounds, and Chapter 8 on childhood family and adult life. But therapists' individual beliefs and current quality of life will be studied next to broaden our portrayal of psychotherapists as persons.

Notes

1 See Table 4.1 in Appendix for a view of "private life" as one aspect of the larger society, based on concepts of the General Theory of Action (e.g., Parsons & Shils, 1954). Although often viewed as the "natural" way to organize human existence, the distinction between "private life" and "public life" is an historically and culturally conditioned construct, essentially descriptive of urban-industrial and post-

industrial society (e.g., Aries, 1962; Berger, Berger & Kellner, 1973; Laslett, 1971; Zaretsky, 1976).

2 One may also have a "secret life", in which illicit or socially shamed prohibited activities and relationships are hidden as much as possible from other spheres of life (always with the risk of being found out).

3 There are other personally important areas of life that overlap with broader social and cultural system contexts, and are sometimes also the focus of patients' concerns; for example, the individual's work life (occupational system), religious/spiritual life (cultural system), neighborhood "social" life (community system), and civic life (political system).

4 Another aspect of private life that was not explored in the DPCCQ, unfortunately, consists of close friendships and circles of friends that mutually sustain one another and can become "intentional families".

5 Other than the data presented here, relatively few studies of the therapist's family life exist except the following: Golden & Farber (1998); Guy (1987); Henry, Sims & Spray (1973); Radeke & Mahoney (2000).

6 Those who indicated they had remarried or were living with a partner after being divorced or widowed were counted, respectively, as currently "married" or "living with a partner".

7 Being "partnered' does not imply that those relationships were all equally intimate or happily committed (see Chapter 6 for more on the latter).

8 However some of those might be living with children as single parents, or if young with their own parents or sharing living quarters with roommates.

9 Table 4.2 shows that the distribution of relationship statuses for this large subsample closely matches that of the total sample, suggesting the plausibility of assuming parental status might also be similar.

10 This brings to mind the familiar line from Tennyson's poem *In Memoriam* which says "'Tis better to have loved and lost than never to have loved at all."

11 It is important to note that these group differences are consistent with there being single and/or childless therapists who, individually, are warm and trusting in close relationships.

12 Wei, Russell, Mallinckrodt & Vogel (2007).

13 The study of attachment has been quite popular recently among psychotherapy researchers, and interested readers can consult the following: Black, Hardy, Turpin & Parry (2005); Degnan, Seymour-Hyde, Harris & Berry (2016); Dinger, Jennissen & Rek (2019); Dinger, Strack, Sachsse & Schauenburg (2009); Mikulincer, Shaver & Berant (2012); Nord, Höger, & Eckert (2000); Rek, Ehrenthal, Strauss, Schauenburg, Nikendei & Dinger (2018); Schauenburg, Buchheim, Beck, Nolte, Brenk-Franz, Leichsenring, … Dinger (2010); Strauss & Petrowski (2017).

14 Profs. M. Schofield (La Trobe University, Melbourne) and J. Grant (Curtin University, Perth) bundled the ECRS-12 with the DPCCQ in their contribution of Australian psychotherapists to our study, and this practice was retained in subsequent data collections in the USA, UK, Canada and a few other countries.

15 One-way ANOVAs showed $F = 6.14$ ($df = 3, 1151$; $p = .000$) for Anxious Attachment, and $F = 9.69$ ($df = 3, 1166$; $p = .000$) for Avoidant Attachment.

References

Ainsworth, M. D. S., Blehar, M. C., Waters, E., & Wall, S. (1978). *Patterns of attachment.* Hillsdale, NJ: Lawrence Erlbaum Associates.

Aries, P. (1962). *Centuries of childhood: A social history of family life* (R. Baldick, trans.). New York: Vintage Books.

Berger, P., Berger, M., & Kellner, H. (1973). *The homeless mind: Modernization and consciousness.* New York: Vintage Books.

Black, S., Hardy, G., Turpin, G., & Parry, G. (2005). Self-reported attachment styles and therapeutic orientation of therapists and their relationship with reported general alliance quality and problems in therapy. *Psychology and Psychotherapy: Theory, Research and Practice,* 78, 363–377.

Bowlby, J. (1969). *Attachment and loss.* Vol. 1: *Attachment.* London: Hogarth Press & Institute for Psychoanalysis.

Degnan, A., Seymour-Hyde, A., Harris, A., & Berry, K. (2016). The role of therapist attachment in alliance and outcome: A systematic literature review. *Clinical Psychology and Psychotherapy,* 23, 47–65.

Dinger, U., Jennissen, S., & Rek, I. (2019). Attachment style of volunteer counselors in telephone emergency services predicts counseling process. *Frontiers in Psychology,* 10: 1936.

Dinger, U., Strack, M., Sachsse, T., & Schauenburg, H. (2009). Therapists' attachment, patients' interpersonal problems and alliance development over time in inpatient psychotherapy. *Psychotheraphy Theory Research and Practice,* 46, 277–290.

Golden, V., & Farber, B. A. (1998). Therapists as parents: Is it good for the children? *Professional Psychology: Research and Practice,* 29, 135–139.

Guy, J. D. (1987). Significant events in the life of the psychotherapist. In *The personal life of the psychotherapist,* pp.147–196. New York: Wiley.

Henry, W. E., Sims, J. H., & Spray, S. L. (1973). The contemporary family. In *Public and private lives of psychotherapists,* pp. 137–162. San Francisco: Jossey-Bass.

Laslett, P. (1971). *The world we have lost: England before the industrial age,* 2nd ed. New York: Charles Scribner's Sons.

Main, M., Kaplan, N. & Cassidy, J. (1985). Security in infancy, childhood and adulthood: A move to the level of representation. In I. Bretherton & E. Waters (Eds.), *Growing points of attachment theory and research* (pp. 66–104). Monographs of the Society for Research in Child Development, vol. 50. University of Chicago Press.

Mikulincer, M., Shaver, P. R., & Berant, E. (2012). An attachment perspective on therapeutic processes and outcomes. *Journal of Personality,* 81, 606–616.

Nord, C., Höger, D., & Eckert, J. (2000). Attachment patterns of psychotherapists. *Persönlichkeitsstörungen Theorie und Therapie,* 4, 76–86.

Parsons, T., & Shils, E. A. (Eds.) (1954). *Toward a general theory of action.* Cambridge, MA: Harvard University Press.

Radeke., J. T., & Mahoney, M. J. (2000). Comparing the personal lives of psychotherapists and research psychologists. *Professional Psychology: Research and Practice,* 31, 82–84.

Rek, I., Ehrenthal, J. C., Strauss, B. M., Schauenburg, H., Nikendei, C. & Dinger, U. (2018). Attachment styles and interpersonal motives of psychotherapy trainees. *Psychotherapy,* 55, 209–215.

Schauenburg, H., Buchheim, A., Beck, K., Nolte, T., Brenk-Franz, K., Leichsenring, F., … Dinger, U. (2010). The influence of psychodynamically oriented therapists' attachment representations on outcome and alliance in inpatient psychotherapy [corrected]. *Psychotherapy Research,* 20, 193–202.

Strauss, B. M., & Petrowski, K. (2017). The role of the therapist's attachment in the process and outcome of psychotherapy. In L. G. Castonguay & C. E. Hill (Eds.), *How and why are some therapists better than others? Understanding therapist effects* (pp. 117–138). Washington, DC: American Psychological Association.

Wei, M., Russell, D. W., Mallinckrodt, B., & Vogel, D. L. (2007). The Experiences in Close Relationship Scale (ECR)-short form: Reliability, validity, and factor structure. *Journal of Personality Assessment*, 88 (2), 187–204.

Zaretsky, E. (1976). *Capitalism, the family, and personal life*. New York: Harper Colophon.

5 Individual Beliefs

D. E. Orlinsky with D. P. Smith

The personal world of psychotherapists, like that of other people, is formed by their private worldviews and values, parallel to and interwoven within the network of intimate relationships in which they express and experience themselves.[1] These worldviews and values consist in large part of the religions that they adhere to, or that they ignore or reject in favor of a secular alternative. Questions about therapists' religious background and their current views and commitments were asked of more than 4,500 therapists as part of the DPCCQ survey. This chapter summarizes and explores their responses.[2]

Secularism, Religion and Spirituality

Perhaps the most common view of psychotherapists is that they are personally non-religious or even anti-religious. This is based largely on writings by prominent psychological authors (e.g., Ellis, 1980; Freud, 1927) who were skeptical and critical of traditional religions. That popular view of psychotherapists is also fed by a sense that psychotherapy itself is a veiled form of religious ministry or pastoral care adapted from religion to help secular people in modern societies cope with their emotional conflicts and ethical dilemmas. The modern psychotherapies, although parallel in some respects, operate under the aegis or cultural authority of psychological science rather than the traditional authority of sacred doctrine.

This common view of psychotherapists as secular is partly—but only partly—supported by the findings of our study. Nearly half (49%) of 4,573 therapists who were asked about the importance of religion in their lives replied that it was "Not at all' or only "Slightly' important (see Figure 5.1, left-hand panel). But the other half (51%) of the sample stands as a major exception to the popular image of non-religious therapists. Indeed, about a quarter (27%) of the therapists reported that religion is "Somewhat or Moderately" important, and another quarter (24%) claimed that religion was currently of "Much or Very much" importance in their lives. Each of the latter two groups is a minority, but rather a substantial minority.

The second major exception to the popular image of therapists as irreligious is that more than half (52%) in our sample described themselves as "Much or

DOI: 10.4324/9781003217572-5

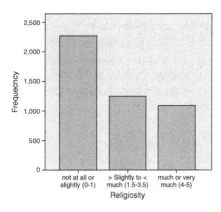 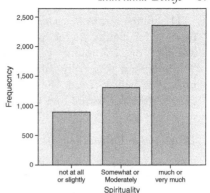

Figure 5.1 Religiosity and Spirituality of Psychotherapists

Very much" spiritual, joined by another 29% who said they were "Somewhat or Moderately" spiritual (see Figure 5.1, right-hand panel). Thus a very large majority (80%) noted that they were spiritual in their own lives, at least to some extent, and just one in five (20%) said they were "Not at all" or only "Slightly" spiritual.

To clarify what "religion" and "spirituality" meant to our therapists, a 10 item list describing experiences that could be viewed as spiritual or religious was included in a version of the DPCCQ that was presented to a subsample of about 2,500 therapists. These respondents were asked to rate each item on a 0–10 scale, where 0 = "Not at all important in my life" and 10 = "The most important part of my life" (see Appendix Table 5.1). The item of highest average importance for all therapists was having "Personal moral and ethical standards" (8.6 of 10). The second highest rated item was having "A sense of spiritual dimension in personal experience" (7.3 of 10). These were important for most therapists.

By contrast, the items that were rated as least important, on average, were "Observing traditional religious holy days" and "Celebrating the beauty and dignity of the worship service" (2.7 and 2.9, respectively). These were of slight importance to most, although clearly more important to the large minority of seriously religious therapists. For example, the correlations of these "least important" items with therapists' ratings of the influence of religion on personal life were $r =.70$ for worship service and $r =.54$ for observing holy days.

A factor analysis was used to further explore the meaning of the 10 rated items, finding two dimensions that could be used to construct reliable multi-item scales of *Spirituality* and *Religiosity* (shown in Appendix Table 5.1). The dimension of Spirituality was defined by four experiences: having "Personal moral and ethical standards", recognizing "A spiritual dimension in personal experience", "Finding a source of discipline and purpose in living", and "Expressing personal devotion through service to others" (the last shared equally by both dimensions).

The dimension of *Religiosity* was defined by six experiences: "Celebrating the beauty and dignity of the worship service", "Participation in a religious fellowship or community", "Observing traditional religious holy days", "Upholding a personally valued historical tradition", having "A specific creed or set of beliefs", and "Seeking inner assurance and communion through prayer" (the last shared to a small extent by Spirituality).

Belief-Value Orientations

That some therapists are both spiritual and religious, and that many others are neither, is suggested by the fact the two dimensions were positively correlated ($r = .52$). Technically however, this correlation indicates that Spirituality and Religiosity share only 25% of their variance, which it is not too high to preclude the dimensions also varying somewhat independently. In other words, many therapists could be high on Spirituality or on Religiosity while being low on the other, while many other therapists could be high on both or low on both. To explore this aspect of the data, each dimension was divided approximately in half and then combined in a 2-by-2 table to define four broad patterns (see Figure 5.2).

The largest single group (38%) of therapists represents a pattern of personal belief which can be called *Ethical Secularism*. In these therapists' lives, religion was "Not at all" to less than "Moderately" important, and spirituality was rated "Not at all" to only "Moderately" important. This group comes closest to the popular image of psychotherapists—but while a plurality of the sample, it is still well short of the majority. Ethical Secularism as a belief-value orientation is described as "ethical" due to the top rating given to that item by almost all therapists.[3]

Two other groups together comprised a majority (55%) of therapists, and both were strongly spiritual. One that was more than "Moderately" high on Spirituality yet low on Religiosity was termed *Secular Spirituality* (27%).

Importance of religion	Importance of spirituality	
	'Not at all' to 'Slightly' or 'Moderate'	More than 'Moderate' to 'Much' or 'Very much'
'Not at all' to 'Slightly' or less than 'Moderate'	ETHICAL SECULARISM 38.4% (n = 1741)	SECULAR SPIRITUALITY 27.2% (n = 1233)
'Moderate' to 'Much' or 'Very much'	CEREMONIAL RELIGION 5.9% (n = 268)	RELIGIOUS SPIRITUALITY 28.4% (n = 1288)

Figure 5.2 Four Belief-Value Orientations

The other was also more than "Moderately" spiritual but "Moderate" to "High" on Religiosity, reflecting a belief-value pattern of *Religious Spirituality* (28%).

There was a fourth belief-value pattern that was "Moderately" to "Much or Very much" devoted to religion but "Not at all" to only "Moderately" spiritual. Because it was focused on traditional worship and observance, this was called *Ceremonial Religion*. It represented the smallest group (6%) of therapists, but if combined with the Religious Spirituality group, showed that about a third (34%) of our therapists would be viewed as seriously religious.

Belief-Value Orientation and Religious Affiliation

How do these belief-value patterns reflect therapists' religious backgrounds and intersect with their current affiliation—including, for some, a lack of religious affiliation? The answer overall is "very diversely", but the details reveal some interesting associations.

Religious Backgrounds

Given the international nature of our sample, it is natural that therapists' backgrounds reflect a broad range of religions: Christian, Jewish, Muslim, Hindu, Buddhist, mixed, and none. The largest group (70%) of therapists came from Christian families. These included various Protestant denominations (45%), typically from English-speaking countries (UK, USA, Canada, Australia and New Zealand) and Roman Catholic/Eastern Orthodox churches (25%) from countries such as Ireland, Chile, Mexico, Slovakia (but with some from Australia, Canada and USA as well). Comparison of therapists' religious backgrounds with their current belief-value orientations showed highly significant variations (see Appendix Table 5.2).

The largest group (61%) among *Unaffiliated* therapists, who had no childhood religious affiliation, held *an Ethical Secular* belief-value pattern, but nearly a fourth (23%) came as adults to have a Spiritual Secular orientation—and a few (16%) even became spiritually or ceremonially religious, suggesting that the latter must have undergone some significant life-changing experiences.

Therapists with a *Protestant Christian* religious background were more evenly divided among Ethical Secular, Spiritual Secular, and Spiritual Religious orientations (37%, 27%, and 33% respectively). However, they were significantly more likely than average to have a Spiritual Religious orientation as adults, and significantly less likely to have a Ceremonial Religious orientation, thus retaining some basic characteristics of their Protestant backgrounds.

Therapists of *Roman Catholic* or *Eastern Orthodox* heritage as adults also divided almost evenly between Ethical Secular (30%), Spiritual Secular (31%), and Spiritual Religious (32%) orientations. However only 39% of therapists who grew up in Catholic or Orthodox families retained a specifically religious orientation as adults, although significantly fewer on average became *Ethical Secular*.

The great majority (62%) of therapists with Jewish backgrounds came from the USA, with smaller numbers from Canada (11%), the UK (10%), and Australia (13%). As adults, the largest group (40%) of Jewish therapists, came to be Ethical Secular in orientation, and 25% were Spiritual Secular—so in effect two-thirds were secular. Therapists from Jewish families were significantly less likely than average to have a Spiritual Religious orientation (21%), but significantly more likely than average to be Ceremonial Religious (15%). The last pattern would most likely characterize adherents of Orthodox Judaism, as distinct from Reform or other branches of the faith.

Therapists with a Hindu religious background were predominantly from India (88%) but also from Malaysia (8%) and the UK (2%). Like the others mentioned, they divided fairly evenly as adults between Ethical Secular (30%), Spiritual Secular (29%), and Spiritual Religious (26%), but mainly stood out as significantly more likely to have a Ceremonial Religious orientation (16%).

Those of Mixed or Other religious backgrounds approximated the total sample base rates, as did the small number of therapists from Muslim and Buddhist backgrounds. A plurality (45%) of therapists from Muslim backgrounds held an Ethical Secular orientation as adults, but a third (33%) remained Spiritual Religious. Although the number of therapists from Buddhist backgrounds was too small to reach statistical significance, half (50%) of them were Spiritual Religious adults—the largest percentage of any religious background.

Current Affiliations

Therapists' religious backgrounds may influence their adult belief-value orientations, but in their current affiliations they may rather gravitate to affiliations that match their adult beliefs and values. The extent of this tendency is suggested by the following analyses (see Appendix Table 5.3).

Nearly half (49%) of the 4,255 therapists who were asked said that they were currently *Unaffiliated*, a figure that differs strikingly from the 12% who said their families had been religiously unaffiliated. A majority (58%) of these "unchurched" therapists held an Ethical Secular belief-value pattern, and another 34% were Spiritual Secular, totaling 92% who were non-religious. Nevertheless, 8% appeared to have religious belief-value orientations even though they didn't identify with a religious community.

By comparison, a third (32%) of the therapists currently identified as *Christian*, which is less than half the number that said they grew up in Christian families. Of those who identified as Christian, 21% named a Protestant denomination and 10% were Roman Catholic or members of an Eastern Orthodox communion. The distribution of belief-value patterns was fairly similar for all: about half had a Spiritual Religious orientation (56% Protestant, 50% Catholic and Orthodox); a minority were Ceremonial religious (7% Protestant, 13% Catholic and Orthodox)—and so basically in a religious orientation. About half of the remaining 37% of Christian therapists exhibited a non-religious orientation, either Spiritual Secular (17% Protestant, 19% Catholic and Orthodox) or Ethical Secular pattern (20% Protestants, 19% Catholics). Those who currently identified as Christian but had an Ethical Secular orientation might view their affiliation as more cultural than personal in nature.

The small number of *Jewish* therapists held diverse belief-value patterns, with none as the majority pattern. The largest group (39%) had an Ethical Secular orientation which, combined with the Spiritual Secular (16%), constituted a slim majority (51%) for the secular orientations. One fourth (26%) were Spiritual Religious and one fifth (19%) fit the Ceremonial Religious pattern, which was significantly more than average. The latter likely reflects the importance of traditional religious observance among Orthodox Jews.

The other current affiliations that had approximately 200 or more therapists were *Buddhists* and those of Mixed or Other religious identity.[4] Approximately half (49%) of the Buddhists had a Spiritual Religious orientation, and nearly a third (30%) fit the Spiritual Secular pattern, reflecting the prevalence of spirituality for most of the Buddhist therapists. Therapists with a Mixed or Other religious affiliation showed a similar pattern, with 46% Spiritual Religious and 37% Spiritual Secular, and a lower than expected proportion (12%) of Ethical Secular therapists.

Changes in Affiliation and Religiosity

Overall it appears that therapists of specific religious affiliations tended to select compatible belief-value orientations, but there was also much evidence of individual variation. In fact, comparison of therapists' religious backgrounds and current affiliations indicate that many therapists experienced a great deal of change in beliefs between childhood and adult life. In looking at overall change in the sample, perhaps the 38% decline in Christian affiliation is most striking, but equally striking was the fourfold increase among therapists claiming no religious affiliation (see Appendix Table 5.4). Additionally, the percentage of therapists identifying as Buddhist saw a nearly six-fold increase, from under 1% by background to nearly 5% by current affiliation.

Patterns of Change

Constructing a matrix to compare therapists' family religious affiliations with their current affiliations allows one to trace the origins and destinations of therapists' transformations (shown in Appendix Table 5.5). Those who retained their background religious identity may be termed Adherents, those who renounced all religious identity are Apostates, and those who chose a different religious identity are typically called Converts.

Among the *Adherents*, both Jewish and Muslim therapists were most likely to maintain their original religious identity (68% and 64%, respectively), as were the small number of Hindu therapists (74%). For many of these therapists, religious identity overlaps significantly with ethnic identity—which is not easily shed. Of those with no religious background, the vast majority (79%) remained Unaffiliated as adults—so, in a sense, they can also be viewed as Adherents.

Among those who can be viewed as *Apostates*, who basically renounced all religious affiliation, Catholic and Protestant therapists were the largest groups (46%, 43%). A large proportion of therapists who had a Mixed or Other background also became Unaffiliated (49%). Being Adherents, the lowest rates of apostasy were observed among Jews (23%), Buddhists (24%), Muslims (32%), and the small group of Hindus (15%) for whom data were available.

Therapists who were *Converts* continued to have a religious affiliation as adults but chose one that differed from their family of origin. The few who grew up as Buddhists had the highest rate of conversion, with 24% becoming Protestant Christians (although this actually only involved 8 individuals). This loss was more than offset by the much larger number of therapists from other religious backgrounds who, as adults, came to identify as Buddhists. These included 100 Protestants, 46 Catholics, 18 from unaffiliated backgrounds, 8 Jews and 7 from Mixed or Other backgrounds. The appeal of Buddhism to many therapists may be related to its often being seen as a "Psychology" more than a religion in the Western sense. However, this degree of outflow and inflow indicates a remarkable fluidity in affiliation as a Buddhist.

Therapists of *Mixed or Other* religious backgrounds had the next highest percentage of converts, most of whom (14%) became Protestant Christians. Possibly the latter had been part of their original mixed religious heritage, with which they aligned more fully as adults. Therapists whose childhood families were Unaffiliated were perhaps the most surprising, with a fifth (21%) who came to identify with a specific religious affiliation as adults—moving in the opposite direction from the majority with religious backgrounds who became unaffiliated as adults. Of those without a religious background, 9% later became Protestants, 3% became Catholics, 4% became Buddhists, 5% identified as Mixed or Other, and a handful (1%) chose to be Jews. All of those therapists "got religion" despite having been raised without one, or possibly even grew up in an atmosphere that was antagonistic to religion.

Periods of Change

Some of the questions included in the DPCCQ asked respondents to rate how important religion was in their lives at three different periods: childhood, adolescence, and currently in adulthood. Answers were given on a scale ranging from 0 ("Not at all important") to 10 ("The most important thing in my life"). For convenience, these assessments were categorized as reflecting "low" (0–5) or "high" (6–10) importance of religion. Overall, religion was rated as highly important in childhood by 45% of the therapists, by 38% in adolescence, and by 35% currently in their adult lives. However, the sense of overall decline implied by these figures doesn't give an adequate picture of change, since at each phase of life, religion increased in importance for some while decreasing in importance for others.

To track the amount and direction of change in the importance of religion, three matrices were constructed. In the transition from *Childhood to Adolescence*, a third (32%) of those for whom religion was highly important in childhood reported that it was no longer so in adolescence, but for a majority (68%) of them religion continued to be highly important (see upper tier in Appendix Table 5.6). Moving in the opposite direction, however, 15% of those for whom religion was not highly important in childhood reported that it had become so in their lives as adolescents, which makes up for about half of those who lost religious fervor. In contrast to those who changed, those not highly religious in childhood were mostly (85%) the same in adolescence. Thus the changes between these two periods of life occur in a context mostly marked by continuity.

Continuity was also the main note in the transition from *Adolescence to Adulthood*, especially at 77% among therapists for whom religion was of relatively low importance (see middle tier in Table 5.6). A smaller majority (55%) of therapists for whom religion had high importance in adolescence remained religious as adults. On the other hand, 45% became less religious as adults, and a surprising counter-trend occurred with nearly a quarter (23%) becoming more strongly religious in adulthood—either regaining the importance that it had for them as children, or finding a serious place for it in their lives for the first time.

Comparing the childhood importance of religion directly with adulthood (in the lower tier in Table 5.6) makes it clear that nearly half (48%) of those who were highly religious as children remained religious as adults, while religion declined in importance for just over half (52%). By contrast, 75% of therapists for whom religion had relatively low importance in childhood remained non-religious as adults—but a significant minority (25%) found religion became more important for them by the time they were adults.

Thus although the overall direction of change in the salience of religion was from greater to lesser importance, a significant countercurrent where religion became more important for some therapists was found at each life-phase transition. Clearly a large number of therapists underwent a lot of change in this respect as they grew from childhood to adolescence and on into adulthood. The contrasting trends leave an impression of fluidity in religious identities, and of therapists as individuals who have been seekers of a personal truth, whether in religion, or spirituality, or in a secular and scientific worldview.

Belief-Value Orientations and Therapists' Characteristics

It is natural to wonder whether and how therapists' personal qualities and professional characteristics might intersect with their individual belief-value patterns. How if at all are those patterns associated with their gender or life course status, their private life situation, their personal self and attachment style, their profession and theoretical orientation? The rest of this chapter seeks answers to these questions.

Personal Demographics

Comparisons of belief-value patterns by gender showed that similarities clearly outweighed the differences between male and female therapists with respect to belief-value patterns (see top tier in Appendix Table 5.7). No pattern has a majority of therapists, but a plurality among both genders had an Ethical Secular orientation (38% women, 40% men). Significantly more women than men had a Spiritual Secular orientation (29% vs. 23%), and more men than women had a Ceremonial Religious pattern—although in both cases the actual difference was relatively small.

In comparing age groups, Younger therapists (ages 21–34) were significantly overrepresented in the Ethical Secular pattern (47% vs. 38% as a sample average)—yet Younger therapists were also more often Ceremonial Religious (see lower tier of Appendix Table 5.7). Thus Younger therapists were distinguished by being more secular but less "spiritually" secular, and also more religious but less "spiritually" religious.

The distribution of belief-value patterns among Midlife therapists (ages 35–54) closely matched the sample, with most being either Ethical Secular (39%) or Spiritual Secular (27%)—a total of 66% secular. However, some significant deviations were observed among the Older therapists (ages 55–85). Fewer than expected were Ethical Secular (34%) and more than expected were Spiritual Secular (31%), twice the proportion of the Younger therapist group. A higher percentage of Older than Younger and Midlife therapists were Spiritual Religious, but the differences were not statistically significant. Overall, the Older therapists tended to be more spiritual, whether religious or secular in orientation.

Private Life

The most striking difference in comparing belief-value patterns across therapists' marital status was the significantly higher rate of cohabiting therapists with an Ethical Secular orientation (53% vs. the average 39%), and the lower rate in that pattern (37%) of married therapists (shown in Appendix Table 5.8)[5]. Cohabiting therapists also were significantly less often Spiritual Religious (14%) in contrast to married therapists who were significantly more so (31%). Overall, married therapists were significantly more religious and less secular in orientation, while cohabiting couples were the reverse, suggesting a trend among the married to be more conventional and among those living with a partner to be less conventional. Curiously, the leading group of divorced or separated therapists was Spiritual Secular in orientation, as if the formerly married had lost the religious element of the married but retained the spiritual aspect. There were no significant differences in personal belief patterns between parents and non-parents, overall and when computed separately for men and women.

Personal Self

Correlations were computed to assess how much therapists' religiosity and spirituality might be related to variations in *personal self* dimensions, with results that indicated the realms of *personal self* and belief-value orientation are largely independent (see top tier of Appendix Table 5.9). The only notable correlations were between Spirituality and the Genial/Caring and Ardent/Expressive dimensions, and these were small ($r = .12$ and $r = .13$ respectively).

For further nuance, mean values on the Genial/Caring and Ardent/Expressive dimensions were compared by belief-value patterns (see Appendix Table 5.10). Ethical Secular therapists had the lowest scores on both Genial/Caring and Ardent/Expressive, and Spiritual Secular therapists had the highest score on both. Ethical Secular therapists stood alone as significantly lower than all others on Ardent/Expressive, and as significantly lower than Spiritual Secular and Spiritual Religious on Genial/Caring. These results suggest a greater level of austerity (i.e., less self-bestowal and self-expression) in close personal relationships among Ethical Secular therapists, although the effects again are relatively small.

Adult Attachment

Therapists' belief-value patterns were also largely independent of their attachment patterns. Only one of the four correlations reached statistical significance, and that was small (see lower tier of Appendix Table 5.9). A negative association ($r = -.08$) between Avoidant attachment and Spirituality suggested that therapists who were less avoidant interpersonally tended to be somewhat more influenced in their lives by spiritual values.

Professional Discipline

Another question is whether therapists with different professional backgrounds tend to embody characteristically different belief-value orientations. Comparison of therapists across professional discipline found the main differences were between Psychologists and Counselors (see Appendix Table 5.11). Psychologists were significantly more likely, and Counselors were significantly less likely, to have an Ethical Secular orientation (46% vs. 30%). Curiously, the Psychologists were also more likely, and Counselors significantly less likely, to have a Ceremonial Religious orientation (8% vs. 3%). Conversely, the Counselors were significantly more likely, and Psychologists were less likely, to have a Spiritual Religious orientation (35% vs. 22%) and a Spiritual Secular orientation (32% vs. 22%). In other words, a majority (54%) of the Psychologists were significantly less spiritual than average, whether they were non-religious or religious, while a majority (67%) of Counselors were significantly more spiritual than the norm, whether they were religious or non-religious. Otherwise, the group of Lay Therapists/Analysts tended to resemble the Counselors and differ from Psychologists, while Psychiatrists and Social Workers did not significantly differ from the total sample norms.

Theoretical Approach

How closely do therapists personal belief patterns tend to match the theoretical orientations which influence their clinical practice? Surprisingly, in exploring these relationships, mono-focal Analytic/Psychodynamic and Cognitive-Behavioral therapists resembled each other, and differed mainly from integrative Broad Spectrum therapists (see Appendix Table 5.12). Majorities of the Cognitive-Behavioral and Analytic/Psychodynamic therapists had an Ethical Secular orientation (59% and 52%, respectively), and were underrepresented in both Spiritual Secular and Spiritual Religious orientations. In other words, both Cognitive-Behavioral and Analytic/Psychodynamic theoretical orientations tended to reflect and/or reinforce a "rationalist" rather than "spiritual" mentality. By contrast, a robust majority (70%) of Broad Spectrum integrative therapists were spiritual in orientation, either as Spiritual Religious (37%) or as Spiritual Secular (34%). The spiritual orientation of Broad Spectrum therapists was twice the rate of their Cognitive-Behavioral colleagues (70% vs. 33%). The openness to diverse theoretical perspectives that Broad Spectrum therapists display professionally seems to be matched by a similar openness in regard to their individual belief-value orientations.[6]

In Sum

Psychotherapists are commonly assumed to be rational, scientifically minded secularists who are either indifferent to or critical of religious beliefs and spiritual values, but the results presented in this chapter show that view to be only partially correct. When several thousand psychotherapists were asked about the importance of religion and of spirituality in their own lives, their answers showed that while religion was not important for about half, religion was moderately or highly important for the other half. Additionally, more than half, including many clearly non-religious therapists, said that spirituality was actually very important in their lives.

Taking reports about religiosity and spirituality together, four distinct personal belief-value patterns were defined as Ethical Secular, Secular Spiritual, Spiritual Religious, and Ceremonial Religious. Each of the first three had a substantial representation among the therapists, while the fourth held for only a small minority. The Ethical Secular pattern characterized the largest group of therapists (38%), for whom neither religion nor spirituality were important although they shared a strong emphasis on personal moral and ethical standards with other patterns. About a quarter (27%) of the therapists had a Secular Spiritual orientation, which was non-religious but still recognized an important spiritual aspect of experience. A similar number (28%) of therapists combined spirituality with an emphasis on the importance of worship, observation of holy days, and participation in a religious community. The last and smallest group (6%) of therapists included those for whom religion involved traditional worship, observation of holy days, and engagement with others in a religious community, but who did not emphasize its spiritual aspect.

Therapists' current religious affiliations were more important than their childhood family backgrounds in relation to their adult belief-value orientations. Moreover, in growing from childhood to adulthood, many therapists experienced changes in religious identity. While some were still Adherents to their religious origins, others were Apostates who ceased to be religious at all, and yet others became Converts to different faiths. This fluidity of religious identities appeared too as change in level of religiosity from childhood to adolescence and from adolescence to adulthood, with change going mainly from more to less, but for a few also from less to more—creating an overall impression of psychotherapists as persons who had been searching for meaning in their own lives.

Compared to religious affiliation, therapists' personal characteristics appeared more as nuances than influences on therapists' beliefs and values. Age, gender and marital status were of that type, although some differences were notable: the tendency of Younger therapists to be more Ethical Secular than Older therapists, and the latter to be more spiritual; the tendency of cohabiting therapists to be more Ethical Secular than married therapists, and the latter to be more religious. The four dimensions of *personal self* and the Anxious and Avoidant dimensions of attachment showed surprisingly little relationship to therapists' belief-value patterns, as if belonging to fairly independent domains (e.g., "personality" versus "mentality").

On the other hand, significant differences in belief-value patterns were found between therapists of different professional backgrounds and theoretical approaches. The main contrast in profession was between Psychologists who more often showed an Ethical Secular pattern and Counselors who were significantly more spiritual than Psychologists. The main contrast in theoretical approach was between Broad Spectrum integrative therapists who were more spiritual and both Cognitive-Behavioral and Analytic/Psychodynamic therapists, who were surprisingly similar in having majorities that each had an Ethical Secular orientation.[7] Although individual exceptions exist as always, the findings indicate a significant and moderately strong intersection between private belief-value patterns and professional theoretical orientations of psychotherapists.

Notes

1 Chapter 5 is based in part on work previous reported in a paper by Smith and Orlinsky (2004).

2 Other studies of psychotherapists' religious and spiritual orientations include: Duggal & Sriram (2021); Gibson & Herron (1990); Henry, Sims & Spray (1971); Hofmann & Walach (2011); Kelly (2001); Norcross & Wogan (1987); Oxhandler, Polson & Achenbaum (2018); Rosmarin, Green, Pirutinsky & McKay (2014); Shafranske & Malony (1990); Walker, Gorsuch & Tan (2004).

3 93% of 2,479 therapists rated this item at 6 or higher on the 0–10 scale; 62% rated it 9 or 10.

4 A total of 168 therapists listed their religious background as Hindu but unfortunately only 24 received a version of the DPCCQ asking for their current affiliation; as did only 43 currently identified Muslim.

5 Separate analyses of male and female therapists showed the same pattern for cohabiting couples in men and women, but the finding for married couples was statistically significant only for women.

6 Nevertheless it is worth noting that many therapists ran counter to type: a third (33%) of the mono-focal Cognitive-Behavioral therapists were either Spiritual Secular or Spiritual Religious in orientation, and a quarter (24%) of Broad Spectrum had an Ethical Secular orientation or reflected little spirituality.

7 This finding converges with professional backgrounds, as most (71%) mono-focal Cognitive-Behavioral therapists were Psychologists, as were a plurality (45%) of mono-focal Analytic/Psychodynamic therapists.·

References

Duggal, C., & Sriram, S. (2021). Locating the sacred within the therapeutic landscape: Influence of therapists' religious and spiritual beliefs on psychotherapeutic practice. *Spirituality in Clinical Practice*, advance copy.

Ellis, A. (1980). *The case against religion: A psychotherapist's view and the case against religiosity*. Cranford, NJ: American Atheist Press.

Freud, S. (1927). The future of an illusion. In J. Strachey & A. Freud, Eds., *The complete psychological works of Sigmund Freud*, Vol. XXI, 3–56. London: Hogarth Press.

Gibson, W. C., & Herron, W. G. (1990). Psychotherapists' religious beliefs and their perception of the psychotherapy process. *Psychological Reports*, 66(1), 3–9.

Henry, W. E., Sims, J. H., & Spray, S. L. (1971). *The fifth profession: Becoming a psychotherapist*, chap. II "Cultural origins and the marginal perspective" & chap. IV "Religious biographies: Genesis of apostasy" (pp. 9–28, 45–71). San Francisco: Jossey-Bass.

Hofmann, L., & Walach, H.(2011) Spirituality and religiosity in psychotherapy: A representative survey among German psychotherapists. *Psychotherapy Research, 21*: 179–192.

Kelly, E. W. (2001). Counselor values: A national survey. *Journal of Counseling & Development*, 73, 648–653.

Norcross, J. C., & Wogan, M. (1987). Values in psychotherapy: A survey of practitioners' beliefs. *Professional Psychology: Research and Practice*, 18, 5–7.

Oxhandler, H. K., Polson, E. C., & Achenbaum, W. A. (2018). The religiosity and spiritual beliefs and practices of clinical social workers: A national survey. *Social Work*, 63(1), 47–56.

Rosmarin, D. H., Green, D., Pirutinsky, S., & McKay, D. (2014). Spirituality/religion: Beliefs, practices, attitudes, and training among ABCT members. *The Behavior Therapist*, 37(7), 193–196.

Shafranske, E. P., & Malony, H. N. (1990). Clinical psychologists' religious and spiritual orientations and their practice of psychotherapy. *Psychotherapy*, 27, 72–78.

Smith, D. P., & Orlinsky, D. E. (2004). Religious and spiritual experience among psychotherapists. *Psychotherapy: Theory, Research, Practice, Training*, 41, 144–151.

Walker, D. F., Gorsuch, R. L., & Tan, S-Y. (2004). Therapists' integration of religion and spirituality in counseling: A meta-analysis. *Counseling and Values*, 49, 69–80.

6 Quality of Life

*D. E. Orlinsky with M. H. Rønnestad and
H. A. Nissen-Lie*

Current Life Quality

A good part of the psychotherapist's work involves helping patients to improve their quality of life. Through therapy, they do this by helping to overcome patients' self-inhibiting, self-demeaning and self-destructive habits; by helping to support them as they cope with painful or conflictual life events; and by helping them find the courage to seek out and explore better opportunities for satisfaction, personal growth, and meaningful involvement with others.

After examining the nature of therapists' private lives and personal beliefs, it is fair at this point to ask about therapists' own quality of life. How much satisfaction do therapists find in their own lives? How stressful are the situations they encounter and in which they live?[1] How much variation in life quality occurs among psychotherapists, and what are the circumstances and concomitants of those variations?[2]

Satisfaction and Stress

The DPCCQ asked questions about therapists' life quality both directly and indirectly. In one section of the questionnaire, therapists were asked directly: "How *satisfying* is your life at present?" and "How *stressful* is your life at present?" Answers to these questions were given on a six-point scale: 0 = Not at all, 1 = Little, 2 = Some, 3 = Moderately, 4 = Greatly, 5 = Very greatly. The response distributions are summarized in Figure 6.1, with some adjacent categories combined due to small proportions in them.

Current Satisfaction Levels

Two-thirds (67%) of therapists reported experiencing a high level of life satisfaction: 50% said they were "Greatly" satisfied and 17% more said they were "Very greatly" satisfied. For the rest, a quarter (26%) of the therapists were "Moderately" satisfied with their lives, and only 7% said they were less than "Moderately" satisfied (5% "Somewhat" so, 2% "Little" or "Not at all"). Overall more than 9 in 10

DOI: 10.4324/9781003217572-6

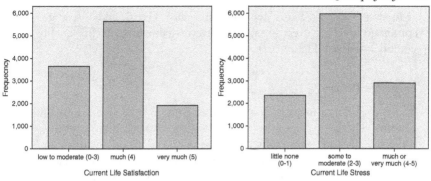

Figure 6.1 Therapists' Current Life Satisfaction and Stress

therapists seemed either quite happy or at least content with their lives, while a few—but perhaps a significant few—were finding their lives to be pretty unsatisfying.

Current Stress Levels

Despite the high level of satisfaction, stress was absent from very few therapists' lives. At its lowest level, only one in five (21%) overall said they currently had "None" (3%) or just a "Little" stress (18%). A combined middle level of stress included more than half (53%) of the therapists, who were experiencing either "Some" stress (22%) or "Moderate" stress (32%); and as many as a quarter (26%) of the therapists reported experiencing the highest level of stress (20% "Greatly" and 6% "Very greatly"). Numerically 2,910 of the 11,200 were in the highest level stress categories. With so many therapists feeling serious stress in their private lives, one may wonder how well they are able to help patients deal with theirs. Any illusions that may have been harbored by patients or the public at large about the presumably idyllic quality of therapists' lives can now be put to rest.

Life Quality Balance

Conceptually, overall quality of life reflects the balance between current satis-factions and stresses. Satisfaction and stress are far from polar opposites, although they are moderately negatively correlated ($r = -.28$), which indicates that extremes of both are unlikely to coexist. Relatively high levels of satisfaction can come with relatively high levels of stress, and relatively high levels stress are compatible with comparatively high levels of satisfaction. To explore patterns of life quality balance, the scales were adjusted as follows. Satisfaction was reduced to two categories: "Great" and "Very great" were combined as High (4–5) and the rest as Low-to-Moderate (0–3). Stress was reduced to three categories: "None" to "Some" were combined as Low stress (0–2),

"Moderate" stress (3) was kept separate, and "Great" and "Very great" were combined as High stress (4–5). When cross-tabulated, six life quality patterns were defined (see Figure 6.2).

Favorable Patterns

Taken together, a majority (54%) of therapists enjoyed two positive life quality patterns. The largest number (33%) of therapists had a high level of satisfaction and low level of stress, which was described as being fortunate or *Fulfilled*. Psychotherapists who enjoyed this life quality balance would have much to applaud and little to complain about in their own lives, and might tacitly convey an optimistic attitude to patients.

The second favorable pattern (21%) was represented by therapists who enjoyed a high level of satisfaction but also experienced a moderate level of stress. The balance here is favorable and the life situation could be described as *Satisfactory*. If the first group were "happy as clams," the second group might be likened to oysters irritated by some grains of sand—some of which could be transforming into pearls. If so, they might be able to offer patients a positive model of coping.

Unfavorable Patterns

By contrast, a quarter (26%) of the therapists appear to be living at high stress levels. About half of those (13%) were experiencing high levels of satisfaction along with high stress and seemed caught up in a very *Hectic* life quality pattern, both intense and impassioned—enduring personally what Dickens described as "the best of times and the worst of times." Their lives are impassioned both in the contemporary sense of passion as joy and the older sense of passion as suffering; yet in living such a tumultuous life, a question might be raised about whether their own compelling issues might distract them from attending empathically to patients' issues.

The other half of high stress therapists (13%) had just a low-to-moderate level of satisfaction, seeming to have a troubled or *Distressed* life quality that

Current Life Satisfaction	Current Life Stress		
	'Not at all' to 'Little' or 'Some'	'Moderate (3)	'Much' or 'Very much'
'Much' or 'Very much'	**FULFILLED**	**SATISFACTORY**	**HECTIC**
	33.2% (n = 3713)	20.9% (n = 2338)	13.3% (n = 1482)
'Not at all' to 'Moderate'	**DULL**	**STRAINED**	**DISTRESSED**
	9.4% (n = 1046)	10.6% (n = 1183)	12.6% (n = 1409)

Figure 6.2 Life Quality Patterns

might not have been very different from that of their patients. One may ask how much these *Distressed* therapists can be aiding their patients while having serious personal troubles of their own.

Mixed Patterns

The remaining one fifth (20%) of the therapists were accounted for by two mixed life quality patterns. About half of those (11%) experienced a moderate level of stress and a low-to-moderate level of satisfaction, being in a life quality pattern that could be described on balance as *Strained*. This is not a happy pattern but hopefully one that could be borne without damage, given sufficient inner resilience and external social support.

Finally, one in eleven (9%) therapists reported living with low stress and only low-to-moderate satisfaction, with a life quality pattern that was not particularly positive or negative but just subdued or *Dull*. These therapists may be surviving well enough in limited circumstances, although the question here is whether therapists whose private lives are limited and dull are able bring much positive energy or zest for life to their encounters with patients.

Characteristics and Dimensions of Life Quality Experience

What specific kinds of experience are linked to therapists' estimates of their overall life satisfaction and stress? To explore this further, therapists were asked in the DPCCQ to rate the frequency of 11 experiences that seemed likely to be linked to personal life quality, and those ratings were correlated with reports about their current life satisfaction and stress. (These are shown in Appendix Tables 6.1 a & b.)

Personal Life Benefits

The strongest correlates of current life satisfaction were experiencing "a satisfying sense of intimacy and emotional rapport" (r =.54), "a sense of being genuinely cared for and supported" (r =.48), and "moments of unreserved enjoyment" (r =.47). What therapists personally valued above all was: loving, being loved, and delight. This emphasizes the importance of adult intimate relationships and focuses attention on how much the configuration of one's private life may determine its quality.

Other experiences that contributed to therapists' current life satisfaction were "a sense of belonging to a personally meaningful community" (r =.37), "being able to freely express your private thoughts and feelings" (r =.33), and "taking opportunities to relax and refresh yourself" (r =.33).

Circumstances that tended to offset and undermine therapists' current life satisfaction were experiencing "a sense of significant personal conflict, disappointment or loss" (r = -.34), having "a heavy burden of responsibility, worry or concern for others close to you" (r = -.25), and being "hassled by the pressures of everyday life" (r = -.25). These corrosive experiences tended to diminish personal life satisfaction, although not so much as the absence of personal love relationships.

Personal Life Burdens

The leading correlates of personal life stress were feeling "hassled by the pressures of everyday life" (r =.61) and bearing "a heavy burden of responsibility, worry or concern for others close to you" (r =.49). Although caring for and being cared for by others seems a precondition of personal life satisfaction, that also creates emotionally significant responsibilities, burdens and vulnerability to worry and concern for them. The word *care* reflects this ambivalence: positively, to affirm, support and enjoy; negatively, to sorrow, grieve, and be "care-worn".

Other experiences contributing to therapists' personal life burdens were "a sense of significant personal conflict, disappointment or loss" (r =.35) and "worry about money or financial security" (r =.34). These may grind down on therapists' lives, as they likely do on other people's. One factor that appears to help in lowering stress is "taking opportunities to relax and refresh yourself" (r = -.27), although it was hardly a panacea and perhaps not readily available to all.

Therapists' worry about their physical health was a relatively minor source of life stress, especially in comparison to daily stress, concerns about loved ones and even worries about financial security, possibly because it was least often experienced. Only 11% experienced worry about their health "often" or "very often"—even among older therapists (ages 55–85).

Commonality of Life Quality Criteria

Do male and female therapists value the same things as contributors to their current life satisfaction and stress? Evidently, they do (based on the correlations in Appendix Table 6.1a). Correlations computed separately for male and female therapists had basically similar results both for life satisfaction and stress.

The same was basically true for therapists in each age group (see Appendix Table 6.1b). Younger (ages 22–34), Midlife (35–54), and Older (ages 55–85) all held essentially the same values regarding the sources of their life satisfaction and stress. The strongest correlations with life satisfaction at each age were "a satisfying sense of intimacy and emotional rapport" (r =.56, .54, and .50), "a sense of being genuinely cared for and supported" (r =.50, .48, and .42), and experiencing "moments of unreserved enjoyment" (r =.47, .46, and. 46). The strongest predictors of life stress at each age were feeling "hassled by the pressures of everyday life" (r =.61, .60, and .60) and bearing "a heavy burden of responsibility, worry or concern for others close to you" (r =.45, .50, and .45). Only the slightest trends might be remarked; for example, a minor decline among older therapists in the impact on satisfaction of intimacy and rapport, and of care and support—but even so, they remained the strongest predictors of life satisfaction.

The overall impression is one of great consistency both in positively and negatively valued life experiences among psychotherapists of all age groups and genders. The main contrast lies between experiences that contribute to current life satisfaction and to current life stress, which may happen concurrently in varying degrees and durations.

Dimensions of Life Quality Experience

A factor analysis of the specific positive and negative life experiences allowed construction of two reliable multi-item scales for further use (shown in Appendix Table 6.2). The positive factor scale was labeled *Personal Satisfactions*, and was defined primarily by intimacy and rapport (.79), care and support (.79), enjoyment (.75), and expression of private thoughts and feelings (.65)—together with current satisfaction (.69). The negative factor scale was labeled *Personal Burdens*, and was defined mainly by daily hassles and pressure (.78), worry and concern for others (.74), and conflict, disappointment or loss (.65)—along with total current stress (.75).

Variations in Life Quality Patterns and Dimensions

Men and women at different ages may value the same life experiences, but they don't necessarily enjoy them to the same extent. The next sections of this chapter are devoted to exploring similarities and differences in how *Personal Satisfactions* and *Personal Burdens* are felt, and how that is reflected in their life quality patterns.

Gender and Age

Long ago, the male and female Greek gods Zeus and Hera are said to have asked the blind prophet Tiresias—whose peculiar fate was to have been both a man and a woman at different times of life—whether men or women were happier (actually, which had the greater pleasure in sex). With respect to psychotherapists at least, the answer in regard to happiness seems to favor women. Independent samples t-tests[3] showed the mean level of Personal Satisfactions was slightly but significantly higher for women than for men (3.72 vs. 3.52 on a 0–5 scale). However, the same did not apply to *Personal Burdens* which were shared equally by both. In terms of life quality patterns, men and women were evenly matched for the most part, except that personal life was slightly less *Dull* (8% vs. 11%) and slightly more *Satisfactory* (22% vs. 20%) for female than for male therapists (see Appendix Table 6.3, left panel).

Therapists' ages were also significantly but marginally correlated with both *Personal Satisfactions* (r =.10) and *Personal Burdens* (r = -.12). Overall, it appears that therapists' lives tended to get a little sweeter and easier with age.[4] Notwithstanding those moderate correlations, several differences did emerge in regard to the incidence of specific life quality patterns (see Appendix Table 6.3, right panel).

Two-thirds (67%) of Older therapists felt their lives were either *Fulfilling* or *Satisfactory*; and correspondingly, their lives were also less *Hectic* (10%), less *Strained* (9%), and less *Distressed* (7%). Most striking was that so many more older therapists' lives were *Fulfilling* (45%) than either Midlife therapists (32%) or especially than Younger therapists (26%). The difference of 20% between Older and Younger therapists is noteworthy. Unfortunately for Younger therapists, their lives were significantly more likely to be *Distressed* (16%) or *Dull* (12%)—and fewer than half (46%) found their own lives *Fulfilling* or *Satisfactory*. By contrast, a majority of the Midlife therapists' lives were either *Fulfilling* (32%) or at least *Satisfactory* (21%), but Midlife therapists' lives were also significantly more *Hectic* (14%)— experiencing both much satisfaction and much stress.

Combining gender and age groups showed that Older female therapists clearly had the highest level of Personal Satisfactions, significantly more so than Younger Women and both Midlife and Younger Men (see Appendix Table 6.4). Younger Women had significantly higher scores than Midlife men, who in turn were significantly higher than Younger Men, who had the lowest level of Personal Satisfactions of all. Older women and Older men both had significantly lower levels of Personal Burdens than other groups, but the burdens experienced by Younger and Midlife men and women did not differ significantly from one another.

The pattern of differences between age groups seemed to vary between men and women.[5] Among female therapists, Personal Satisfactions were about the same for Younger and Midlife groups (3.67 and 3.71). Personal Satisfactions were already high for Younger and Midlife groups and only significantly increased for the Older women (3.79). On the other hand, the level of Personal Burdens dropped significantly from one age group to the next: Younger (2.55) to Midlife (2.44) to Older (2.19). To the extent that life improved for Midlife women (35–54), it was through a reduction of Personal Burdens—which conceivably might reflect most of their children having reached adulthood.

By contrast, life quality improved among male therapists through a steady age-to-age increase in Personal Satisfactions: Younger (3.30) to Midlife (3.52) to Older (3.73), but levels of Personal Burdens remained the same for Younger (2.44) and Midlife (2.42) men, with a significant drop coming only for the Older (2.20) ones—possibly reflecting fewer worries about money and less daily hassles regarding career advancement.[6] To the extent that life improved for Midlife men (35–54), it was through enhancement of Personal Satisfactions—possibly resulting from increased frequency of marriage and parenthood (see section on Private Life Status, below).

Viewed in terms of life quality patterns (see Appendix Table 6.5), the outstanding fact was that life was Fulfilling for a very large plurality of older women (46%) and older men (43%), and a much smaller proportion of Younger men (25%) and women (26%). The picture looked particularly bleak for Younger men, whose quality of life was significantly more Dull (17%),

Distressed (16%) or Strained (14%)—a total of 47%—due to their relatively low levels of Personal Satisfactions. Younger women were also more prone than older groups to experiencing a Distressed quality of life.

One has to wonder how well those less than happy Younger therapists are able to help their patients if their own personal lives are not going well. What kind of personal energy, optimism and confidence can they possibly convey as they relate with patients during therapy sessions? How much of a subtle "downbeat vibe" do they unconsciously radiate through their posture, mannerisms, vocal quality and facial expressions? More practically, what can be done to help this group of Younger therapists so they can be more helpful to their patients? These questions will be considered again in Chapter 10 when examining how therapists experience their work in clinical practice.

Private Life Status

It seems obvious that life quality experiences must be at least partially determined by the kinds of relationships that embody the therapist's private life situation, which include both adult intimate relationships and parental relationships. With regard to marital status (see Appendix Table 6.6), single therapists had significantly lower Personal Satisfactions than all other groups, and both married and cohabiting couples had significantly higher Personal Satisfactions, with divorced or separated therapists in the middle.

Combining marital status and gender makes clear that it was single men who were lowest and significantly lower than other groups in Personal Satisfactions, whereas single women were at a moderately higher level. Divorced or separated men were a step higher in Personal Satisfactions than single men, but still lower than men who were married or living with a partner. Women who were married or living with a partner reported having the most rewarding lives, at levels significantly higher than all others groups (including married men).

There were fewer significant differences in Personal Burdens among marital statuses (see Appendix Table 6.7). Married therapists experienced significantly fewer burdens than divorced or separated therapists, but neither differed significantly from either single or cohabiting therapists. The same relative positions were held when gender was combined with relationship status, although specific groups were not significantly differentiated from one another.

From the perspective of life quality patterns that reflect both satisfaction and stress (see Appendix Table 6.8), a clear majority of married therapists experienced lives that were either Fulfilling (36%) or Satisfactory (23%), both significantly above average. By contrast, nearly half the single therapists had lives that were significantly more likely to be Distressed (17%), Dull (15%) or Strained (15%)—as were the lives of divorced or separated therapists.[7]

Therapists who were parents had significantly more Personal Satisfactions in their lives than non-parents but, strikingly, no more Personal Burdens.[8] Similar results were found for the combination of parental status and gender: no difference in Personal Burdens; and a slightly more differentiated view for Personal

Satisfactions, with mothers significantly higher than fathers and childless men but not childless women. On its face, the finding that having children imposes no greater Personal Burdens may seem counter-intuitive, but the number of cases in these analyses is large enough to detect very small differences; the likelihood of a chance "false negative" finding (i.e., no difference) is very slight.

Clearly, being married or living with an intimate partner affords more frequent opportunities to experience emotional rapport, care and support—the leading features of therapists' Personal Satisfactions—than being single or being divorced. This advantage extends to those who are parents over those who are not, at least in regard to experiencing intimacy and emotional rapport (recognizing there is a significant overlap between marital status and parental status). But this apparently doesn't extend to the experiences that correlated most strongly with life stress. Differences in life quality between therapists in diverse private life patterns evidently depend more on the disparate opportunities they offer for Personal Satisfactions than on the Personal Burdens they tend to impose.

Belief-Value Patterns

Another question is whether therapists' religiosity, spirituality and their joint belief-value patterns were associated with variations in quality of life. Direct correlations between the respective dimensions indicate no association either of religiosity or of spirituality with level of Personal Burdens, and slight but significant correlations of each with Personal Satisfactions: with Religiosity, $r = .10$ (n = 4,541); for Spirituality, r =.17 (n = 3,542). A significantly higher level of Personal Satisfactions was experienced principally by therapists for whom Spirituality was of "Great" or "Very great" importance.[9]

The limited association of therapists' life quality with their religiosity and spirituality was reflected in a comparison of life quality patterns and belief-value patterns, where only the Ethical Secular pattern diverged significantly from average (see Appendix Table 6.9). Ethical Secular therapists were significantly underrepresented among those with a Fulfilling life quality (35%) and overrepresented among those whose quality of life was Distressed (13%) or Dull (8%). The main contrast was with Spiritual Religious therapists, significantly fewer of whom had a Distressed (7%) or Dull (4%) quality of life. Overall, the differences between therapists of various belief-value orientations were small, but were least favorable for Ethical Secular therapists.

Personal Self

Therapists' life quality was quite strongly associated with their scores on the dimensions of *personal self*, in contrast to the findings for belief-value patterns (see Appendix Table 6.10, upper panel). This was especially the case for Personal Satisfactions, which was strongly correlated with being Genial/Caring $(r = .42)$.[10] The more that therapists experienced themselves as self-bestowing (i.e., warm, friendly, nurturant, tolerant, receptive and accepting) in close personal relationships, the more they also had a sense of intimacy and emotional rapport, a sense of being genuinely cared for and supported, a sense of belonging to a personally meaningful community, and moments of unreserved enjoyment. This was reinforced by their being more openly self-expressive, as implied by the parallel positive correlation between Personal Satisfactions and being Ardent/Expressive ($r = .30$).[11]

Personal Satisfactions also had a significant negative correlation with being Reclusive/Remote ($r = -.22$), implying that the more therapists experienced themselves as reserved, skeptical, private and guarded in close personal relationships, the *less* likely they tended to experience a sense of intimacy and emotional rapport, a sense of being genuinely cared for and supported, a sense of belonging to a personally meaningful community, and moments of unreserved enjoyment. The moral of this story is that those who "hold back" from others often find the rewards of being close to others are held back from them.

Personal Burdens were not as strongly associated with the dimensions of *personal self*, but the correlations were statistically significant and psychologically interesting. Therapists who experienced themselves as Forceful/Exacting (e.g., directive, demanding, authoritative and critical) tended to experience modestly higher levels of Personal Burdens ($r = .16$). Similarly, therapists who were Reclusive/Remote also were somewhat more likely to experience more Personal Burdens ($r = .13$). Another small but significant correlation with Ardent/Expressive ($r = .10$) suggests that self-expressiveness can also add to one's burdens, perhaps by being too outspoken or emotionally demonstrative in circumstances that may require tact.

The impression created by these findings is of a cyclical and reflexive association between *personal self* and life quality dimensions, both positively and negatively. An old saying has it that "Life is a mirror: If you frown at it, it frowns back; if you smile, it returns the greeting."[12] That seems to be at least partially the case here, where the lives of therapists who are Genial/Caring and Ardent/Expressive in personal relationships are lifted up by Personal Satisfactions, while the lives of therapists who are Forceful/Exacting and Reclusive/Remote in their close relationships bear a heavier weight of Personal Burdens. It is not clear if being more self-bestowing in relationships gave therapists satisfaction directly or evoked more satisfying responses from others—or whether, having the good fortune of a satisfying life situation, they naturally tended to have a "sunnier" (i.e., more cheerful and optimistic) personal disposition. Likewise, it isn't clear if being more self-assertive and self-protective in close relationships is the result of having more Personal Burdens to bear or tends to elicit more stress and conflict in those relationships. In both cases the alternatives are not logically incompatible, and there may well be benign and detrimental self-reinforcing cycles of influence at play. For whatever reasons, the strongest finding was that the more Genial/Caring the therapists' *personal self*, the more satisfactions they currently found in their lives.

Attachment Style

Evidence congruent with the above findings comes from an additional data source: the subgroup of about 1,250 therapists who completed a measure of adult attachment style (the brief ECRS described in Chapter 4) along with the DPCCQ. Correlations of Personal Satisfactions and Personal Burdens with Anxious Attachment and Avoidant Attachment were quite substantial (see Appendix Table 6.10 lower panel). Personal Satisfactions was negatively related both to Anxious Attachment (r = -.36) and to Avoidant Attachment (-.41). Personal Burdens was positively related both to Anxious Attachment (r =.37) and to Avoidant Attachment (r =.20).

The inverse of Anxious and Avoidant attachment styles is understood to be a capacity for Secure attachment in intimate relationships, and these findings with psychotherapists indicate a notable positive association of Secure attachment with the life quality dimension of *Personal Satisfactions*, and nearly equivalent negative association of Secure attachment with the life quality dimension of *Personal Burdens*. Evidently, securely attached individuals experience their lives as more Fulfilling (or at least more Satisfactory).

If attachment style is largely determined early in life, as theoretically supposed, then it has a causal priority in this association. The capacity for Secure attachment seems to facilitate and enhance a sense of intimacy and emotional rapport, and a sense of being genuinely cared for and supported, in adult life—presumably by enabling individuals to engage in and sustain close personal relationships. Contrariwise, acquiring either type of insecure attachment, anxious or avoidant, seems to predispose individuals to more often encounter adult situations of conflict, disappointment and loss, of worry and concern, and a tendency to feel stressed and hassled by pressures of everyday life. Personal self and attachment disposition— as two partially overlapping aspects of the therapist's psychological makeup—clearly are important sources for the therapist's quality of life, even more than their age, gender, beliefs patterns, and the circumstances of their life situations.

Professional Discipline

It seems fair to ask whether psychotherapists' quality of life may be linked to professional as well as personal characteristics. How much, if at all, is a therapist's chosen professional discipline or theoretical approach to practice related to their personal satisfactions and burdens?

Psychotherapists of all professional backgrounds except Psychiatrists had basically similar levels of Personal Satisfaction (see Appendix Table 6.11, upper panel). Psychiatrists, as a group, were significantly lower in Personal Satisfactions on average than those in other professions.[13] It is possible that two sampling factors help to explain this: they are younger on average, and experienced less work satisfaction due to more extensive inpatient practice, than our other professional samples.[14] Given the lack of differentiation among other professions, it seems plausible to interpret the lower level of Personal Satisfactions among Psychiatrists as due at least partly to their lower age and work satisfaction, and to expect that older Psychiatrists working in private practice might experience as many Personal Satisfactions as their professional counterparts. On the other hand, Psychiatrists were the lowest of all groups in Genial/Caring and in Ardent/Expression (per Appendix Table 3.10)—personal characteristics that were just found to correlate substantially with Personal Satisfaction—so a mixture of causes may prove to offer the best explanation.

More differentiation between professions was found in regard to Personal Burdens (see Appendix Table 6.11, lower panel). The lives of Social Workers appeared to be significantly more burdened than other groups, and similar results were found when analyzed separately by gender. Psychologists were the next most heavily burdened, similar to Psychiatrists but significantly more so than Counselors and Lay Therapists/Analysts. A possible explanation may lie in the fact that Psychologists and especially Social Workers were significantly more often single in their marital status, and single persons have just been found to have significantly poorer life quality than other therapists (see Appendix Table 4.4 top panel, and Table 6.8).

Apparently the answer to why therapists of diverse professions tend to differ in their personal life quality lies in some combination of their private life circumstances and *personal self* characteristics.[15]

Theoretical Approach

Correlations between therapists' theoretical orientations and life quality dimensions indicated little to no connection with their personal life quality (see Appendix Table 6.12). All of the correlations with Personal Burdens were close to zero, and some were not statistically significant despite the very large sample size. Likewise, Personal Satisfactions was basically unrelated to therapists' use of Analytic/Psychodynamic approaches to treatment, and was slightly but positively related to other orientations—with the highest being only r =.13 for Broad Spectrum integrative therapists. What may be more interesting is that all correlations with Personal Satisfactions were positive except for the Analytic/Psychodynamic orientation, which was also the orientation that had the only significant positive correlation with Personal Burdens. This reversal of pattern might conceivably reflect a tendency of Analytic/Psychodynamic therapists to view experiences (and their own lives) through the lens of psychopathology. Nevertheless, with such thin support from the data, it would be wise not to give much weight to such conjectures. The safest conclusion is that therapists' theoretical orientations have little impact on, and are not influenced by, their personal quality of life.

In Sum

People who seek professional help from psychotherapists typically do so because their quality of life has become intolerable to them; because there is either malaise and misery or a dearth of meaningful satisfactions in their personal lives. From this perspective, the therapist's aim is to foster a significant improvement in the patient's quality of life. But of course psychotherapists are people too, and as such have their own life quality issues to manage—which, at times, may affect how well they can help patients to manage theirs. The ideal therapeutic situation is one in which therapists whose own personal lives are well-managed help patients learn how to better manage their lives and improve their life quality. This chapter explored the first part of that proposition by examining the personal life quality that is actually experienced by psychotherapists.

Initially, a survey of therapists' global experience of satisfaction and stress in their lives found that two-thirds reported high levels of current personal satisfaction, but that a fourth also reported high levels of stress. Since quality of life reflects a balance between satisfaction and stress, a measure combining them was fashioned to describe six alternative life quality patterns. The patterns for more than half of our therapists were primarily positive, being either *Fulfilling* (high satisfaction, low stress) or *Satisfactory* (high satisfaction, moderate stress). A smaller group of therapists experienced a high or very high satisfaction but also a high level of stress.

Unfortunately about a third of the therapists had less favorable life quality patterns. Those with moderate stress but low to moderate satisfaction were described as *Strained*. For others with low stress but also low satisfaction, life appeared *Dull*. More worrisome were the one-of-eight therapists who seemed to have really *Distressed* lives, with high stress levels and only low to moderate satisfaction—probably not unlike the lives of many patients.

Specific kinds of experience that tend to promote current satisfaction and stress were identified. Satisfaction was associated mainly with their close personal relationships: feelings of intimacy and emotional rapport, being genuinely cared for and supported, having moments of unreserved enjoyment. Giving and receiving love mattered most to the therapists. Current life stress, on the other hand, related mostly to feeling hassled by pressures of everyday life, but also to feeling burdened by responsibility, worry and concern for others close to them—the somber side of caring. Moreover, therapists of varied age groups and genders—young and old, men and women—responded similarly about which life experiences were satisfying or stressful.

Yet though the same life experiences were valued positively and negatively by all therapists, clearly not all enjoyed them to the same extent, as shown by differences in their life quality patterns. The next step was to learn which factors differentiated therapists whose personal lives were more and less favorably endowed. Categorical life quality patterns were compared for various therapist groups, and scales of Personal Satisfactions and Personal Burdens were constructed to correlate and contrast with diverse therapist characteristics.

The first characteristics analyzed were therapist gender and age group. Viewed separately, a small gender difference favored female therapists and a larger difference favored older therapists, but age and gender combined was more revealing. Older women and men (ages 55 to 85) enjoyed the highest levels of Personal Satisfactions as well as the lowest levels of Personal Burdens. Life for them appeared to have reached its "golden" years. For Midlife (ages 35–54) and Younger (21–34) therapists, gender differences were notable. Moderately high levels of Personal Satisfaction were experienced by Midlife and Younger women, while Midlife and especially Younger men had the lowest satisfaction. Personal Burdens were in the moderate range for both Midlife women and men, but fell most heavily on Younger therapists of both genders. Youth was not a carefree time of life for many young therapists.

Given the value placed on intimacy and support in close relationships as a source of satisfaction, it was reasonable to suppose that therapists' current life quality would be associated with the configuration of relationships in private life, as was indeed the case. Those without active adult close relationships—divorced and especially single therapists of both sexes—had the lowest level of Personal Satisfaction, while those who were married or living with a partner had the highest levels. Concurrently, therapists who were married or living with a partner experienced the lowest levels of Personal Burdens, while those who were single, but especially those who were divorced or separated, had the highest levels. In terms of group averages, having an intimate adult partner was clearly the condition associated with the most favorable quality of life, even allowing that some married or partnered individuals might be less than fully happy. As for parenthood, therapists who were fathers and mothers experienced significantly higher levels of Personal Satisfactions, yet reported no more Personal Burdens than those without children. On average, having children added to their net quality of life.[16]

The most notable differentials among therapists both in Personal Satisfactions and in Personal Burdens were associated with the dimensions of *personal self*— and (where data were available) with the dimensions of adult attachment. Personal Satisfactions were most strongly and positively correlated with being Genial/Caring (self-bestowing) in close relationships. Those who experienced themselves as most warm, friendly and nurturant in close relationships tended also to experience higher levels of life satisfaction. Those also tending to be Ardent/Expressive (self-expressive) in close relationships also experienced more Personal Satisfactions. On the other hand, being Reclusive/Remote (self-protective) in close relationships correlated negatively with Personal Satisfactions and positively with Personal Burdens. Being Forceful/Exacting (self-assertive) in close relationships also correlated with Personal Burdens. In effect, therapists who experienced themselves as kindly, generous and expressive enjoyed life more, while therapists who tend to be distant or dominant in close relationships tended to experience life as more burdened.

Information on adult attachment style was available for about 1,250 therapists. Anxious Attachment and Avoidant Attachment were strongly and negatively correlated with Personal Satisfactions—the more anxious and avoidant, the less satisfying life was. Moreover, Anxious Attachment was strongly and positively correlated with Personal Burdens—the more anxious in close relationships, the more stressful life was.[17] Since Secure attachments are viewed as a relative absence of anxious and avoidant styles, the findings suggest that having a secure attachment style is key to experiencing a favorable quality of life.

Finally, as the persons who participated in this study were all working psychotherapists, it was interesting to know whether differences in professional discipline or theoretical orientation related to variations in personal life quality. The answer seems to be "not much." Correlations of Personal Satisfactions and Personal Burdens with theoretical approach to practice were either statistically non-significant or so small as to be negligible. The only significant differences between therapists' professional disciplines were that Psychiatrists on average enjoyed less Personal Satisfactions, and Social Workers on average felt more Personal Burdens—but these differences seemed at least partly explained by other factors like age and gender distributions. The conclusion is that personal quality of life was associated mainly with therapists' personal characteristics.

Notes

1 Aspects of this chapter were presented in a paper by Nissen-Lie, Orlinsky and Rønnestad (2021).
2 Some other studies related to this topic are those by Brugnera, Zarbo, Compare, et al. (2020); Coster & Schwebel (1997); Guy, Poelstra & Stark (1989); Linley & Joseph (2007); Nissen-Lie, Havik, Høglend et al. (2013); Schröder, Wiseman & Orlinsky (2009).
3 For *Personal Satisfactions,* $t = 12.9$, $df = 8664$, mean difference $=.20$, $p =.000$, where female therapists scored $M = 3.72$, $sd =.78$ and males scored $M = 3.52$, $sd =.80$. For *Personal Burdens,* $t = 1.91$, $df = 8880$, mean difference $=.04$, $p =.06$, where female therapists scored $M = 2.41$, $sd =.98$, and males scored $M = 2.38$, $sd =.97$.
4 The alternative hypothesis of "cohort difference" is that this heterogeneous group of older therapists was more satisfied and less burdened even when they were younger, which is logically possible but less plausible.
5 The comparisons are based on 1-way ANOVAs computed separately by gender ($p =.000$), with significance of differences between age groups determined by Scheffe test set at $p \geq .01$.
6 Two 1-way ANOVAs of specific items shown in Table 6.2 showed Older therapists to be significantly less worried about money ($F = 40.4$, $df = 2$, 4525, $p =.000$) and less hassled by pressures of everyday life ($F = 58.44$, $df = 2$, 4370, $p =.000$) than Midlife and Younger age groups.
7 Nevertheless, keep in mind that 42% of single therapists had a Fulfilling or Satisfactory quality of life, as did 46% of divorced or separated therapists. Mean differences between groups are consistent with substantial overlap at the individual level.
8 For *Personal Satisfactions,* t = -4.40, df = 3953, mean difference = -1.13, p = 000, where parents scored M = 3.76, sd =.74, and non-parents scored $M = 3.64$, $sd =.78$. For *Personal Burdens,* $t = 1.45$, $df = 3956$, mean difference $=.05$, $p =$.ns, where parents scored $M = 2.32$, $sd =.94$, and males scored $M = 2.36$, $sd =.96$.

9 $F = 70.2$, $df = 2$, 4528, $p = .000$ in a 1-way ANOVA.
10 This association is notable not just for its size, but because correlates for the Genial/ Caring dimension had previously proved elusive when sought in Chapter 3.
11 Ardent/Expression was positively correlated with Genial/Caring, but still accounted for a small amount of additional variance when both were entered in a regression model predicting Personal Satisfactions.
12 The saying is attributed to the satirical English writer William Makepeace Thackeray (1811–1863), and is one of which my mother was annoyingly fond.
13 Similar results were found when analyzed separately by gender.
14 At an average age of 43, Psychiatrists happened to be the youngest profession in the study. Only 16% in the older and significantly happier group of therapists (ages 55–85) were Psychiatrists—as compared to 33% of Counselors, 30% of Lay Therapists/ Analysts, and 21% of Social Workers. Psychologists were on average just a year older but another factor to consider is the work setting and work satisfaction of the different professions. Psychiatrists worked significantly more hours in inpatient settings than any other profession (8.8 hours/week vs. 3.8 hours for Psychologists and Social Workers, and 1.6 hours for Counselors). Psychiatrists also had significantly lower scores on work satisfaction than any other group, and in our sample work satisfaction was positively correlated with Personal Satisfaction ($r = .37$, $N = 10,212$, $p = 000$). A link between inpatient treatment and work satisfaction was previously reported in Orlinsky and Rønnestad (2005).
15 Again, it should be remembered that these findings reflect group-level differences; and because groups tend to overlap despite mean differences, at the *individual* level there are surely Psychiatrists who enjoy much Personal Satisfaction, and Social Workers who experience few Personal Burdens.
16 These findings should not be viewed as an endorsement of traditional "bourgeois" values that esteem marriage and parenthood as indicators of social respectability. What is essential is positive emotional connection in securely attached relationships, which may take many forms. Therapists above all know—from their patients' lives and sometimes from their own—that marriages empty of mutual caring are often arenas of misery, and parenthood can become a trial and an affliction.
17 The potency of these attachment dimensions is underscored by the large proportion of variance they accounted for when entered along with other variables in multiple regression analyses. Optimal Scaling Categorical Regression (CATREG) was used to allow inclusion of nominal as well as ordinal and numeric variables, with results shown in Appendix Tables 6.13 and 6.14. Up to a third of the variance in Personal Satisfactions and up to a fifth of the variance in Personal Burdens were accounted for by combinations of the variables analyzed in this chapter.

References

Brugnera, A., Zarbo, C., Compare, A., Talia, A., Tasca, G. A., De Jong, K., Greco, A., Greco, F., Pievani, L., Auteri, A., & Lo Coco, G. (2020). Self-reported reflective functioning mediates the association between attachment insecurity and well-being among psychotherapists. *Psychotherapy Research*, 31, 247–257.

Coster, J., & Schwebel, M. (1997). Well-functioning in professional psychologists. *Professional Psychology: Research and Practice*, 28, 5–130.

Guy, J. D., Poelstra, P. L., & Stark, M. J. (1989). Personal distress and therapeutic effectiveness: National survey of psychologists practicing psychotherapy. *Professional Psychology: Research and Practice*, 20, 48–50.

Linley, P. A., & Joseph, S. (2007). Therapy work and therapists' positive and negative well-being. *Journal of Social and Clinical Psychology*, 26, 385–403.

Nissen-Lie, H. A., Havik, O. E., Høglend, P. A., Monsen, J. T., & Rønnestad, M. H. (2013). The contribution of the quality of therapists' personal lives to the development of the working alliance. *Journal of Counseling Psychology*, 60, 483–495.

Nissen-Lie, H. A., Orlinsky, D. E., & Rønnestad, M. H. (2021). The emotionally burdened psychotherapist: Personal and situational risk factors. *Professional Psychology*, Advance of publication.

Orlinsky, D. E., & Rønnestad, M. H. (2005). *How psychotherapists develop: A study of therapeutic work and professional growth*. Washington, DC: APA Books.

Schröder, T. A., Wiseman, H., & Orlinsky, D. E. (2009). "You were always on my mind": Therapists' professional characteristics, and quality of life. *Psychotherapy Research*, 19, 42–53.

7 Family Background

D. E. Orlinsky with M. H. Rønnestad and T. A. Schröder

It is generally understood that the childhood family in which someone grows up—their "family of origin"—is the first and frequently most foundational arena for developing their emotional attachments, their core sense of self, and their basic expectations about how to interact with others in safe and satisfying ways. In other words, childhood family experiences are the mold that shapes us as persons and that provides the platform on which we learn to become adults. This view is broadly shared in modern psychology and social sciences, as well as among the diverse theoretical approaches to psychotherapy. Given this understanding, it is relevant in a study of psychotherapists as persons to examine (a) the kinds of family groups that therapists grew up in with respect to their size and stability, (b) their economic and cultural/religious family backgrounds, and (c) their experiences while growing up, in terms of their family's psychological functioning and the quality of care they received.

Family Situation

An individual's family situation is shaped in large part by the number of siblings and their birth order among those siblings.[1] Families can be large or small and the children in them can be first-born, last-born or somewhere in the middle if there are three or more. Growing up as an "only child", having no one as an ally or a rival (or both), is surely conducive to a different early experience than growing up as the oldest child and natural leader of two or more younger siblings; or growing up the youngest, either "picked on" or favored and indulged as the "baby of the family"; or just as one in a crowd of several who might be overlooked in the middle of a large family. The particular family context in which one grows up is part of the initial "hand that one is dealt" by life, optimizing or limiting the strategies available for gaining attention and power, safety and satisfaction.[2]

Family Size

In modern societies where nuclear families are the norm, consisting basically of parents and their dependent children, family size depends mainly on the number of siblings. Figure 7.1 shows the wide range of size in the childhood families of our therapists.

DOI: 10.4324/9781003217572-7

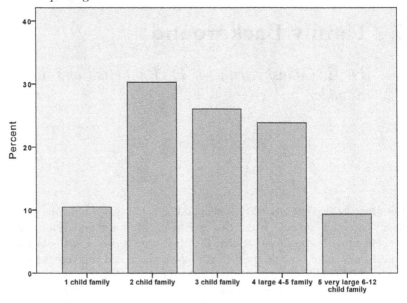

Figure 7.1 Therapists' Childhood Family Size (N = 4799)

Relatively few therapists grew up as "only" children (11%) or in very large families with anywhere from 6 to 12 children (9%). A majority of therapists had one or two siblings: 30% had one brother or sister, and 26% had been one of three children in the family. About a quarter (24%) of the therapists had been one of four or five children—large but not a crowd in which one could easily get lost.

Birth order

One's early environment is shaped not only by the number of other children in the family but also by one's position in the order of birth. Figure 7.2 shows a wide range in birth orders among our therapists.

Overall, about 35% of the therapists were oldest children. However, the majority of therapists were either the youngest child in the family (29%) or a "middle" child with both older and younger siblings (26%).[3] As noted above, very few of the therapists in our sample were "only" children. It is conceivable that psychotherapy as a profession does not attract many "only" children, as therapeutic practice demands a high level of interpersonal skills—social skills of a sort that may be best learned through early and long experience developing adaptive strategies for dealing with one's siblings. In addition, contemporary models of psychotherapeutic relationships in Western cultures emphasize a peer-like quality evocative of relations between older and younger siblings, rather than a hierarchic authoritative quality resembling that of parent and child.[4]

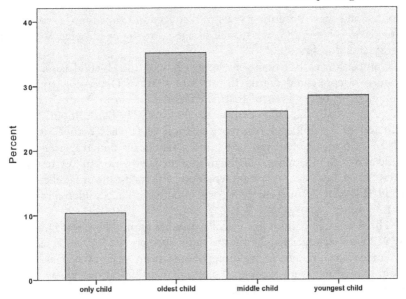

Figure 7.2 Therapists' Birth Order (N = 4844)

Birth Order and Family Size

Combining family size and birth order shows a wide range of specific situations. For example, even the largest of the 12 combinations shown in Appendix Table 7.1 has only 16% of the sample: being the older child in a 2-child family. The next most frequent combination (14%) was being the younger child in a 2-child family. Therapists raised in 2-child families were followed, in descending order of frequency, by middle children in 4- or 5-child families (12%); oldest children in 3-child families (10%); and "only children" (10%). These five combinations of birth order and family size together accounted for 62% of the sample, with each of the remaining combinations representing smaller groups.

Gender and Generation

As for gender, no significant differences were detected between male and female therapists, either with respect to family size, birth order, or the combination of those variables. Given the large sample (N ≈ 4,800), the lack of statistical differentiation seems definitive. Percentages of men and women in each family category were virtually identical.

However, there were some differences in family size based on the generation (birth year cohort) of therapists.[5] Three generations of therapists were distinguished: those born between 1927 and 1946 (N = 2,422), whose early years were influenced by the Great Depression and World War 2; those born between 1947 and 1966 (N = 6,967) who were part of the post-war "Baby

Boom" and grew up during years of recovery and expansion[6]; and those born after 1966 (N = 2,285) who came of age in an era of growing Western prosperity and globalization.

Comparison of different generations showed that 1-child families (at 14%) were overrepresented during the stressful years of Depression and war, even though a majority (57%) of that generation came from 2- or 3-child families (see Appendix Table 7.2). During the Post-WW2 "Baby Boom" years, there was indeed a significant overrepresentation of families with 4 or 5 children (28%) or 6 to 12 children (12%), and a significant underrepresentation of 1-child and 2-child families. Finally, during the later period of Western prosperity there was a significant overrepresentation of therapists from families with just 1 child (14%) or 2 children (37%), and a corresponding underrepresentation of large families.

The reversal in pattern from smaller families during the Great Depression and WW2 years to larger families in the immediate post-WW2 era is relatively easy to understand. Young men coming home from years of war and separation from loved ones were eager to "catch up with life" as quickly as possible and return to "normalcy" following the demands and deprivations that had interrupted their development. They were also able to find jobs in the post-war economy, enabling them to support larger families. It is less clear why the pattern reversed again in the succeeding era of Western prosperity. Part of the reason must be the introduction and widespread adoption of oral contraceptives in the early 1960s which made choice of family size an effective option; but families of the preceding "Baby Boom" generation must also have been motivated to limit the number of children. It may be plausible to find that motivation in the reputation of "Boomers" as the "Me-generation",[7] one that was invested in their own growth and "self-realization" as adults, as well as in that of their children. Moreover, given the new ethos of "personal growth" it was clearly easier to invest in each child as an individual if there were just a few in the family.[8]

Family Disruption

Few events in the life of a family can affect a child as much or as adversely as the death of a parent, or as disruption due to divorce or separation between the parents. Later versions of the DPCCQ survey included questions about both types of event and the therapist's age at the time if that occurred.

Parental Death

Our data showed, as would be expected, that most (65%) of the Older therapists (55+ years) had already lost both parents, and more than a quarter (28%) had lost one parent (see Appendix Table 7.3). By contrast, most (85%) of Younger therapists (under 35) still had both living parents. These findings appear quite normal given the natural succession of generations. Those who had lost only one parent were overrepresented (38%) among Midlife therapists (35–54 years), three times more often than for Younger therapists (12%). Typically, it was also the case that substantially more of those therapists had lost fathers than had lost mothers.

The psychological and emotional impact of parental mortality on offspring must depend to a great extent on how early in life that occurred. Most (65%) of therapists who had lost one or both parents were already 30 or more years old and very likely independent at the time their first parent died (see Appendix Table 7.4).[9] Of those who had lost a parent at a younger age, 7% were children (age 12 or less), at the time, 8% were adolescents (ages 13–19), and 20% were young adults (ages 20–29). Children and adolescents are certainly ill equipped to cope with a parent's death, but even for young adults the loss would likely feel untimely and potentially traumatic.[10]

Parental Divorce

Another major source of disruption occurs when parents in a family divorce or separate. This had happened to about a fifth (20%) of the therapists. Moreover, contrary to the circumstances with parental mortality, the older that therapists had become the less frequently had their parents divorced or separated (see Appendix Table 7.5). In fact the highest proportion of parental divorce or separation occurred when therapists were children 12 or younger (47%); fewer when they were adolescents ages 13 to 19 (26%); fewer still when they were young adults ages 20 to 29 (17%); and least of all when therapists were over 30 years old (10%). Thus if therapists had experienced their parents' divorce or separation, they most likely were still young and emotionally vulnerable at the time.

This finding might reflect the relative resilience and durability of the marital bond between therapists' parents, since those with brittle or unstable relationships would likely have ended sooner, at a time when their children were younger—or, if they had several children, before having their youngest child. The latter effect was observed in a significant association of parental divorce with therapists' birth order, such that therapists who were only children or oldest children were more likely to have divorced parents (24%, 22%) than those who were youngest children (15%).[11] Most parents of youngest children stayed together at least long enough to have multiple children.

However, the observed trend might also reflect a historical change in cultural norms across generations, especially with legal obstacles to divorce having diminished in many countries in recent years and social acceptance of divorce having increased. This is illustrated by a significant trend across birth-cohort generations, with the incidence of parental divorce increasing from 17% in the Depression/WW2 era to 20% in Post-WW2/Baby Boom era, and to 24% in the later generation of Western prosperity and globalization.[12]

The family's economic status (see below) may also be related to parental divorce or separation. Analysis of a small subsample for which data were available indicated that divorce or separation was significantly more likely to occur in economically Challenged families (36%) than in either Secure or Affluent families (24% and 22% respectively).[13] It might be that emotional distress over material scarcity and financial crises undermined the bond between parents, or alternatively that families destabilized through divorce or separation were more likely to have become economically unstable. In fact both might be true, with the weight of those factors varying according to other circumstances.

Additionally (as expected) there was a higher proportion of economically challenged families in the Depression/WW2 generation (31%) than in either of the succeeding generations (18%), complemented by increasing percentages of economically Secure families across the subsequent generations (31% vs. 45% vs. 53%).[14] Which of these interpretations ultimately has most influence—relative marital stability of parents, generational cultural change, or economic hardship—is not discernible, but they are not logically incompatible and may all play a part.

Therapists' family religious background also affected the likelihood of their parents having divorced or separated, although possibly not as might be expected. Overall, a significantly higher rate of divorce (28%) occurred among non-religious families than among families of Protestant (17%), Catholic (20%) or Jewish (19%) background.[15] However, there were no significant differences between religious backgrounds in the older birth-cohort generation (1927–1946) or even in the youngest generation (1967–1990)—although in each generation non-religious families led the divorce statistic, which might reflect a trend to greater social cohesion among families with a religious affiliation.

Family Economic Background

An important feature influencing a family's situation is their economic status.[16] For adults, economic status is a matter of income, resource management, occupational prestige and perhaps work satisfaction. Economic status primarily links adults to the larger social world outside of the family. However, children's experiences of their family's economic status would almost surely be primarily reflected in terms of consumption. Children whose life-world is largely internal to the family are more likely to be affected by the relative abundance or scarcity of material resources (shelter, food, clothing, toys and "treats"), and by their parents' feelings of economic confidence and security, or anxiety and stress, which would likely diffuse into the family's emotional atmosphere.

Accordingly, a question was eventually added to the DPCCQ about childhood family economic status focusing on the consumer and security aspects of family life. Framed in this way, the question had the further advantage of transcending the considerable differences between countries with respect to monetary systems, occupational rankings and educational institutions—an important advantage in a broadly multinational study. The question introduced to the DPCCQ asked therapists: "How materially comfortable or difficult were the economic circumstances in which you grew up?" The distribution of respondents on this is illustrated in Figure 7.3.

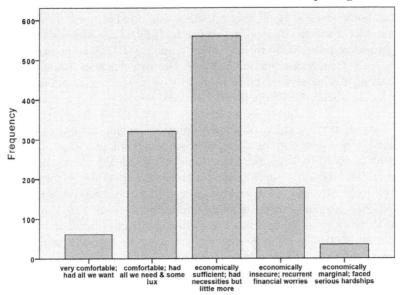

Figure 7.3 Therapists' Childhood Family Economic Status (N = 1155)

Basically half (49%) of the therapists indicated that their families' resources were: "Economically sufficient; we had the basic necessities but little more." This reflects a materially *Secure* but not affluent condition, which in modern societies would indicate a lower-middle class or skilled working class situation. By comparison, a third (33%) of the therapists came from families that can be considered *Affluent*, whose resources were either "Comfortable; we had all that we needed and some luxuries as well" (28%) or "Very comfortable; we always had all we wanted" (5%). These therapists were raised in upper-middle or upper class families, where they likely were not just materially secure but perhaps also indulged or pampered. (Whether they also felt emotionally well cared for and secure is a question to be explored later and in Chapter 8.)

At a lower socioeconomic level, about one in six (18%) of the therapists grew up in families that were economically *Challenged*, describing their backgrounds mainly as: "Economically insecure; my family had recurrent financial worries" (15%) or even as "Economically marginal; we had real financial worries or faced serious hardships" (3%). These would generally be from unskilled working class or for some reason marginally employed economic backgrounds. Thus overall there was a fairly wide range of economic statuses (and implicitly, of social classes) among therapists' families of origin.

Economic Status and Family Situation

No significant associations were found between family economic status and birth order, nor the combination of birth order and family size. However, a small but statistically significant association was found between family economic background and family size (see Appendix Table 7.6). Affluent families were significantly more likely to be 2-child families (41%) as compared with economically Challenged families (26%). By contrast, therapists from economically Challenged families were more likely to have grown up in very large families of 5–12 children (20%), in contrast to very few (8%) of those from Affluent families.

Affluent families could obviously afford to provide for more children but typically had just two or three, whereas economically Challenged families could ill afford to have more than one or two children but tended to have many. The thought that families at different economic levels might have different cultural values about child-bearing led to examining those families' religious backgrounds, but no significant relationships were found in this regard. An alternative possibility is that the greater resources of Affluent families might have enabled them to more effectively manage their fertility and choose the number of children they wished to have.

Gender, Age and Generation

As expected, neither therapist age nor gender appeared related to childhood family economic background. Male and female therapists were equally likely to be from Affluent, Secure or Challenged families. There was a close to zero correlation of family economic status with therapist age, although there was a slight but statistically significant association of family economic status with therapists' birth year cohort, indicating that those born in the era of Western prosperity (1967–1990) were more likely to come from economically Secure families (53%), especially as compared with those raised in the Great Depression and WW2 era (31%).[17] By contrast, the percentages of therapists from economically Affluent families did not change significantly across birth cohorts (being respectively 38%, 37%, 30% of therapists).

Family Religious Background

The religious origins of the psychotherapists were partly reported in Chapter 2 and Chapter 5 in connection with therapists' individual belief and value orientations, but religious backgrounds are also important as a potential cultural influence on childhood family life. The distribution of the many psychotherapists (N = 4,319) who provided data on their family's religious background is illustrated in Figure 7.4, which shows that most (70%) were raised in a Christian context, either in a Protestant denomination (45%) or in the Roman Catholic or Eastern Orthodox tradition (25%). The next largest groups consisted of therapists from non-religious families (12%), Jewish families (8%), or families with mixed religious backgrounds (5%).[18] Religious backgrounds of a small number of non-Western therapists included Hindu (4%), Buddhist (1%), and Muslim (1%).[19]

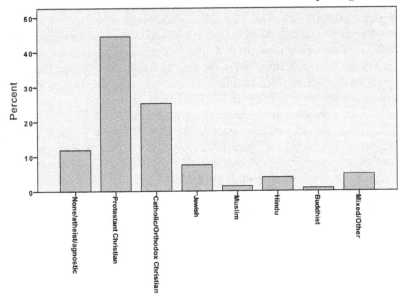

Figure 7.4 Therapists' Childhood Family Religious Backgrounds (N = 4319)

Gender and Age

The composition of religious background groups varied significantly by generation, age, and gender (see Appendix Table 7.7). There were two significant differences in religious background by therapist gender: non-religious background (14% women vs. 10% men) and those from Jewish families (12% men vs. 7% women). No gender differences were found for Protestant, Catholic/Orthodox, and mixed background families.

As for age, non-religious and Catholic/Orthodox therapists were significantly younger than those from mixed and Protestant backgrounds, and those in turn were younger than therapists from Jewish families. The average age of therapists from different family backgrounds was: non-religious, 47.5 years; Catholic/Orthodox, 47.8 years; mixed background, 51.4 years; Protestant, 52.5 years; and Jewish, 55.2 years. Approximately the same differences appeared for men and women separately, except the number of therapists of Jewish background was too small when divided by gender to be statistically significant.

Generation

Perhaps of greater interest are changes in the family religious backgrounds of therapists over different generations or birth year cohorts. A significantly higher proportion of therapists born between 1927 and 1946 were from Protestant and Jewish backgrounds, while those from Catholic/Orthodox and non-religious backgrounds were significantly underrepresented in that generation (see Appendix Table 7.8). This pattern reversed among therapists born from 1967 to 1990: therapists from Catholic/Orthodox and from non-religious families were significantly overrepresented, while those from Protestant and Jewish backgrounds were significantly underrepresented in this more recent cohort. Rather large generational differences were evident: decreases from 54% to 31% for therapists with Protestant backgrounds, and from 13% to 3% for those from Jewish families; increases from 19% to 41% among Catholic/Orthodox therapists, and from 8% to 21% among those from non-religious families. It is tempting to interpret these differences as reflecting historical change in the psychotherapeutic professions (e.g., the progressive fading away of Jewish therapists), but a more cautious view would attribute these variations at least in part to data collections being conducted in different countries at different times over the past 30 years.

Religiosity

Therapists from each of these religious backgrounds varied among themselves in how important religion was for them during their childhood and adolescence,[20] and also differed significantly in that respect between religious groups. Both in childhood and adolescence, religion was significantly more important for therapists raised in Roman Catholic or Eastern Orthodox families than all other groups, and (as expected and reassuringly) had significantly least importance for therapists from families having no religious affiliation (see Appendix Table 7.9). Protestants, Jews and those of mixed background were between the two but did not differ significantly from each other.

For the older generation (born 1927–1946), religion was also significantly more important in the childhood of those raised in Catholic/Orthodox families than all other groups, and least important for those from non-religious families.[21] However, in both succeeding generations (1947–1966 and 1967–1990) the only significant difference was between the non-religious and religious groups, although Catholic/Orthodox therapists were consistently the most religious.

Family Situation

Significant differences in childhood family size were observed between therapists who grew up in families with different religious backgrounds, both overall and in each of the three successive birth cohort generations. For all therapists with relevant data, a majority (50%) of those of Catholic/Orthodox background grew up in large (4–5 child) or very large (6–12 child) families, as compared to only 32% of Protestant and 16% of Jewish therapists (see Appendix Table 7.10).

By contrast, two-child families predominated among therapists from Jewish backgrounds (45%) as well as those from non-religious backgrounds (42%), and majorities in both groups either had just one sibling or were "only" children.

Most Catholic/Orthodox therapists came from large or very large families in the 1927–1946 and 1947–1966 generations (49% and 57%, respectively), but in the 1967–1990 generation most (60%) came mainly from large (4- or 5-child) and medium (3-child) families. Jewish therapists in the older birth-cohort generation (1927–1946) came largely from two-child families (57%), but in the two subsequent generations most grew up in 2- or 3-child families (77% and 72%, respectively). Thus the number of children in Catholic/Orthodox families decreased slightly over the generations of therapists, while the number of children in Jewish families increased slightly. Among therapists from Protestant backgrounds, a majority (58%) grew up having one or two siblings, and this was consistent across each of the three birth-cohort generations.

The findings on birth order naturally reflected the facts of family size. Therapists from large or very large families would have a surplus of middle children, while therapists from 1- or 2-child families would have none. This was in fact the case for therapists overall and clearly in the two older generations (1927–1946 and 1947–1966), with most Catholic/Orthodox families containing more middle children—except in the youngest generation, where therapists in somewhat smaller Catholic families were more often oldest or youngest children.

Religion and Economic Status

Relatively few therapists provided data on both religious and economic backgrounds ($N = 462$), and the statistical significance of results was marginal. Descriptively, 50% of Protestant therapists, 46% of Catholic/Orthodox therapists and 45% of non-religious therapists came from Affluent families, as compared to 38% of Jewish families and 20% from mixed religious backgrounds. By contrast, 38% of Jewish therapists came from economically Challenged families, but only 15% of the non-religious and 12% of Protestant therapists did so. More therapists of Protestant and non-religious families came from the most privileged strata.

Childhood Family Functioning

Beyond the internal structural aspects and social backgrounds of therapists' childhood families is the important subjective aspect of the family's emotional and psychological functioning. This aspect of their patients' childhood family life is a familiar and theoretically meaningful concern in the professional work of psychotherapists—so perhaps their view of their own childhood families may be regarded as involving an experienced expert assessment. If lacking the same degree of impartiality as their assessments of patients' families, therapists views of their own childhood families nevertheless reflect a deep subjective reality. Based on this, the following question was added to the DPCCQ and presented to the most recent 6,347 therapists who participated in this study: "Overall, when growing up, how much … Did the family you grew up in function well, psychologically and emotionally?" To answer, therapists checked one of the following options: 0 = Not at all, 1 = Slightly, 2 = Somewhat, 3 = Moderately, 4 = Much or 5 = Very much. The distribution of responses that therapists gave is illustrated in Figure 7.5.

Surprisingly and rather gloomily, only a third (32%) of the therapists rated the emotional and psychological functioning their own childhood families as "Very good" (8%) or "Good" (24%)—meaning that two-thirds viewed their own family's psychological functioning as less than good.

Nearly half (49%) rated their family's functioning as mediocre, as either "Moderately" (29%) or only "Somewhat" (20%) positive, and a significant minority (20%) of the therapists—yet over 1,200 in our sample—rated their family's emotional and psychological functioning as only Somewhat functional, or as "Poor" (15%) or slightly or not at all functional, or "Very poor" (5%). It is unclear how much this is comparable with other occupational groups[22] or how much it may reflect therapists' heightened self-reflection and insight.

In either event, the thought arises that there may well be a sense of personal mission in the vocational choice and motivation of many if not most professional psychotherapists. That it might be so is supported by a significant correlation between therapists' ratings of their own family functioning and how much they indicated (in another part of the DPCCQ) that their "development as a therapist has been influenced by motivation to explore and resolve your personal problems." The poorer their childhood family functioning, the more

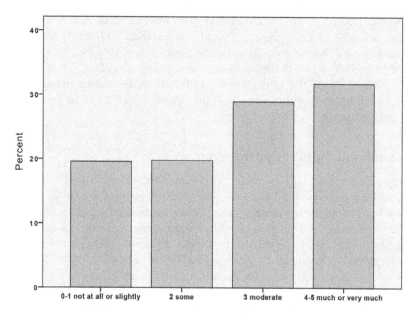

Figure 7.5 "How much did the family you grew up in function well, psychologically and emotionally?" (N = 6347)

their development as therapists was likely to be personally motivated (r = -.27, p =.000, N = 2032). (See Chapter 10 on therapists' Healing Types.) What follows is a review of childhood family features that might contribute to therapists' assessments of their emotional and psychological functioning.

Family Structure

Evidently a family's emotional and psychological functioning is independent of family size, therapist birth order, and the combination of those features. With ample Ns sufficient to detect even small effects (about 4,800 therapists), none of those characteristics were significantly associated with family functioning.

Family Disruptions

There were very small but statistically significant negative correlations between family functioning and death of a parent (r = -.05), but a more substantial negative correlation with parents' divorce or separation (r = -.23). One might think that the death of a parent is objectively a greater loss, but in fact death may occur due to unrelated causes in well-functioning as in poorly functioning families. It is also a singular event, possibly deeply traumatic when it occurs but an occurrence delimited in time, which often elicits sympathy and support for the family, and to which family members learn to adapt through mourning. On the other hand, divorce or separation typically only occur in more poorly functioning families, and may represent only an inflection point in long-term and ongoing conflict between one's parents.

Age at Time of Loss

If therapists had experienced a major family disruption while growing up, either through the death of a parent or parents' marital breakup, the age of the therapist at the time would likely have had a significant impact on their view of the family's emotional and psychological functioning. Overall, the younger the therapist was at the time of the disruption, the greater was its negative impact (r =-.20). More specifically, the impact was most acute if the disruption had occurred when the therapist was a child of 12 or less, and it had the least impact on family functioning if the therapist was a mature adult (see Appendix Table 7.11). Ratings of family functioning were better if disruption was experienced as a teen than as a child, better as a young adult than as a teen, better as a mature adult than as a young adult, and best if one's family was not disrupted at all than if disrupted when a mature adult.

Gender, Age and Generation

There was a small but significant negative correlation of therapist age with family functioning, indicating that younger therapists tended to have more favorable views of their childhood families (r = -.13, p =.000, N = 6,242). Comparing age and gender showed both women and men among Younger therapists (ages 21–34) gave positive reports about their family's emotional and psychological functioning significantly more than other groups (46% and 45%), and at 12% and 10% least often reported poor family functioning (see Appendix Table 7.12). By contrast, women but not men at Midlife (ages 35–54) rated their family's functioning as "poor" significantly more often (22%) and as "good" significantly less often (29%). Women but not men among Older therapists (55–85) also rated their family's functioning as "good" significantly less often (26%). Younger women viewed their family's functioning as "good" at nearly twice the rate of the Older women (46% vs. 26%).

This may again reflect the statistically significant differences between successive generations, in which 44% of the Depression/WW2 generation and 43% of the Post-WW2 generation felt their families had functioned *poorly*, whereas the same percentage of the Western prosperity generation (42%) thought their families had functioned *well* (see Appendix Table 7.13). In the two earlier generations, childhood family function was viewed less favorably from the women's perspective than from the men's. This could well reflect a historical reality in earlier generations: an expectation that daughters would be raised more strictly than sons; should more readily make sacrifices on behalf of the family; and could be given fewer opportunities than sons for individual development. In that case, brothers and sisters in the same family might well have divergent assessments of their family's functioning. The most recent generation (born 1967 to 1990) may have been treated with a greater sense of gender equality, as well as a greater investment in each child as an individual.

Economic Background

Although data reflecting the economic backgrounds of early family life are limited to about 1,200 therapists, the findings with respect to their assessments of emotional and psychological functioning are particularly striking.[23] Those who grew up in Affluent families overwhelmingly (62%) rated their family's functioning as mediocre (i.e., "somewhat" or "moderately" positive), whereas only a quarter (27%) viewed their family's functioning as good (see Appendix Table 7.14). A very different pattern was observed in economically Challenged families. Although they rated their family functioning as poor significantly more (21%) than other therapists, twice as many (43%) rated their family functioning as good. Actually those from Challenged families had the highest incidence of good or very good ratings: 43% as compared to 38% for those from economically Secure families and only 27% for Affluent backgrounds. There was clearly a split effect for therapists from the least well-off families: a small but statistically overrepresented minority who viewed their family as functioning quite poorly vs. a plurality of twice as many who viewed their family as functioning quite well! What might make such a large difference for therapists from economically Challenged families? Similarly, the results for

Affluent families is far from what might be naively expected—which would have been that upper and upper-middle class families, having few material wants, would also enjoy psychological and emotional abundance. What might make these therapists take such a dim view of their Affluent families?

Of therapists who grew up in economically Secure middle or lower-middle class families, the most favorable aspect was perhaps their being the *least likely* to view their families as functioning poorly. Only 7% did—so, in effect, nearly all were raised in families that were at least tolerably well-functioning, and more than a third (38%) in quite well-functioning families.

Religious Background

Therapists of different religious backgrounds had essentially the same numbers of well-functioning, mediocre and poorly functioning families, both overall and in each of the three birth-cohort generations.

Childhood Experiences

Care and Trauma

The lasting impact of their family's psychological and emotional environment on children is perhaps most vividly expressed in their lasting memories of being loved or being hurt. These two aspects of childhood experience were surveyed in the DPCCQ with the following questions: (1) "Overall, when growing up, how much did you experience a sense of being genuinely cared for and supported?" and (2) "Overall, when growing up, how much did you experience any emotionally significant trauma or abuse?" The responses of therapists to these questions are illustrated in Figures 7.6 and 7.7.

On the positive side, more than half (54%) of the therapists felt they had been well loved as children—that is, felt "Much" or "Very much" genuinely cared for and supported. Nearly a quarter (22%) felt that they were only "Moderately" cared for and supported, or just maintained but not fully cared for by their families. Taken together, three-fourths (76%) of the therapists could be said to have received a "good enough" level of care and support as children. Sadly, the remaining quarter (24%) of our therapists felt that they received just "Some" (14%) or even "Little or no" (10%) care and support, and were largely neglected or disregarded as children.

In terms of childhood trauma and abuse, nearly half (47%) of the therapists recalled experiencing "Little or none", and felt they had been well protected when growing up. However, nearly a third (31%) said they experienced "Some" or "Moderate" trauma or abuse, and remembered feeling distressed in childhood. Most disturbing, however, was that nearly a quarter (22%) of therapists reported having experienced "Much" (14%) or "Very much" (8%) trauma or abuse. Those therapists felt they had been seriously hurt and clearly not protected when they were growing up.[24]

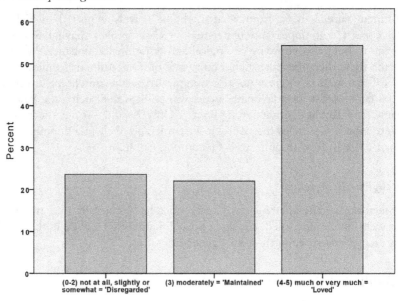

Figure 7.6 "How much did you experience a sense of being genuinely cared for and supported?" (N = 6351)

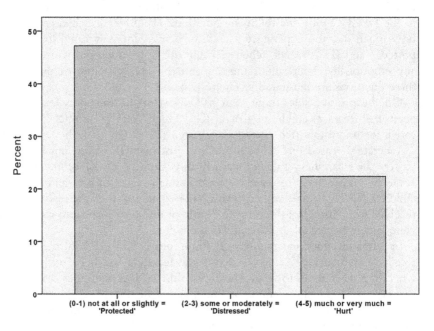

Figure 7.7 "How much did you experience any emotionally significant trauma or abuse?" (N = 4143)

Both the positive experiences of love and support, and the negative experiences of trauma or abuse, contributed separately though not equally to therapists' ratings of their childhood family's emotional and psychological functioning. Childhood experience of love and support correlated very strongly with family functioning ($r = .71$). Childhood experience of trauma or abuse also correlated substantially but negatively with family functioning ($r = -.48$).

Childhood Experience Patterns

Therapists' assessments of positive and negative experiences were significantly and inversely correlated, but not so highly as to be mutually exclusive ($r = -.43$, $p = .000$, $N = 4133$). It would certainly be possible to have had a mix of both positive and negative experiences in varying degrees, making it plausible to define patterns of childhood experience based on the joint distribution of two variables (see Appendix Table 7.15).

Reassuringly, the largest proportion of therapists felt they had been both loved and protected as children, but this was just one-third (33%) of the sample. Others had experienced emotional distress but still felt that they had been loved (13%), or that they were maintained without much love but had been well protected (9%). These represent the majority of therapists who felt their childhood experience was really good or at least "good enough".

Unfortunately, about one in eight therapists (12%) felt they had been both hurt and disregarded as children, and on this account seem to have had rather dreadful childhoods. About as many of the therapists felt they had either been disregarded and distressed as children (8%) or hurt but at least maintained (5%).

A simpler but meaningful arrangement of these patterns can be reached by combining cells that seem sufficiently similar, as illustrated in Figure 7.8. For

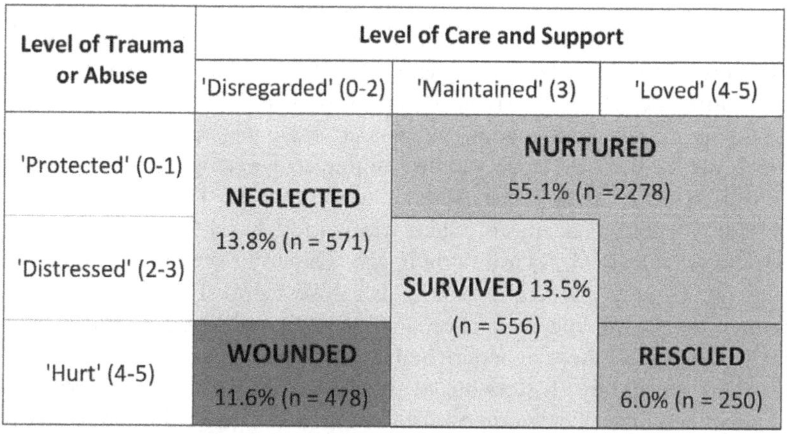

Level of Trauma or Abuse	Level of Care and Support		
	'Disregarded' (0-2)	'Maintained' (3)	'Loved' (4-5)
'Protected' (0-1)	NEGLECTED 13.8% (n = 571)	NURTURED 55.1% (n =2278)	
'Distressed' (2-3)		SURVIVED 13.5% (n = 556)	
'Hurt' (4-5)	WOUNDED 11.6% (n = 478)		RESCUED 6.0% (n = 250)

Figure 7.8 Childhood Experience Patterns

example, it seems reasonable to combine those who were loved and protected, those who had been just maintained but protected, and those who had been distressed but loved, and describe them as having been *Nurtured*. Likewise, it seems reasonable to regard as *Neglected* those who had been disregarded but protected or disregarded and distressed (but not hurt) as children. Another group could combine those who were distressed but maintained, or hurt but maintained, as having at least *Survived* their childhoods without having been too harmed.

Those who had been really harmed comprised two different patterns: the *Wounded*, who had been both disregarded and hurt; and the *Rescued*, who had been hurt but also experienced love. Both those who were *Wounded* and those who were *Rescued* in childhood, having become therapists as adults, are candidates for being viewed as "wounded healers". The difference between them apparently is that the *Wounded* children likely had to wait until adulthood to find healing for the hurt and disregard they had experienced as children, while the *Rescued* children found sources of care and support in childhood to help heal their trauma or abuse. The next task is to explore how these patterns of childhood experience may be connected to therapists' other background characteristics and qualities.

Variations in Childhood Experience

Gender and Generation

No significant differences were found between men and women in the incidence of childhood experience patterns. Overall, 54% of the women and 57% of the men felt they had been well *Nurtured* in childhood. However, generational differences were more apparent (see Appendix Table 7.16). A majority of therapists in each birth-year cohort were *Nurtured* as children, but significantly more were in the latest birth cohort (1967–1990) and significantly fewer felt they had been *Neglected* or *Wounded*. By comparison, statistically significant minorities of therapists from both earlier birth cohorts had felt *Wounded* as children. It appears that the treatment of children may have improved over time.[25]

Looking at the combinations of gender and generation revealed that it was principally women therapists of the most recent generation (1967–1990) who were most likely to have felt *Nurtured* (see Appendix Table 7.17), especially in contrast to earlier generations, when women felt *Nurtured* significantly less often (68% vs. 48% and 49%). Correspondingly, women in the most recent generation were significantly less likely to have felt *Neglected* or *Wounded*—in contrast to women in the middle generation (1947–1966), who were significantly more likely to have had those experiences. It was the childhood experiences of women therapists specifically that produced significant differences in all but one comparison: men as well as women in the most recent generation were significantly less often *Wounded*. These findings suggest that generational changes affected the childhood experiences of women more than men.

Family Structure and Family Disruption

Family size and birth order proved to influence childhood experience in one specific way: therapists who grew up in large (4–12 child) families were significantly more likely to have been *Wounded* and less likely to have felt *Nurtured* than those who grew up in smaller families.[26] The same applied to therapists who were middle-children, who of course mostly belonged to large families.

Family disruption through the death of a parent had little discernible effect on therapists' childhood experience pattern when controlling for therapist age group. However, for those who had lost a parent, the age at which that occurred had a differential impact. Only a third (33%) who experienced the death of a parent during childhood (age 12 or below) reported having been well *Nurtured*, as compared with more than half (52%) of those who were adults at the time.[27] Those who were children whose parent died were also twice as likely to have felt *Wounded* as those who were adults (23% vs. 12%).

The effect of parental divorce or separation on childhood experience was even more dramatic. Therapists whose parents had divorced or separated were significantly more likely to have felt *Neglected* (20% vs. 14%) or *Wounded* (21% vs. 11%) than for those with parents who remained together, and the incidence for having felt *Nurtured* was significantly lower (38% vs. 57%).[28]

The therapists' age when parents divorced or separated also made a significant difference for their childhood experience pattern, but in a more differentiated manner than for a parent's death (see Appendix Table 7.18). Adolescents (ages 13–19) were most broadly affected, with nearly half having felt either *Neglected* (26%) or *Wounded* (22%), and with even fewer having felt *Nurtured* (28%). Children of divorced parents were also higher than average in feeling *Wounded* (23%) and lower than average in feeling *Nurtured* (35%). Even therapists who had become young adults (ages 20–29) when their parents parted were adversely affected, with a higher than average number also feeling *Neglected* (27%). Indeed, adolescents and young adults would have been exposed to more years of parental discord than younger children, and likely would have been more acutely conscious of it than children. Moreover, none of the therapists in any age group whose parents had divorced or separated had a majority who felt *Nurtured*. Family disruption due to parental conflict was even more damaging than the death of a parent.

Family Economic Background

Just one significant result was found with respect to the therapists' family economic status. Growing up in an economically Challenged family increased the likelihood of having been *Wounded* in childhood, 14% vs. 3% for economically Secure families (see Appendix Table 7.19). In addition, there was a tendency for therapists from Affluent families to have felt *Neglected* (19% vs. 13% and 12%

respectively in Secure and Challenged families), which might help explain the seemingly counterintuitive finding that significantly fewer therapists from Affluent families rated their family's functioning as good (recall Appendix Table 7.14). Although materially well-off, it appears they were more likely to feel disregarded even though they rarely came from large (i.e., multi-sibling) families. By contrast, therapists who grew up in economically marginal Challenged families, often in large (4+ child) families, were more likely to rate their family's functioning as poor, due not to neglect but rather to trauma or abuse.

Religious Background and Religiosity

A majority (52% to 55%) of therapists from each religious background felt *Nurtured* in childhood, except for those from mixed backgrounds who were slightly but not significantly lower (49%). Differences were small but significant overall, and significant only for one specific comparison: those from Protestant families were more likely than expected, and those from Catholic/Orthodox families were less likely to have felt *Neglected* (17% vs. 10%).[29]

On the other hand, there were some interesting differences between therapists' childhood experience patterns and their levels of religiosity in childhood and adolescence (see Appendix Table 7.20). Religion in childhood was most important for therapists who *Survived* or felt they had been *Rescued*—significantly more so than therapists who felt *Neglected*. Religion in adolescence was again most important for therapists who felt *Rescued*—and again significantly more so than for those who felt *Neglected*. These findings suggest the importance of religious faith as a potential source of support for children growing up in emotionally toxic situations.

In Sum

The family of origin is literally the starting point and, for many years, also the principal matrix of individual development. Knowing the psychotherapist's family of origin is one route to knowing the psychotherapist as a person. This chapter explored both objective and subjective aspects of the families in which the therapists grew up. Objective aspects included the family structure, reflected in the number of siblings and birth order of the therapist; disruptions of family life due to the death of a parent, or divorce or separation between the therapist's parents; the family's economic status in terms of material resources available to children; and the family's religious background, including the importance that religion had in therapists' lives while they were growing up. The subjective aspect of therapists' family backgrounds focused on how well the family functioned, emotionally and psychologically, and on the patterns of childhood experience based on the two dimensions of care and support versus trauma or abuse. The extent to which various factors contributed to each of those aspects was also explored.

Family Situations

Therapists were reared in a remarkable variety of family structures, ranging from single child families to families with as many as 6 to 12 children. No one family structure could be described as characteristic of most or even many psychotherapists. Neither of the two largest groups, the middle child of 4 or more and the older child of 2, accounted for as many as 1-in-5 of the therapists. Further, as our samples were collected over several decades and always contained therapists of varied ages, there was an opportunity to examine three successive "generations" or birth year cohorts: the oldest, born during the Great Depression and World War 2 (1927–1946); the middle, Post-WW2 "Baby Boom" generation (1947–1966); and the youngest generation (born 1967–1990, including most so-called "Gen X" and some "Gen Y" members) who grew up in a period of increasing Western prosperity and globalization that were also years of cultural change and social transformation. In terms of family size, 1-child families were significantly overrepresented, and 4–5 child families were underrepresented, in the Depression/WW2 generation; large (4–5 and 6–12 child) families were overrepresented, and 1- and 2-child families underrepresented, in the Post-WW2 Boom generation; and, in an interesting reversal, the 1- and 2-child families were again overrepresented while large families were under-represented in youngest generation.

Family Disruption

The study of family disruption focused on deaths of a parent and parental break-up through divorce or separation. Naturally, most (85%) of the Younger therapists (ages 21–34) had both living parents, many (42%) therapists in Midlife (ages 35–54) did too, as compared to hardly any (7%) of the Older therapists (ages 55 and up). Relatively few had lost a parent when children (7%) or when teens (8%), yet the impact of early loss on the subjective aspects of family life was significant, both with respect to ratings of the family's emotional and psychological functioning and the impact on therapists' childhood experience patterns.

Family disruption also had a major impact on therapists whose parents had divorced or separated. Parental break-up was significantly more common for those born in the most recent generation (1967–1990) than in either of the two preceding generations, especially the Depression/WW2 birth cohort. It was also a more common experience for therapists growing up in economically Challenged families. Although adverse for therapists who were still children at the time, the impact of divorce seemed to fall most heavily if it happened when therapists were adolescents, or even young adults.

Economic Background

Therapists' family economic backgrounds were defined in terms of material resources and consumption because this aspect most directly impacts the life of children within the family. Families were classified into three broad levels: Affluent (33%), economically Secure (49%) and economically Challenged (18%). Family size varied to some extent with economic background, with 2-child families favored by the Affluent (41%) as compared to Challenged families (26%). Larger (5–12 child) family groups were overrepresented in economically Challenged families (20%) in contrast to Affluent families (8%), a finding that needs to be interpreted in connection with religious background.

Religious Background

Most therapists grew up in families they identified as Christian, primarily as Protestants (47%) or as Roman Catholic or Eastern Orthodox (27%). Others grew up in unaffiliated or non-religious families (13%), in families with mixed religious backgrounds (5%), or in Jewish families (8%). More therapists from Catholic/Orthodox backgrounds tended to come from larger families, in contrast to Jewish and non-religious therapists who mainly came from small families. Personally, therapists varied in how important religion had been in their lives as children and adolescents, within as well as between different backgrounds. Religion on average was most salient for therapists growing up in Catholic/Orthodox families, and was of little or no importance for therapists reared in non-religious families.

Family Psychological Functioning

When asked to rate how well their childhood families had functioned emotionally and psychologically, only a third (32%) thought that their family's functioning had been good or very good, and a fifth (20%) said their families had functioned poorly. There were no significant differences between the assessments of family functioning made by men and women, and no differences based on family size or birth order. However, disruption of the family's life by the death of a parent, especially in childhood, or by parents' divorce or separation, did significantly and negatively affect therapists' assessments of their family's functioning.

In addition, nearly half (45%) of those born during the Depression/WW2 period said their families functioned poorly, as did many in the Post-War generation—in contrast to in the most recent generation (1967–1990) in which a plurality (43%) said their families functioned well. The greater relative prosperity of families of the later generation may have been one factor in that shift, as those therapists had grown up economically Secure significantly more often than those of the preceding generations (57% vs. 45% and 37% respectively). Generally, most therapists from economically Secure backgrounds rated their family's functioning as moderate or good. This stood in contrast to therapists from economically Challenged backgrounds whose ratings largely split between the extremes of poor (37%) and good (43%). It also contrasted with therapists from Affluent families who overwhelmingly (62%) rated their family's functioning as mediocre, and fewer than expected (26%) rated it as good. A clue about the ratings of Affluent families came from analysis of childhood experience patterns: more therapists from Affluent families had felt *Neglected* as children.

Childhood Experience

A majority (54%) of therapists felt they had been genuinely cared for and supported as children, but that left substantial minorities feeling they had just been maintained (22%) or were largely disregarded (24%). The fact that more therapists felt they were well cared for than had rated their family's functioning as good (54% vs. 32%) suggests that many may have found caring and supportive persons outside their immediate family. Less favorably, almost a third (30%) of the therapists reported having experienced moderate trauma or abuse, and nearly a quarter (22%) said they were really hurt when growing up, which suggests that many therapists have had to overcome significant aspects of their own childhood experience. Fewer than half (47%) said they had experienced little or no emotionally significant trauma or abuse.

Five childhood experience patterns were defined by combining levels of care and support with levels of trauma or abuse: *Nurtured* (55%), *Survived* (14%), *Neglected* (14%) *Wounded* (12%) and *Rescued* (6%). Children in large families were less likely than others to have felt *Nurtured* (51%) and more likely to have felt *Wounded* (15%). Apparently middle children in large families were more likely to be overlooked and less likely to be well protected. Family disruption during the therapist's childhood and adolescence also had significant adverse effects on childhood experience, evident in significantly lower rates of feeling *Nurtured* (i.e., loved and protected) and higher rates of *Wounded* and *Neglected*. Adverse effects of parental divorce or separation were most acute if it occurred when therapists were in their teens. These disruptions among therapists' parents clearly cast a shadow over their children's lives.

There were no differences in childhood experience patterns related to family religious backgrounds, but there were in regard to levels of religiosity. For therapists who felt they had been *Rescued* (i.e., traumatized or abused, but also loved and supported), religion was significantly more important in their lives during childhood and adolescence.

Therapists from economically Secure families were significantly less likely than others to have felt *Wounded* as children (3%), especially as compared with economically Challenged families (14%), raising a question as to whether the parents in many economically Challenged families were too distressed to adequately keep their children from being hurt. Therapists from Affluent families on the other hand were relatively more likely to feel *Neglected* (19%), raising a question as to whether the parents in many affluent families were too busy with their own work or pleasures to devote much time to their children. The majority of therapists from all economic backgrounds had felt *Nurtured*, but the exceptions raise unsettling questions. How much therapists' childhood family backgrounds and experiences also affected their lives as adults will be explored in the next chapter.

Notes

1 Parental relationships are the other large part in defining one's childhood family situation, and will be analyzed later in the chapter.
2 Some other studies of therapists' family backgrounds include: Henry, Sims & Spray (1973); Johnson, Campbell & Masters (1992); Softas-Nall, Baldo & Williams (2001); Trusty, Skowron, Watts & Parrillo (2004).
3 These figures partly reflect the fact that 2-child families (the largest single group) contain just one older and one younger child, whereas families of 4 or larger have multiple middle children.
4 By contrast, psychotherapeutic and counseling relationships in some non-Western societies are clearly more authoritative and hierarchic in structure (Elsass, Rønnestad, Jensen & Orlinsky, 2017; Kassem, 2012; Kakar, 1994; Joo, Kim & Orlinsky, 1994), as perhaps was also true in 19th and early 20th century Western countries.
5 It was possible to use birth year cohort or "generation" rather than therapist age because data collection for the study extended over three decades, resulting in therapists of similar age having been born in historically different eras. Although the two variables are correlated (-.20), using generation rather than age was given preference when it produced statistically clearer results.
6 Obviously post-war recovery and expansion occurred earlier in countries whose homelands were not directly impacted by war than in others that experienced much deprivation and destruction (e.g., Germany and the U.K.).
7 From: wikipedia.org/wiki/Me generation.
8 It can be argued that this ethos of "personal growth" was itself both reflective of, and to a significant degree responsible for, the widespread acceptance of psychotherapy in contemporary culture.
9 Percentages did not differ significantly for either the older or middle birth-cohort generations, while the number who had already lost a parent in the younger generation was too small ($N = 136$) for a meaningful comparison.
10 There were no differences in reports of parental mortality among therapists whose families were at different economic levels or of different religious backgrounds. Death does not respect either.
11 The Chi-square values were: $\chi^2 = 33.1$, df = 3, p =.000; N = 4,270.
12 The Chi-square values were: $\chi^2 = 15.2$, df = 2, p =.001; N = 4,252.
13 Economic status categories are discussed next under Family Background. The Chi-square values were: $\chi^2 = 8.4$, df = 2, p =.015; N = 657.
14 The Chi-square values were: $\chi^2 = 18.5$, df = 4, p =.001; N = 1,133.
15 The Chi-square values were: $\chi^2 = 30.5$, df = 4, p =.000; N = 3,934.
16 Socioeconomic status (SES) surely is one of the most common variables studied by sociologists, but it is only rarely reported in research by psychologists. Undoubtedly this reflects psychology's typical focus on the functioning of individuals, and on interpersonal relationships whose scope seldom goes beyond the small face-to-face group. The potential value of studying therapists' SES was further obscured by the fact that, simply by virtue of the professional status therapists had attained as adults, relatively little variation would be expected in SES as typically construed. It was not until the study of therapists' childhood families was included in the DPCCQ that it seemed there would likely be significant variability in family economic backgrounds. Thus the present study had been in progress for several years before data on childhood family SES started to be collected, with the consequence that data are only

available for the most recent 10% of respondents (N = 1,155). Therapists who received this question were mainly from Canada, China, Denmark and the US.

17 The Chi-square values were: χ^2 = 20.9, df =4, p =.000; N=945.
18 Henry, Sims & Spray (1971) provided some data on the religious/cultural backgrounds of American therapists.
19 Due to their small Ns, the non-Western therapists are often omitted in further analyses by religious background.
20 The standard deviation for childhood was SD = 3.1 and for adolescence was SD = 3.2 on a 0–10 scale of the importance of religion in their lives during each period.
21 In childhood, the mean for religiosity of those from Catholic/Orthodox backgrounds in the 1927–1946 birth cohort was 7.6 out of 10, higher than (Sheffe *p* =.01) 5.4, 5.3 and 4.8 for those of Mixed, Protestant and Jewish backgrounds.
22 The only partially relevant cross-professions studies identified are those by Burton & Topham (1997) and Elliott & Guy (1993).
23 Henry, Sims & Spray (1971) provided some data on American therapists' socioeconomic backgrounds.
24 A number of studies have been done of therapists' childhood experiences, focusing mainly on the traumatic aspect, including: Burton & Topham (1997); Elliott & Guy (1993); Fussell & Bonney (1990); Little & Hamby (2001); Nutall & Jackson (1994); Poal & Weisz (1989); Pope & Feldman-Summers (1992). A recent study by Nivison, Lowe Vandell, Booth-LaForce & Roisman (2021) does offer some caution on the veridicality of adult memories about the quality of childhood experiences of parenting.
25 At least in the US and perhaps other countries, this coincides with the fading of John Watson's (1928) behaviorist philosophy in pediatric thinking and the rise of Benjamin Spock's (1946) widely followed and more humane approach—a shift in perspective that seems to reflect, and may also have contributed to the apparent improvement in childcare.
26 The Chi-square values were: χ^2 = 25.4, df = 12, *P* =.000; *N* = 4,036.
27 The Chi-square values were: χ^2 = 38.5, df = 12, *P* =.000; *N* = 2,053.
28 The Chi-square values were: χ^2 = 93.1, df = 4, *P* =.000; *N* = 3,590.
29 The Chi-square values were: χ^2 = 45.2, df = 16, *P* =.000; *N* = 3,255.

References

Burton, M., & Topham, D. (1997). Early loss experiences in psychotherapists, Church of England clergy, patients assessed for psychotherapy, and scientists and engineers. *Psychotherapy Research*, 7, 275–300.

Elliott, D., & Guy, D. (1993). Mental health professionals versus non-mental health professionals: Childhood trauma and adult functioning. *Professional Psychology: Research and Practice*, 24, 83–90.

Elsass, P., Rønnestad, M. H., Jensen, C. G., & Orlinsky, D. E. (2017). Warmth and challenge as common factors in Eastern and Western counselors? Buddhist Lamas' responses to Western questionnaires. *International Journal of Psychosocial Rehabilitation*, 21, 57–69.

Fussell, F. W., & Bonney, W. C. (1990). A comparative study of childhood experiences of psychotherapists and physicists: Implications for clinical practice. *Psychotherapy*, 27, 505–512.

Henry, W. E., Sims, J. H., & Spray, S. L. (1971). *The fifth profession: Becoming a psychotherapist* [Chapter 2, "Cultural origins and the marginal perspective"; Chapter 3, "Social class origins and career mobility" (pp. 9–44)]. San Francisco: Jossey-Bass.

Henry, W. E., Sims, J. H., & Spray, S. L. (1973). *Public and private lives of psychotherapists* [Chapter 6. "The historical family," (pp. 163–193)]. San Francisco: Jossey-Bass.

Johnson, M. E., Campbell, J. L., & Masters, M. A. (1992). Relationship between family-of-origin dynamics and a psychologist's theoretical orientation. *Professional Psychology: Research and Practice*, 23, 119–122.

Joo, E., Kim, H. A., & Orlinsky, D. E. (1994). The psychotherapeutic relationship in different cultures. In *Proceeding of the 16th International Congress of Psychotherapy* (Revised Edition) (pp. 70–78). Seoul: Korean Academy of Psychotherapies.

Kakar, S. (1994). Modern psychotherapies in traditional cultures: India, China and Japan. In Proceeding of the 16th International Congress of Psychotherapy (Revised Edition) (pp. 79–85). Seoul: Korean Academy of Psychotherapies.

Kassem, L. (2012). *Psychotherapy between two cultures: A portrait of psychotherapists in Egypt.* Doctoral dissertation, Department of Comparative Human Development, University of Chicago.

Little, L., & Hamby, S. (2001). Memory of childhood sexual abuse among clinicians: Characteristics, outcomes, and current therapy attitudes. *Sexual Abuse: A Journal of Research and Treatment*, 13, 233–248.

Nivison, M. D., Lowe Vandell, D., Booth-LaForce, C., & Roisman, G. I. (2021). Convergent and discriminant validity of retrospective assessments of the quality of childhood parenting: Prospective evidence from infancy to age 26 years. *Psychological Science.*

Nutall, R., & Jackson, J. (1994). Personal history of childhood abuse among clinicians. *Child Abuse and Neglect*, 18, 455–472.

Poal, P., & Weisz, J. R. (1989). Therapists' own childhood problems as predictors of their effectiveness in child psychotherapy. *Journal of Clinical Child Psychology*, 18, 202–205.

Pope, K. S., & Feldman-Summers, S. (1992). National survey of psychologists' sexual and physical abuse history and their evaluation of training and competence in these areas. *Professional Psychology: Research and Practice*, 23, 353–361.

Softas-Nall, B. C., Baldo, T. D., & Williams, S. C. (2001). Family-of-origin, personality characteristics, and counselor trainees' effectiveness. *Psychological Reports*, 88, 854–856.

Spock, B. (1946). *The common sense book of baby and child care.* New York: Duell, Sloan & Pearce.

Trusty, J., Skowron, E. A., Watts, R. E., & Parrillo III, A. L. (2004). Modeling the effects of counselor-trainees' perceptions of early childhood on trainees' social influence attributes. *The Family Journal: Counseling and Therapy for Couples and Families*, 12, 6–13.

Watson, J. B. (1928). *Psychological care of infant and child.* New York: Norton.

8 From Childhood to Adult Life

D. E. Orlinsky

After exploring a broad range of therapists' personal characteristics as adults—their self-experience, private lives, beliefs and values, and quality of life—and then examining their childhood families and experiences—a question naturally arises as to how those features of early family life may relate to the therapist's personal characteristics as adults.[1] To explore this open-mindedly but systematically (i.e., without prior expectations), each of the areas of therapists' adult personal life will be analyzed for potential links with the characteristics surveyed in the preceding chapter: childhood family situation (structure and disruption); family economic and religious background; family psychological functioning and childhood experience patterns.

Personal Self

Therapists' descriptions of their self-experiences in close personal relationships led to defining four dimensions of *personal self*: Genial/Caring, or varying levels of self-bestowal; Forceful/Exacting, or degrees of self-assertion; Reclusive/Remote, or extent of self-protection; and Ardent/Expressive, or amplitude of self-expression. The question here is which if any aspects of therapists' family background and experience may have influenced these four dimensions of adult personal self.[2]

Family Situation

Neither therapists' birth orders nor the size of the families in which they grew up showed any significant association with the four dimensions of adult personal self, so it seems that family structure was not a significant influence. However, there was one respect in which the combination of family size and birth order seemed to have an effect on *personal self*. In large families of 4+ children, first-born therapists (as the oldest of siblings) were most Ardent/Expressive, significantly more so than the youngest of 4+ children, whereas those last-born (i.e., youngest of siblings) were least Ardent/Expressive.[3] Additionally, "only children" (without siblings) and youngest children in 2- or 3-child families were among the least Ardent/Expressive, while oldest and middle children in

DOI: 10.4324/9781003217572-8

larger families were among the most Ardent/Expressive. These findings suggest a plausible though speculative answer to the question of who had to be loudest in the family to get attention.

Family disruption due to the death of a parent (controlling for therapist age) was not directly related to personal self. Disruption due to parents' divorce or separation was also unrelated except for being Ardent/Expressive, which was slightly but significantly higher among those whose parents had parted.[4] Again, this could reflect circumstances in which a child needs to be more intensely expressive to gain attention. For those who experienced a family disruption, the therapist's age when it occurred seemed also not directly related to the dimensions of *personal self*. However, indirect effects of family disruption may occur through the impact (noted in Chapter 7) that parental death or divorce at an early age has both on ratings of family functioning and patterns of childhood experience (e.g., fewer Nurtured, more Wounded).

Family Background

Somewhat surprisingly, several dimensions of therapists' *personal self* were significantly associated with their childhood family's economic status. Small but significant negative correlations suggested that the wealthier the economic background, the less therapists were inclined to be Genial/Caring ($r = -.16$, $p = .000$) or Ardent/Expressive ($r = -.11$, $p = .000$) in their close personal relationships—perhaps related to having had a materially indulged or "privileged" childhood. By contrast, therapists who grew up in economically Challenged families were most Genial/Caring and Ardent/Expressive; that is, they grew up to be most self-bestowing and self-expressive in close relationships. Remembering the divergent impact of poverty on family functioning (see Chapter 7) this may reflect the survival value of cohesion and love in adverse circumstances.

Differences in *personal self* were also observed in relation to therapists' religious backgrounds. Therapists from Jewish backgrounds had significantly higher scores on Genial/Caring than those from non-religious, Protestant or Catholic/Orthodox families (see Appendix Table 8.1). Those from Jewish backgrounds were also significantly more Ardent/Expressive than therapists from non-religious and Protestant families, as were those from mixed religious and Catholic/Orthodox backgrounds. In addition, therapists from Jewish and mixed religious backgrounds were significantly more Forceful/Exacting than those from Protestant families.

Therapists from Protestant families and those from non-religious backgrounds appear to be more restrained overall in their close personal relationships: less Ardent/Expressive, less Forceful/Exacting, and less Genial/Caring. These differences are probably best interpreted as reflections of families' cultural norms regarding emotions and expressiveness in interpersonal relationships, and not necessarily of their inner feelings.

There were also small but statistically significant correlations of adult *personal self* with therapists' religiosity in childhood and adolescence. Those for whom religion had been important while growing up were slightly more inclined to experience themselves as Genial/Caring (r =.08, p =.000) and Ardent/Expressive (r =.09, p =.000), but also as more Reclusive/Remote (r =.08, p =.000). At least for the backgrounds represented in our samples, childhood religiosity may be a marginal influence on self-experience.

Family Psychological Functioning

Therapists who viewed their family's emotional and psychological functioning as good or very good tended to be significantly more Genial/Caring (r =.13, p =.000, N = 6,038) and less Ardent/Expressive (r = -.10, p =.000, N = 6,032); that is, more loving but less loud in expressing it. These small but significant linkages attest to the value of an emotionally well-functioning family in personality development, and are even more pronounced when computed separately (with reduced Ns) by family economic status. For example, among those who grew up in Affluent families the correlation of family functioning with Genial/Caring was just a nonsignificant r =.09 (p = ns), but for the economically Secure it was r =.22 (p =.000) and for those from economically Challenged families it was r =.37 (p =.000). This dramatically highlights the importance of good family functioning in economically disadvantaged families, especially in view of the split effect of poverty on family psychological functioning, providing the highest levels of both good and poor functioning (see Appendix Table 7.14).

Childhood Experience Patterns

Given the close association of family functioning with childhood experience patterns,[5] it is not surprising to find that these were also reflected in therapists' adult self-experience. Therapists who felt Neglected while growing up were the least Genial/Caring and least Ardent/Expressive as adults (see Appendix Table 8.2). Those who felt they had been Nurtured as children were the least Forceful/Exacting as adults in intimate relationships. However, the real surprise, unanticipated but understandable in retrospect, is that those who felt they had been Rescued (i.e., were traumatized or abused but managed to find a source of care and support) were, as adults, the most Genial/Caring, most Ardent/Expressive, and also most Forceful/Exacting in close personal relationships. Somehow they had found love and support when hurt as children, and afterwards became the most self-bestowing and self-expressive of adults, and the most self-assertive too.

In sum: the psychological and experiential aspects of early family life left the clearest impressions on therapists' adult self-experience, but subtler traces of influence were also found among the economic and religious/cultural aspects of therapists' family backgrounds.

Private Life

The question here is whether aspects of the therapist's early family experience seemed to influence the intimate pattern of adult private life. How much does one's original family situation cast a light, or a shadow, on one's family circumstances as an adult, at least as reflected in the presence or absence of conjugal and parental relationships? Moreover, do childhood family features have an impact on adult attachment styles?

Family Situation

No significant associations were found between either birth order or childhood family size (as separate variables) and adult marital/relationship status. However, therapists' birth order and childhood family size converged in one effect regarding therapists' parental status (see Appendix Table 8.3). Although most therapists did become parents, those who had been "only children" (without siblings) and youngest were significantly less likely to have children than those who were oldest or middle children; that is, therapists who had no younger siblings were less likely to become parents themselves than those who grew up with (and likely helped to take care of) younger siblings. This effect was more prominent among women therapists, but was significant overall for men as well. Most (75%) first-born women (i.e., those who had grown up as oldest sister) had become mothers, in contrast to women who grew up as "only children" (62%). Growing up as the oldest sister with responsibility for younger siblings (or alternately as an "only" daughter without that responsibility) may have been one influence on whether to have one's own children (recognizing, certainly, that motherhood is not always a matter of deliberate choice).

No association was found between having lost a parent through death and current marital/relationship status, when examined separately by therapists' age group. Nonetheless, therapists' parents having separated or divorced did have a small but statistically significant impact on therapists' own marital/relationship status, both overall and particularly for women therapists. Only half (50%) of the women whose parents parted were currently married, as compared to three-fifths (59%) of those whose parents had remained together.[6] Parallel to this, significantly more of the women therapists whose parents were divorced were themselves divorced (17% vs. 12% for those whose parents remained together). Why this affected women more strongly than men is an open question. However, parents' divorce or separation had no effect on therapists' own inclination to become a parent, either for women or men.

The therapist's age when a family disruption occurred did have an impact both on adult marital and parental status. Those who lost a parent or experienced parental divorce when they were children were twice as likely to remain single than therapists who were adults when their childhood family was disrupted (19% vs. 9%), reflecting a linear decline across age groups (see Appendix

Table 8.4). Likewise, those who lost a parent or experienced parental divorce when they were children were less likely to have children of their own as compared to therapists who were adults at the time of disruption (18% vs. 29%).[7]

These two converging findings suggest a heightened caution about engaging in family life as an adult among those who, as children, had suffered a serious disruption in their own families. However, the therapist's age at the time of family disruption did not appear related to adult attachment styles.

Family Background

The therapist's childhood family economic status was significantly associated with their adult marital/relationship status, but not their parental status. Overall, a majority (62%) of therapists were married, but those who had grown up in economically Secure families were significantly overrepresented (69%) among them while therapists from Affluent families were significantly underrepresented (53%) (see Appendix Table 8.5). On the other hand, therapists from Affluent families were more likely to be living with a partner: 19% vs. 9% of those from economically Secure families. Why this might be is unclear. The apparent hesitation to marry and the tendency to cohabitation among therapists from Affluent families is not due to marital instability of their own parents, as their rate of divorce or separation was actually lower than for other economic statuses.

Family religious background was significantly associated both with therapists' adult relationship status and parental status. As just noted, most therapists were married but significantly more of those from Jewish families (72%) and Protestant families (65%) were, in contrast to only 56% of those from Catholic/Orthodox families (see Appendix Table 8.6). The latter were more likely to be single (21%). Even controlling for differences in age, therapists from Catholic/Orthodox backgrounds were more likely to be single: 50% of Catholic/Orthodox among Younger therapists compared to 26% of Protestants, and 17% of Catholic/Orthodox among Older therapists were single compared to 9% from Protestant and 4% from Jewish backgrounds. Interestingly, no differences in rates of divorce were observed based on family religious background.

Differences in parental status based on religious background reflected those found for marital/relationship status. Significantly more therapists from Jewish (83%) and Protestant (80%) backgrounds were parents than from Catholic/Orthodox families (64%).[8]

No differences on either the Anxious or Avoidant dimension of adult attachment were found based on family structure, economic background, childhood religiosity; or, on the Anxious dimension, among therapists of different religious backgrounds. However, therapists from Jewish families tended to be least Avoidant, and were significantly less so than therapists from non-religious families.[9]

Family Psychological Functioning

Therapists who said the emotional and psychological functioning of their childhood family was "good" or "very good" were significantly more likely to be married as adults than those who indicated their families functioned poorly (67% vs. 55%). (See Appendix Table 8.7.) In comparison to those from well-functioning families, therapists who said their childhood family functioned poorly were significantly more likely to be divorced or separated (14% vs. 7% for well-functioning families). They were also slightly but significantly more likely to be living with a partner (17% vs. 12%). Nevertheless, childhood family functioning was unrelated to therapists' adult parental status.

The impact of childhood family functioning also extended to adult attachment dimensions. The better the therapists' early family functioning, the less they tended to show Anxious Attachment ($r = -.16$, $p = .000$) or Avoidant Attachment ($r = -.17$, $p = .000$). Although not the main determinants, therapists who grew up in well-functioning families tended to have a better capacity for establishing Secure attachments as adults, which may explain why they more often had a marital commitment and were less often divorced or cohabiting.

Childhood Experience Patterns

The main impact of early experience patterns on therapists' adult marital/relationship status was a contrast between those who had felt Nurtured and those who felt Wounded in childhood. Therapists who felt Nurtured in childhood were significantly more likely to be married (64%), and at only 8%, were significantly less likely to be divorced or separated (see Appendix Table 8.8). By contrast, those who were Wounded as children (i.e., suffered serious trauma or abuse, as well as neglect) were significantly more likely to be divorced (15%) and significantly less likely to be married (53%). Despite this, there was no difference between childhood experience patterns in the likelihood of having children—a realm where biology may have more influence than psychology.

Childhood experience patterns also had an impact on therapists' adult attachment style, adding specificity to the findings regarding family functioning. Therapists who experienced being Wounded while growing up scored highest on both Anxious Attachment and Avoidant Attachment (see Appendix Table 8.9). They were also significantly more Anxious than those who felt Nurtured, and significantly more Avoidant than both the Nurtured and those who had felt Rescued. The Nurtured and Rescued experience patterns both involved receiving strong care and support during childhood, and despite the trauma associated with the Rescued pattern, both fostered a capacity for Secure attachment in adulthood.

In sum, both the societal and experiential aspects of therapists' childhood family backgrounds exerted an influence upon their adult relationships, and on their aptitude for forming secure intimate attachments.

Individual Beliefs

Therapists' personal beliefs as individuals were described in terms of varying levels of religiosity and spirituality in their current lives, and the belief-value patterns arising from combinations of the two. Those patterns were Ethical Secular (low religiosity and low spirituality), Spiritual Secular (low religiosity and high spirituality), Spiritual Religious (high religiosity and high spirituality), and Ceremonial Religious (high religiosity and low spirituality). The possible impact of family background and experience on the adult belief patterns of therapists will be explored through these measures.

Family Situation

When examined overall, a significant association was found between therapists' belief-value patterns and their childhood family size. Therapists from 2-child families were significantly more likely to have an Ethical Secular orientation (45%) than those from larger (4+ child) families (32%). Therapists from larger (4+ child) families were significantly more likely to be Spiritual Religious (34%) while those from 2-child families (24%) were significantly less likely.[10]

However, the therapists who more often came from 2-child families tended to be from non-religious or Jewish backgrounds (42% and 45% respectively), and therapists with non-religious backgrounds were significantly more often Ethical Secular (61%), while those from Jewish families were second in order and most commonly, although not significantly more often, Ethical Secular (see Appendix Table 5.2). Unfortunately this explanation, which seems so plausible for the first result, works only partially for Spiritual Religious therapists. Therapists from families with 4+ children were significantly more often Catholic/Orthodox, but it was therapists from Protestant backgrounds who were significantly more often Spiritual Religious (33%), yet significantly less often from 4+ child families (32% vs. 50% for those from Catholic/Orthodox backgrounds). Therapists from Catholic/Orthodox backgrounds were Spiritual Religious about as often but no more than expected (as will be seen in Appendix Table 8.11). The size of families that therapists grew up in, and the family's religious background, may separately or jointly influence therapists' adult belief-value orientations but it seems likely that those are not the only (or even the main) variables in the process.

Neither the death of a parent (controlled for therapist age group) nor parents' divorce or separation had an effect on therapists' adult levels of religiosity or spirituality. However, the age of therapists at the time when their families were disrupted was significantly associated with both adult religiosity and spirituality overall, although specific groupings were not significantly differentiated. Therapists who experienced family disruption as children were the least spiritual and, after those in their teens, next to least religious as adults; those who were already adults at the time of family disruption were relatively the most religious and spiritual as adults.[11] At least for our therapists, this trend suggests a reduced capacity for religious feeling and spiritual feeling among those who suffered a major loss earliest in life.

Family Background

Statistically significant differences based on childhood family economic status were found, despite the relatively small sample available, showing therapists from economically Challenged families having higher levels of religiosity and spirituality as adults (see Appendix Table 8.10). This was also reflected in a greater proportion of therapists from Challenged economic backgrounds having a Spiritual Religious pattern (29%) rather than Ethical Secular (12%) pattern as adults. Something about childhood economic deprivation seems to stimulate or strengthen adult faith.

Therapists from different childhood religious backgrounds varied considerably in how often they reported having a religious affiliation as adults, which may reflect a social or cultural identification if not greater piety. Most (78%) of those from Jewish families reported a religious affiliation (almost always Jewish; see Appendix Table 5.5); those from Protestant and Catholic/Orthodox families did to a lesser extent (57% and 55% respectively); those from families with mixed religious background even less so (51%); yet as adults, even some from non-religious families also came to identify with an affiliation (22%).[12]

As noted above, therapists' current belief-value patterns were also predicted by their family's religious background. Although the greater number from Protestant families in the total sample led to Protestants being the most numerous in each pattern, they were significantly overrepresented only in the Spiritual Religious orientation (see Appendix Table 8.11). By comparison, therapists from Jewish families were overrepresented among the Ceremonial Religious, implying that a certain number were traditionally observant as adults. Therapists from non-religious backgrounds were overrepresented among Ethical Secular therapists (61%), as would be expected; although the remaining 39% came as adults to adopt a more religious and/or spiritual orientation, showing that the process of orientation change can work in both directions.

Family Psychological Functioning

Little relationship was noted between the level of emotional and psychological functioning in therapists' childhood families and adult religiosity or spirituality.[13] In terms of belief-value patterns, therapists from well-functioning families were significantly overrepresented among both Ceremonial Religious and Spiritual Religious therapists (35% and 30%, respectively; see Appendix Table 8.12). In contrast, therapists from poorly functioning families were significantly overrepresented among Spiritual Secular therapists (31%), in contrast to those from well-functioning families (21%). It appears that well-functioning childhood families may tend to encourage religious adherence, while dysfunctional childhood families rather tend to foster a sense of individual spirituality.

Childhood Experience Patterns

Particular patterns of childhood experience were also significantly associated with levels of religiosity and spirituality. Therapists who had been Rescued or Nurtured as children had the highest levels of Religiosity as adults, both significantly higher than those who had been Neglected and were at the lowest level (see Appendix Table 8.13). Partially reversing this order, therapists who had been Nurtured were at the lowest level of Spirituality, while those who had been Rescued or Wounded were at the highest level, and both were significantly higher in Spirituality than those who were Nurtured. The quality that both the Rescued or Wounded shared was experiencing serious trauma or abuse as children; the difference is that the Rescued had also found a strong source of care and support.

Another view of this association shows the distribution in percentages (see Appendix Table 8.14). A majority (65%) of therapists who felt Nurtured in childhood were secular, but the Spiritual Secular were significantly underrepresented; while among the 35% who were religious, a significantly larger minority (6%) were Ceremonial Religious—thus having a relative deficit in spirituality in both secular and religious orientations. An even larger majority (70%) of therapists who felt Wounded in childhood were secular, but in their case the Spiritual Secular were significantly overrepresented and the Ethical Secular were underrepresented, more or less reversing the distribution among the Nurtured. Like the Wounded, therapists who felt Rescued in childhood (i. e., traumatized or abused but also loved and supported) also were significantly underrepresented among Ethical Secular adults, and were strongly but not significantly present among the Spiritual Secular, reinforcing the impression that early trauma or abuse tended to foster a sense of spirituality. Finally, with a 74% vs. 26% split, therapists who had felt Neglected as children were the most secular and least religious group of all.

In sum, childhood family experiences exert more influence than family structure upon therapists' development of their adult belief and value orientations. The overall impression of how childhood experience informed adult religious and spiritual sensitivities is that religion, grounded in having felt loved, inspired an attitude of acceptance towards a cosmic "benign order"; while spirituality, grounded in having been wounded, inspired a search for alternative sources of meaning and healing later in life.

Quality of Life

The quality of life currently enjoyed or endured by adult therapists was assessed with scales of Personal Satisfactions and Personal Burdens constructed by factor-analysis, and was described qualitatively in terms of six patterns based on varied levels of overall life satisfaction and stress. Those patterns depicted life alternatively as "Fulfilling" (high satisfaction, low stress), "Satisfactory" (high satisfaction, moderate stress), "Hectic" (high satisfaction, high stress), "Distressed" (high stress, low satisfaction), "Strained" (moderate stress, low satisfaction), or just "Dull" (low stress, low satisfaction). How much are these measures of current life quality influenced by therapists' childhood family characteristics and experiences?

Family Situation

Little evidence was found for an association between adult life quality and childhood family structure.[14] With therapist age group controlled, no significant association either between Personal Satisfactions or Personal Burdens and parent loss were observed. Also, no significant association was found between Personal Satisfactions or Personal Burdens and parental divorce or separation. More surprisingly, no significant direct effects were observed for age at the time when family disruption occurred.

Family Background

There was a small but significant inverse relationship between childhood economic background and adult life quality. Personal Satisfactions in adulthood were significantly higher for those from economically Challenged backgrounds than from Secure and Affluent families ($r = -.13$, $p = .000$, $n = 1,147$), while therapists from Affluent families tended to feel more Personal Burdens as adults ($r = .09$, $p = .002$, $n = 1,155$). Some 47% of therapists from Affluent backgrounds experienced a less than moderate level of Personal Satisfactions as compared with only 11% of those from economically Challenged backgrounds; 50% of those from Affluent backgrounds experienced frequent Personal Burdens, as compared with only 16% of those from economically Challenged backgrounds. This could conceivably reflect the influence of high or low expectations from childhood experiences on one's standards for evaluating adult life experiences as much as actual differences in Personal Burdens.

Small but statistically significant differences appeared between therapists from different religious backgrounds. Those from non-religious and from Protestant families experienced less Personal Satisfactions but also felt less Personal Burdens than colleagues from Jewish backgrounds (see Appendix Table 8.15). At the risk of trading in stereotypes, Jewish therapists seem to have a somewhat higher level of satisfactions, significantly more so than non-religious therapists, but also feel significantly more heavily burdened than therapists from all of the other backgrounds; what might be called, as it were, a mild "best of times, worst of times" complex, or at least a set of expectations that might heighten both.

Family Psychological Functioning

Modest but significant effects of childhood family functioning were found both for adult Personal Satisfactions ($r = .15$, $p = .000$) and Personal Burdens ($r = -.11$, $p = .000$)—a reversal of the pattern for economic background. Having grown up in an emotionally and psychologically well-functioning family offered a small but not negligible boost to adult life quality, adding a bit to life's positive and diminishing a bit of its negative side.

Childhood Experience Patterns

Even stronger associations with adult life quality were found with respect to the positive and negative aspects of therapists' childhood experiences. The level of felt care and support that therapists experienced when growing up was moderately correlated with their adult Personal Satisfactions (r =.22, p =.000, n = 6,321). Similarly, the level of trauma or abuse experienced while growing up had a significant although smaller effect on therapists' adult Personal Burdens (r =.17, p =.000, n = 4,133). Although clearly not the main determinant of adult life quality, the influence of early childhood experience on adult life quality seems evident here.

These effects are illustrated by the differences between childhood experience patterns. The significantly highest levels of Personal Satisfactions in adult life belonged to those who had been Nurtured or Rescued in childhood, and the significantly lowest levels to those who had felt Neglected (see Appendix Table 8.16). However, while the Nurtured and the Rescued shared in high satisfaction, they differed in terms of Personal Burdens. Therapists who felt Nurtured as children were significantly lowest in Personal Burdens even while highest in Personal Satisfactions, being 61% of those with "Fulfilling" lives. Therapists who were Rescued in childhood (i.e., suffered serious trauma or abuse but also found good care and support) were highest as adults both in Personal Satisfactions *and* in Personal Burdens, seemingly both redeemed from yet still bruised by their childhood experience.

In sum, therapists' adult lives contain strong resonances of childhood family experiences as well as nuances resulting from family economic and cultural backgrounds.

Professional Characteristics

Therapists' family background and experiences have been linked thus far to various aspects of their adult personal life. It also seems worth asking whether and how childhood family features may be associated with their primary professional characteristics; that is, their training background or professional identity, and their theoretical approach to therapeutic practice. Any findings may illuminate what those professional characteristics mean to the therapists, and what implications they might have for clinical practice.

Family Situation

Neither family size nor birth order appear specifically associated with the professions that were chosen by therapists as their source of training to qualify for clinical practice. The same was true for the extent to which therapists' favored different theoretical orientations, with one interesting exception: therapists from larger families (e.g., 4+ children) relied significantly more on family systems theory in practice than did therapists who were "only children" (see Appendix Table 8.17). Evidently therapists who participated as children in complex family systems acquired a greater appreciation of systems-theory as a resource in treatment. This was also true for therapists who were middle children in their families if due only to the fact that middle children (neither oldest nor youngest) are necessarily more numerous in larger families.

Among Midlife therapists (ages 35–44), differences between therapists' professions were significant overall but specifically indicated only that those with two living parents were overrepresented among psychologists (47% of 893).[15] For Older therapists (ages 55+), differences again were significant overall but specifically indicated only that those whose mother had died were overrepresented among social workers (15% of 94).[16] These mixed results and relatively small numbers suggest the results could be attributable to sample instabilities. Whether therapists' parents had divorced or separated had no apparent relationship either to their eventual choice of profession or their theoretical approach to practice. Also, among therapists who had experienced family disruption through parental death or divorce, neither professional identity nor theoretical orientation were associated with the age at which the disruption had occurred.

No differences in theoretical approach based on parental loss were observed among Mature and Older therapists, but two significant effects were noted among Younger therapists. The very few Younger therapists (ages 21–34) who had lost both parents were significantly more inclined towards Humanistic and Broad-Spectrum integrative modes of practice than those whose parents were both still living.[17] Again, the small numbers involved in these comparisons suggest caution in interpreting the results.

Family Background

Therapists' chosen professional identity was significantly linked to their childhood family's economic status. A great majority (69%) of those from Affluent families had become Psychologists, in contrast to 41% of those growing up in Secure families or 39% in economically Challenged families (see Appendix Table 8.18). Also, relatively few of the Affluent became Counselors as compared to those from economically Secure backgrounds (12% vs. 33%).

The effect of family economic background on therapists' theoretical approach was primarily related to the number of theoretical orientations they endorsed as guides to clinical practice. The poorer their economic circumstances when growing up, the more they tended to be Broad-spectrum integrative-eclectic as practitioners ($r = -.14$, $p = .000$). Those from economically Challenged backgrounds were Broad-spectrum therapists twice as often as those from Affluent backgrounds (48% vs. 22%). It seems as if those who experienced material scarcity in their early years favored theoretical abundance as adults, or perhaps they were just more pragmatic and less ideological in their therapeutic work.

Family religious background also differentiated therapists' professional training choices. Those from families with Protestant and mixed religious affiliations were both overrepresented among Counselors (48% and 52%, respectively), especially in contrast to a mere 15% of those of Jewish background (see Appendix Table 8.19). Therapists from Jewish families largely became Psychologists (61%), as did a majority of those from non-religious backgrounds (53%). The finding with respect to therapists of Jewish background must be understood in geographical context, as three-quarters of Jewish therapists in the sample lived in North America—in the US (64%) and Canada (11%)—samples that included a disproportionately large number of Psychologists. This overlap of country and religious background likely explains much of the observed effect.

Two theoretical approaches were significantly differentiated in terms of therapists' religious backgrounds: Jewish therapists were more likely than others in the sample to say they drew on Analytic/Psychodynamic theory in practice, and more likely than those from non-religious backgrounds to draw on a Systems-theoretic approach.[18] Preferences for other theoretical orientations—Cognitive-Behavioral, Humanistic, and Broad-spectrum—were evenly distributed among therapists of different religious backgrounds.

Family Psychological Functioning

The therapeutic professions on average differed significantly among themselves with respect to how therapists viewed their childhood family's emotional functioning. Therapists from well-functioning families were overrepresented in Psychiatry and underrepresented in Counseling and as "Lay" Therapists/Analysts (see Appendix Table 8.20). Those who judged their family's function to have been mediocre (i.e., as "lacking" or "moderate" at best) were overrepresented in Psychology and underrepresented in Counseling. On the reverse side, therapists from poorly functioning families were overrepresented in Counseling and as "Lay" Therapists/Analysts, and were underrepresented in Psychology and Psychiatry. One implication is that therapists' early experiences and life stories incline them towards training in different professional disciplines. Another implication is that therapists who experienced different levels of family functioning in their own early lives may tend to bring different expectations and priorities to their therapeutic work with patients—with unknown advantages or disadvantages for their ability to provide effective help.

The only link found between childhood family functioning and theoretical orientation was that good family functioning was modestly and positively correlated with adherence to a Cognitive-Behavioral approach ($r = .13$, $p = .000$, $n = 6051$).

Childhood Experience Patterns

The main association of specific childhood experience patterns with professional disciplines was a contrast between therapists who were Nurtured vs. those who had felt Wounded as children. Psychologists and Psychiatrists were overrepresented among Nurtured therapists; Counselors and "Lay" Therapists/Analysts were over-represented among Wounded therapists.[19] This basically replicates and reflects the findings about family functioning noted above. Therapists with other patterns of childhood experience matched the average sample distribution of professions.

The main influence of childhood experience patterns on theoretical approach again focused on Cognitive-Behavioral Theory (CBT). Reliance on CBT practices by therapists was significantly higher among those who felt Nurtured as children than among those who were Wounded, Neglected or felt they just Survived (see Appendix Table 8.21). The tendency to rely on a Cognitive-Behavioral approach in working with patients was modestly but significantly related positively with childhood experience of Care and Support ($r =.13$, $p =.000$, $n = 6,055$) and negatively with childhood experience of Trauma or Abuse ($r = -.11$, $p =.000$, $n = 3,863$).

Both in childhood family functioning and the related patterns of early experience, these findings almost seem to echo William James's (1902) classic distinction between the "healthy-minded" and "sick-soul" types of persons and religious experience. Having been Nurtured as children might incline psychotherapists to develop an optimistic "healthy-minded" perspective on life and a correspondingly confident and practical problem-solving approach which are both reflected in the outlook and methods of the Cognitive-Behavioral approach. Conversely, psychotherapists who were Wounded or Neglected as children (having the lowest scores on the Cognitive-Behavioral scale) might tend to develop a pessimistic or "sick soul" view of life, and adopt approaches to therapy that emphasize melioration and healing, and are grounded in what has been termed a tragic sense of life (e.g., Rubens, 1992), focusing more on reframing and adapting constructively to difficult realities than on fixing them.[20]

Adult Life Aspects

This chapter presented many findings about childhood family features that seem to influence therapists' adult lives, and also specified which aspects of adult life were involved. The challenge now is to review and weave together our interpretations. A summary chart has been constructed to help in this effort: a matrix in which the columns represent aspects of adult life and the rows represent the features of childhood family life that were found to affect them (see Figure 8.1).

Personal Self

The Ardent/Expressive dimension of *personal self*—how intense, energetic, and demonstrative therapists tend to be as adults in close personal relationships—

Childhood Family Features	Aspects of Adult Life				Professional Characteristics
	Personal Self	Private Life	Individual Beliefs	Quality of Life	
FAMILY SITUATION					
Family Structure Family size Birth order	Unrelated except: Oldest of 4+ most, youngest of 4+ & only child least *Ardent/Expressive*	Unrelated except: only children less (esp. women), oldest sisters more often had children	Unrelated except: 2-child fam tend more *Ethical Secular*; 4+ child more *Spiritual Religious*	Unrelated except: Only child less *Pers. Satisfaction*, more *Personal Burdens* than 4+ child family	Unrelated to prof. & orientation, except 4+ child fam child more *Systemic* than only children
Family Disruption Parental death Divorce Age occurred	Unrelated except: Divorced, more *Ardent/Expressive*	If parents divorced, women less married, more divorced; if early disruption, more single & non-parents	Unrelated except: earlier disrupted, least spiritual & less religious; disrupted in adulthood most religious & spiritual	Unrelated.	Unrelated.
FAMILY BACKGROUND					
Economic Status Material level	*Affluent* least, Challenged most *Genial* & *Ardent*; *Affluent* more *Forceful*	Economically *Secure* more, *Affluent* less often married; *Affluent* cohabited more	Economically *Challenged* more *Spiritual Religious*	*Challenged* more *Pers. Satisfaction*. *Affluent* more *Personal Burdens*	*Affluent* more *psychologists*; *Secure* more *counselors*; *Challenged* more *Broad-spectrum*
Family Religion Affiliation Early religious importance	Jewish more, Protestant less *Genial* & *Ardent* & *Forceful*; early religious too, Catholic most religious early	Jewish, Protestant more married & parents; Catholic more single & non-parents; Jewish less *Fearful Avoidant*	Protestant, Catholic less adult relig. affiliation; Protestant more *Spiritual Religious*; Catholic more *Spiritual Secular*; no family relig. more *Ethical Secular*	Non-relig. & Protestant less *Pers. Satisfaction* & less *Personal Burdens* than Jewish; early relig. more *Pers. Satisf.*	Protestant & mixed more *counselors*, Jewish & non-relig. more *psychologists*; Jewish more *Analytic* Jewish & non-relig. more *Systemic*
FAMILY EXPERIENCE					
Family Functioning Emotional & psychological level	Better functioning more *Genial*, less *Ardent*—esp. for economically *Challenged*	Well-functioning more married, & securely attached; poor-functioning more divorced, cohabiting, & more *Anxious, Avoidant*	Well-functioning more *Ceremonial Religious*; *Spiritual Religious*; poorly functioning more *Spiritual Secular*	Well-functioning more *Pers. Satisf*, less *Pers. Burdens*, (more *Fulfilling*); poorly functioning more *Distressed, Strained, Dull*	Well-functioning more *psychiatry*, mediocre more *psychology*, poor more *counselors*; well-functioning more *CBT*
Childhood Experience Care/Trauma Early experience patterns	*Neglected* were least *Genial* & *Ardent*; *Nurtured* least *Forceful*; *Rescued* most *Genial/Caring, Ardent/Expressive & Forceful/ Exacting*	*Nurtured* more, *Wounded* less married; *Wounded* more divorced, most *Anxious, Avoidant*; *Nurtured* & *Rescued* less *Avoidant*	*Rescued, Nurtured* most adult religiosity; *Neglected* least; *Rescued, Wounded* most adult spirituality *Nurtured* least; more *Wounded*, fewer *Nurtured* among *Spiritual Secular*	*Care/support* more *Pers. Satisfaction*, trauma/abuse more *Personal Burdens*; *Nurtured*, *Rescued* more *Personal Satisfaction*, but *Rescued* most *Personal Burdens*	*Nurtured* more *psychol* & *psychiatry*, *Wounded* more *counselors*, 'lay' ther.; Care more *Systemic*; Trauma more *Analyt, Humanist, Broad- spectrum*

Figure 8.1 Influences of Childhood Family Background/Experience on Adult Life

was influenced by many features of childhood family life. If they were the oldest in a large family; if their parents had divorced; if they came from a poor family; if they grew up in a Jewish family; if the family wasn't emotionally and psychologically well-functioning; or if they experienced a Rescued (traumatized but loved) childhood: then they tended to be more Ardent/Expressive as adults. However, if they were the youngest in a large family, or on the other hand an "only child" with no siblings; if their parents had remained together; if they came from an Affluent family; if they grew up in a Protestant family; if their childhood family functioned well emotionally and psychologically; or if they experienced a Neglected childhood: then they tended to be less Ardent/

Expressive as adults. Each of these factors seems to make sense as heightening or modulating a person's self-expressiveness. Possibly the more conditional factors that applied, the more the outcome was influenced in one or the other direction; but whether each factor had the same weight or some had more than others isn't clear.

Perhaps more important, how Genial/Caring a therapist had become as an adult appears to have been influenced more by family background and early experience than by family structure. Therapists were more Genial/Caring: the more their childhood families functioned well emotionally and psychologically; if they had been Rescued in childhood; if they came from poorer families; and if they grew up in Jewish families. Therapists who grew up in emotionally poorly functioning families; had felt Neglected in childhood; had come from materially more Affluent families; and had grown up in Protestant families: tended to be less (though not necessarily deficiently) Genial/Caring or self-bestowing in close relationships. Given that these were all working professional therapists as adults, the difference in "warmth" may actually just be a difference between "moderate" and "much". Nevertheless, receiving care and support consistently—and especially when it is most needed—appears to be a recipe for developing self-bestowal, for giving back by "giving forward" to others.

The other *personal self* dimension associated with family background and early experience was being Forceful/Exacting. Therapists who came from Affluent families, from Jewish backgrounds, or had a Rescued pattern of childhood experience, as adults tended to be more self-asserting in close relationships. Those who came from economically Secure or Challenged families, from Protestant backgrounds, or felt Neglected during childhood, tended to be less Forceful/Exacting. Hypothetically, it is possible to see these features of family background and experience as conditions for learning how far it is acceptable and/or necessary to push oneself forward in order to gain satisfaction and be safe as a person in relationships.

Curiously, there were no associations of the Reclusive/Remote (or self-protective) dimension of adult self-experience with childhood family features. Clearly this was not due to lack of valid measurement, as Reclusive/Remote had a very strong positive correlation with Avoidant Attachment ($r = .42$) as well as a moderate correlation with Anxious Attachment ($r = .21$). Moreover, childhood family features were associated with both of those attachment dimensions. This suggests that the Reclusive/Remote dimension may reflect more an inherent trait than part of the self that is influenced by development—unlike Genial/Caring, Ardent/Expressive, and Forceful/Exacting dimensions.

Private Life

The marital and parental status of women therapists seemed more strongly affected by certain childhood family alignment and disruption features than was the case for men. Women who had been first-born among several siblings, and thus likely to have had some "big sister" childcare responsibilities, more often became mothers than did those who grew up as an "only child" without siblings. This might seem a relatively natural outcome of expectations grounded in early learning. Another aspect of early learning might be seen in the fact that women therapists whose parents had been divorced were as adults themselves somewhat more often divorced, or else not married—and, if that parental disruption had occurred when they were children, they tended to remain single and not to have children. In this respect, what they may have learned was a determination to "avoid the mistakes" that their parents made while they were growing up. The question is why women therapists might be more prone to (or perhaps more adept at) applying lessons learned from their family history; or possibly the question should be phrased as to why men were less likely to learn these childhood lessons and apply them in their adult lives. Did women's development tend to be more "embedded" as girls in the context of family life, placing them more "under the influence" of events, or did men rather tend as boys to be more oblivious or indifferent to the events of family life?

Family economic and religious backgrounds seemed to influence therapists of both genders. Those who grew up in economically Secure families tended to be married more often than those from really Affluent families, while more of the latter cohabited with partners. Those who came from Protestant or Jewish backgrounds tended more often than those from Catholic/Orthodox families to be married and parents, even controlling for age-group differences. Although the meaning of these trends is not clear, they remain a distinctive effect as no other overlap was found in the sample between families' economic status and religious backgrounds.

The impacts of childhood family experience on private life in adulthood seem clearer. Therapists from emotionally and psychologically well-functioning families tended more often to be married, in contrast to those from poorly functioning families who were more often cohabiting or divorced. In terms of specific patterns of childhood experience, Nurtured therapists tended to be married as adults, whereas Wounded therapists were more often divorced. Thus, it seems that childhood family experience laid a foundation, solid or shaky, for family relations in adult life.

Childhood family experience evidently also influenced adult attachment behavior more generally. Therapists from emotionally and psychologically well-functioning families seemed to have a greater capacity for forming secure adult attachments (i.e., had significantly lower scores on Avoidant and Anxious attachment) than those from poorly functioning families. By extension, therapists who had been Wounded (i.e., seriously traumatized and disregarded) as children were more often Avoidant and Anxious in attachments as adults, and more often divorced; while those who had felt Nurtured and Rescued during childhood were less Avoidant as adults. These alternate developmental outcomes seem particularly important for the selection of psychotherapists, given that the therapeutic bond or alliance they are able to form in treatment is well known to be a major predictor of patient improvement.

Individual Beliefs

Therapists' individual beliefs were configured formally in this study as belief-value patterns based on varying degrees of religiosity and spirituality, rather than in terms of particular theological or philosophical contents. The religiosity dimension was divided into "religious" versus "secular"; the spirituality dimension, into "spiritual" versus "ethical/rational". The resulting patterns were Spiritual Religious, Spiritual Secular, Ceremonial Religious, and Ethical Secular. In some analyses, variations in religiosity and in spirituality were also treated as separate continuous dimensions.

Childhood family structure seemed to be only marginally related to the individual beliefs that defined therapists as adults. Those who grew up in 2-child families (i.e., had 1 sibling) tended more towards the non-religious and non-spiritual Ethical Secular pattern. Therapists from larger families with 4+ children tended more towards both as reflected in the Spiritual Religious pattern. This might be partly explained by the fact that a significantly higher proportion of non-religious childhood families (but also Jewish ones) were 2-child families, while a significantly higher proportion of Catholic/Orthodox families had 4+ children—but therapists from Protestant, Catholic and Jewish backgrounds did not differ significantly among themselves as adults, either in their levels of spirituality or religiosity, so the issue remains moot.

Among therapists whose families had been disrupted by a parent's death or by divorce, the earlier it occurred in the therapist's life, the more it tended to lessen the development of religiosity and spirituality in adulthood—all the more so if they had felt Neglected in childhood.

Childhood family poverty appeared to promote a stronger likelihood of becoming a Spiritual Religious adult. So too did growing up in a Protestant family—yet Protestant families were least often economically Challenged, so the two findings seem independent. Therapists who were raised in Catholic/Orthodox families tended to become Spiritual Secular adults, rejecting formal religion but retaining a sense of spirituality. In general, nearly half the therapists from Protestant and Catholic families identified no religious affiliation as adults. For many Catholics, at least, a heightened sense of spirituality may be the heir to a childhood faith.

Childhood experiences clearly seemed to influence adult belief-value patterns. Therapists who felt Nurtured or Rescued as children were significantly more religious as adults, while those who had been Neglected were least religious. Therapists who had been Wounded or Rescued as children were significantly more spiritual, but those who were Nurtured were least spiritual. This difference between the Nurtured and the Rescued—between those who were protected and loved vs. those who were traumatized but somehow still found love—hinted at possibly different functions of religiosity and spirituality, the former fostering an "affirmative/optimistic" worldview and the latter a "meaning/healing seeking" worldview. Generally, therapists from emotionally and psychologically well-functioning families were more likely to be Spiritual

Religious or Ceremonial Religious adults, while those from poorly functioning families tended to be Spiritual Secular; and although many therapists fit the Ethical Secular pattern as adults, the largest group of those were recruited from childhood families that had no religious affiliation.

Quality of Life

Personal Satisfactions included a satisfying sense of intimacy and emotional rapport; a sense of being genuinely cared for and supported; experiencing moments of unreserved enjoyment; having occasions to freely express one's private thoughts and feelings; belonging to a personally meaningful community; taking opportunities to relax and refresh oneself; and an overall sense of current life satisfaction. Personal Burdens included feeling hassled by the pressures of everyday life; carrying a heavy burden of responsibility, worry or concern for others close to oneself; experiencing significant personal conflict, disappointment or loss; worry about money or financial security; and worry about one's physical health.

Satisfactions and Burdens in adult life each were significantly associated with childhood family features. An aspect of family structure seemed to predispose therapists who were an "only child" to feel less Personal Satisfactions and more Personal Burdens than those who were one of 4+ children. Family economic background also influenced adult life quality, with therapists from materially Challenged families tending to be more Satisfied with adult life, and those from Affluent families tending to feel more Burdened as adults. Culturally, therapists from non-religious or Protestant families tended to feel lower Satisfactions but also lower Burdens as adults, while those from Jewish backgrounds experienced both more Satisfactions and more Burdens. Different norms and expectations about how much good it *ought* to take to be satisfied, and how much ill it *ought* to take to feel burdened, may lie behind these findings. Additionally, having had more religious involvement as children and adolescents tended to foster a greater sense of Personal Satisfactions in adult life. This may be explained in part by the fact that therapists who felt Neglected in childhood were less religious as children and adolescents, and those who felt Rescued in childhood had been more religious.

Emotional and psychological family functioning and childhood experience patterns provide more direct correlations to adult life quality. Therapists from psychologically well-functioning childhood families tended to experience more Personal Satisfactions as adults and to feel less Personal Burdens. The better their early family's functioning, the more they found current life Fulfilling and the less their lives felt Distressed, Strained or Dull. The more care and support they received as children, the more likely they were to find satisfaction as adults. The more trauma and abuse they received as children, the more likely they were to feel burdened as adults. But even if experiencing trauma or abuse, those who also found sources of care and support in childhood—who had been Rescued—were able to find Personal Satisfactions as adults, like those who were Nurtured; although unlike the Nurtured, as adults they also had the strongest sense of Personal Burdens. (This divergence of effects on quality of life between Nurtured and Rescued childhoods seems to resemble the divergence found with respect to religion and spirituality, and William James's contrast between "healthy-minded" and "sick-soul" religious attitudes.)

Professional Characteristics

Psychotherapists' main professional characteristics are their professional discipline and their theoretical approaches or orientations. Only one specific aspect of theoretical orientation was related to childhood family structure: therapists who grew up among many siblings in 4+ child families were significantly more likely to draw on Family Systems theory in practice than were therapists who grew up as the only child in their family. (No further explanation seems required.)

On the other hand, family backgrounds and childhood experiences were more richly related both to therapists' professional identities and therapeutic approaches. More Psychologists came from Affluent families, while more Counselors were from less well-off but still economically Secure families. More Counselors were from Protestant and mixed religious backgrounds, as compared to Psychologists who more often grew up in non-religious or Jewish families. Psychiatrists tended to come more often from psychologically well-functioning families, Psychologists more from mediocre or moderately functioning families, and Counselors disproportionately from poorly functioning families. Yet Psychologists and Psychiatrists both tended to have been Nurtured (i.e., protected and loved) while growing up, whereas more Counselors tended to feel Wounded as children. Thus psychotherapists entering their careers through different professional trainings and having different professional identities tend to come from different backgrounds and bring different childhood family experiences with them to their therapeutic practice.[21]

Therapists' family backgrounds and childhood experiences also appeared to influence their predilection for different theoretical orientations. Therapists from poor, economically Challenged families were more inclined to a pragmatic Broad-Spectrum integrative or eclectic approach. Therapists from Jewish and non-religious backgrounds, and therapists who felt well cared for and supported as children, tended to work more with Family Systems theories (like therapists from large families). Many therapists from Jewish backgrounds were also more inclined to Analytic/Psychodynamic theories. By contrast, therapists from psychologically well-functioning families, especially those who felt Nurtured as children, were drawn more to Cognitive-Behavioral theories. But therapists who experienced trauma or abuse in childhood were instead drawn more to Analytic/Dynamic, Humanistic, and Broad-Spectrum approaches. These diverse treatment orientations are not just different sets of methods and techniques; they also embrace contrasting metaphors and assumptions with respect to the nature of human personality, human potential and fulfillment.[22]

In that sense, they can be better understood as linked to therapists' personal backgrounds, experiences and mentalities.

Sources of Childhood Influence

The findings presented in this chapter make clear the numerous and pervasive, if generally subtle, influences of therapists' childhood families on their adult personal and professional lives. Individually those influences represent mostly quite small or occasionally moderate effects; but cumulatively, taken together, they reflect a surprisingly long afterglow or shadow (as the case may be) cast by experiences in their first learning environment: the network of early family relationships. A final look at the rows in Figure 8.1 provides an impression of the relative influence of different childhood family features.

Family structure was analyzed in terms of the therapists' family configuration (number of siblings and birth order) and its stability or disruption (due to a parent's death or divorce). As influences on adult life, these childhood family features were typically "unrelated, except for" one or two small or limited (e. g., gender-specific) effects. Having grown up in a small (1- or 2- child) family vs. a large (4+ child) family did make a difference in various spheres of life. In the long term, parental divorce seemed more disruptive than a parent's death, and together with the therapist's age at time of disruption, did leave a mark on the therapist's adult personal self, private life, and individual beliefs. However, these traces seem relatively slight when compared to family economic and religious backgrounds and childhood experiences.

Family economic and religious background exerted a surprising amount of influence, not only on therapists' personal but also professional adult characteristics. Perhaps the surprise is due largely to the fact that psychotherapists and psychotherapy researchers have rarely dealt with those social and cultural "background" variables, so that they are relatively unfamiliar; but the findings probably would not be either surprising or unfamiliar to other social scientists. Family economic background appeared to have an impact across the board on therapists' adult personal self, private life, belief-value orientation, quality of life, professional identity and theoretical approach. So too did family religious background. The practical take-away for therapists, and especially for researchers, is that these background features do matter, and need to be taken into account.

Psychotherapists and psychotherapy researchers will be on more familiar ground and more readily acknowledge the importance of families' emotional and psychological functioning, and of childhood experiences, as influences on adult life. All of the personal aspects of psychotherapists that were surveyed in the DPCCQ appeared to reflect nuances and impacts of childhood family experiences. Even some professional aspects of psychotherapists did, and a detailed consideration of them will be the main topics of Chapters 9 and 10.

Notes

1 Only three studies were found of psychotherapists on this important topic, including: Firth-Cozens (1992); Elliott & Guy (1993); Jackson & Nutall (2001).
2 It seems more plausible to view early family situation, background and experiences as influences in the shaping of *personal self* than the opposite, but also necessary to recognize that correlations are not evidence of causality.
3 The values for this 1-Way ANOVA were: $F = 2.65$; $df= 8, 4583$; $P =.007$; $N = 4,591$.
4 The values for this independent samples t-test were: $t = -3.18$, df $= 1303.2$, $p =.001$.
5 The joint prediction of family psychological functioning by care/support and trauma/abuse is: R $=.73$, Adjusted $R^2 =.53$; $F = 584.9$, $p =.000$, $N = 4,124$.
6 The Chi-square values were: $\chi^2 = 110.1$, df $= 3$, p $=.000$; $N = 2,980$.
7 The Chi-square values were: $\chi^2 = 29.7$, df $= 3$, p $=.000$; $N = 2,809$.
8 The Chi-square values were: $\chi^2 = 110.1$, df $= 4$, p $=.000$; $N = 3,974$.
9 The values for this 1-Way ANOVA were: $F = 3.17$; df $= 4, 1047$; $P =.01$; $N = 1,051$.
10 The Chi-square values were: $\chi^2 = 62.5$, df $= 9$, $p =.000$; $N = 4,100$.
11 The values for these 1-Way ANOVA were: $F = 3.49$; df $= 3, 2736$; $P =.02$ for Religiosity; $F = 4.6$; df $= 3, 2108$; $P =.003$ for Spirituality.
12 The Chi-square values were: $\chi^2 = 283.2$ df $= 4$, p $=.000$; $N = 3,965$.
13 Although adult religiosity and adult spirituality are positively correlated ($r =.52$, $p =.000$), they each had a small but significant correlation—in *opposite* directions—with therapists' ratings of their childhood family's emotional and psychological functioning. Therapists from well-functioning families modestly inclined to be a bit more religious as adults ($r =.07$, $p =.000$); therapists from poorly functioning families modestly inclined to be a bit more spiritual ($r = -.05$, $p =.003$).
14 Only one aspect of childhood family structure was marginally significant (at $p =.05$ but not $p =.01$): "only children" (without siblings) tended to experience a higher level of Personal Burdens as adult than therapists who had many siblings in 4–12 child families. This was reflected in a correlation of $r = -.06$ ($p =.000$, $n = 4,780$) between family size and Personal Burdens: the smaller one's childhood family, the (slightly) higher the adult sense of burden.
15 The Chi-square values were: $\chi^2 = 39.1$, df $= 12$, p $=.000$; n $= 2,117$.
16 The Chi-square values were: $\chi^2 = 29.0$, df $= 12$, p $=.004$; n $= 1,559$.
17 The values for these 1-Way ANOVA were: $F = 3.7$; df $= 3, 453$; $P =.01$ for Humanistic; $F = 3.2$; df $= 3, 452$; $P =.02$ for Broad-spectrum.
18 The values for these 1-Way ANOVA were: $F = 9.3$; df $= 4, 4011$; $P =.000$ for Analytic/Dynamic orientation; $F = 6.5$; df $= 4, 4004$; $P =.000$ for Systemic orientation.
19 The Chi-square values were: $\chi^2 = 98.7$, df $= 16$, p $=.000$; $N = 3,899$.
20 These interpretations of group differences reflect statistical trends that would characterize individuals to differing degrees. Individuals might well embody both tendencies in various measure, in ways that either conflict or are balanced in creative tension. These trends would also constitute one set of developmental influences among many, not strong enough by themselves to be regarded as "determinants".
21 How much difference these childhood family differences make in psychotherapists' experiences while treating patients is examined in Chapter 10.
22 See, for example: Browning (1987), London (1964), Lowe (1969); Orlinsky (2009, 2017).

References

Browning, D. S. (1987). *Religious thought and the modern psychologies*. Philadelphia, PA: Fortress Press.

Elliott, D. M., & Guy, J. D. (1993). Mental health professionals versus non-mental-health professionals: Childhood trauma and adult functioning. *Professional Psychology: Research and Practice*, 24, 83–90.

Firth-Cozens, J. (1992). The role of early family experiences in the perception of organizational stress. *Journal of Occupational and Organizational Psychology*, 65, 61–75.

Jackson, H., & Nutall, R. L. (2001). A relationship between childhood sexual abuse and professional sexual misconduct. *Professional Psychology: Research and Practice*, 32, 200–204.

James, W. (1902). *The varieties of religious experience*. London: Longmans, Green.

London, P. (1964). *The modes and morals of psychotherapy*. New York: Holt, Rinehart & Winston.

Lowe, C. M. (1969). *Value orientations in counseling and psychotherapy*. San Francisco, CA: Chandler Publishing.

Orlinsky, D. E. (2009). The "Generic Model of Psychotherapy" after 25 years: Evolution of a research-based metatheory. *Journal of Psychological Integration*, 19 (4), 319–339.

Orlinsky, D. E. (2017). Unity and diversity among psychotherapies. In A. Consoli, L. Beutler & B. Bongar, *Comprehensive textbook of psychotherapy: Theory and practice*. (2nd ed.), pp.11–30. Oxford, New York: Oxford University Press.

Rubens, R. (1992). Psychoanalysis and the tragic sense of life. *New Ideas in Psychology*, 10 (3), 347–362.

9   Personal Therapy

D. E. Orlinsky with M. H. Rønnestad and
H. Wiseman

The phrase "personal therapy" refers not to a particular theoretical approach or type of psychotherapy but rather to psychotherapists' engagement as clients or patients in their own therapy. To judge from our survey, it appears that psychotherapists themselves are indeed avid users of personal therapy. Information from all relevant questions in the DPCCQ indicates that as many as four of five (80%) of 11,340 therapists had engaged in personal therapy at least once; and of those, nearly two-thirds (65%) had been in personal therapy two or more times (see Figure 9.1).

Moreover, personal therapy was not just something experienced in the past: as many as a fourth (26%) of those surveyed indicated they were currently receiving therapy at the time.[1]

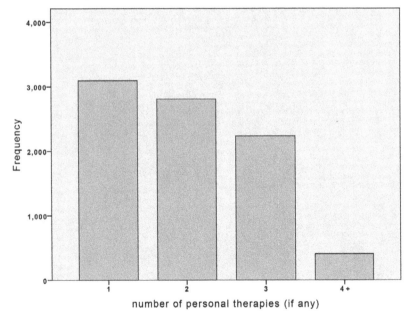

Figure 9.1 Total Number of Personal Therapies Reported (N = 8,544)

DOI: 10.4324/9781003217572-9

Understandably, a high proportion (31%) of those were Novices or trainees in their first three years of practice, and a similar proportion (31%) were Graduate therapists with three to ten years in practice (see Appendix Table 9.1)—although a fifth (21%) of the Novices and a fourth (25%) of the Graduates also had been in therapy before. A substantial number of therapists who had been in practice longer were also currently in therapy: 25% of the Established therapists with 10 to 20 years in practice, and even 16% of the Senior therapists with more than 20 years in practice.

As an occupational group, professional psychotherapists may well be proportionally the largest consumers of their own services. Yet psychotherapists on the whole are probably as happy or happier with their lives than most other people: they hardly portrayed themselves as poorly functioning, emotionally struggling or maladjusted individuals who would typically be viewed as needing to have therapy. As seen in Chapter 6 (Figure 6.1), two-thirds (67%) of 11,201 therapists reported experiencing great or very great life satisfaction and only one-fourth (26%) said they were feeling great stress. Then why do so many therapists have their own personal therapy, many of them not just once? Which therapists do and which don't? What reasons do they give for undertaking personal therapy, and what benefit do they seem to derive from it? And what does all this indicate about psychotherapists as persons and as professionals?

Who Uses Personal Therapy?

The "Adjustment" Question

Clearly, a subjective sense of emotional distress and coping with life is one factor that might lead therapists to be in personal therapy. Relatedly, about 5,500 of the therapists were asked point-blank in the DPCCQ: "How would you describe your present state of emotional and psychological wellbeing?" and were offered the following six response alternatives:

1   Quite poor; I am barely managing to deal with things.
2   Fairly poor; life is pretty tough for me at times.
3   So-so; I manage to keep going with some effort.
4   Fairly good; I have my ups and downs.
5   Quite good; I have no major complaints.
6   Very good; I get along much the way I would like to.

About two-thirds (65%) of those surveyed reported their psychological wellbeing was "quite good" or "very good", 29% said "fairly good", and only 6% said it was less than that (see Figure 9.2).

The small group of therapists whose psychological wellbeing would be considered "Poor" (i.e., less than "Fairly good") were currently in therapy at nearly twice the rate as those who rated their wellbeing as "Very good" (39% vs. 21%) (see Appendix Table 9.2).[2] The somewhat larger group (29%) who rated their

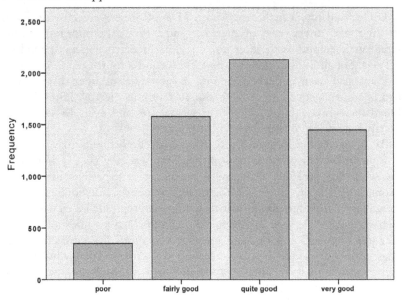

Figure 9.2 Therapists' Current Psychological/Emotional Well-Being (*N* = 5,501)

emotional and psychological wellbeing as "Fairly good" (but having "ups and downs") were also in therapy at a relatively high rate (32%). Yet as many as a fifth (21%) of therapists with a "Very good" sense of wellbeing were also currently in therapy, as were a fourth (24%) of the many whose wellbeing was "Quite good".

Thus while a disproportionate percentage of therapists who said they were not doing well psychologically and emotionally were currently in therapy, so were a large number of those who "had no major complaints" or felt they got "along much the way [they] would like to". Indeed, a majority (56%) of those currently in therapy were not the ones whose emotional and psychological state would suggest that they needed it most. It seems reasonable to conclude that the high rate of personal therapy engaged in by psychotherapists does not reflect a corresponding level of psychopathology or need for treatment. This point was reinforced by an analysis of current personal therapy use with respect to therapists' current life quality patterns (see Chapter 6). Over a fifth (22%) of those whose lives were Fulfilling (high satisfaction, low stress) were in therapy, as compared to 35% of those whose lives were Distressed (low satisfaction, high stress).[3] Why are therapists even with Fulfilling lives engaging in personal therapy?

A Professional Norm

Historically, undergoing personal therapy was seen as a part of the process of becoming a therapist. This had its origin in Freud's (1912) recommendation that psychoanalysts need to be analyzed (and possibly reanalyzed about every five years) in order to convince themselves of the efficacy of therapy through the positive impact it has on them, to avoid pitfalls in relations with patients based on their own unconscious reactions ("counter-transference"), and to refine their ability to use their subjective reactions during sessions effectively as part of the treatment process. This became an established norm, initially for analytic and psychodynamic orientations, but eventually for others too (with the main exception having been Cognitive-Behavioral approaches).[4]

Given this background, it was natural to ask in the DPCCQ: "How important, in your opinion, is it for therapists themselves to have an experience of psychotherapy, analysis, or counseling (individual, group, etc.)?" As illustrated in Figure 9.3, more than half (56%) of the 6,760 therapists asked this replied "It is essential and should be required for all therapists". Another 30% felt "It is definitely desirable for most therapists, but should not be required"—their reservation about requiring it is possibly due to ethical and clinical convictions that undertaking therapy should be the result of a voluntary decision. In other words, 86% agreed that personal therapy was an essential or at least very desirable experience for psychotherapists, while fewer than 2% thought that it was irrelevant or undesirable.

This degree of consensus reflects the normative quality of this view—that therapists not only often have personal therapy as a matter of fact, but that therapists *ought* to have personal therapy. This professional norm contributes to

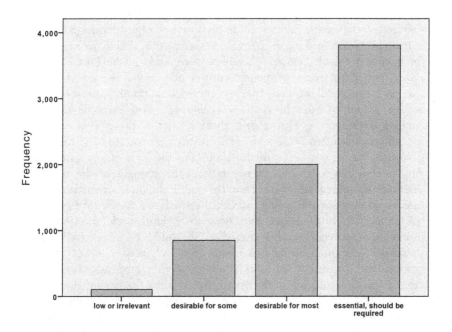

Figure 9.3 Importance of Personal Therapy for Psychotherapists? (*N* = 6,760)

the commonality of therapists found to be currently in their own treatment: 36% of therapists who agreed personal therapy was "essential" were actually in treatment, as compared to 21% of those who felt it was "desirable for most", 7% who said it was "desirable for some", and 4% who thought it "irrelevant".[5] This may account for at least some of the therapists in personal therapy who felt that their current emotional wellbeing was "Quite good" or "Very good".

Professional Characteristics

The norm of having personal therapy as an essential part of training and a desirable aspect of continuing education derived from classical psychoanalysis and is most adhered to in those therapeutic professions and approaches that are more closely tied to that tradition. Significant variations between therapists with different theoretical orientations were clearly evident, both with regard to their views of the necessity of personal therapy for all or almost all therapists, and in terms of their own utilization of personal therapy. The highest endorsements of the norm were among mono-focal Analytic/Dynamic therapists and Analytic/Dynamic + Humanistic therapists (96% and 94%, respectively), with correspondingly high rates of utilization: 91% for both (see Appendix Table 9.3). (The term mono-focal indicates having one strong or salient orientation; bifocal indicates two salient orientations; broad-spectrum indicates three or more salient orientations.) Mono-focal Humanistic therapists were next highest, both in endorsement of the norm (90%) and in utilization of personal therapy (88%). The lowest endorsement of the norm was among mono-focal Cognitive-Behavioral therapists (60%), with a correspondingly low rate of utilization (52%).[6]

It is also worth looking at the reasons therapists of different orientations gave for having personal therapy. Therapists were asked in the DPCCQ to report about their experiences of specific courses of personal therapy, including the reasons for undertaking each therapy: professional training, personal problems, and/or individual growth (as many as applied). Both Analytic/Dynamic and Analytic/Dynamic + Humanistic therapists cited professional training significantly more often (76% and 75%), in sharp contrast to C-B therapists who gave that reason only 40% of the time (and the least of any orientation; see Appendix Table 9.4). This clearly reflects the strength of the norm among orientations influenced by the Freudian tradition. Those orientations also were significantly strongest in giving individual growth as a reason for having therapy, this time with bi-focal Analytic/Dynamic + Humanistic therapists ahead of mono-focal Analytic/Dynamic therapists (86% and 80%, respectively), with C-B therapists least often citing this reason (55%). Unlike those of other orientations, and consistent with its problem-solving emphasis, these therapists cited personal problems more than other reasons for having therapy.

The fact that a strong majority in every therapeutic approach viewed personal therapy as essential or desirable for most therapists, even among C-B therapists and those having no salient orientation, attests to the normative quality associated with it. Another fact to note is the discrepancy between the number who endorsed the norm and those who implemented it; for example, 96% of Analytic/Dynamic therapists endorsed vs. 91% utilized. This gap between attitude and action may be an inevitable feature of human nature. However, the greatest discrepancy between attitude and behavior occurred among theoretically "uncommitted" therapists, for whom no orientation was salient: 82% endorsed vs. 59% utilized. Feeling committed to almost any orientation may well enhance the norm's effect.

Variations in personal therapy based on therapists' professional discipline are similar to those based on theoretical orientation. Consensus on the essential or highly desirable quality of personal therapy was nearly unanimous among Lay Therapists/Analysts (96% endorsement, 93% utilization), and was also significantly higher among Counselors (91% endorsement, 86% utilization) (see Appendix Table 9.5). The other professions trailed along: Psychiatry (87% endorsement, but only 70% utilization); Social Work (86% endorsement, 79% utilization); and significantly least, Psychologists (83% endorsement, 81% utilization). Psychologists were likely lowest due in part to the concentration of C-B therapists among them.

The reasons for having therapy that were cited by members of the different professions also differed. Significantly more (73%) of the Psychiatrists than all other professions cited training as their reason for having therapy, and were in fact the only profession to make this their leading reason for doing so, significantly down-playing individual growth and personal problems (see Appendix Table 9.6). By contrast, Counselors gave individual growth as their leading reason for therapy, as well as personal problems, both of which were significantly higher than in other groups. Social Workers cited personal problems significantly more often and professional training significantly less often than all of the other professions. Apparently for Psychiatrists, having personal therapy was more about their profession than about themselves, while for Social Workers and Counselors it was more about themselves than their profession.

Interestingly, clinicians who identified as Lay Therapists/Analysts and as Counselors were significantly higher than Psychologists, Social Workers and Psychiatrists in endorsing the importance of personal therapy, and also in their utilization of personal therapy. One reason for this likely is that being in therapy was a major gateway to their becoming professional practitioners. The other therapeutic professions are more solidly institutionalized, either in medicine or in academia, and therapists acquire their basic professional identity by graduating from a "parent" training program (e.g., medical school). With that basic certification, about a fifth of Psychologists and Social Workers (19% and 21% respectively) were able to function as psychotherapists without having personal therapy, as were nearly a third (30%) of the Psychiatrists. Nevertheless, the importance of personal therapy as essential or highly important for therapists was endorsed by large majorities from all professional backgrounds and theoretical orientations, and was almost as widely used.

Personal Characteristics

Age and Gender

Several personal characteristics of therapists beyond current emotional distress are related to the rates at which personal therapy was used, both present and past. Naturally age is one factor to control, since the older therapists are, the more time and perhaps more occasions they would have had to engage in therapy. As an example: 64% of Younger therapists, 83% of Midlife therapists, and 90% of Older therapists had or were having personal therapy.

Gender is one factor. Although majorities of men and women in every age group had or were engaged in personal therapy, in every age group women were significantly more likely to have done so than their male counterparts. Among Younger therapists, 67% of women but only 59% of men were or had been in therapy;[7] among Midlife therapists, 86% of women compared to 77% of men;[8] and among Older therapists, 92% of women and 86% of men had been or were again in therapy.[9] The greater propensity of women therapists to have personal therapy was also observed when compared separately by profession within Psychology and Psychiatry, and marginally within Counseling, but not in Social Work or among Lay Therapists/Analysts.

Some of the difference between men and women therapists may be due to the different reasons they gave for seeking treatment. Male therapists were slightly but significantly more likely to cite professional training (65% vs. 61%),[10] whereas women were more inclined than men to cite personal problems (71% vs. 63%)[11] and individual growth (79% vs. 71%)[12] as reasons for having therapy. The differences are small but telling: men leaned toward professional reasons, women inclined towards personal reasons.

Personal Self

Dimensions of *personal self* were another factor that significantly differentiated between therapists who didn't and did have personal therapy at least or more than once, but in diminishing scope based on age. Among the Younger therapists, those who weren't or hadn't been in therapy were significantly less Genial/Caring, less Forceful/Exacting, more Reclusive/Remote and less Ardent/Expressive than others (see Appendix Table 9.7). Therapy users tended to be more self-bestowing, more self-asserting, more self-expressive and less self-protective. By contrast, the only significant difference among the Midlife and Older therapists was that those who had still not been in therapy were significantly less Ardent/Expressive (i.e., more reticent) than others. At every age level, those therapists who were least self-expressive or self-disclosing were also those who avoided having personal therapy.

Private Life

Aspects of private life also tended to differentiate therapists' use of personal therapy, with respect to marital status but not parental status. Among Younger therapists, a great percentage (83%) of those already divorced or separated had been in therapy, far more than those who were married (59%).[13] A comparatively high rate of personal therapy also typified those who were living with a partner (70%). Midlife therapists showed much the same pattern: 89% of the divorced as well as 88% of the cohabiting had been in therapy—about two-thirds of each group more than once—compared with just 79% of married therapists.[14] Of the Older therapists, significantly more of the divorced and of those living with a partner had experienced personal therapy (95% and 94% respectively) than the married therapists (87%).[15] Indeed 73% of the divorced and 76% of cohabiting therapists had done so two or more times.

It is understandable that therapists who had been divorced or separated, and presumably had experienced significant emotional conflict, might turn to therapy as a source of help. It is equally understandable that therapists who were more successful in marriage would find a reliable source of support in that relationship, and would have a correspondingly smaller need to seek it from therapy. However, it is not as clear why therapists who had an intimate live-in partner would have personal therapy more often than those who were married, and quite as often as those who had been divorced or separated. One possibility is that some cohabiting therapists may have had emotional reservations about committing to marriage, introducing a potentially problematic instability into their private lives. Another possibly related alternative might be that cohabiting relationships might have been more temporary or transitional arrangements than long-term marital bonds. Laws regarding cohabitation vary from country to country but, in some, cohabiting couples have fewer rights vis-à-vis each other (e.g, respecting finances, inheritance, etc.) than married couples, which may build more insecurity into the relations of cohabiting couples. What is clear at least is that significantly more of divorced and cohabiting therapists cited personal problems as a reason for therapy (78% and 74%, respectively) than did married therapists (65%),[16] and significantly more of the divorced cited individual growth than did married therapists (81% vs. 75%),[17] while married therapists were more likely than others to use professional training as their reason for having personal therapy.[18]

Attachment Patterns

Attachment patterns reflect the psychological foundation of intimate relationships in therapists' private lives. There were too few Younger therapists in the subsample for whom Attachment data was available to make a valid analysis, but consistent significant results were found for Midlife and Older therapists. Among Midlife therapists, those with higher levels of Anxious Attachment were more likely to have been in therapy one or more times.[19] Among Senior therapists, those with higher levels of Anxious Attachment were more likely to have been in therapy two or more times.[20] Unsurprisingly, therapists predisposed to an Anxious mode of engagement in adult relationships were more likely to have sought help in personal therapy and, as previously shown (Chapter 4), married therapists had the lowest levels of Anxious attachment and were least Avoidant interpersonally; single and divorced therapists had the highest levels.

Childhood Family Experience

If childhood family experience is as pervasive or subtle an influence on adult life as shown in the preceding chapter, one would expect to find some of that influence also in regard to therapists' uses of personal therapy—which, indeed, proved to be the case. In every age group, therapists' ratings of the emotional and psychological functioning of their childhood family significantly differentiated between those who never sought personal therapy and viewed their family's functioning most positively, those who had one personal therapy and a more moderate view of their family's functioning, and those who engaged in their own therapy two or more times while viewing their family's functioning least favorably (see Appendix Table 9.8). Clearly, therapists who grew up in poorly functioning families seemed to experience greater need for personal therapy than those who came from well-functioning families.[21]

The different patterns of childhood experience reflected this in more detail. The results were the same for each age group, allowing for an overall summary. Nearly all (97%) of the Wounded had sought personal therapy, 84% of them two or more times (see Appendix Table 9.9). Next were therapists who had felt Neglected (91% utilization, 68% twice or more), followed by those who just *Survived* their childhood (88% utilization, 67% twice or more). By contrast, only four in five (79%) of those who felt Nurtured had gone for personal therapy—a substantial majority, but still significantly fewer than all other groups.

The reasons cited for having personal therapy also differed based on childhood experience patterns, other than for the purpose of professional training. Therapists who had been Wounded in childhood said they had sought therapy to deal with personal problems most often (89%), followed by those who had felt Neglected (78%), both citing problems significantly more often than therapists who were Nurtured (63%) (see Appendix Table 9.10). Psychotherapists who felt they had just Survived as children were not unusually high in citing personal problems but were the most frequent (85%) in giving individual growth as a reason for therapy, while Wounded therapists also frequently cited individual growth (84%), and both did so significantly more often than Nurtured therapists (76%).

The different reasons that therapists give for engaging in personal therapy and their differential participation in it make clear that professional training is not the primary factor, even though a majority in each group did it and cited it.

The greater prominence given to personal problems as a reason for personal therapy instead emphasizes its use—especially by the Wounded and Neglected—to repair emotional and interpersonal deficits left over from childhood. And the greater prominence given to individual growth—especially by those who just Survived as well as the Wounded—highlights the use of therapy to refine the personal assets derived from prior life experiences, like empathy and resilience, that therapists bring to their functioning as conductors and conduits of treatment. How much benefit therapists seemed to get from their experiences in therapy is the focus of the next section.

Effects of Personal Therapy

Each time therapists described one of their personal therapies, they were asked in the DPCCQ to rate its "value to you as a person". The response options were: 0 = None, 1 = Little, 2 = Some, 3 = Moderate 4 = Great, and 5 = Very great. Therapists were able to describe up to three or four separate experiences, depending on which DPCCQ version they received.

Outcomes of First-Listed Therapy

To get an overall view of treatment outcomes with equal contributions from all persons, the first therapy that each person listed was selected, with the result shown in Figure 9.4. The largest group (44%) of therapists rated the value of therapy to them as "Very great", and the next largest group (29%) rated its value as "Great". Taken together, nearly three-fourths of 8,175 therapists indicated they had what can be fairly described an "excellent" experience. About one in six (16%) felt their first-listed therapy was of "Moderate" value, and an even smaller group (7%) said it only had "Some" value, amounting to just under a fourth (23%) that had a "middling" experience. Last and least, about one in 20 had a really "poor" outcome, with that therapy experience being of "Little" (4%) or "No" (1%) value to them. This is a strong testimonial to the importance of personal therapy for psychotherapists, even allowing for possible bias due to retrospectively justifying their engagement in therapy by overestimating its value.

Factors Associated with First-Listed Outcome

The therapist's age and gender are among several factors that appear to have had a small but statistically significant impact on therapists' ratings on the value of therapy: Older women were most likely, and Younger men were least likely, to have an excellent experience (76% vs. 64%), with other age and gender combinations in between (see Appendix Table 9.11 9.11). Younger and Midlife male therapists were more likely than expected to have a "middling" experience, although large majorities (64% and 69%) among even these lowest-on-average groups did have an " excellent " experience.

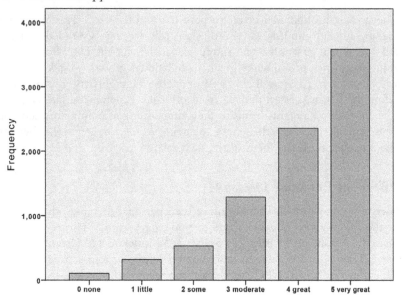

Figure 9.4 First Listed Personal Therapy: "Value to you as a person?" (*N* = 8,175)

No significant differences were observed between specific therapeutic professions in the personal value attributed to their first-listed therapy, with "excellent" outcomes ranging from 71% to 78%. However, a major difference was observed among adherents of alternate theoretical approaches, both overall and when analyzed separately for men and women. More than a third (39%) of Cognitive-Behavioral therapists failed to have an "excellent" outcome, tending instead either toward a "middling" result (29%) or a really "poor" experience (11%) (see Appendix Table 9.12). This personal disappointment may well account for an attitude of skepticism or antipathy towards more traditional approaches found among some adherents of Cognitive-Behavioral therapy. By contrast, relatively few therapists of other orientations experienced "poor" outcomes in their first-listed therapy, ranging from 3% of Analytic/Dynamic to 6% among Humanistic therapists. Only therapists who had no salient orientation had a rate of excellent outcomes as low as C-B therapists (59% and 61% respectively).

As parallels were found between therapists' theoretical orientations and individual beliefs in Chapter 5, it seemed relevant to check the latter in relation to personal therapy outcomes. Significantly fewer therapists having an Ethical Secular belief-value orientation had an "excellent" outcome than others (69%), while significantly more of them had a "middling" outcome (26%).[22] This seemed mainly to reflect the difference between orientations, as C-B therapists tended to have more of an Ethical Secular and less of a Spiritual Secular orientation. By contrast, significantly more of the therapists with a Spiritual

Secular pattern had an "excellent" outcome than expected (77%), as was also typical of Broad-Spectrum therapists. There was no difference in frequencies of "poor" outcome, which hovered around 5% for all four patterns.

Few other personal factors had more than a small but statistically significant association with the outcomes of first-listed therapies. This included small correlations (r =.08, p =.000) with the Genial/Caring and Ardent/Expressive dimensions of personal self. With respect to childhood family functioning, therapists who suffered more trauma or abuse experienced more benefit (r =.11, p =.000). Another small but significant correlation (r =.11, p =.000) suggests that therapists who found more benefit in therapy enjoyed a somewhat higher level of Personal Satisfactions. Outcome of the first-listed personal therapy was unrelated both to marital status and parental status, and also to adult attachment dimensions. The fact that only a few and relatively small associations between therapists' characteristics and the outcomes of their first-listed personal therapy is likely due to whether therapists chose to rate their first or most recent or most impactful personal therapy. A more relevant view of personal therapy influences may be had by taking the therapist's history with it into account.

Cumulative Effect of Personal Therapies

Nearly two-thirds (65%) of the 8,281 therapists who had been in personal therapy had done that two or more times, raising the likelihood of having experienced over time at least one "excellent" outcome (see Appendix Table 9.13). Three-fourths (75%) of those with one personal therapy such had an outcome, leaving the remaining fourth to have a "middling" or "poor" outcome. By contrast, 90% of those with two or more personal therapies had at least one "excellent" outcome, and 60% had two or more "excellent" outcomes. It seems that many who might have been disappointed with only a "middling" or even a "poor" outcome in their first course of therapy may have ultimately enhanced their experience of what personal therapy can offer by being persistent. Nevertheless, one in ten of those remained disappointed.

Factors Associated with Cumulative Outcome[23]

Age and Gender. Women in each age group tended to rate their experiences in personal therapy more positively than their male counterparts, although the difference narrowed and became less significant among Older therapists (see Appendix Table 9.14, right column). The combinations of age and gender showed significantly higher satisfaction among Older women (88%, with 50% having 2+ excellent outcomes) and among Midlife women (87%, with 43% having 2+ excellent outcomes). Lower (but still high) levels of satisfaction with personal therapy were experienced by Younger men (75% with at least one excellent outcome) and Midlife men (82% with at least one excellent outcome). Despite being somewhat behind their female colleagues, most male therapists clearly experienced a highly positive benefit from personal therapy.

Profession and Orientation. No significant differences in experiencing at least one excellent therapy outcome were observed between members of the different therapeutic professions. However, in terms of theoretical orientations, Cognitive-Behavioral therapists in all age groups were significantly less likely than others to experience at least one excellent personal outcome (see Appendix Table 9.15). Overall, just 70% of the C-B therapists succeeded in having a positive outcome, as compared to 90% of Analytic/Dynamic and hybrid Analytic/Dynamic + Humanistic. Something about traditional therapy and/or something about therapists inclined to the C-B approach seems not to mix well at a personal level. Still, even with this disparity, a large majority of C-B therapists did have at least one excellent outcome.

Two other points are worth noting in passing. First, therapists without a strong commitment to any theoretical orientation also lagged in their responsiveness to personal therapy; and second, significantly more Broad-Spectrum therapists and bifocal Analytic/Dynamic + Humanistic had 2+ "excellent" outcomes. In this case, the difference seems to reflect their relative breadth of theoretical commitment in therapeutic practice, mediated by their difference in therapy utilization: only 59% of the "uncommitted" therapists had a personal therapy, as compared with 91% of the Analytic/Dynamic + Humanistic and 81% of the Broad-Spectrum therapists (previously noted in Appendix Table 9.3).

Individual Beliefs. The relation of cumulative outcomes to individual belief-value patterns (see Appendix Table 9.16) repeats that found regarding the first-listed therapy. A statistically significant contrast between Spiritual Secular and Ethical Secular therapists (88% vs. 82% with at least one excellent outcome),[24] probably reflecting a more frequent use of personal therapy by Spiritual Secular therapists (92% vs. 84%). The rate of use among Ceremonial Religious therapists (84%) was as low as for Ethical Secular therapists, and their likelihood of at least one excellent outcome (79%) was even lower.[25] This suggests that therapists' spirituality or the factors that heighten it promote both more utilization and better eventual results, though the differences overall were fairly small. Perhaps the most important fact is that utilization and benefit from personal therapy are both quite high even for therapists who are religious.

Personal Self. The higher that therapists were on Ardent/Expressive and Genial/Caring dimensions of *personal self,* the more they had an excellent cumulative experience of personal therapy, as was also seen in regard to first-listed personal therapies. However, the self-expressive dimension promoted therapists' use of personal therapy in all age groups, while the Genial/Caring (self-bestowing) dimension did so only among Younger therapists. Overall, more (88%) of the "ardent" (i.e., most self-expressiveness) therapists attained at least one excellent outcome, as compared to 76% of the "reticent" (i.e., least self-expressive) therapists (see Appendix Table 9.17). Significantly more (45%) of the "ardent" therapists also attained two or more excellent outcomes, as compared to only a fourth (24%) of the "reticent". Therapists who were more open and intense in their close relationships (and among the Younger, also more "devoted") tended to have a more favorable record of using and benefiting from their own personal therapy—possibly reflecting both their need and ability to invest in meaningful relationships. Similarly, therapists who reported the highest ("devoted") level of Genial/Caring were significantly more likely to experience two or more excellent outcomes, while those at the lowest ("sympathetic") level were significantly more likely not to have had personal therapy at all (see Appendix Table 9.18). Notwithstanding those apparent advantages, the recurrent finding is that a great majority of therapists sought and benefitted from having personal therapy.

Private Life. Differences between therapists in marital status and between those who were or weren't parents also did not reach statistically significant levels. Neither did differences in levels of Anxious Attachment and Avoidant Attachment, despite the significant tendency of the former to seek therapy more often.

Childhood Family. No significant differences in cumulative outcome were found based on family structure (size, birth order) or family background (economic, religious) or childhood or adolescent religiosity. However, fewer of therapists who came from families that functioned well, emotionally and psychologically, had multiple excellent outcomes.[26]

Childhood Experience. However, childhood experience patterns did show significant and suggestive differences, particularly with respect to the "Wounded Healer" concept (see Chap. 10). Overall, therapists who had been Wounded as children (i.e., disregarded and traumatized) were most frequent in having one or more excellent personal therapy outcomes (90%), with significantly more of them also having two or more excellent therapies (57%) (see Appendix Table 9.19). In fact, coming from such a dire childhood experience, they almost certainly needed to have more benefit from therapy in order as adults to be capable of functioning as psychotherapists. Almost all (97%) had been in personal therapy, and most (84%) had been in therapy two or more times (as was seen in Table 9.9). Even just among Younger therapists, those who had been Wounded as children already had nearly twice the average number of 2+ excellent outcomes as other therapists (53% vs. 28%). They were "coming from behind" and had need of "catching up" with those whose childhoods had been more fortunate.[27]

The most fortunate were the largest group of therapists who had felt Nurtured (i.e., cared for and protected) as children. These may be described as "normals" both for their benign childhood and for their majority status (55% overall, and 51% of those with data shown in Appendix Table 9.19). As many as one in five (21%) of Nurtured therapists apparently didn't feel a need for personal therapy (noted in Appendix Table 9.9), and significantly more of those who did have therapy did not experience an excellent outcome (17% as compared with 10% of no excellent outcome among the Wounded). Perhaps the psychological and emotional foundation established among the Nurtured as children was sufficient as a base for their functioning as psychotherapists in adulthood.

Among the others there was a small group of therapists who, like the Wounded, had been seriously traumatized in childhood but managed somehow to find care and support while growing up, and were thus viewed as Rescued. Psychologically they seem to share some characteristics both with the Wounded and the Nurtured, and most of them were close to average in seeking therapy (87%) and receiving benefit (87%) from it. Another group of therapists had a different kind of negative experience in childhood, being Neglected rather than Wounded—sinned against more by "omission" than by "commission", either because they were one among too many children and "got lost in the crowd", or because their caregivers were absent or preoccupied. Although not seriously traumatized, they likely felt disregarded with their needs and feelings left unattended. Like the Wounded, most (91%) sought therapy, and many—although fewer—attained at least one excellent outcome over time (84%).

Finally, there are therapists who felt they had just Survived their childhood. Having experienced trauma or abuse at moderate ("distressed") or serious ("hurt") levels, they still were able to get a moderate level of care and support, and were, in effect, midway between Wounded and Rescued. Yet like the Wounded and the Neglected, they were significantly more likely to seek personal therapy two or more times, and were second only to the Wounded in having at least one excellent outcome. Overall, a very high proportion of therapists coming from each kind of childhood had experienced at least one highly beneficial outcome. Some clearly needed personal therapy to repair omissions and deformations of childhood experience more than others, but all (even the "normals") needed the refinement of their social-emotional sensitivity and skill provided by personal therapy.

Personal and Professional Benefits

Thus far, the outcomes of personal therapy have been defined in terms of therapists' subjective ratings about the personal benefit they received, which could be counted under the heading of "consumer satisfaction". In and of itself, this would likely serve to reinforce a confident, optimistic attitude about the effectiveness of treatment that therapists bring to their therapeutic work, and implicitly convey to their patients. Yet two other sources of evidence that might confirm therapists' subjective ratings of outcome can be drawn from information collected by the DPCCQ: one, already familiar, based on therapists' current life quality; the second, to be introduced, focused on the influence of personal therapy on their professional development.

Personal Life Quality

Does having been in personal therapy, especially with one or more excellent outcomes, have a positive impact on the therapist's current quality of life? The answer is that therapists in each age group who had at least one excellent outcome in personal therapy recorded a significantly higher level of Personal Life Satisfactions than those who did not (See Appendix Table 9.20). Among

Midlife therapists, those with two or more excellent outcomes had a significantly higher level than those with only one. Generally, of course, most (68%) of our therapists enjoyed a high level of current life satisfaction (as shown in Chapter 6). However, significantly more (71%) of those with two or more excellent therapy outcomes did so, while significantly fewer (62%) with no excellent outcome did (see Appendix Table 9.21). Moreover, twice as many therapists with no excellent outcome experienced a "less than moderate" level of life satisfaction than those who had two or more excellent therapy outcomes (10% vs. 5%). Yet although cumulative positive outcomes are reflected in therapists' Personal Life Satisfactions, therapy did not diminish their Personal Life Burdens. It appears that effective personal therapy only lessens therapists' self-inflicted (i.e., neurotic) burdens, but not the burdens and griefs imposed by life. Even so, raising therapists' life satisfactions without diminishing their burdens enhances their quality of life overall.

Professional Development

Therapists were asked in the DPCCQ to rate "How much influence (positive and/or negative) each of the following [experiences] has had on your overall development as a therapist?"—with personal therapy included as one of the influences they were asked to rate. Overall, a majority (54%) of those who had personal therapy said that it had a "very" positive influence on their professional development, 22% said it was "moderately" positive, and another 14% said "slightly" positive (totaling 90% positive). However, having experienced one or more excellent outcomes had a major impact. Among therapists who experienced two or more excellent outcomes, significantly more rated personal therapy as a "very" positive influence (71% vs. 54%), as did those with one excellent outcome (55% vs. 22%).[28]

The opposite was found concerning a possible negative influence of personal therapy on therapists' development. Overall, nearly 6% of therapists who had no excellent outcome felt their therapy had a negative effect on their development (4% slightly, 1% moderately, 1% very negative); but among therapists who had two or more excellent outcomes, less than 2% felt any negative impact (0.9% slightly, 0.6% moderately, 0.3% very).[29] Thus in therapists' judgments at least, their personal therapy had professional benefits as well as personal benefits, and the benefits far outweighed the drawbacks.

In Sum

Most people who go for therapy do so essentially because they are suffering emotionally or psychologically; because they are discontented or dismayed with their lives, their relationships, their behavior or themselves. Psychotherapists do this too, like other people—when and as the occasion arises. But psychotherapists go for personal therapy more consistently for other reasons, not only to *repair* their dysphoria, dysfunctions, and deficiencies in order to attain or return to states that are considered "normal". Unlike most other people, they also need to *refine* their personal capacity to sense and respond empathically to the emotions and implicit interpersonal messages of others, and—in the process—to retain a clear sense of their own identity and boundaries, resources and limitations, at a level that goes above and beyond what is generally experienced as "normal". The work of being a psychotherapist demands that therapists serve the best interests of their patients without imposing their own personal needs on those relationships, yet at the same time knowing and protecting their own essential and legitimate interests. And in the nature of the case—psychotherapists being humans not angels—this goal is never finally achieved but must be constantly striven for with the capacity to do so recurrently upgraded. And so the evidence reviewed in this chapter shows. There is a very widespread conviction among psychotherapists of most theoretical persuasions that personal therapy is either essential or extremely important as a condition of therapeutic practice. This is true not just for purposes of training or only in the initial phases of professional work; it is critical for repairing or resolving personal problems, and for refining the therapist's individual growth recurrently, as needed, and at all career levels. Individual growth was the most common reason cited for engaging in personal therapy.

Their own personal therapy, or some "non-clinical" equivalent to enhance self-awareness and reflectivity, is highly desirable or a necessity for most persons who practice psychotherapy because of what the best practice of psychotherapy demands. As stated in Chapter 2:

> Every psychotherapy operates through the medium of an interpersonal relationship between patient and therapist, developed over time typically through a series of person-to-person encounters (or "therapy sessions"). What makes the relationship "therapeutic" is a consistently empathetic, discerning, caring and resiliently committed engagement of the therapist with the patient, matched by the patient's awareness of it and acceptance of its sincerity (or "genuineness").

That is the description of an ideal circumstance, an ideal that is in fact higher than is managed by most "normal" people in their close relationships. Psychotherapists may, by some innate talent, be better than most people at empathy; or, through past experiences of their own, be more highly motivated than most people to listen and respond caringly to emotionally distressed persons— but, however talented and however motivated, no one is consistently able to maintain high levels of empathy and genuine caring. Therapists too have emotional knots and conflicts, biases and blindspots—even if most of the time at levels that are low enough for "normal" relationships in everyday life. All of this is true no less of therapists whose therapeutic approaches appear to focus more on techniques and procedures than of those who focus explicitly on nuances of feeling and relationship: the therapist must be able to read and respond, accurately and appropriately, to what clients implicitly present in their moment-to-moment encounters. Naturally, all therapists do not start at the same level of personal ability, or at the same level in all aspects of personal and therapeutic functioning. Some have further to go than others in repairing and refining their capabilities, as shown by the data on different childhood experience patterns. The psychotherapists' most general need for personal psychotherapy is to repair and refine their capacities for empathy and genuine caring. To *repair*, by gradually coping with the traumas, emotional conflicts, and imperfect strategies to survive them devised in childhood, and to remove the biases and resolve the blind spots in their responsiveness to others. To *refine*, by gradually enhancing these capacities to a higher level effectiveness than most "normal" persons, in their usual relationships, are called upon or expected to attain.

This is not a recent discovery, nor an original one, but nevertheless it is an important one that probably needs to be remade and reinforced at intervals. In a study of the patients' and therapists' experiences in therapy sessions nearly 50 years ago (Orlinsky & Howard, 1975), the title given to a final chapter was *The Therapist as an Instrument of Treatment*. The idea that therapists as persons are themselves an important part of psychotherapeutic treatment seems as relevant and useful now as it was then, especially with the recent interest in exploring "the therapist effect" (e.g., Baldwin & Imel, 2012). The idea that psychotherapies involve "an emotionally charged, confiding relationship with a helping person" clearly implies that the therapist (as the "helping person" in the relationship) is an instrument of treatment, and as such the therapist has a dual responsibility: to be an effective and appropriate instrument (e.g., empathically "attuned" and emotionally "present"), and to be wisely skillful in knowing how to make the best use of self as an instrument of treatment.[30]

The evidence further suggests that most of those who undertake personal therapy feel that they experience significant personal benefit most of the time, but that—being a perfectly human and therefore imperfect process—there are relatively rare occasions when therapy fails to deliver much if any benefit, and very rare occasions when it is experienced as harmful and a negative influence on development. Over time, many therapists engage more than once in personal therapy, and if an excellent outcome is not experienced in one personal therapy there is a good likelihood that it will be experienced in another—giving the therapist, when that happens, a personal conviction about the power of therapy to make a positive impact on the lives and selves of patients. There is evidence as well that having positive experiences of personal benefit in treatment extends, beyond the subjective estimates of those who have had it, into their own private lives by contributing moderately to their current life satisfactions. This is the personal take-away from the therapists having had their own successful therapy. But in psychotherapy, the personal is the professional. The next chapter considers more broadly what, and how, the therapist's personal characteristics and qualities appear to contribute to their professional work as psychotherapists.

Notes

1 Additional major sources on research related to psychotherapists' personal therapy can be found in the book edited by Geller, Norcross & Orlinsky (2005) and the review chapter by Rønnestad, Orlinsky & Wiseman (2016). Also of interest are papers by Bike, Norcross & Schatz (2009); Curtis, Field, Knaan-Kostman & Mannix, (2004); Orlinsky, (2014), and Orlinsky, Schofield, Schröder & Kazantzis (2011).

2 However, three-fifths (61%) of the therapists experiencing the most serious personal difficulties were not in therapy when they probably should have been, which is a worry.

3 The Chi-square values were: χ^2 = 107.6, df = 5, p =.000; N = 10962.

4 Many contemporary Cognitive-Behavioral therapists recognize the importance of, and participate in practices like, "self-experience" or "encounter" groups, role-play with peers, or individual self-reflection, as ways of obtaining feedback from others on the social and personal qualities that are communicated to clients, and may have a positive or negative impact on them in therapy (e.g., Bennett-Levy & Finlay-Jones (2018)).

5 The Chi-square values were: χ^2 = 383.9, df = 3, p =.000; N = 6,590.

6 Although the lowest rate of personal therapy was observed among Cognitive-Behavioral therapists, it should be noted that this reflects a historical situation which may no longer apply to the same extent in contemporary C-B practice.

7 The Chi-square values were: χ^2 = 13.6, df = 1, p =.000; N = 2,459.

8 The Chi-square values were: χ^2 = 72.1, df = 1, p =.000; N = 6,375.

9 The Chi-square values were: χ^2 = 18.0, df = 1, p =.000; N = 2,262.

10 The Chi-square values were: χ^2 = 13.3, df = 1, p =.000; N = 8,183.

11 The Chi-square values were: χ^2 = 43.0, df = 1, p =.000; N = 8,183.

12 The Chi-square values were: χ^2 = 64.3, df = 1, p =.000; N = 8,183.

13 The Chi-square values were: χ^2 = 34.2, df = 6, p =.000; N = 2,280.

14 The Chi-square values were: χ^2 = 107.5, df = 6, p =.000; N = 5,927.

15 The Chi-square values were: χ^2 = 39.15, df = 6, p =.000; N = 2,071.

16 The Chi-square values were: χ^2 = 79.7, df = 3, p =.000; N = 7,895.

17 The Chi-square values were: χ^2 = 18.7, df = 3, p =.000; N = 7,895.

18 The Chi-square values were: χ^2 = 27.3, df = 3, p =.000; N = 7,895.

19 The values for this 1-Way ANOVA were: F = 9.70, df = 2, 575, p =.000.

20 The values for this 1-Way ANOVA were: F = 8.59, df = 2, 564, p =.000.

21 Regarding family background: (a) no significant association of therapy use was found with religious background, and (b) a marginally significant (p =.05) effect of greater use by those from Affluent families was found in the small subsample (n = 1,085) with economic status data.

22 The Chi-square values were: χ^2 = 22.7, df = 3, p =.001; N = 3,434.

23 Comparing the characteristics of therapists who did or didn't succeed in personal therapy may aid in understanding its function in their lives. However, because time is entailed in the accumulation of outcomes, analyses are computed separately for different age groups although shown for the whole sample when results are the same across age.

24 The Chi-square values were: χ^2 = 22.5, df = 3, p =.000; N = 3,477.

25 The small number of Ceremonial Religious in this analysis limited the statistical significance.

26 The values for this 1-Way ANOVA were: F = 52.4, df = 2, 4847; P =.000.

27 The 7% gap between Wounded children who had sought personal therapy (97%) and had experienced at least one very beneficial outcome (90%) is a potential cause for worry in terms of how capable they might be of functioning effectively as therapists (see Chapter 10).

28 The Chi-square values were: χ^2 = 1577.1, df = 6, p =.000; N = 8,088.
29 The Chi-square values were: χ^2 = 60.5, df = 6, p =.000; N = 8,085.
30 Preverbal empathic resonance is the main channel of communication during the first two years of life, when the most basic lessons of human relatedness are being learned—lessons of critical survival value to the individual and the species. It is also the period of life when attachment patterns are first crystallized. This basic channel of communication by empathic resonance continues in later life as the experiential ground underlying "higher' verbal and symbolic levels of interpersonal perception and communication—a source of comfort, discomfort, intuition and "spirituality" (cf. Martin Buber, 1965, on "the Interhuman"). At a most basic level of relating, humans effectively are like *emotional tuning-forks* capable of "sympathetic vibrating" at the level of preverbal sensorimotor affect—to the extent, and in areas of experience, where developmentally later overlays of dissonant defenses, cognitive bias, or normative social expectation do not interfere.

References

Baldwin, S. & Imel, Z. I. (2012). Therapist effects: Findings and methods. In M. J. Lambert (Ed.), *Bergin & Garfield's handbook of psychotherapy and behavior change*, 5th ed. New York: Wiley.

Bennett-Levy, J., & Finlay-Jones, A. (2018). The role of personal practice in therapist skill development: a model to guide therapists, educators, supervisors and researchers. *Cognitive Behaviour Therapy*, 47, 185–205.

Bike, D. H., Norcross, J. C., & Schatz, D. M. (2009). Processes and outcomes of psychotherapists' personal therapy: Replication and extension 20 years later. *Psychotherapy*, 46, 19–31.

Buber, M. (1965). Elements of the interhuman. In M. Friedman (Ed.), *Martin Buber: The knowledge of man*, 72–88. New York: Harper & Row.

Curtis, R., Field, C., Knaan-Kostman, & Mannix, K. (2004). What 75 psychoanalysts found helpful and hurtful in their own analyses. *Psychoanalytic Psychology*, 21, 183–202.

Freud, S. (1912). Recommendations to physicians practicing psycho-analysis. In J. Strachey (Ed.), *The standard edition of the complete psychological works of Sigmund Freud*, vol. XII, 111–120. London: Hogarth Press, 1958.

Geller, J. D., Norcross, J. C., & Orlinsky, D. E. (2005). *The psychotherapist's own psychotherapy: Patient and clinician perspectives*. New York: Oxford University Press.

Orlinsky, D. E. (2014). Reasons for personal therapy given by psychoanalytically-oriented psychotherapists and their effects on personal wellbeing and professional development. *Psychoanalytic Psychology*, 30, 644–662.

Orlinsky, D. E., & Howard, K. I. (1975). *Varieties of psychotherapeutic experience: Multivariate analyses of patients' and therapists' reports*. New York: Teachers College Press.

Orlinsky, D. E., Schofield, M. J., Schröder, T., & Kazantzis, N. (2011). Utilization of personal therapy by psychotherapists: A practice-friendly review and a new study. *Journal of Clinical Psychology: In Session*, 67, 828–842.

Rønnestad, M. H., Orlinsky, D. E.; Wiseman, H. (2016). *Professional development and personal therapy*. In *APA Handbook of Clinical Psychology, Vol. 5., Education and Profession*, 223–235. Washington: American Psychological Association.

10 Psychotherapists as Persons: Doing Psychotherapy

D. E. Orlinsky with A. Hartmann, M. H. Rønnestad and U. Willutzki

Many individual variations in the personal characteristics of psychotherapists have been delineated in previous chapters, including their experiences as patients engaged in their own personal psychotherapy. In this chapter, we look at therapists as they switch chairs in the consulting room and move back to the professional chair that brought them into our study. This time, in contrast to the first chapter, therapists are viewed not just in terms of their profession and orientation but as varied and complex persons. Having explored their lives, selves, and origins as persons, it is possible to see psychotherapists as persons who, like the actors in classical Greek drama, create the parts they play behind and within the outer "mask" of their professional role. The question addressed in this chapter is how much (if at all) therapists' own personal qualities and characteristics influence how they experience their therapeutic work with patients—their confidence, effectiveness, and personal satisfaction in practicing their therapeutic role?

A first step in exploring this question requires focusing on how psychotherapists typically experience their therapeutic work. The main outline and details of this were presented previously in *How Psychotherapists Develop* (Orlinsky & Rønnestad, 2005), a study of therapeutic work that also used the Development of Psychotherapists Common Core Questionnaire (DPCCQ). Continued data collection since that earlier report has more than doubled our sample size from 4900 to over 12000, allowing for re-testing prior analyses and establishing their results on an even broader empirical base. The next section presents findings about the ways that therapists experience their therapeutic work with clients.

Experiences of Psychotherapeutic Practice

In addition to questions about individual qualities and personal backgrounds of therapists that were explored in prior chapters, other parts of the DPCCQ asked about their professional characteristics, clinical practices, and work experiences. Those parts of the DPCCQ focused in separate sections on topics such as therapists' typical treatment goals; their clinical skills for reaching those goals; their relationships with patients as role-partners in treatment; the difficulties that they encounter working with patients; the coping strategies they use when encountering difficulties; and what their own feelings are like during therapy sessions with

DOI: 10.4324/9781003217572-10

their patients. Each section included a dozen or more specific questions with rating scales or checklists used as response formats.[1] These sections, devoted to therapeutic work and professional growth, provided the empirical data analyzed in *How Psychotherapists Develop*; reanalyzed and confirmed with the now much larger data base, they form the criterion variables for the present chapter.

Method of Analysis

To derive the relevant variables empirically, data analyses were conducted successively at several levels, each building on results of the one preceding it. At the *first level*, the items were analyzed separately within each DPCCQ section that focused on a different facet of practice experience. These item analyses (e.g., means and medians, standard deviations and response ranges) represent therapists' explicit awareness of the topic in question. A *second level* of analysis examined the interrelations of items within each section using factor analysis to determine the number and nature of the dimensions underlying therapists' responses to items, and involved constructing internally consistent multi-item scales that reliably assessed these dimensions. These intra-section factor dimensions represent implicit, often not fully conscious aspects of therapists' experiences, and reduce the number of variables needed in later analyses. A *third level* of analysis included these reliable intra-section dimension scales as variables in a factor analysis across various DPCCQ sections, in order to delineate the overall dimensions of therapists' therapeutic work experience. The results of this third-level analysis presented a statistical view of the deeper structural dimensions of psychotherapeutic work experience that are presumably a further step away from therapists' direct awareness although still rooted in their specific experiences of what transpires in therapy. Finally, a *fourth level* of analysis concerns the patterns made by differential combinations of the third-level dimensions, distinguishing groups of therapists based on shared patterns of experience in therapeutic practice.

Dimensions and Patterns of Therapeutic Work Experience

Healing Involvement and Stressful Involvement

The successive analyses described above of our DPCCQ data resulted in the empirical definition of two broad (third-level) dimensions of therapeutic work experience: Healing Involvement and Stressful Involvement (see Figure 10.1). *Healing Involvement* reflects the therapist's positive sense of warm and effective engagement with clients, a high level of clinical skillfulness, an ability to take constructive measures if and when difficulties arise, and personal feelings of "Flow" or deep interest and involvement in the process.[2] The higher a therapist's Healing Involvement score, the more they experienced the professional role-ideal of helpfulness.[3]

Stressful Involvement, by contrast, reflects the therapist's disturbing sense of frequent difficulties with patients, of coping ineffectively with difficulties (e.g.,

Level-3: Therapeutic Work Experience Dimensions	Healing Involvement[1]		Stressful Involvement[1]	
Level-2: Therapy Process Facet Dimensions	.71	*Relating with Clients:* Warm/Affirming	.81	*Difficulties in Practice:* Frequent Difficulties
	.70	*Relating with Clients:* Effective	.73	*Own In-session Feelings:* Anxiety (e.g., anxious, pressured)
	.68	*Own In-session Feelings:* 'Flow' (e.g., inspired, stimulated)	.67	*Coping with Difficulties:* Avoidant Coping
	.64	*Coping with Difficulties:* Constructive Coping	.60	*Own In-session Feelings:* Boredom (e.g., bored, inattentive)
	.61	*Current Clinical Skills:* High skill level		
Level-1: DPCCQ—Therapy Process Item Scales	....		....	

[1] Numbers reflect third-level factor loadings.

Figure 10.1 Derivation of Therapeutic Work Experience Dimensions

by being critical of patients, or avoiding dealing with problems), and feeling anxiety and/or boredom during sessions. Taken together, these show the therapist under emotional pressure and failing to perform effectively. Therapists at high levels of Stressful Involvement may be at risk for burnout. The items and algorithms for computing Healing Involvement and Stressful Involvement are presented at the end of this chapter, enabling readers who wish to assess their own current therapeutic work involvements to do so.

Four Practice Patterns

Although the content of these dimensions contrast sharply with each other, the negative correlation between them is rather modest ($r = -.22$, $p = .000$). They are contrasting aspects of the therapist's work experience but not mutually exclusive (except at very high levels), and can be felt as concurrent positive and negative aspects of an overall experience. The therapist's overall practice experience is jointly defined by their respective levels of Healing Involvement and Stressful Involvement. To determine patterns that approximate the practice experience of large numbers of therapists, the score levels on each dimension (in principle, 0 to 15) were simplified to "high" or "low" and combined to make a 2x2 table defining four basic patterns of practice experience: Effective Practice, Challenging Practice, Disengaged Practice, and Distressing Practice (see Figure 10.2).[4]

Healing Involvement		Stressful Involvement		Total
		Little (≤ 4.4 on 0-15 scale)	More than a little (> 4.4 on 0-15 scale)	
Much (> 6.8 on 0-15 scale)		*Effective Practice*	*Challenging Practice*	
	n	5464	2396	7860
	%	51.9%	22.8%	74.6%
Not much (≤ 6.8 on 0-15 scale)		*Disengaged Practice*	*Distressing Practice*	
	n	1532	1139	2671
	%	14.5%	10.8%	25.4%
Total	n	6996	3535	10531
	%	66.4%	33.6%	100.0%

Figure 10.2 Therapists' Work Experience Practice Patterns

Effective Practice describes a combination of "much" Healing Involvement with "little" Stressful Involvement—a seemingly optimal pattern that included more than half (52%) of the therapists. *Challenging Practice* also involved therapists' experiences of much Healing Involvement, but combined with more than a little Stressful Involvement. This pattern included just under a fourth (23%) of the therapists, which, combined with those in an *Effective Practice*, means that three-fourths (75%) of the therapists experienced much Healing Involvement in their work with patients.[5] A pattern of *Distressing Practice* described the work of therapists who experienced "more than a little" Stressful Involvement, but (unlike those in a *Challenging Practice*) also experienced "not much" Healing Involvement. About one in nine (11%) of our therapists felt ineffective in their work with patients and instead found themselves daunted and disturbed by it.

Disengaged Practice seemed the best way to describe the situation of therapists who experienced "not much" Healing Involvement and also relatively "little" Stressful Involvement. These therapists appeared to be uninvested in, and unaffected by, their therapeutic work with patients, as if just "going through the motions". About 15% of therapists seem to experience themselves as just "doing their job" without being personally engaged.

Predictors of Therapists' Work Experience: Baseline Predictors

The quest to see whether therapists' personal characteristics and qualities intersect with, and possibly influence, their experiences in therapeutic practice needs to start with an analysis of baseline predictors, which include professional characteristics like career level, professional background and theoretical orientation. Any influence of therapists' personal characteristics would have to be shown to occur above and beyond the baseline predictors, which would also reasonably include demographic variables like therapists' age and gender.

Healing Involvement

The following baseline predictors for Healing Involvement were entered together in an Optimal Scaling Categorical Regression (CATREG) model: Practice duration (years in therapeutic practice); professional background/identity; scales of theoretical influence on current practice for Analytic/Psychodynamic, Behavioral, Cognitive, Cognitive-Behavioral, Humanistic, and Systemic orientations, as well as theoretical breadth (number of salient orientations); plus therapist gender and years of age.[6] The result shows that 21% of the variance in Healing Involvement was predicted by these baseline variables, and that all but a few of the orientation scales were statistically significant predictors (see Appendix Table 10.2).[7] The aggregate of retained theoretical orientation scales accounted for the largest share (43%) of predicted variance, followed almost equally by professional background and career level cohort (19% and 18%, respectively). Therapists' professional characteristics thus accounted for 80% of the baseline predicted variance, with the remainder accounted for by therapists' age (14%) and gender (6%).

Theoretical breadth (measured by number of salient orientations) accounted for the largest amount of variance attributable to theoretical orientations. With respect to Healing Involvement, having at least one strong theoretical commitment was clearly better than having none, and two or more was better than only one—but no specific orientation seemed significantly superior to others. The approximate parity of orientations, their superiority to lack of any theoretical commitment, and their reflection of theoretical breadth is well illustrated in Figure 10.3, drawn from a preliminary analysis that used theoretical orientation categories rather than separate orientation scales.[8]

The fact that both age and years in practice contributed independently to the baseline prediction of Healing Involvement is another interesting result, considering that the two are strongly correlated ($r = .70$). Practice duration was a somewhat stronger predictor than age, but what is interesting is the complementary quality of their association with Healing Involvement (compare Figures 10.4 and 10.5). Healing Involvement shows an early steep but negatively accelerated increase with growing years in practice, indicating that even a small amount of initial clinical experience produces a relatively large increase in experienced competence and confidence. That was succeeded by a levelling out at around 10 years and then followed by a second positively accelerated increase after 20 years in practice that suggests a sense of therapeutic mastery. On the other hand, when compared with increasing age, Healing Involvement

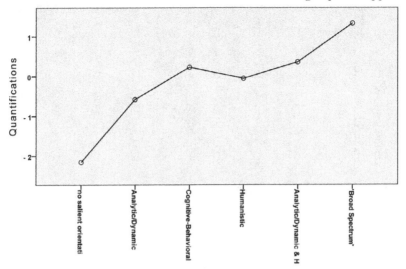

Figure 10.3 Healing Involvement by Main Theoretical Orientations

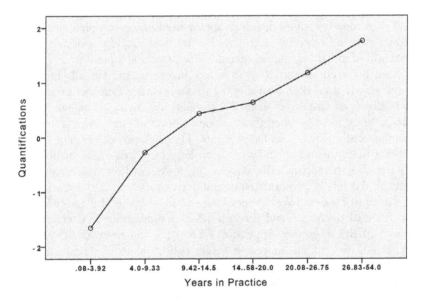

Figure 10.4 Healing Involvement by Practice Duration

shows a relatively slow start in Younger practitioners (ages 21–34) succeeded by a positively accelerated increase in early Midlife (ages 35–54) up to about age 48, after which there is a second phase of negatively accelerated or slowing increase continuing into later years.

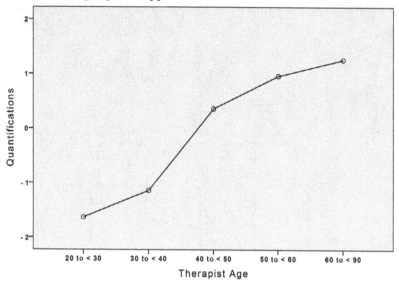

Figure 10.5 Healing Involvement by Therapist Age

Taken together, these functions appear to illustrate complementary effects of experience and maturity. Experience is relatively rapidly acquired at first as a function of initial years in practice duration, reaching a presumed "expert" level plateau between 10 and 20 years before increasing substantially but somewhat more slowly thereafter. Maturity, as an approximate function of age, accumulates slowly at first (e.g., from 20s through 40), makes a bigger impact from about 40 to mid-50s when the additional impact of experience is low, and then continues at a slowing and slower rate. Higher levels of Healing Involvement among older therapists who have been long in practice may or may not indicate greater therapeutic effectiveness, but it does at least reflect ease and assurance in the role of psychotherapist and deep satisfaction in the work of therapy.

Levels of Healing Involvement scores were compared by career level cohort, professional discipline, and theoretical orientation categories which include at least 500 therapists (see Appendix Table 10.3, top three tiers). As would be expected, each of the successive career cohorts showed a significantly higher level of Healing Involvement than its predecessors. By contrast, there were no significant differences between different professional discipline, with the exception of Psychiatrists in our sample whose scores were comparatively low.[9] As for theoretical orientations, significant differences were observed between therapists who were Uncommitted (i.e., had no salient orientation), therapists who had a single or blended orientation, and Broad Spectrum therapists (i.e., 3 + salient) orientations. Healing Involvement levels associated with the single or blended bifocal orientations were basically the same, except for mono-focal Analytic/Psychodynamic therapists at a slightly but significantly lower level.

Within each age group, women experienced significantly higher levels of Healing Involvement than their male colleagues (see Appendix Table 10.3, bottom tier). The least Healing Involvement, on average, was felt by Younger men (ages 21 to 34), and the most by Older women (ages 55 to 85). Midlife men (ages 35 to 54) had about the same scores as Younger women, and Older men had about the same scores as Midlife women. Only the difference between Older men and Older women was no longer statistically significant.

Stressful Involvement

The prediction of Stressful Involvement using only the baseline variables accounted for just a disappointing 7% of the total variance, in contrast to the 21% predicted for Healing Involvement.[10] Another contrast was that personal demographics accounted for nearly half (49%) of Stressful Involvement, with therapist age being by far the strongest individual predictor (see Appendix Table 10.4). Among the professional characteristics that proved significant predictors were: practice duration (years in therapeutic practice); professional discipline; Analytic/Psychodynamic influence on clinical practice; and theoretical breadth (i.e., number of salient orientations).

Both therapist age and practice duration stood out as predictors of Stressful Involvement, as illustrated in Figures 10.6 and 10.7. While practice duration

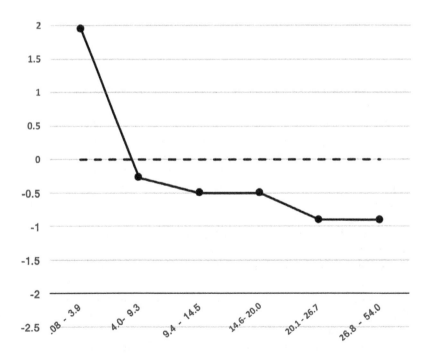

Figure 10.6 Stressful Involvement by Practice Duration

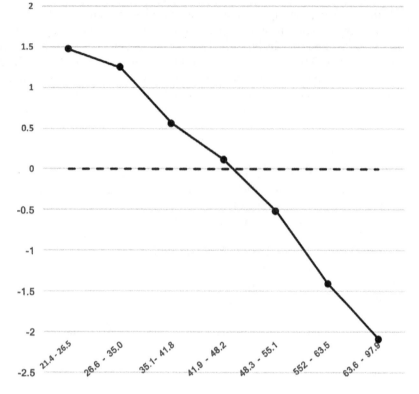

Figure 10.7 Stressful Involvement by Therapist Age

was the stronger predictor of the two in regard to Healing Involvement, therapist age is four times stronger than practice duration in accounting for Stressful Involvement, but the shape of the curves is very different too. Stressful Involvement is highest among younger therapists (e.g., in their 20s) and diminishes in a linear fashion with increasing age. Stressful Involvement is highest among new therapists (e.g., in their first three years of practice) and then declines precipitously with increasing experience. One implication is that therapists who begin training and practice somewhat later in life may be less susceptible than young trainees to experiencing high levels of Stressful Involvement.

Professional characteristics (career level cohort, professional background, and theoretical orientation) jointly predicted about half (51%) of the explained variance in Stressful Involvement, which still was much less than the 80% they accounted for in Healing Involvement.

Differences in Stressful Involvement between career level cohorts reflect what has already been noted, showing Apprentice therapists (>0 to 3 years practice) highest and both Established and Senior therapists statistically tied in experiencing the least (see Appendix Table 10.5, top three tiers). Differences between professions again showed Psychiatrists at a disadvantage with the highest level of Stressful Involvement, and Counselors and Lay Therapist/ Analysts statistically tied at the lowest levels—which may partly reflect the fact that the latter were significantly older than other groups (49 years old on average, as compared to 43 years old for Psychiatrists). Differences between theoretical orientations showed that "uncommitted" therapists (having no salient orientation) experienced the most Stressful Involvement and least Healing Involvement, while the opposite was true for those with a Broad Spectrum orientation (practice influenced by 3+ salient orientations).[11] Given the small role of theoretical orientations in predicting Stressful Involvement, it may not be necessary to search further for explanations.

Therapist gender was a relatively weak although statistically significant predictor of Stressful Involvement (5% variance), as it was of Healing Involvement (6% variance), but in both cases women therapists were consistently favored over their male colleagues. Women had higher scores on Healing Involvement and lower scores on Stressful Involvement. In terms of age and gender combinations, Older women experienced the least Stressful Involvement; Midlife women and Older men were next higher; Midlife men had still higher scores; while Younger men and Younger women both experienced the highest levels of Stressful Involvement (see Appendix Table 10.5, bottom tier). The only consolation worth offering in this regard is that "Things get better" for both genders—although more quickly for women than for men.

Predictors of Therapeutic Work Experience: Personal Characteristics

Having identified the relative influence of these baseline predictors, the more important question concerns which (if any) of the personal qualities and characteristics of psychotherapists studied in previous chapters additionally predict the work experience of those therapists? How much, cumulatively, do they aid in understanding psychotherapy as a professional practice that is conducted by diverse and at times dissimilar kinds of persons? Each personal aspect will be considered in turn.

Personal Self

The amount of variance predicted in Healing Involvement increased rather substantially from 21% to 38% by the inclusion of therapists' *personal self* dimensions along with the established baseline (see Appendix Table 10.6, top tier). Genial/Caring and Ardent/Expressive together accounted for two-thirds of the predicted variance, with Genial/Caring twice as potent and by far the most important in the whole set of predictors. Healing Involvement increased in a linear fashion at increasing levels of both dimensions.

The amount of variance predicted in Stressful Involvement also increased with the inclusion of therapists' *personal self* (from 7% to 14%) but through the involvement of different dimensions (see Appendix Table 10.6, bottom tier). Being Reclusive/Remote in close personal relationships was by far the strongest predictor of experiencing therapeutic work as a Stressful Involvement. Smaller amounts of variance were predicted by being Forceful/Exacting in personal relationships (intensifying) and being Genial/Caring (minimizing). The relation of Stressful Involvement to Reclusive/Remote and Forceful/Exacting were approximately linear (i.e., the more Reclusive and the more Forceful in close relationships, the higher the level of Stressful Involvement in doing therapy). By contrast, Genial/Caring showed a gently curving, positively accelerating increase indicating that increments from high to higher levels had greater impact in helping to minimize Stressful Involvement.

Adding the *personal self* dimensions as predictors to the categorical regression led to excluding gender as a baseline predictor for both Healing Involvement and Stressful Involvement, which suggests that the apparent difference between male and female therapists may be attributable to average differences in *personal self* rather than gender *per se*. On the other hand, practice duration and professional discipline remained as significant predictors, with newer therapists and Psychiatrists faring relatively poorly. Another continuing baseline predictor of Stressful Involvement was having a strongly Analytic/Psychodynamic orientation. Based on correlations computed separately for each profession, this seems largely due to the reactions of Counselors in the database, who were consistently the least inclined of professions to be analytically oriented (shown in Appendix Table 2.1). Interestingly, being analytically oriented had a relatively protective effect for Psychiatrists with respect to Stressful Involvement.

Analysis of therapists' work practice patterns also shows the impact of their leading predictors on Healing Involvement and Stressful Involvement (see Appendix Table 10.7). In terms of Genial/Caring, two-thirds (68%) of the therapists highest ("devoted") on that dimension were significantly more likely to be in an Effective Practice, and least likely to be in a Distressing Practice (4%) or a Disengaged Practice (5%). By contrast, only one-third (34%) of those at the lowest (merely "sympathetic") level of Genial/Caring in close relationships were experiencing an Effective Practice, and they were most likely to be in a Distressing Practice (21%) or a Disengaged Practice (25%). Adding Effective Practice and Challenging Practice together, almost all (91%) of personally "devoted" therapists but only 55% of the "sympathetic" felt they were helping their patients. Likewise, therapists who were least Reclusive/Remote (i.e., "approachable") in close relationships were more likely to be in an Effective Practice (65%) and least likely to be in a Distressing Practice (5% compared with 18% among the "wary" or most Reclusive/Remote). From all angles, the therapists who experienced the most Healing Involvement and least Stressful Involvement in their therapeutic work were those whose self-experience personally was most Genial/Caring and least Reclusive/Remote.

Private Life

Healing Involvement was not significantly predicted either by the therapists' marital status or parental status, whether tested separately or combined with the therapist's gender. Similarly, neither Anxious Attachment nor Avoidant Attachment were significant predictors beyond the *personal self* dimensions and baseline variables in the smaller sample (about 1250 therapists) for whom relevant data were available.

Differences in relationship status and parental status also were not significant as predictors of Stressful Involvement, but the two attachment dimensions added substantially to the variance accounted for by *personal self* and the baseline measures, raising the amount of variance predicted to a total 24%, as compared with 14% in the preceding model (see Appendix Table 10.8). Anxious attachment and a Reclusive/Remote *personal self* were the strongest predictors, but Avoidant Attachment was also a strong predictor independently of Reclusive/Remote (despite their positive correlation with one another: $r = .34$, $p = .000$, $n = 1,235$).

In this iteration of the Categorical Regression, Avoidant Attachment took over about half the variance previously accounted for by Reclusive/Remote but did not wholly replace it, showing that they are distinct though related concepts. Both Forceful/Exacting and Genial/Caring remained as significant predictors of Stressful Involvement, the former increasing it and the latter counteracting it. Professional discipline also remained a predictor, showing Psychiatrists and Psychologists both at relatively high levels. However, the inclusion of the attachment dimensions resulted in eliminating practice duration, Analytic/Dynamic orientation, and therapist age *per se* as sources of significant variance. Stressful Involvement emerged from this analysis as more reflective of therapist personality traits.

Considering therapists' work practice patterns, the impact of Anxious Attachment and Avoidant Attachment was virtually the same, reflecting their relatively strong correlation to each other ($r = .48$, $p = .000$). The best interpretation of the findings is to recall that low scores on both reflects a Secure Attachment. Thus it is understandable that the large majority (69%) of the therapists who were low on both Anxious Attachment and Avoidant attachment experienced their therapeutic work as an Effective Practice, as compared to little more than half (53%) of those with moderate to high scores (see Appendix Table 10.9). By contrast, therapists with moderate to high scores on the Anxious and Avoidant attachment were significantly more often in a Challenging Practice, at about three times the frequency of Securely attached therapists. Reassuringly, most therapists showed a good capacity to form Secure attachments: 70% low Anxious Attachment; 78% low Avoidant Attachment.

Individual Beliefs

Exploration of therapists' beliefs involved measures of their current religiosity, spirituality, and the belief-value orientations based on them, as well as therapists' religious backgrounds and current affiliations. Their further exploration here concerns whether and how any of those are associated with their experiences of therapeutic work.

Therapists' belief-value orientations, as categorical variables, are best compared to the categories of work involvement patterns. Among those, a significantly higher percentage of therapists with a Spiritual Secular orientation, and a significantly low proportion of Ethical Secular therapists experienced an Effective Practice (69% vs. 59%) (see Appendix Table 10.10). The same two belief-value orientations contrasted in the less favorable practice patterns: Ethical Secular therapists were significantly more often in a Disengaged Practice (15% vs. 9%), and also were significantly more often in a Distressing Practice (8% vs. 3%). No significant differences were found for Spiritual Religious and Ceremonial Religious therapists, highlighting the impact of therapist spirituality among secular therapists.

This was also reflected in the fact that neither Healing Involvement nor Stressful Involvement were correlated with therapists' current religiosity, while spirituality did have a small positive association with Healing Involvement ($r =.16$, $p =.000$, $n = 3,412$) and a slight negative association with Stressful Involvement ($r = -.08$, $p =.000$).[12] These findings suggest a limited protective value for spirituality, but not one strong enough to meet the inclusion criterion in predicting Healing Involvement or Stressful Involvement.

There was no significant differentiation between therapists of various family religious backgrounds. In regard to current religious affiliations, differences were significant overall (results of a 1-way ANOVA: $F = 11.6$, $df = 5, 4004$; $p =.000$) but with substantial overlap between groups. Curiously, therapists from Jewish backgrounds had the highest scores on Healing Involvement as well as the highest scores on Stressful Involvement, although not significantly higher than the large group of therapists who had no religious affiliation. Accordingly, they were somewhat but significantly more likely than average to experience a Challenging Practice (27% vs. 20%), and less likely than average to experience a Disengaged Practice (6% vs. 11%).[13]

Quality of Life

The total prediction of Healing Involvement was increased to a small but significant extent (from 37.7% to 39.4%) by the inclusion of Personal Life Satisfactions, but not Life Burdens (see Appendix Table 10.11, upper tier). The Genial/Caring and Ardent/Expressive dimensions of *personal self* were still the strongest predictors, but Personal Life Satisfactions was close behind. Therapists who were more self-bestowing, self-expressive and fulfilled in their personal relationships were also the ones more likely to experience their therapeutic work as Healing Involvement.

The total prediction of Stressful Involvement was also increased to a small but significant extent (from 13.7% to 19.4%) but this time by Personal Life Burdens rather than Personal Life Satisfactions (see Appendix Table 10.11, lower tier). In this iteration, Personal Life Burdens also became the single strongest predictor of Stressful Involvement (in the full sample, without attachment data), displacing but not eliminating the Reclusive/Remote aspect of *personal self*. Therapists who were heavily burdened in private life, especially if personally Reclusive/Remote and young, were those most likely to experience therapeutic work as a Stressful Involvement. Being older and personally

Genial/Caring were mitigating factors. Using the smaller sample that also contained attachment data led to a modified result: Personal Life Burdens (but not Life Satisfactions) still added significantly to the prediction, with the total rising from 23.5% to 25.5%, but Anxious Attachment and Avoidant Attachment together yielded the strongest prediction (35% of predicted variance), with similar weight for Reclusive/Remote and Personal Life Burdens added together (see Appendix Table 10.12).

The impact of therapists' life quality patterns on their work practice experience can be seen in the significantly higher levels of Effective Practice among therapists whose lives are Fulfilling (62%) or Satisfactory (57%), as compared to the significantly lower levels (39%) among those who found their private lives Dull, Strained or Distressed (see Appendix Table 10.13). The therapists whose lives felt Dull, Strained or Distressed were significantly more likely to experience their therapeutic work as Distressing (18% to 20%), in contrast to therapists who felt their lives Fulfilled or Satisfying (6% or 7%). Therapists whose personal life was Hectic (high in both stress and satisfaction) were overrepresented among those in a Challenging Practice (33%), but underrepresented among those in a Distressing or Disengaged Practice (8% and 7%).

Surprisingly, therapists whose personal lives just seemed Dull, without much satisfaction or even a moderate level of stress, experienced as much or more Disengaged Practice and Distressing Practice as did Strained or actively Distressed therapists. Evidently having a life of limited personal satisfaction is not a good foundation for helping others.

Family Structure and Background

Healing Involvement was not significantly associated with any structural aspects of therapists' childhood families: neither family size nor birth order; neither parental divorce, parental death, nor therapists' age when family disruption occurred (if it did). Their childhood family's economic and religious background also did not add meaningfully to the set of previously established predictors. Stressful Involvement was also unrelated to these structural and background facets of therapists' families. Whatever other effects they may have on therapists' lives, they clearly made no difference regarding how therapists experienced their work with patients.

Childhood Family Experience

Given the significant associations of therapists' childhood family experiences with *personal self*, and given the strong connection of *personal self* with therapists' experiences of therapeutic work, it would seem that childhood family experiences might relate strongly to therapeutic work. There was apparently no direct association; a result with potentially interesting implications.

Healing Involvement was unrelated to the emotional and psychological functioning of therapists' childhood families, and to the level of care and support they received as children. However, there was a small but significant *positive* correlation (r =.15, p =.000) between Healing Involvement and levels of trauma and abuse that therapists' experienced in childhood, indicating a modest (and surprising) tendency for therapists with distressed childhoods to experience more Healing Involvement in their work as adults. That association was not strong enough to add meaningfully to the overall prediction of Healing Involvement, but it did show up when comparing levels of Healing Involvement by childhood experience patterns. Therapists who were Rescued as children experienced the highest level of Healing Involvement in doing therapy as adults, significantly higher than therapists who had just Survived, or had been Nurtured or Neglected (see Appendix Table 10.14, upper tier). Wounded therapists in turn were significantly higher than those who had just Survived or were Neglected, and the lowest level of Healing Involvement occurred for therapists who had been Neglected as children.

Stressful Involvement also was unrelated directly to family functioning and levels of care and support in childhood, and levels of trauma and abuse as well. Differences between childhood experience patterns were significant overall but not significantly differentiated among themselves (see Appendix Table 10.14, lower tier) although descriptively, therapists who were Rescued as children, and those who were Neglected, seemed to experience less Stressful Involvement than those who were Nurtured or had just Survived through childhood.

Differences in work practice patterns between therapists with various childhood experience patterns were significant overall, but with very few significant specific associations. Interestingly, therapists who had been Neglected as children were significantly more likely than average to experience therapeutic work as a Disengaged Practice, mirroring their low level of Healing Involvement and relatively low level of Stressful Involvement (see Appendix Table 10.15). Descriptively, the lowest rate of Effective Practice (56%), and a significantly higher rate of Distressing Practice (10%) was experienced by therapists who just Survived childhood, while the highest rates of Effective Practice (at 68% and 66% respectively) were experienced by therapists who had been Rescued as children (i.e., seriously harmed, but also finding love and support) and by those who were Wounded (i.e., harmed but with no corrective childhood care)—which suggests that therapists apparently disadvantaged as children managed to overcome their handicaps.

Personal Therapy

The psychotherapists' own personal therapy is one of the ways that they can come to terms with their past. Clearly they often engaged in this option, and the evidence to follow shows its effectiveness. Differences in Healing Involvement clearly reflected their utilization of and outcomes in their personal therapy.[14] The 20% of therapists who missed having personal therapy on average showed the least Healing Involvement, significantly less than those with one course of therapy, who in turn showed less than those with two or more personal therapies (see Appendix Table 10.16, upper tier). The same progression was observed in terms of personal outcomes: those who were in therapy but had no more than moderate benefit showed the least Healing Involvement, those with one excellent outcome showed significantly more, and those with two or more excellent outcomes had the highest average level of Healing Involvement (see Appendix Table 10.16, lower tier). However, neither utilization nor personal therapy outcomes added significantly to the set of predictors for Healing Involvement. Presumably their observed links to Healing Involvement were indirect, especially through the impact of therapy on Ardent/Expressive and Genial/Caring dimensions of *personal self*, as well as on Personal Life Satisfactions, and the important contribution of those in the prediction of Healing Involvement.

Therapy utilization and personal outcomes were also not significant predictors for Stressful Involvement. Their impact on Stressful Involvement was also slighter than on Healing Involvement. Therapists who were never in personal therapy experienced significantly higher levels of Stressful Involvement on average than those who had personal therapy, but the number of times in therapy did not further differentiate among the latter (see Appendix Table 10.17, upper tier). By contrast, therapists who experienced two or more excellent outcomes experienced significantly less Stressful Involvement in doing therapy. Evidently it takes more successful personal therapy to lower Stressful Involvement than it does to raise Healing Involvement.

In terms of work practice patterns, a majority (58%) and significantly high proportion of therapists who experienced two or more excellent outcomes in personal therapy had an Effective Practice, and significantly lower proportions (11% and 7%) of Disengaged or Distressing Practice (see Appendix Table 10.18). By contrast, therapists who had never engaged in personal therapy were significantly lowest in Effective Practice and Challenging Practice (45% and 21%), and significantly highest in rates of Disengaged and Distressing Practice (17% each). Additionally, majorities of Effective Practice were found only among therapists who had at least one excellent personal outcome.

Notably, the impact of personal therapy on work practice patterns varied among therapists with different patterns of childhood experience. Among *Wounded* therapists, 70% of those with two or more excellent outcomes, and 60% of those with one, were in an Effective Practice, in contrast to 53% of those with no excellent outcome, the latter being also twice as often as others in a Disengaged Practice (20% vs. 10%). Among *Rescued* therapists, 73% of those with two or more excellent outcomes, and 69% of those with one, were in an Effective Practice, in contrast with 63% of those with no excellent outcome; few (8%) were in a Disengaged Practice, and virtually none (2 of 189) were in a Distressing Practice. Among *Nurtured* therapists, 67% of those with two or more excellent outcomes, and 62% of those with one, were in an Effective Practice, in contrast with 53% of those with no excellent outcome. In contrast to the Wounded, Rescued and Nurtured, 62% of *Neglected* therapists experienced an Effective Practice but unrelated to personal therapy outcome.

Those *Neglected* therapists may have found sources of nurture elsewhere in their lives, but nearly a quarter (22%) of those who had no excellent personal outcome were in that curious category of Disengaged Practice. Finally, 57% of those who *Survived* childhood experienced an Effective Practice, with a minor (statistically non-significant) impact of therapy: 53% of those with no excellent outcome had an Effective Practice, as compared with 58% of those with one or more.

Therapist "Healer" Types

The results of this study, from first chapter to last, amply demonstrate that therapists vary considerably among themselves both in their professional and personal characteristics. In fact, the results described thus far seem to suggest an empirically-based typology of different sorts of "healers" among psychotherapists. These types are distinctive patterns that reflect what is personally motivating and emotionally meaningful to therapists as reflected in their mode of involvement in therapeutic work. The types are conceptualized as *experiential dynamisms* not as categories of persons; so it is possible that a therapist may evolve in "healer" type over time (e.g., as they gain more clinical experience, or as a result of successful personal therapy). At any time, most therapists may be characterized as predominantly in one or another of the following four "healer" types.

Wounded Healers

Perhaps the most venerable, mythic image[15] that is sometimes applied to psychotherapists is that of the "Wounded Healer". Are Wounded Healers to be found among the large number of therapists in our study, and if so how do they qualify for that portrayal? In our study, both the Wounded and the Rescued children had experienced high levels of trauma or abuse in childhood, and both clearly qualify for the traditional sobriquet of "wounded healer"—healers who became such after they themselves were healed sufficiently from their own wounds. As just seen, they engaged extensively in personal therapy, benefited substantially from it, and also attained the highest levels of Effective Practice.

As persons, therapists who were Rescued or Wounded in childhood were also significantly highest in levels of spirituality, and the Rescued were highest in religiosity. Significantly more Wounded children had a Spiritual Secular belief-value orientation, and significantly fewer had an Ethical Secular pattern. Significantly fewer of the Rescued children also had an Ethical Secular orientation, and most were about evenly divided between Spiritual Religious and Spiritual Secular. They differed in this respect from therapists who had been Nurtured, Neglected or just Survived, among whom the largest pluralities had Ethical Secular orientations.

By profession, a strikingly large majority (71%) of Wounded children in our sample became psychotherapists by training as Counselors (56%)[16] or as Lay

Therapists/Analysts (15%)—rather than through academic training in Psychology or Psychiatry. A majority of the Rescued were also Counselors (50%) or Lay Therapists/Analysts (10%). Their taking a relatively nontraditional path of entry to therapeutic practice was complemented by a tendency to avoid a narrowly traditional theoretical identification: about a third of the Rescued and Wounded had a Broad Spectrum approach to treating patients, drawing saliently on the concepts and methods of three or more orientations.

Overall, the "Wounded Therapists" in our study—those who were *Wounded* or *Rescued* as children and largely overcame their pasts—comprise a minority of only 18%, and thus are not typical of most psychotherapists.

Normal Caring Healers

A much larger group of therapists is the 55% majority who had a Nurtured childhood experience, and who may be called "Normal Caring Healers" both for their culturally normative childhood, their large numbers, and the importance of Genial/Caring (self-bestowal) as a source of motivation.[17] The following is a brief sketch of characteristics that tend to differentiate them.

By professional background, Normal Caring Healers became psychotherapists significantly more often than expected through primary training in the traditional academic/medical disciplines of Psychology and Psychiatry. A large plurality (46%) of these Nurtured children were Psychologists or Psychiatrists, as compared with only 26% of Wounded children and 34% of Rescued children. In terms of theoretical approach to practice, significantly more than expected (16%) had a Cognitive-Behavioral orientation, although numerically more were Broad Spectrum (30%) or mono-focal Analytic/Psychodynamic (24%) in approach. Being most numerous, they anchored the sample average in their work practice patterns: 61% Effective Practice and 19% Challenging Practice (i.e., 80% high Healing Involvement), with 13% in a Disengaged Practice and 7% in a Distressing Practice.

As persons in close relationships, Normal Caring Healers were significantly more Genial/Caring (self-bestowing), less Ardent/Expressive (self-expressive), and of all groups least Forceful/Exacting (self-assertive). In attachment pattern, they were significantly lowest on Anxious Attachment and among the lowest on Avoidant Attachment, indicating they generally formed Secure attachments. Likely reflecting that, they also were significantly more often married, and significantly less often divorced or separated. They had a significantly high level of Personal Life Satisfactions and significantly lowest level of Personal Life Burdens. Accordingly, they were significantly highest of all in enjoying a Fulfilling quality of life, and significantly lowest in having a Strained or Distressed quality of life. Ideologically, they were significantly least likely of all groups to have a Spiritual Secular belief-value orientation; and, although significantly more likely than others to be in the small group of Ceremonial Religious, numerically their largest group (42%) was Ethical Secular. It appears that this most common type of therapist, who can well be described as Normal Caring, are themselves mainly normal individuals trained in more traditional, prestigious helping professions, leading successful and basically happy private lives. Their motivation as therapists to be psychological healers may not draw from deep sources of redeemed personal trauma, as among the Wounded Healers. Instead, the motivation of these therapists as Normal Caring Healers probably draws on their own extensive experience as participants in and beneficiaries of past and present caring and nurturing relationships that foster personal development (Nissen-Lie & Orlinsky, 2014), build a deep attitude of self-bestowal toward cared-for others in return, and create a strong sense of positive morale able to be put in service to the typically "demoralized" patients who come for therapy (Frank, 1974).

Both Wounded Healers and Normal Caring Healers were mostly in an Effective Practice or a Challenging Practice, and were (by definition) experiencing high levels of Healing Involvement in their therapeutic work. Overall, about three-quarters (75%) of therapists were in those two work practice pattern groups. However, the remaining minority who were not in those groups represent an uncomfortable number of psychotherapists who were *not* experiencing much Healing Involvement when working with patients. Those therapists in a Disengaged Practice and in a Distressing Practice were previously identified and discussed in a chapter on the clinical implication of results that concluded the first book on this study (Rønnestad & Orlinsky, 2005). There the context was mainly professional and the focus was how to help those therapists. Here we can briefly add some of the personal characteristics associated with those therapists who were disengaged or distressed by doing therapy.

Indifferent Healers

Normal Caring Healers and Wounded Healers together accounted for nearly three-fourths (73%) of the therapists in our study, but what of the remaining fourth (27%)? Some likely were those who experienced their therapeutic work as a Disengaged Practice, with relatively low levels both of Healing Involvement and Stressful Involvement. That group comprised about 15% of the 10,531 therapists for whom data were available, and might conceivably be described as Indifferent Healers in the sense that they practiced psychotherapy—not necessarily without success—but apparently without much inner involvement in the process. Certainly, sufficiently well-motivated patients are able to benefit from having therapy with those therapists (cf. Orlinsky, Rønnestad & Willutzki, 2004) if the therapist does little to undermine their patients' progress, whether by emotionally tone-deaf responses that distract the patient or by unconscious counter-transference that distorts the relationship. However, with patients who aren't well-motivated, these Indifferent Healers might not be able to engage them, possibly increasing the chance of the patient "dropping out" or else remaining in a dull de-energized relationship that seems to "go nowhere".[18]

Professionally, therapists who were Indifferent Healers were significantly more likely to have entered the field through training in medicine and Psychiatry (23%)[19] and either to have no salient theoretical orientation (28%) or a mono-focal Analytic/Psychodynamic orientation (20%).[20] Individually, they were significantly more often Younger men (23%) and Midlife men (17%), although the gender disparity had disappeared among Older therapists.[21] Personally, Indifferent Healers were significantly less Genial/Caring and less Ardent/Expressive in their close relationships (in both cases, second lowest to Distressed therapists); significantly more Reclusive/Remote than those in Effective Practice (but less than those in Distressing Practice); and least Forceful/Exacting.[22] Indifferent Healers were moderately secure in attachment style, being second lowest on both Anxious and Avoidant Attachment after those in Effective Practice. They were significantly more likely than average to have an Ethical Secular orientation, and least likely of all groups to be Spiritual Secular.[23] They had a relatively low level of Personal Life Satisfactions, the lowest level of Personal Life Burdens, and accordingly were significantly more likely (25%) to have a Dull or limited quality of life.[24] They were moderately but significantly more likely than average (17%) to have experienced a Neglected childhood.[25] All in all, Indifferent Healers seemed reasonably normal but emotionally constricted as persons: having started life with less; giving and receiving less in adult life; and as therapists, probably being able to offer less of themselves to motivate their patients.

Troubled Healers

A small group, comprising about 11% of our therapists, experienced their therapeutic work as a Distressing Practice, an ordeal that was difficult and disturbing for them. It seems reasonable to describe this group as Troubled Healers, despite its sounding (and perhaps too often being) something of a contradiction. Troubled Healers suffered a high level of Stressful Involvement, which was defined by frequent difficulties in practice; non- and perhaps antitherapeutic attempts to cope with their difficulties by criticizing or rejecting patients, or helplessly hoping the difficulties will pass; and were therapist's with feelings of anxiety and boredom during treatment sessions.

Professionally, these Troubled Healers most often (23%) had no salient theoretical orientation to practice, which likely left them without clear guidance about how to respond to patients. A significantly higher proportion (30%) were still Apprentices with less than three years in practice. Very many (44%) were Psychiatrists in their Apprentice years, but this percentage dropped rapidly with clinical experience to 20% among Graduates, 15% among Established practitioners, and 10% among Senior therapists (a progression *not* seen among Disengaged therapists).

As individuals, Troubled Healers were especially Younger men (28%) and to a lesser extent Midlife men (13%), but *not* Older men (only 5%). Younger women (16%) were also at a significantly higher risk of Distressing Practice, emphasizing the vulnerability of young practitioners. Personally, they were the least Genial/Caring, least Ardent/Expressive, and most Reclusive/Remote of all in their close relationships. They were also the most insecurely attached group, having the significantly highest levels on measures of Anxious Attachment and Avoidant Attachment. One is forced to ask how these persons were accepted and retained in psychotherapy training programs.

A small but significantly higher than expected proportion (10%) of Troubled Healers had just Survived in childhood, and almost none (3 of 233) had been Rescued. As adults, Troubled Healers had the significantly least amount of Personal Life Satisfactions and a significantly high level of Personal Burdens, making a majority (57%) among them in one or another of the low life quality groups: Dull (16%), Strained (19%), or Distressed (22%). Only a fourth (24%) had Fulfilling or Satisfactory quality of life—yet, more than any other group, a third (32%) had never been in personal therapy, or were in personal therapy only for the first time (9%); and among those who did have therapy, significantly more (20%) experienced no great personal benefit.

It is understandable that therapists with these characteristics would find their therapeutic work to be a Distressing Practice. As noted some time ago, "Practitioners in this state are at risk of being harmed by their practice and of being potentially harmful to their patients" (Rønnestad & Orlinsky, 2005). Where possible, prior assessment of some of the characteristics related to trainee personality (e.g., attachment measures, low scores on Genial/Caring and Ardent/Expressive, high Reclusive/Remote) might be part of the screening process used by training programs when selecting candidates. Another selection criterion might be seeking older candidates, especially in regard to male trainees, if this can be done without violating laws on age and gender discrimination. For those already trained and in practice, the best that can be done is probably applying the greatest range of available resources to enhance their work morale: practice-focused, theory-based training to increase clinical skills; caseload adjustment to increase the likelihood of experiencing Healing Involvement; sharing of distressing experience in a supportive peer-group setting; constructive supervisory input; effective personal therapy. If all else fails, the seriously Troubled Healer might be counseled to consider a different career alternative.

In sum, there appears to be a sound empirical basis for differentiating four "Healer Types" among the Psychotherapists we have studied: *first*, Normal Caring Healers (55%) who function as therapists with an abundance of goodwill (Genial/Caring, self-bestowal) and optimism based on their own life experience, so that they are willing and able to invest in helping others; *second*, Wounded Healers (18%) who function as therapists with a sense of dedication to repairing the hurt and harms suffered by others, based on their having suffered and overcome hurt and harm in their own lives; *third*, Indifferent Healers (15%) who have become psychotherapists through specialization in one of the traditional academic professions, who are approximately normal but emotionally limited persons, and who practice their profession without much inner involvement (as a "job" not a "calling"); and *fourth*, Troubled Healers (11%)

some of whom are beginners (especially men) who need a lot of support and constructive supervision, and may with tutoring and positive clinical work, come to experience fewer difficulties and less emotional stress, along with some who probably should have not become psychotherapists, both for their own and their patients' sake.[26]

Additional Predictors of Therapeutic Work Involvement

This book has explored many personal qualities and characteristics of psychotherapists, and in this chapter has focused on links between therapists as persons and their experiences as professionals working with patients in psychotherapy. Therapists' personal characteristics and qualities were employed to predict—with reasonable success[27]—the extent to which therapeutic work was experienced as a Healing Involvement and a Stressful Involvement. It is worth noting, however, that other aspects of the therapeutic situation also contribute to predicting Healing Involvement and Stressful Involvement, and help to further explain factors that influence therapists' experiences of therapy. Aspects of the practice setting in which therapists work can be counted among those additional factors: the *social support* that therapists have in those settings; their *professional autonomy* in managing treatment parameters (e.g., number and choice of patients, theoretical orientation, treatment schedule and duration); and positive and negative aspect of therapist's *work morale*. Positive work morale has been previously assessed (Orlinsky & Rønnestad, 2005, chap. 8) through development of a reliable scale called Currently Experienced Growth, reflecting deepened understanding of psychotherapy, increased enthusiasm for doing therapy, a sense of overcoming past limitations, and becoming more skillful in practice. Negative work morale was reliably assessed by a scale of Currently Experienced Depletion, reflecting the therapists' sense of growing doubt about the effectiveness of therapy, losing the capacity to respond empathically, performing in a routinized way, and becoming impaired as a therapist. Adding the variables of social support, professional autonomy, and work morale to the predictors of Healing Involvement and Stressful Involvement significantly expanded the amount of variance accounted for in each.

The prediction Healing Involvement increased to a total variance of nearly 48% with the consideration of contextual factors (see Appendix Table 10.19, upper tier). Importantly, the largest portion of predicted variance (53.2%, equal to 25.5% of the total variance) was still defined by therapists' personal characteristics, especially being Genial/Caring (self-bestowing) in close personal relationships. Therapists' professional characteristics (professional discipline, career level, and theoretical breadth) together accounted for another 21.5% of predicted variance (equal 10.4% of total variance) in Healing Involvement. The work setting conditions of social support, professional autonomy, and positive work morale together contributed 25.4% of the predicted variance (equal to 12.2% of total variance), with positive morale as a particularly important contributor, second only to experiencing oneself as Genial/Caring.

The prediction of Stressful Involvement is even more enhanced by the inclusion of work setting variables, raising the amount of total variance predicted from 25% to 33% (see Appendix Table 10.19, lower tier). The inclusion of work setting variables made therapists' professional characteristics (professional discipline, theoretical orientation) redundant, as were both measures of insecure attachment. In addition to the major impact of negative work morale (17.4% of the total variance), and the moderating effects of professional autonomy and Healing Involvement, two therapists' personal characteristics still fostered Stressful Involvement: Personal Life Burdens, and being Reclusive/Remote in close personal relationships, together accounting for 33.9% of the predicted variance. Among the work setting factors, lack of professional autonomy and the inability to experience Healing Involvement each promoted Stressful Involvement. But therapists' negative work morale, reflected in their Currently Experienced Depletion, was a huge factor, accounting by itself for more than half (52.5%) the predicted variance.

The hopeful implication of this analysis is that much can be done to alleviate Stressful Involvement by modifying adverse work setting conditions, which are not part of who the therapist is, personally or professionally. Expanding a therapist's professional autonomy in controlling treatment parameters could help, as would enhancing the likelihood of experiencing Healing Involvement by selecting cases within the therapist's clinical competence. However, by far the greatest effect in reducing Stressful Involvement would come from improvement of the therapists' work morale. Helping young, overwhelmed or bewildered therapists to discover—and older but exhausted therapists to rediscover—a sense of inspiration regarding the beneficial impact of therapeutic work, for their patients and for therapists themselves, should be an urgent task and principal responsibility, not just for individual supervisors but for the psychotherapeutic community itself (e.g., via training workshops and mutually supportive professional meetings).

In Sum

Psychotherapists experience the conduct of their therapeutic work with patients, to varying degrees, both as a Healing Involvement and as a Stressful Involvement. For the most part, the therapists we studied experienced much Healing Involvement: for half of them with little Stressful Involvement (in an Effective Practice), and for a fourth with more than a little Stressful Involvement (in a Challenging Practice). Less favorably, nearly one in seven therapists experienced both little Stressful Involvement and not much Healing Involvement (in a Disengaged Practice), and about one in nine experienced more than a little Stressful Involvement as well as not much Healing Involvement (in a Distressing Practice). The figures presented and the concepts they represent reflect the psychotherapists' perspective on their therapeutic practice, and of course how much the therapist's perspective converges with the observational perspectives of patients, supervisors, and researchers is a highly important topic that urgently needs to be studied (see Chapter 11). Nevertheless, psychotherapists themselves are a distinctive and essential component of psychotherapy,[28] and their perspective on therapeutic work has its own interest and value.

The leading exemplars of Healing Involvement were therapists who experienced themselves as Genial/Caring and Ardent/Expressive in their close relationships (self-bestowing and self-expressive aspects of *personal self*), and who had a comparative abundance of Personal Life Satisfactions. The leading exemplars of Stressful Involvement were therapists who experienced themselves as Reclusive/Remote (self-protective) even in close relationships, who had insecure (Anxious or Avoidant) attachments, and who experienced heavy Personal Life Burdens. The quality of the therapists' own personal relationships and the happiness, distress or dreariness of their private lives, significantly predicted and possibly influenced the quality of their professional work.

In addition, therapists' experiences of significant benefit in their own personal therapies clearly contributed to their positive involvement in conducting therapy with their own patients. Therapists who had no personal therapy appeared disadvantaged in comparison to those who had gained much from their own therapists. Examination of personal therapy in relation to different patterns of therapists' childhood experience led to defining therapists as different types of "healers". Some had successfully overcome significant trauma or abuse in their early family life and could legitimately be called Wounded Healers. Most therapists experienced good care and support and had been protected from serious harm in childhood, and were inspired to share the care from which they benefited with others in their lives, as persons and as Normal Caring Healers. Some others seemed only to have wandered into professional work as therapists, hopefully doing no harm, by being Indifferent Healers; and a few, sadly, seemed to be Troubled Healers, overwhelmed by the personal demands of therapeutic work.

The main finding of this exploration has been showing the very salient role of therapists' personal qualities and characteristics as predictors of, and presumably influences on, how they experience their work with patients. Although some professional characteristics were found to be predictors, they were minor contributors to Healing Involvement, and not predictors of Stressful Involvement if work setting conditions are included. Taken together, these personal qualities and characteristics of therapists may help to understand the consistent statistical differences in effectiveness between therapists that researchers now refer to as "the therapist effect" (e.g., Baldwin & Imel, 2013). Are therapists who appear to be Normal Caring Healers or Wounded Healers really more effective, when assessed by traditional outcome measures? Are therapists who appear to be Indifferent Healers really a source of indifferent outcomes? And are therapists who appear to be Troubled Healers really a source of negative outcomes for patients who may actually deteriorate?

The answers, to be determined by future research, will likely not reflect a simple correspondence with the four "healer" types that emerged in this study. Those are empirical constructs, derived from data analyses, but they are collective constructs based on average characteristics of very many psychotherapists. As individuals, particular psychotherapists will conform to the "healer" type they approximate only to varying degrees. It would be rare for any given individual to display all the characteristics associated with a particular "healer" type. Thus the search for therapist characteristics that underlie those variations in outcomes called the "therapist effect" might best focus[29] on the specific variables on which individuals vary but that jointly defined the "healer" types, such as childhood experience patterns, *personal self* dimensions, attachment styles, quality of life, belief-value orientations, and personal therapy benefit, among other features of psychotherapists as persons both covered in this book and yet to be discovered.

For readers who only wanted to know what this study has learned about psychotherapists as persons, this is "the End". For researchers who are interested in studies that also used the DPCCQ together with other instruments, the next chapter explores how far the DPCCQ may be valid beyond the psychotherapists' perspective. Here below are the DPCQ items and algorithms used to compute Healing Involvement and Stressful Involvement.

Healing Involvement and Stressful Involvement: Item Scales and Scoring Algorithms

HEALING INVOLVEMENT
Scale range 0 to 15 (combining items of HI-1 though HI-5)

MANNER OF RELATING (multiply item scores by 5)
Factor HI-1: AFFIRMING: 1+ 4 + 6 + 7 + 11 + 12
Factor HI-2: EFFECTIVE: 2 + 3 + 5 +8+ 9 +10

How would you describe yourself as a therapist – your actual style or manner with clients?

Item	Content	Not at all	Some	Much	Very much
1	Accepting	0	1	2	3
2	Committed	0	1	2	3
3	Effective	0	1	2	3
4	Friendly	0	1	2	3
5	Intuitive	0	1	2	3
6	Involved	0	1	2	3
7	Nurturant	0	1	2	3
8	Organized	0	1	2	3
9	Skillful	0	1	2	3
10	Subtle	0	1	2	3
11	Tolerant	0	1	2	3
12	Warm	0	1	2	3

IN-SESSION FEELINGS (multiply item scores by 5)
Factor HI-3: **"FLOW"**: 1 + 2 + 3 + 4

Recently in sessions with clients, how often have you found yourself feeling...

Item	Content	Not at all	Some	Much	Very much
1	**Creative**	0	1	2	3
2	**Focused**	0	1	2	3
3	**Inspired**	0	1	2	3
4	**Stimulated**	0	1	2	3

CLINICAL SKILLS (multiply item scores by 3)
Factor HI-4: **CURRENT SKILL LEVEL**: 1 + 2 + 3 + 4 + 5 + 6 + 7

Overall, at the present time...

Item	Content	Not at all	Slight- ly	Some- what	Moder- ately	Much	Very much
1	How effective are you at engaging clients in a working alliance?	0	1	2	3	4	5
2	How "natural" (authentically personal) do you feel while working with clients?	0	1	2	3	4	5
3	How empathic are you in relating to clients with whom you had relatively little in common?	0	1	2	3	4	5
4	How effective are you in communicating your under-standing and concern to your clients?	0	1	2	3	4	5
5	How well do you understand what happens moment-by-moment during therapy sessions?	0	1	2	3	4	5
6	How much mastery do you have of the techniques and strategies involved in practicing therapy?	0	1	2	3	4	5

| 7 | How much precision, subtlety and finesse have you attained in your therapeutic work? | 0 | 1 | 2 | 3 | 4 | 5 |

COPING STRATEGIES (multiply item scores by 3)
Factor HI-5: **CONSTRUCTIVE COPING**: 1 + 2 + 3 + 4 + 5 + 6 + 7 + 8 + 9

When in difficulty, how often do you...?

Item	Content	Never	Rarely	Occasionally	Moderately	Often	Very often
1	Try to see the problem from a different perspective.	0	1	2	3	4	5
2	Discuss the problem with a colleague.	0	1	2	3	4	5
3	Consult relevant articles or books.	0	1	2	3	4	5
4	Involve another professional or agency in the case.	0	1	2	3	4	5
5	Review privately with yourself how the problem has arisen.	0	1	2	3	4	5
6	Just give yourself permission to experience difficult or disturbing feelings.	0	1	2	3	4	5
7	See whether you and your client can together deal with the difficulty.	0	1	2	3	4	5
8	Consult about the case with a more experienced therapist.	0	1	2	3	4	5

| 9 | Sign up for a conference or workshop that might bear on the problem. | 0 | 1 | 2 | 3 | 4 | 5 |

STRESSFUL INVOLVEMENT

Scale 0 to 15 (combining items of SI-1 though SI-6)

DIFFICULTIES IN PRACTICE (multiply item scores by 3)

Factor SI-1: **PROFESSIONAL SELF-DOUBT**: 1+ 4 + 6 + 7 + 11 + 12

Factor SI-2: **FRUSTRATING TREATMENT CASE**: 2 + 3 + 5 +8+ 9 +10

Factor SI-3: **NEGATIVE PERSONAL REACTION**: 2 + 3 + 5 +8+ 9 +10

How would you describe yourself as a therapist – your actual style or manner with clients?

Currently, how often do you feel…?

Item	Content	Never	Rarely	Occa-sion-ally	Mod-erately	Often	Very often
1	Lacking in confidence that you can have a beneficial effect on a client.	0	1	2	3	4	5
2	Afraid that you are doing more harm than good in treating a client.	0	1	2	3	4	5
3	Unsure how best to deal effectively with a client.	0	1	2	3	4	5
4	In danger of losing control of the ther-apeutic situation to a client.	0	1	2	3	4	5
5	Unable to have much real empathy for a client's experiences.	0	1	2	3	4	5
6	Distressed by your powerlessness to affect a client's tragic life situation.	0	1	2	3	4	5
7	Unable to generate sufficient momentum to move therapy with a client in a con-structive direction.	0	1	2	3	4	5
8	Irritated with a client who is actively blocking your efforts.	0	1	2	3	4	5

9	Demoralized by your inability to find ways to help a patient.	0	1	2	3	4	5
10	Unable to comprehend the essence of a client's problems.	0	1	2	3	4	5
11	Unable to withstand a client's emotional neediness.	0	1	2	3	4	5
12	Unable to find something to like or respect in a client.	0	1	2	3	4	5
13	Angered by factors in a client's life that prevent a beneficial outcome.	0	1	2	3	4	5
14	Conflicted about how to reconcile obligations to a client with equivalent obligations to others.	0	1	2	3	4	5
15	Bogged down with a client in a relationship that seems to go nowhere.	0	1	2	3	4	5
16	Frustrated with a client for wasting your time.	0	1	2	3	4	5

COPING STRATEGIES (multiply item scores by 3)
Factor SI-4: **AVOIDANT COPING**: $1 + 2 + 3 + 4 + 5 + 6 + 7 + 8$

When in difficulty, how often do you...?

Item	Content	Never	Rarely	Occasionally	Moderately	Often	Very often
1	Seek some form of alternative satisfaction away from therapy.	0	1	2	3	4	5
2	Simply hope that things will improve eventually.	0	1	2	3	4	5
3	Criticize a client for causing you trouble.	0	1	2	3	4	5
4	Seriously consider terminating therapy.	0	1	2	3	4	5

5	Express your upset feelings to somebody close to you.	0	1	2	3	4	5
6	Avoid dealing with the problem for the present.	0	1	2	3	4	5
7	Show your frustration to the client.	0	1	2	3	4	5
8	Explore the possibility of referring the client on to another therapist.	0	1	2	3	4	5

IN-SESSION FEELINGS (multiply item scores by 5)
Factor SI-5: **BORED** = 1 + 3 + 4 + 5
Factor SI-6: **ANXIOUS** = 2 + 6 +7+ 8

Recently in sessions with clients, how often have you found yourself feeling...

Item	Content	Not at all	Some	Much	Very much
1	Absent	0	1	2	3
2	Anxious	0	1	2	3
3	Bored	0	1	2	3
4	Drowsy	0	1	2	3
5	Inattentive	0	1	2	3
6	Overwhelmed	0	1	2	3
7	Pressured	0	1	2	3
8	Tense	0	1	2	3

Notes

1 A few open-format questions were also included to gather narrative data for qualitative analyses. Those questions include "What do you feel is your greatest strength as a psychotherapist?" and "What do you feel is your most problematic limitation as a psychotherapist?"
2 "Flow" is the commonly recognized term denoting a state of intense interest, subjective immersion, focused attention, altered time sense, and creativity in a process, whether solitary (e.g., painting, playing music, solving puzzles) or social (e.g., dancing, dueling, conversing). The term was introduced by M. Csikszentmihalyi (1990).
3 The therapists' experience of Healing Involvement is not a measure of overall effectiveness in practice; its relation to therapist effectiveness gauged by average outcomes across cases over time remains to be determined.
4 As described in *How Psychotherapists Develop* (Orlinsky & Rønnestad, 2005), meaningful cut-offs for each dimension were set by combining clinical judgment with examination of both the median of the therapists' score distribution and the anchors associated with the 0–15 scale of each dimension (based on the 0–3 and 0–5 scales that were used to rate the included DPCCQ items). As a result, the cut-off used for

Healing Involvement was rounded to 6.8 (75% high vs. 25% low), and the cut-off for *Stressful Involvement* was rounded to 4.4 (66% low vs. 33% high).

5 The percentages of therapists in each pattern would naturally be altered if the cut-points for dividing *Healing Involvement* and *Stressful Involvement* into high and low categories were changed, and so are inherently a matter of judgment. The percentages are very close to those described in *How Psychotherapists Develop* (2005), based on a sample half the present size, and so are at least consistent.

6 Major advantages of CATREG are its ability to combine nominal, ordinal and interval measures in a single set of predictors; to select those that are statistically independent as well as statistically significant, to provide a controlled estimate of the variance contributed by each significant predictor, and to chart the shape of the association between predictor and criterion variables.

7 The statistically non-significant exceptions that were dropped from the final analysis were the scales for Analytic/Psychodynamic, Behavioral, and Cognitive orientations.

8 The rationale for using orientation scales rather than the categorical variable of main orientations (N > 500 each) is that it allowed inclusion of 9,442 therapists, in contrast to only 6,534 cases.

9 As will be seen, the gap between Psychiatrists and other professional disciplines narrows over successive career level cohorts.

10 The same set of potential baseline predictors as used in the initial CATREG model of Healing Involvement were entered together again in an initial model to predict Stressful Involvement, and again were winnowed down according to the same criteria of statistical significance and relative importance (e.g., about 5% of the predicted variance).

11 When using the variable of main orientation categories (i.e., those of N > 500 cases each), considerable overlap between orientations was noted. Mono-focal Analytic/ Psychodynamic therapists and Analytic/Psychodynamic + Humanistic therapists did not differ significantly from those with no salient orientation at the high end of Stressful Involvement. Mono-focal Humanistic, Broad Spectrum, and Cognitive-Behavioral therapists were statistically tied at the low end of Stressful Involvement. Even greater overlap between orientations was observed in an analysis using a broader categorical variable including groups with N > 300 therapists.

12 The positive impact of high levels of spirituality contributed too little variance to meet the criterion for inclusion in the cumulative set of predictors. Differences in religious background and current affiliation were so marginally significant statistically that they also contributed negligibly to the overall prediction of Healing Involvement. Therapists from non-religious backgrounds had the lowest scores on Healing Involvement, but they were not significantly differentiated from the great majority of therapists who had Protestant or Roman Catholic/Orthodox backgrounds (overall result of a 1-way ANOVA: $F = 19.0$, df = 4, 3795, $p = .000$). Therapists of different current religious affiliations were not specifically differentiated in terms of Healing Involvement, with the exception of Jewish therapists whose scores were higher (overall results of a 1-way ANOVA: $F = 10.7$, df = 5, 3914; $p = .000$).

13 The Chi-square values were: $\chi^2 = 36.3$, df = 12, p = .000; AsR at $p = .01$ for 20 cells, cut-off = ± 3.48 ($p = .05$, ± 3.01).

14 Given therapists' generally high ratings of their personal benefit (see Chapter 9), utilization and outcome are positively correlated ($r = .53$).

15 Referring to the Greek myth of the centaur Chiron.

16 These figures are not necessarily representative of professional Counselors as such, but only of the relative large sample (N=2,193) in our composite database, two-thirds of whom were from the UK or Australia.

17 There was a total of 4,133 therapists for whom information on childhood experience patterns was available.

18 These interpretations are offered as hypotheses to be assessed in future research testing the links between the psychotherapist's experience of therapy and patient outcomes measured from alternate observational perspectives (see Chapter 11).

19 The Chi-square values were: χ^2 = 633.4, df = 12, p =.000; AsR at p =.01 for 20 cells, cut-off = ± 3.48 (p =.05, ± 3.01).

20 The Chi-square values were: χ^2 = 634.5, df = 15, p =.000; AsR at p =.01 for 24 cells, cut-off = ± 3.53 (p =.05, ± 3.08).

21 The Chi-square values were: χ^2 = 722.3, df = 15, p =.000; AsR at p =.01 for 24 cells, cut-off = ± 3.53 (p =.05, ± 3.08).

22 The One-Way ANOVA values were all at p =.000: for Genial/Caring, F = 603.5; for Ardent/Expressive, F = 270.7; for Reclusive/Remote, F = 221.5; for Forceful/Exacting, F = 85.8.

23 The Chi-square values were: χ^2 = 81.2, df = 9, p =.000; AsR at p =.01 for 16 cells, cut-off = ± 3.42 (p =.05, ± 2.96).

24 The Chi-square values were: χ^2 = 809.7, df = 15, p =.000; AsR at p =.01 for 24 cells, cut-off = ± 3.53 (p =.05, ± 3.08).

25 The Chi-square values were: χ^2 = 54.9, df = 12, p =.000; AsR at p =.01 for 20 cells, cut-off = ± 3.48 (p =.05, ± 3.01).

26 In a very recent report, Willutzki et al. (2021) presented cluster analyses of data from an independent sample of 1,010 trainees in 15 countries designed to determine their personal and professional pathways to training in psychotherapy, using questionnaires similar to the DPCCQ, distinguishing five personal pathways with a striking resemblance to the "healer" types among practicing psychotherapists that were identified in this chapter. Cluster 1 ("Grown up in a mainly positive environment and yet vulnerable") and cluster 2 ("Young trainees with a privileged background") together accounted for 61% of the trainees—and were comparable in content to the 55% of Normal Caring Healers. Cluster 3 ("Wounded Healers") represented 18% of the trainees—comparable in content and numbers to the 18% of practicing therapists also identified as Wounded Healers. Cluster 5 ("Material background ok, emotionally dysfunctional") comprised 8% of the sample—similar to the 11% of Troubled Healers in our therapist sample. Finally, Cluster 4 ("All in all not so comfortable background"), which involved 12% of the trainees, was more ambiguous with regard to "healer" types but seemed at least to overlap with the 15% of Indifferent Healers among practicing therapists. Future analysis of the relations of trainees' personal and professional pathways should further clarify their convergence with the four "healer" types defined in this chapter.

27 The total variance predicted for Healing Involvement thus far was 39.4% (Appendix Table 10.11), and was 25.5% for Stressful Involvement (Appendix Table 10.12).

28 Even computer programs that are designed to provide help-seekers with an interactive "psychotherapy" experience must be designed by persons with expert knowledge of therapeutic processes and principles, the mastery of which would define them as psychotherapists.

29 The practical wisdom of this suggestion is reinforced by the studies reviewed in Chapter 11 which showed that specific component variables defining Healing Involvement and Stressful Involvement often were more significantly related to non-DPCCQ measures than were the composite measures of Healing Involvement and Stressful Involvement.

References

Baldwin, S. A., & Imel, Z. E. (2013). Therapist effects: Findings and methods. In M. J. Lambert & A. E. Bergin (Eds.), *Bergin and Garfield's Handbook of Psychotherapy and Behavior Change* (6th edition), 258–297. New York: Wiley.

Csikszentmihalyi, M. (1990). *Flow: The psychology of optimal experience.* New York: Harper & Row.

Frank, J. D. (1974). Psychotherapy: The restoration of morale. *American Journal of Psychotherapy,* 131, 271–274.

Nissen-Lie, H., & Orlinsky, D. E. (2014). Growth, love, and work in psychotherapy: Sources of therapeutic talent and clinician self-renewal. In R. J. Wicks & E. A. Maynard (Eds.), *Clinician's guide to self-renewal: Essential advice from the field,* 3–24. New York: Wiley.

Orlinsky, D. E., & Rønnestad, M. H. (2005). *How psychotherapists develop: A study of therapeutic work and professional growth.* Washington, DC: American Psychological Association.

Orlinsky, D. E., Rønnestad, M. H., & Willutzki, U. (2004). Fifty years of psychotherapy process-outcome research: Continuity and change. In M. J. Lambert (Ed.), *Bergin and Garfield's Handbook of psychotherapy and behavior change* (5th edition), 307–389. New York: Wiley.

Rønnestad, M. H., & Orlinsky, D. E., (2005). Clinical implications: Training, supervision, and practice. In D. E. Orlinsky & M. H. Rønnestad, *How psychotherapists develop,* 181–201. Washington, DC: American Psychological Association.

Willutzki, U., Rønnestad, M. H., Orlinsky, D. E., Heinonen, E., Pirke, J. & Hartmann, A. (2021). *Psychotherapy trainees' pathways into the profession.* Paper presented at the 52nd annual meeting of the Society for Psychotherapy Research, Heidelberg, Germany, June 24.

11 Research From Within and Beyond the Psychotherapist's Perspective

D. E. Orlinsky

The book that I set out to write is done. Chapters 2 through 10 have described the personal characteristics, qualities, backgrounds and experiences of a very large number of psychotherapists, as recorded by them in a survey conducted with the Development of Psychotherapists Common Core Questionnaire (DPCCQ). After a previous study with the same instrument that focused on therapeutic work and professional growth (Orlinsky & Rønnestad, 2005), this book aimed to focus on psychotherapists as persons, rather than as professionals: their intimate selves, private lives, personal beliefs, quality of life, family backgrounds, childhood experiences, personal therapy, and finally (back into the office or consulting room) as *persons* doing therapy. On most topics, data were available from ten to twelve thousand therapists; on some topics, from just a few thousand. These are far from all the psychotherapists in the world, and no claim has been made that those in this study are a representative sampling of all therapists—if indeed such a sample could even be drawn from a profession whose boundaries are ill-defined and porous. But it is a large enough number to command attention and, from a statistical point of view, to detect small effects (i.e., significant nuances as well as major differences).

Observational Perspectives in Research

These things have a certain interest of their own, yet one more question remains to be answered or at least explored, a question that is sure to be of prime interest to psychotherapy researchers. *How much do the findings based on psychotherapists' experiences of therapy correspond to data generated from other observational perspectives?* The other perspectives in question, to which the therapists' perspective would be compared, are those of patients as participant-observers, and of research raters or clinical supervisors as non-participant observers. Observations made from these alternative perspectives sometimes fail to agree. This poses a dilemma for some researchers who tacitly assume that—as in physical and biological sciences—there is a single "objective reality" which ideally should be viewed in the same way by different observers. Typically, this dilemma is resolved by privileging the perspectives of patients and non-participant observers while adopting a skeptical attitude towards the experiences of

DOI: 10.4324/9781003217572-11

therapists and data based on therapists' experiences. Reason to doubt therapist-based data is sometimes cited from a study that found most of the therapists in the sample who were asked to rate themselves felt that they were "above average"—even though, in a statistically normal distribution, only half can be literally "above average" (when the median is the "average")—without reflecting on the implications of being "only average" for therapists' work morale. Some researchers' doubts about the accuracy or objectivity of therapist-based data in general overlook the important distinction between judgmental and descriptive data. Some therapist-reported data—such as that typically found in the methods section of journal articles—is accepted without question: age, gender, profession, length of time in practice, and so forth. Therapist-based data also goes beyond simple descriptions to include dimensions of meaning inferred and measured through statistical analyses of particular experiences that are described in specific detail without self-assessment or evaluation, and findings established on such therapist-based data have validity as representing the therapists' perspective, whether or not that agrees with other perspectives. It would be obvious to any clinician who has done couples therapy, or family therapy, that interpersonal realities are inherently defined by multiple perspectives, even among persons who share their daily lives with each other.

Yet accepting that the phenomena of psychotherapy are multi-dimensional and often differentially accessible from different perspectives, a practical question remains about how much, and in what ways, the therapists' observational perspective connects with or corresponds to observations from beyond the therapists' perspective. More specifically in the present context, how well do the measures and findings about therapists derived from the DPCCQ correspond to research measures based on other observational perspectives? In so far as there are cross-perspective correspondences, the research on therapists that has been reported here may not only be relevant to psychotherapists, but stand as a meaningful contribution to knowledge about the sources, processes and outcomes of psychotherapy.

This chapter is addressed to colleagues in the field of psychotherapy research, and consists in a brief overview of studies done over the past decade using the DPCCQ, or the specific sections of it contained in the so-called Therapist Work Involvement Scales or TWIS (Orlinsky & Rønnestad, 2005, Appendix E) that assess Healing Involvement and Stressful Involvement. These studies examined the relations of variables drawn from the DPCCQ or TWIS to varied aspects of therapeutic process, outcome, and training. The main question is whether those studies found associations between measures based on the psychotherapist's perspective and measures from other perspectives.

Therapy Process

Six studies were published during the past decade comparing Healing Involvement, Stressful Involvement, and other psychotherapeutic processes from therapists' and patients' perspectives. The latter focused almost exclusively on the "working alliance" in the relationships between patient and therapist. As defined in Bordin's (1979) original model, the working alliance has three components: agreement on treatment goals, treatment methods, and the quality of emotional bond that develops between patient and therapist over time. Three papers were published by Nissen-Lie and her colleagues in Norway (2010, 2013, 2015); two papers were published by Hartmann and Zeeck in Freiburg, Germany (2012, 2014); one paper was published by Heinonen and colleagues in Helsinki, Finland (Heinonen, Lindfors, Härkänen et al., 2013).

Norwegian Studies

Between 1996 and 2000, data were collected from 68 therapists, treating 335 patients at 16 outpatient clinics in the Norwegian Public Health Care system as part of a naturalistic, longitudinal research program called the Norwegian Multisite Study of Psychotherapy Process and Outcome (Havik, Monsen, Høglend, Lippe, Lyngstad, Stiles, et al., 1995). During that time therapists completed the DPCCQ up to six times. Assessments of change in the patients' condition (to be described in the following section on outcome) were made using the Symptom Check List (SCL-90-R; Derogatis, 1983) and the Inventory of Interpersonal Problems (IIP-64; Horowitz et al., 2000). Assessments of the working alliance were made using both the patient and therapist forms of the Working Alliance Inventory (WAI-P, WAI-T; Horvath & Greenberg, 1989). These instruments have been used in very many studies and have become standard measures in the field of psychotherapy research.

In their first study examining therapist predictors of the early (3rd session) working alliance, Nissen-Lie, Monsen & Rønnestad (2010) conducted factor analyses of items within different sections of DPCCQ and of first-level factor dimensions across DPCCQ sections for the limited sample of Norwegian therapists, with results very comparable to the original analyses reported by Orlinsky and Rønnestad (2005)—including the dimensions of Healing Involvement and Stressful Involvement. Contrary to expectations, the global dimensions of Healing Involvement and Stressful Involvement had no significant influence on patient alliance ratings. However, specific first-level DPCCQ factors did appear related to patient alliance ratings. For example, two components of Healing Involvement ("Relational Skills" and "Warm Affirming Manner") had a positive but complex association with patient alliance ratings. More potently, two first-level dimensions of the DPCCQ section on Difficulties in Practice ("Professional Self-Doubt" and "Negative Personal Reaction") were significantly associated with patients' early alliance ratings, but in different directions. When the shared variance of the two difficulties dimensions (i.e., the overall frequency of difficulties) was statistically controlled, the remaining unique contribution of therapist "Professional Self-Doubt" was positive in how patients experienced the alliance, whereas the relation of therapist "Negative Personal Reactions" to patients was highly negative.

In their second study, Nissen-Lie, Havik, Høglend, Monsen & Rønnestad (2013) examined the impact of therapists' personal quality of life (Personal

Satisfactions and Personal Burdens; see Chapter 6 above) on the development of the working alliance. In summarizing their main findings, the authors wrote: "The Personal Burdens scale was strongly and inversely related to the growth of the alliance as rated by the patients, but was unrelated to therapist-rated alliance. Conversely, the factor scale of therapists' Personal Satisfactions was clearly and positively associated with therapist-rated alliance growth, but was unrelated to the patients' ratings of the alliance." Patients appeared to be particularly sensitive to their therapists' distress in private life, which even though it was not discussed openly by therapists and did not affect therapists' own alliance ratings, nevertheless was somehow subtly but potently communicated through their in-session behaviors. By contrast, the therapists' judgments of alliance quality positively reflected their own sense of personal wellbeing, which perhaps was not a significant signal to patients because it does not deviate from their expectations that therapists should project a sense of their own wellbeing.

In a third study, Nissen-Lie and colleagues (Nissen-Lie, Havik, Høglend, Rønnestad & Monsen, 2015) focused on the potential of therapists' practice experiences to predict the development of patient and therapist alliance ratings over the course of treatment. The "practice experiences" considered were Healing Involvement, Stressful Involvement and some first-level dimensions among their components (e.g., Difficulties in Practice with respect to Stressful Involvement). Neither of the two global work involvement dimensions predicted patient average alliance levels (as previously reported) but the therapists' Stressful Involvement negatively influenced the slope of patients' alliance ratings assessed at sessions 3, 12, 20 and 40. That is, the more the therapists experienced their therapeutic work as a Stressful Involvement, the more their patients' alliance measures tended to decline over time. With a statistical model that used scores for therapists' "Professional Self-Doubt" and "Negative Personal Reaction" (two Difficulty dimensions that are components of Stressful Involvement), the authors obtained a complex set of results. The therapists' "Negative Personal Reaction" negatively predicted patients' alliance levels but not their development over time, whereas "Professional Self-Doubt" negatively predicted patients' alliance development but not levels; and (similar to the first study) "Professional Self-Doubt" positively predicted patient alliance level. Finally, when that statistical model used scores for therapists' in-session feelings, the development of patients' alliance scores over time was negatively predicted by the first-level dimension of therapist "Anxiety" (another component of Stressful Involvement).

Helsinki Study

A parallel investigation of therapists' professional and personal characteristics as predictors of working alliance was conducted in Finland by Heinonen and his colleagues (Heinonen, Lindfors, Härkänen, Virtala, Jääskeläinen & Knekt, 2013), where 70 experienced therapists treated 333 patients suffering depressive and/or anxiety disorders. Therapists were assessed via the DPCCQ, focusing primarily on the global dimensions of Healing Involvement and Stressful Involvement, the dimensions of *personal self* (see Chapter 3 above), and the first-level dimensions that were components of them. The Helsinki Psychotherapy Study followed a quasi-experimental design that included both long-term and short-term treatments (Knekt & Lindfors, 2004). Therapist and patient versions of the Working Alliance Inventory (Horvath & Greenberg, 1989) were administered at the third session and after seven months in treatment. (Outcome measures included in the study will be described in the following section.)

In their initial basic statistical model, the authors compared groups of practitioners that had either high, medium or low scores on therapist characteristics, and found numerous professional and personal therapist characteristics that predicted early (3rd session) alliance as rated by therapists, but not as rated by patients. Significant variables related to therapist-rated alliance included both work involvement dimensions and their specific components among professional characteristics, and being "Reclusive" among personal characteristics. The lone therapist variable significantly associated with patient-rated alliance was therapists' level of "Basic Relational Skills"—and this only for short-term treatments. There were also few significant predictions for change over time in both the therapist-rated and patient-rated alliances, differentiated in terms of treatment length. The authors noted that: "Improvement of patient alliances was predicted specifically in short-term therapies by engaging and encouraging qualities ("Invested" relational agency and "Affirming" relational manner). They predicted, however, alliance deterioration in long-term therapies." Like many studies, the findings seemed to raise more questions than they answered.

Freiburg Studies

Taking a different tack, the first of two studies by Hartmann, Zeeck and their colleagues focused on therapists' Stressful Involvement as their dependent variable and examined the therapist, patient and treatment process characteristics associated with it (Zeeck, Orlinsky, Hermann, Joos, Wirsching, Weidmann & Hartmann, 2012). The 26 therapists studied were conducting private outpatient therapy (*n* = 49 patients) or therapy in a public day-hospital setting (*n* = 49 patients) in Freiburg, Germany. As each therapist had from 2 to 4 patients, the DPCCQ instructions were modified from "Overall, in your practice" to "Recently, with this patient" to accommodate the research design. Differing from the Norwegian and Helsinki studies, the treatment process measures used were the Helping Alliance Questionnaire (Luborsky, Crits-Christoph, Alexander, Margolis, & Cohen, 1983), the Session Evaluation Questionnaire (Stiles, Gordon & Lani, 2002), and the Intersession Experience Questionnaire (Orlinsky, Geller, Tarragona & Farber, 1993). Interestingly, most of the therapists also took the Inventory of Interpersonal Problems (Horowitz, Strauss & Kordy, 2000), which is typically used as a patient outcome measure.

As in the studies reviewed above, a significant inverse relationship was found between Stressful Involvement and therapists' alliance ratings (high alliance with low Stressful Involvement), but only a weak (though statistically significant) association with patients' alliance ratings—despite the use of a different alliance measure in this study. The therapists' experience of therapy as a Stressful Involvement also appeared to be unrelated to the patients' level of symptom severity. Yet other interesting therapist-rated process measures were associated with Stressful Involvement, such as good "flow" in and positive evaluation of therapy sessions with *low* Stressful Involvement, and therapists' negative feelings (especially feeling "discouraged" about treatment) in the times between sessions with *high* Stressful Involvement. Therapists' personal characteristics similar to those analyzed in Chapter 3 above were also associated with Stressful Involvement: globally, with total level of interpersonal problems assessed with the IIP; and specifically, with being "nonassertive/submissive" (*low* Forceful/Exacting), "socially inhibited/avoidant"(*high* Reclusive/Remote), and "vindictive" (not assessed in the DPCCQ).

A second paper from the Freiburg team sought to understand variations in the extent of divergence between the alliance ratings of therapists and their patients (Hartmann, Joos, Orlinsky & Zeeck, 2014). Drawing on the study described above, data included treatments of 98 patients by 26 therapists where both participants used the Helping Alliance Questionnaire to rate the quality of their patient–therapist relationship. Other available measures were the Therapist Work Involvement Scales (a subset of the DPCCQ items used to compute Healing Involvement and Stressful Involvement; see the box included at end of Chapter 10), the Session Evaluation Questionnaire, and the Intersession Experience Questionnaire. Analyses focused on the means of multiple scores over blocks of sessions, thus "omitting session-by-session variability and using values to represent the average of each process variable rated by patient of therapist" (p. 5)—from which patient–therapist difference scores were computed. Although the authors found that "Overall, therapists clearly underestimated their patients' ratings of the therapeutic alliance", there were also instances of therapists overestimating their patients' alliance ratings. Healing Involvement and Stressful Involvement each were significantly related to the different patterns of divergence. The more that therapists experienced therapeutic work as a Healing Involvement, the more they tended to overestimate their patients' alliance ratings. By contrast, therapists tended to underestimate patients' alliance ratings only when experiencing high levels of Stressful Involvement. These results demonstrate that therapists' experiences, as assessed with the DPCCQ, had significant relationships beyond the psychotherapists' perspective, but as usual in a rather complex way.[1]

Therapy Effects

Psychotherapy is intended to have a positive effect on patients, but effects also occur for psychotherapists (e.g., improved clinical skill; positive or negative work morale). How, if at all, are those effects associated with psychotherapists' qualities and experiences as assessed by the DPCCQ? Inevitably the main concern focuses on patients, with the hope and expectation that participation in psychotherapy will result in improvements in their condition. This is referred to as patient "outcome", and while it is well established that most patients improve at least moderately on average (i.e., have a positive outcome) there is a small minority of cases in which the patient's condition deteriorates (has a "negative outcome")—either due to the inability of therapy to arrest a patient's downward decline or, even worse, due to a toxic quality of the therapist's interventions. Generally less noticed, however, is the fact that conducting psychotherapy as professionals can also have an impact on psychotherapists themselves. This is not termed "outcome"—but a class of negative impacts of practice on therapists is well-known under the name of "burnout".[2] The contrasting positive impacts of a therapist's participation in therapy is professional "development"—experienced in the near term as "Currently Experienced Growth" and in the long term as "Overall Career Development".[3] The next section reviews six studies on the relation of patient outcome to DPCCQ-measured therapist variables, and the following reviews two studies relating DPCCQ variables to therapist burnout.

Patient Outcomes

Helsinki Studies

Two early studies of patient outcomes and therapist factors were reported by Heinonen and his colleagues in the Helsinki Psychotherapy Study, both of which focused on comparing therapies of different length and type. The first paper compared long-term and short-term treatments (Heinonen, Lindfors, Laaksonen & Knekt, 2012) in connection with therapists' professional and personal characteristics. Because the main independent variable was an "interaction term between therapy group (short or long), the therapist measure, and time", the results as reported were especially complex. However, both professional and personal therapist characteristics assessed by the DPCCQ had measurable impacts on patient outcomes in the different treatment conditions. The professional characteristics included Healing Involvement, Stressful Involvement, and their components (e.g., first-level factor dimensions of "Basic Relational Skills" and "Difficulties in Practice"). Results were clearest for first-level factors; for example, patients of therapists with higher "Basic Relational Skills" experienced relatively fast and lasting improvement in both short-term and long-term therapy, whereas therapists who felt "Flow" (immersive interest) during therapy sessions *less* frequently had patients who experienced *less* symptom reduction in short-term therapy. Both of those therapist qualities are components of Healing Involvement. The personal characteristics were dimensions of *personal self* (described in Chapter 3). For example, the patients treated in long-term therapy by therapists more Genial/Caring and less Forceful/Exacting in their close personal relationships had fewer symptoms at the 3-year follow-up, while the patients treated in short-term therapy by less

Reclusive/Remote therapists had faster symptom reduction in short-term therapy.

In their second paper, Heinonen and colleagues compared their project's two long-term treatments, psychodynamic psychotherapy and psychoanalysis (Heinonen, Knekt, Jääkesläinen & Lindors, 2013). Once again the focus was on interactions of therapist characteristics and treatments rather than on therapist characteristics as main effects, and once again the complex results showed significant differential effects with DPCCQ variables.

Norwegian Studies

In addition to focusing on the working alliance as a measure of treatment process, the Norwegian Multisite Study made use of three outcome measures: the Global Assessment of Functioning (GAF) scale, rated by the clinic directors; the Symptom Check List Global Severity Index (SCL-90/GSI); and patients' global scores on the Inventory of Interpersonal Problems (IIP). Nissen-Lie, Monsen, Ulleberg, & Rønnestad (2012) assessed both the level and the rate of change in these measures in relation to certain first-level dimensions of therapists' characteristics that the authors were able to independently replicate even with their limited sample of 70 clinicians. Those included two dimensions of therapist difficulties, "Professional Self-doubt" and "Negative Personal Reaction to a Client", both of which are components of Stressful Involvement; and one dimension of current clinical skill ("Advanced Relational Skill"), together with one dimension of relating with patients ("Warm Interpersonal Style"[4]), which are both components of Healing Involvement. As it turned out, none of these variables showed any direct association with client outcomes in the statistical analyses that the authors conducted, although one puzzling interaction effect reached a statistically significant level: patients with higher levels of interpersonal problems (on the IIP) did less well in treatment with therapists who rated themselves higher on Advanced Relational Skills.

In a further analysis of the same data, Nissen-Lie and colleagues (Nissen-Lie, Rønnestad, Høglend, Havik, Solbakken, Stiles & Monsen, 2015) found another unexpected interaction effect between the first-level Difficulty dimensions previously studied and therapists' self-affiliation, as assessed with a modified version of the well-known SASB Intrex (Benjamin, 1983, 1995), an instrument based on the Structured Analysis of Social Behavior (Benjamin, 1974). Two first-level dimensions of coping strategies derived from the DPCCQ were also included: "Constructive Coping" and "Avoidant" or non-constructive coping[5]—the former a component of Healing Involvement and the latter a component of Stressful Involvement. As in their earlier study, the authors used "a three-level, hierarchically nested random effects growth model to analyze the effect of therapist predictors on change in IIP and GSI." For the IIP index of interpersonal problem severity, the main finding was an interaction between DPCCQ-based "Professional Self-doubt" (PSD) and SASB-based therapist self-affiliation, such that "the most change was obtained by patients treated by therapists who were high on both PSD and self-affiliation, while the least change was observed in those treated by therapists who combined low scores of PSD with high scores on self-affiliation." There was also a nearly significant direct positive impact of therapist PSD on patient outcomes, and therapists' "Constructive Coping" was directly and positively related to patient improvement (but showed no interaction with self-affiliation). Still, different and somewhat contradictory results were obtained when using the Symptom Checklist GSI as the measure of patient outcome. Both "Professional Self-doubt" and self-affiliation, and their interaction, and also both "Constructive Coping" and its interaction with self-affiliation, were *not* significantly associated with patient outcome. On the other hand, therapist "Avoidant" or non-constructive coping had a significantly deleterious effect on patient outcome, unmoderated by therapist self-affiliation. Thus different aspects of the DPCCQ related significantly to the two outcome criteria, and perhaps the most intriguing finding of the study (which gave its name to the paper's title, "Love yourself as a person, doubt yourself as a therapist") emerged only, but importantly, where specifically interpersonal problems were concerned.

A German Study

Partly inspired by the foregoing Norwegian study, as well as an earlier study (Willutzki, Hernandez Bark, Davis & Orlinsky, 1997) that related therapist difficulties and coping strategies to patient outcomes, Willutzki and colleagues attempted a replication based on data from 40 German therapists, each with multiple patients, during their training in Cognitive Behavioral Therapy (Odyniec, Probst, Margraf & Willutzki, 2017). In their study, the DPCCQ scales were used to assess overall therapist trait-based at one time when they enrolled in the study, and a session-focused adaptation of the same scales was used as a repeated measure to assess therapist state-based difficulties. Outcomes were assessed with the Inventory of Interpersonal Problems (IIP) and the Global Severity Index of the Brief Symptom Inventory (BSI; Derogatis, 1975), a shorter version of the Symptom Check List-90. The two first-level Difficulties factors of "Professional Self-doubt" (PSD) and "Negative Personal Reaction" (NPR) were independently replicated for their German therapists. As therapist overall trait-based measures, neither of the two Difficulties dimensions had an effect over time on patients' symptom reduction (GSI). However, both showed a beneficial effect on patients' interpersonal problems over time (IIP)—except, contrary to the Norwegian study, NPR was associated with positive patient change and *higher* PSD was negatively related to patient change. As session-by-session state-based measures, "higher psychological symptom severity in a given patient was associated with higher PSD of their patient's therapist at the start of treatment"—an effect that was statistically significant for the larger BSI sample ($n = 40$ therapists), and near-significant for the smaller IIP sample ($n = 18$ therapists). For the BSI sample, *increases* in therapist PSD over time was associated with less favorable patient outcome. That is, trainees experienced more "Professional Self-doubt" with more severely impaired patients at first, and that self-doubt increased if and as patients got worse over time. With the smaller IIP sample (n = 18 therapists), neither therapist "Professional Self-doubt" nor "Negative Personal Reaction" seemed related to patient outcome.

Given the striking differences in results between the Norwegian and German studies, it is worth quoting the discussion by Odyniec et al. (2017) at some length:

> The contrary results in our study and Nissen-Lie et al.'s studies may be caused by the different therapist characteristics, considering the years of experience (trainees vs. 10 years of experience) and theoretical orientation (CBT vs. psychodynamic/psychoanalytic). This indicates that the difficulty scales may have different meanings for therapists at different career stages and are influenced by the therapist's theoretical background. Even though the level of trait-based difficulties in our sample was similar to that in Nissen-Lie et al. (2013), it could be hypothesized that NPR towards patients might have a different function between experienced therapists as investigated by Nissen-Lie et al. and the rather inexperienced trainees analyzed in the present study. At the beginning of their psychotherapeutic work, trainees might be very reluctant to allow themselves to experience NPR towards their patients, since such feelings might not be helpful to build a positive image of oneself as a future therapist.

These diverse findings and possible explanations illustrate the deep complexity of relationships between the psychotherapist's perspective (as assessed by the DPCCQ) and patient-based measures of outcome, as well as the diversity of findings presented by different outcomes instruments.

A British Study

The last of the studies relating DPCCQ therapist measures to outcome was reported by Schröder, Steel and Macdonald (2016), which included data from an internet-based cross-sectional survey in the United Kingdom of 116 therapists in eight IAPT[6] services. Routinely collected data about client characteristics and treatment outcome were linked to therapist data (including a focus on burnout to be described below). Outcome measures of patient depression (PHQ-9) and anxiety (GAD-7) were derived from the Patient Health Questionnaire Anxiety-Depression Scale (Kroenke, Spitzer, Williams & Lowe, 2010). The DPCCQ dimensions used to assess therapist characteristics were the Total Difficulties scale that was part of Stressful Involvement and the full dimension of Healing Involvement along with its factor components. Most of the therapists in the study practiced Cognitive-Behavioral therapy. Controlling for patients' pre-treatment scores on the outcome measures and the number of therapy sessions they had, therapist Healing Involvement was a significant predictor of patient improvement on both depression and anxiety. The effects proved particularly attributable to the first-level therapist dimension of "Affirming" relational manner both for depression and anxiety, and for the latter also the relational agency component dimension of therapist "Efficacy". Further, when analyzed in terms of the four therapist work practice patterns based on Healing Involvement and Stressful Involvement (see Chapter 10 above), therapists with the best outcomes across a variety of patients were more likely than therapists with the worst outcomes to show the pattern of Effective Practice. Thus for this sample at least, the relationship between the therapist's perspective and patient-based outcomes seemed both more direct and closer to expectation.

Therapist Burnout

British Studies

The negative impact of psychotherapy on therapists has been much studied as therapist burnout, especially with the Maslach Burnout Inventory (Maslach & Jackson, 1981) which typically uses three subscales: Emotional Exhaustion (EE, or emotionally depleted), Depersonalization (DP, becoming routinized or "robotic" in work), and Personal Accomplishment (PA, feelings of competence and success). The first two appear to overlap with some components in Stressful Involvement, and the third with some in Healing Involvement. The British study of outcome just cited (Schröder et al., 2016) had a major focus on therapist burnout as well as patient outcome. As reported there and in a prior publication (Steel, Macdonald, Schröder & Mellor-Clark (2015), Stressful Involvement contributed significantly to the prediction of Emotional Exhaustion for their 94 therapists. More fine-grained analysis of Stressful Involvement component factors showed the dimension of therapist feeling in-session "Anxiety" contributed significantly to both the EE and DP aspects of burnout. On the positive side, Healing Involvement contributed significantly to the prediction of Personal Accomplishment (PA), especially by the first-level dimension of therapist feeling in-session "Flow" (immersive interest and creative responsiveness).

Another British study which did not include DPCCQ variables may nevertheless be mentioned here for its relevance to the relation of therapist burnout to patient outcome (Delgadillo, Saxon & Barkham, 2018). Using the Oldenburg Burnout Inventory (Demerouti, Bakker, Vardakou & Kantas, 2003), those authors found that higher levels of burnout "detachment" predicted poorer patient outcomes to a substantial degree. This finding, based on data from 2223 patients, nested within 49 therapists, provides additional if indirect evidence of a link between the psychotherapist's perspective (in this case, reports of burnout) and "external" clinical perspectives.

Therapist Training

One further application of the DPCCQ has been made in addition to process and outcome studies, and that is as a kind of outcome measure for therapist training. In these studies, time itself is the "objective" measures to which the psychotherapist's perspective is compared. Presumably, if training is effective then trainees' experiences of their work with clients as a Healing Involvement (or its components) should increase, and their experiences of Stressful Involvement (or its components) should decrease over time. To date, four studies have explored this idea.

A Swedish Study

In a study by Dennhag & Ybrandt (2013) the DPCCQ was administered to 76 inexperienced but highly motivated undergraduate psychology students in Sweden who were enrolled in a two-semester clinical practicum. Each trainee treated one patient, either in Cognitive-Behavioral or Psychodynamic therapy, and each was assessed with the DPCCQ five times during their training experience, at sessions 2, 8, 16, 22 and at the end. Data analyses focused on the factor components of Healing Involvement and Stressful Involvement that showed adequate reliability in their sample. These were the Healing Involvement components "Basic Relational Skills", "Technical Expertise", and "Constructive Coping", as well as the Stressful Involvement components "Total Difficulties in Practice", and in-session feeling dimensions of therapist "Anxiety" and "Boredom".

Overall for Healing Involvement, the trainees as a group showed a linear increase over time in "Basic Relational Skills", "Technical Expertise" and "Constructive Coping"—although significant differences existed among individual trainees. Moreover, reliable change (assessed by the statistical method of Jacobson and Truax, 1991) was evident only in some trainees. Only eight trainees (10.5%) experienced a positive change in "basic Relational skills" while 67 remained unchanged and 1 trainee seemed to decline. Also, 24 trainees (31.6%) experienced a reliable positive change in "Technical Expertise" while 50 showed no change, and two regressed. Positive change in use of "Constructive Coping" occurred in eight trainees, negative change for two, and 66 remained unchanged on this dimension. Similarly complex results were found for the component dimensions of Stressful Involvement. Trainees varied individually among themselves with respect to in-session feelings of "Boredom" and "Anxiety"; some increased, some decreased, most remained unchanged—but as a group, the changes did not reach statistical significance. There was a small but significant overall decrease in "Total Difficulties in Practice", but more so among trainees following Cognitive-Behavioral than Psychodynamic models of practice. Once again, only some trainees experienced fewer difficulties, most remained unchanged, and a small minority experienced more difficulty over time. The general impression is that trainees tended to change positively in the components of Healing Involvement that were analyzed, but that change in the components of Stressful Involvement was minimal or null.

Three German Studies

By contrast, in a cross-sectional study of 171 more advanced trainees in Germany, Taubner and colleagues found that Stressful Involvement in therapy sessions was lower for those who had previously completed more years in training (Taubner, Kächele, Visbeck, Rapp & Sandell, 2010). The students were enrolled in postgraduate training institutes teaching either Psychoanalytic, Psychodynamic or Cognitive-Behavioral therapies. The authors also found that Healing Involvement was higher among female than male trainees, but not among trainees who had more years in training. Thus while also finding relations between time in training and DPCCQ-based dimensions, the findings were almost the reverse of those later found in the Swedish study.

Taubner and colleagues followed up their cross-sectional study with a longitudinal study involving 71 of the same students who had been initially assessed with a series of instruments at the start and end of a three-year period (Taubner, Zimmermann, Kächele, Möller & Sell, 2013). Those instruments included the Work Involvement Scales of the DPCCQ, with scores on Healing Involvement viewed by the authors as a measure of therapist self-efficacy. Other measures included the SASB-Intrex questionnaire (Benjamin, 1983) to assess therapist self-affiliation, and a scale of personal satisfaction with trainees' own psychotherapy. The main finding of relevance for our context is that Healing Involvement increased significantly over time, indicating that trainees felt more effective after three years of therapy training. These findings agreed with those of the Swedish study, but not with the results of their own previous cross-sectional study. (Trainees were not assessed for change in levels of Stressful Involvement.)

A recent and similar but more expansive study by Taubner's group reinforces their earlier findings (Evers, Schröder-Pfeifer, Möller & Taubner, 2019).[7] The sample included 130 students, recruited from several psychotherapy training institutes in Germany, who were tested at different points in their training and once more three years later. Over that time, overall scores for Healing Involvement increased significantly even though high at first, with 66% of the sample showing "much" Healing Involvement initially, rising to 87% above the criterion for "much" Healing Involvement at the second assessment. Employing a statistically derived Reliable Change Index that is frequently used in therapy outcome studies (Jacobson & Truax, 1991), the authors found that 19% of the trainees showed a reliable improvement whereas 81% did not reach the statistical criterion, while none declined.[8] By contrast, Stressful Involvement did not change significantly over time. Initially, 39% of the trainees showed "more than a little" Stressful Involvement and after three years 42% did as well.[9] This was reflected as well in results for the Reliable Change Index: only 10% improved (i.e., experienced *less* Stressful Involvement), 77% remained relatively unchanged, and some 13% deteriorated significantly (experienced *more* Stressful Involvement).

It is, of course, gratifying to see that therapist trainees in Germany show evidence of increase in Healing Involvement or its components over time, as did trainees in Sweden over an even shorter period. It is sobering to note that not all trainees improved significantly on the statistical criteria employed. It is also sobering to see that Stressful Involvement did not decline significantly in any of the trainee studies, but this might have been due to the relatively short period involved. In the Collaborative Research Network database with therapists at all career levels, 48% of those having less than three years in practicing therapy (who most likely were still trainees) experienced practice with "more than a little" Stressful Involvement. The percentage in that category declined significantly over career cohorts to 35% for those with 3 to 10 years of practice, 30% for those with 10 to 20 years of practice, and 25% for those with 20 to 50 years of practice—suggesting a significant residual of Stressful Involvement that is probably due to patient or practice characteristics. The studies of trainees nevertheless add to evidence showing that the measures of therapists' qualities and characteristics based on the DPCCQ correspond, however complexly, to measures of therapy and therapists based on other observational perspectives.

Observational Perspectives and Levels of Analysis in Research Measures

This book differs from previous studies of therapists' lives and personalities by its analyses of a massive and broad-ranging collection of empirical data. All of the data (collected with the DPCCQ) are based on therapists' own reports and observations, as distinct from observations made by others, and thus uniquely reflect the psychotherapist's observational perspective. This final chapter, addressed to researchers, has reviewed a number of studies that used the DPCCQ along with measures from other observational perspectives, in order to assess how much measures from those other perspectives coordinate with therapists. This seemed a valuable task even though the studies reviewed mostly focused on therapists' professional activities rather than their personal qualities and characteristics. Taken together, the studies reviewed showed many significant relationships between DPCCQ measures such as Healing Involvement or Stressful Involvement (or their component dimensions) and several commonly used measures of therapeutic process and outcome, indicating that therapists' views are not methodologically isolated or unrelated to clinical processes. Psychotherapists do not live in "a world of their own" but rather in a shared reality, however multifaceted the latter may be. Yet the relationships these studies established were clearly complex and not always consistent, both within and across different studies. Thus it seems worthwhile to end by reflecting a bit on the challenges of measurement involved in psychotherapy research.

One point of comparison that draws our attention is the difference in levels of conceptual analysis or focus of the various research instruments. For example, the DPCCQ focuses clinically on the therapist's current professional practice, experienced as including all clients in all treatment modalities and in all settings; and focuses individually on the therapist as a person engaged in many areas of personal life beyond that of professional practice. By contrast, the conceptual level of analysis of other measures focus sometimes on individual treatment cases within the therapist's practice (e.g., the working alliance trajectory over time), and sometimes on characteristics of specific therapy sessions within a treatment case (e.g., the working alliance level), or sometimes even on attributes of specific segments within therapy sessions (e.g., particular therapist interventions). This concept of different analytic levels of focus is illustrated in Figure 11.1.

The levels can range from a highly "microscopic" focus on specific actions or behaviors in sessions where patient–therapist interactions are studied (Level 1),

Level of Analysis	Observational Perspective			Focus of Action		
	Therapist	*Patient*	*Observer*	*Therapist*	*Patient*	*Context*
Level 6: *Community*	Therapist 'expert helper' role	Patient help-seeking 'sick' role	Sociology, Anthropology, Economics etc.	Professional 'mental health' manpower & networks	Community 'mental health' patient populations	'Mental health' care systems: culture & institutions
Level 5: *Person*	DPCCQ, TBIF[1], Intrex-T[2], MBI[3]	SCL90-R[4] IIP[5], Intrex-P	Th. & Pt. 'demographic' attributes	Th.'s professional skill, manner & motivations	Pt's personal 'disorders' & 'assets'	Intersecting life-course & social networks
Level 4: *Practice*	DPCCQ, TCPR[6]	Pt.'s treatment record	Professional practice review board	Th.'s supervisory & support resources	Pt's personal support network	Treatment setting
Level 3: *Case*	WAI-T[7], slope+level, TCPR-C[8]	WAI-P, slope+level,	TSPR[9]	Th.'s counter-transference & case management	Pt. treatment progress course	Therapy relationship: quality & trajectory
Level 2: *Session*	SEQ-T[10], WAI-T level, TSR-T[11]	SEQ-P, WAI-P level, TSR-P	Whole session ratings/themes	Th. session management & role performance	Pt. session experience & impact	Sequential interaction patterns
Level 1: *Action*	Process recall analysis[12]	Process recall analysis	Session segment ratings/themes	Therapist intervention	Patient response	Specific interactions

[1] *Trainee Background Information Form* (based on DPCCQ), used in SPRISTAD Study.
[2] Structured Analysis of Social Behavior *Intrex* (Benjamin, 1983), therapist (T) & patient (P) versions.
[3] *Maslach Burnout Inventory* (Maslach).
[4] *Symptom Check List 90-R* (Derogatis).
[5] *Inventory of Interpersonal Problems* (Horowitz).
[6] *Trainee Current Practice Report* (based on DPCCQ), used in SPRISTAD Study.
[7] *Working Alliance Inventory* (Horvath & Greenberg) therapist (T) & patient (P) versions.
[8] *Trainee Current Practice Report-Case*, case-based version of trainee TCPR.
[9] *Trainee's Supervisor Practice Report*, case-based version of trainee TCPR-C.
[10] *Session Evaluation Questionnaire* (Stiles) therapist (T) & patient (P) versions.
[11] *Therapy Session Report* (Orlinsky & Howard), therapist (T) & patient (P) versions.
[12] Post-session interview reviewing specific tape-recorded session segments (e.g., Elliott).

Figure 11.1 Therapy Research Measures: Levels of Analysis, Observational Perspectives, and Focus of Action

to a highly "macroscopic" focus (Level 6) at which social, cultural and institutional patterns related to "mental health" ideals and practices in particular communities are studied (e.g., Ulvik & Rønnestad, 2013). The instruments used in the studies that have been reviewed in this chapter lie between these extremes, with a focus on sessions at Level 2 (e.g., Odyniec et al. 2017), with a focus on cases at Level 3 (e.g., Heinonen et al., 2013; Nissen-Lie et al., 2013), with a focus on the therapist's professional practice a Level 4 (e.g., Schröder et al., 2016; Taubner et al., 2013), or with a focus on the personal lives and attributes of participants in therapy at Level 5 (e.g., the DPCCQ). It does not seem reasonable to expect that measures focused at different conceptual levels would show consistent or statistically significant associations, whether comparing observational perspectives or in other respects. When the therapist's perspective is focused on one level and measures used to assess the patient's perspective are focused at a different level, there are sound reasons to think that the associations between them may be attenuated or obscured. This may be why the factor scales that are components of Healing Involvement or Stressful Involvement were often found to be significant in studies while the broader dimensions themselves were not. Healing Involvement or Stressful Involvement are statistically derived composites at the level of overall practice, whereas dimensions of therapists' difficulties are closer to the level of analysis focused on by instruments that rate "smoothness" or "depth" as qualities of specific sessions, or that assess the development of working alliance across sessions in specific cases. The Practice Patterns based jointly on Healing Involvement or Stressful Involvement are even more general categories which, like the "Healer" types identified in Chapter 10, will closely fit a subgroup of cases but only approximately fit most of the individual cases which resemble them. Even with these disparities in levels of analysis tending to confound the comparison of the psychotherapist's perspective with other observational perspectives, the numerous if sometimes oblique correspondences between the DPCCQ and other measures provide some assurance that what our therapists reported about their lives and selves does represent one aspect of a manifold reality that is worthy of research interest.

Finally, a last word of commendation is reserved for the Development of Psychotherapists Common Core Questionnaire as the wide-ranging research instrument used in this study. Unlike most instruments that focus on a single topic and yield limited information, the DPCCQ includes multiple topics exploring many aspects of psychotherapists' professional and personal lives. The breadth of information harvested with the DPCCQ has made it possible to recognize meaningful statistical patterns in the multiple data-points drawn from what psychotherapists have told us. So finally, then, thanks to the 12,000 therapists who told us so much about themselves; thanks to the many colleagues in the SPR Collaborative Research Network who used the DPCCQ over 30 years to gather that data; and thanks to the original group of collaborators who developed the DPCCQ from their own diverse experiences as psychotherapists.

Notes

1 The fact that therapists typically underestimated their patients' ratings of the therapeutic alliance would imply that they tend to experience high levels of *Stressful Involvement* and low levels of *Healing Involvement*, which seems contrary to the levels reported for this sample by Zeeck et al. (2012), where the mean level of *Healing Involvement* was above 8 and that of *Stressful Involvement* was just above 3 (each on a 1–15 scale).
2 Another recognized category of negative impact is "vicarious traumatization" in which therapists suffer from their exposure to and empathy with narratives of the traumas and suffering their patients have experienced.
3 The relation of therapists' work experiences to professional development was examined at length in Orlinsky & Rønnestad (2005), *How Psychotherapists Develop*. It is also currently a main focus of the large-scale, international, longitudinal multisite study of psychotherapy trainees being conducted by the Society for Psychotherapy Research Interest Section on Therapist Training and Development (SPRISTAD; Orlinsky, Strauss, Rønnestad et al., 2015).
4 Called "Affirming" by Orlinsky & Rønnestad (2005).
5 Termed "Avoiding Therapeutic Engagement" by Orlinsky & Rønnestad (2005).
6 IAPT = the "Improving Access to Psychological Therapies" program of the UK National Health Service.
7 The study by Evers et al. included a wide array of measures assessing training context variables (e.g., theoretical orientation), professional attributes (e.g., work satisfaction), and personal attributes (e.g., neuroticism, introject affiliation), as well as age, sex, and training semester.
8 Since many trainees were already at a comparatively high level initially, a ceiling effect may have constricted the amount of possible improvement in the measure.
9 Unfortunately, Evers et al. did not combine those percentages in a way that permitted seeing change in overall practice pattern (as Schröder et al. had done in their UK studies). Possibly the increase in Healing Involvement had moved some trainees from a Distressing Practice to a Challenging Practice even without the level of Stressful Involvement having been reduced.

References

Benjamin, L. S. (1974). Structural analysis of social behavior. *Psychological Review*, 81(5), 392–425.
Benjamin, L. S. (1983). *The Intrex user's manual*. Madison, WI: Intrex Interpersonal Institute.
Benjamin, L. S. (1995). *SASB Intrex short form user's manual*. Salt Lake City, UT: University of Utah.
Bordin, E. S. (1979). The generalizability of the psychoanalytic concept of the working alliance. *Psychotherapy: Theory, Research and Practice*, 16, 252–260.
Delgadillo, J., Saxon, D., & Barkham, M. (2018). Associations between therapists' occupational burnout and their patients' depression and anxiety treatment outcomes. *Depression and Anxiety*, 35(9), 844–850.
Demerouti, E., Bakker, A. B., Vardakou, I., & Kantas, A. (2003) The convergent validity of two burnout instruments: A multitrait-multimethod analysis. *European Journal of Psychological Assessment*, 18, 296–307.
Dennhag, I., & Ybrandt, H. (2013). Trainee psychotherapists' development in self-rated professional qualities in training. *Psychotherapy*, 50(2), 158–166.
Derogatis, L. R. (1975). *Brief Symptom Inventory*. Baltimore: Clinical Psychometric Research.

218   *Beyond the Psychotherapist's Perspective*

Derogatis, L. R. (1983). *SCL-90-R: Administration, scoring and procedures manual* (2nd ed). Towson, MD: Psychometric Research.

Evers, O., Schröder-Pfeifer, P., Möller, H., & Taubner, S. (2019). How do personal and professional characteristics influence the development of psychotherapists in training: Results from a longitudinal study. *Research in Psychotherapy: Psychopathology, Process and Outcome*, 22, 389–401.

Hartmann, A., Joos, A., Orlinsky, D. E., & Zeeck, A. (2014): Accuracy of therapist perceptions of patients' alliance: Exploring the divergence. *Psychotherapy Research*, 25 (4), 408–419.

Havik, O.E., Monsen, J.T., Høglend, P., Lippe, A.L. von der, Lyngstad, G., Stiles, T., et al. (1995). *The Norwegian Multisite Study on Process and Outcome of Psychotherapy (NMSPOP)*. Research protocol available from Odd E. Havik, Department of Clinical Psychology, University of Bergen, Christiesgt. 12, 5015 Bergen, Norway.

Heinonen, E., Knekt, P., Jääskeläinen, T., & Lindfors, O. (2013). Therapists' professional and personal characteristics as predictors of outcome in long-term psychodynamic psychotherapy and psychoanalysis. *European Psychiatry*, 29(5), 265–274.

Heinonen, E., Lindfors, O., Härkänen, T., Virtala, E., Jääskeläinen, T., & Knekt, P. (2013). Therapists' professional and personal characteristics as predictors of working alliance in short-term and long-term psychotherapies. *Clinical Psychology & Psychotherapy*, 21(6), 475–494.

Heinonen, E., Lindfors, O., Laaksonen, M. A., & Knekt, P. (2012). Therapists' professional and personal characteristics as predictors of outcome in short- and long-term psychotherapy. *Journal of Affective Disorders*, 138(3), 301–312.

Horowitz, L. M., Strauss, B., & Kordy, H. (2000). *Inventar zur Erfassung Interpersonaler Probleme (IIP-D) Deutsche Version* (2nd ed.) [Inventory of Interpersonal Problems (IIP) German version]. Göttingen: Beltz.

Horvath, A. O., & Greenberg, L. S. (1989). Development and validation of the Working Alliance Inventory. *Journal of Counseling Psychology*, 36, 223–233.

Jacobson, N. S., & Truax, P. (1991). Clinical significance: A statistical approach to defining meaningful change in psychotherapy research. *Journal of Consulting and Clinical Psychology*, 59(1), 12–19.

Knekt, P., & Lindfors, O. (Eds.). (2004). *A randomized trial of the effect of four forms of psychotherapy on depressive and anxiety disorders. Design, methods, and results on the effectiveness of short-term psychodynamic psychotherapy and solution-focused therapy during a one-year follow-up.* Studies in social security and health 77. Helsinki: The Social Insurance Institution.

Kroenke, K., Spitzer, R. L., Williams, J. B., & Lowe, B. (2010). The Patient Health Questionnaire Somatic, Anxiety, and Depressive Symptom Scales: A systematic review. *General Hospital Psychiatry*, 32(4), 345–359.

Luborsky, L., Crits-Christoph, P., Alexander, L., Margolis, M., & Cohen, M. (1983). Two helping alliance methods for predicting outcomes of psychotherapy: A counting signs vs. a global rating method. *Journal of Nervous and Mental Disease*, 171, 480–491.

Maslach, C., & Jackson, S. E. (1981). The measurement of experienced burnout. *Journal of Occupational Behavior*, 2(2), 99–113.

Nissen-Lie, H. A., Havik, O. E., Høglend, P. A., Monsen, J. T., & Rønnestad, M. H. (2013). The contribution of therapists' personal life quality to the development of the working alliance. *Journal of Counseling Psychology*, 60(4), 483–495.

Nissen-Lie, H. A., Havik, O. D., Høglend, P. A., Rønnestad, M. H., & Monsen, J. T. (2015). Patient and therapist perspectives on alliance development: Therapists' practice experiences as predictors. *Clinical Psychology and Psychotherapy*, 22, 317–327.

Nissen-Lie, H. A., Monsen, J. T., & Rønnestad, M. H. (2010). Therapist predictors of early patient-rated working alliance: A multilevel approach. *Psychotherapy Research*, 20 (6), 627–646.

Nissen-Lie, H. A., Monsen, J. T., Ulleberg, P., & Rønnestad, M. H. (2012). Psychotherapists' self-reports of their interpersonal functioning and difficulties in practice as predictors of patient outcome. *Psychotherapy Research*, 23(1), 86–104.

Nissen-Lie, H. A., Rønnestad, M. H., Høglend, P. A., Havik, O. E., Solbakken, O. A., Stiles, T. C., & Monsen, J. T. (2015). Love yourself as a person, doubt yourself as a therapist? *Clinical Psychology & Psychotherapy*, 24(1), 48–60.

Odyniec, P., Probst, T., Margraf, J., & Willutzki, U. (2017). Psychotherapist trainees' professional self-doubt and negative personal reaction: Changes during cognitive behavioral therapy and association with patient progress. *Psychotherapy Research*, 29(1), 123–138.

Orlinsky, D. E., Geller, J. D., Tarragona, M., & Farber, B. (1993). Patients' representations of psychotherapy: A new focus for psychodynamic research. *Journal of Consulting and Clinical Psychology*, 61, 596–610.

Orlinsky, D. E., & Rønnestad, M. H. (2005). *How psychotherapists develop: A study of therapeutic work and professional growth*. Washington, DC: APA Books.

Orlinsky, D. E., Strauss, B., Rønnestad, M. H., et al. (2015). A collaborative study of development in psychotherapy trainees. *Psychotherapy Bulletin*, 50(4), 21–25.

Schröder, T., Steel, K., & Macdonald, J. (2016). *Psychotherapists' process experiences predict client treatment outcomes: The work experience of British IAPT therapists in relation to staff burnout and client outcomes*. Paper presented at the Paper presented at the 47th annual conference of the Society for Psychotherapy Research, Jerusalem, Israel.

Steel, K., Macdonald, J., Schröder, T., & Mellor-Clark, J. (2015). Exhausted but not cynical: *Burnout* in therapists working within Improving Access to Psychological Therapy Services. *Journal of Mental Health*, 24(1), 33–37.

Stiles, W. B., Gordon, L. E., & Lani, J. A. (2002). Session evaluation and the Session Evaluation Questionnaire. In G. S. Tryon (Ed.), *Counseling based on process research: Applying what we know*, 325–343. Boston, MA: Allyn & Bacon.

Taubner, S., Zimmermann, J., Kächele, H., Möller, H., & Sell, C. (2013). The relationship of introject affiliation and personal therapy to trainee self-efficacy: A longitudinal study among psychotherapy trainees. *Psychotherapy*, 50(2), 167–177.

Taubner, S., Kächele, H., Visbeck, A., Rapp, A., & Sandell, R. (2010). Therapeutic attitudes and practice patterns among psychotherapy trainees in Germany. *European Journal of Psychotherapy and Counselling*, 12(4), 361–381.

Ulvik, O. S., & Rønnestad, M. H. (2013). Cultural discourses of helping: Perspectives on what people bring with them when they start training in therapy and counsel-ing. In M. H. Rønnestad & T. M. Skovholt, *The developing practitioner: Growth and stagnation of therapists and counselors*, 37–51. New York: Routledge.

Willutzki, U., Hernandez Bark, G., Davis, J., & Orlinsky, D. E. (1997, June). Client outcomes as a function of the therapist's difficulties and coping strategies in the course of psychotherapy: Initial results. Paper presented at the 28th Annual International Conference of the Society for Psychotherapy Research, Geilo, Norway.

Zeeck, A., Orlinsky, D. E., Hermann, S., Joos, A., Wirsching, M., Weidmann, W., & Hartmann, A. (2012). Stressful involvement in psychotherapeutic work: Therapist, client and process correlates. *Psychotherapy Research*, 22(5), 543–555.

12 Statistical Appendix

David E. Orlinsky

The Appendix consists of approximately 150 statistical tables showing results of data analyses that were presented and discussed in Chapters 2–10.

Notes to Chi-square tables:

1. The term AsR = Adjusted standardized Residual.
2. Cell percentages in **bold** type are significantly higher than expected by chance; cell percentages in *italic* type are significantly lower than expected by chance.
3. Percentages in **bold** type or underlined *italic* type, without parentheses, indicate cell $p \leq .01$; **bold** type and *italic* type within parentheses indicates cell $p \leq .05$.

Notes to Factor tables:
(1) Criterion for factor rotation: Eigenvalue ≥ 1.
(2) α = Cronbach's alpha.

Notes to Correlation tables:

1 Correlations of $r \geq .20$ in bold type, but not $r \leq .19$ even if statistically significant.

DOI: 10.4324/9781003217572-12

Table 2.1 Professions by Theoretical Orientation (N ≥ 300)

Theoretical Orientation		Psychology	Psychiatry	Counsel-ing	Social Work	Lay Therapist/ Analyst	Total
Analytic/ Psychodynamic	n	1,159	830	284	103	208	2,584
	%	27.2%	**44.6%**	*16.8%*	*18.4%*	**36.7%**	28.9%
	AsR	-3.4	16.8	-12.2	-5.7	4.2	
Cognitive-Behavioral	n	558	109	69	18	37	791
	%	**13.1%**	*5.9%*	*4.1%*	*3.2%*	6.5%	8.9%
	AsR	13.5	-5.1	-7.7	-4.9	-2.0	
Humanistic	n	335	86	388	40	56	905
	%	*7.9%*	*4.6%*	**23.0%**	7.1%	9.9%	10.1%
	AsR	-6.8	-8.9	19.4	-2.4	-.2	
Systemic	n	170	34	51	53	19	327
	%	4.0%	*1.8%*	3.0%	**9.5%**	3.4%	3.7%
	AsR	1.6	-4.7	-1.6	7.6	-.4	
Analytic/ Psychodynamic + Humanistic	n	373	139	77	41	38	668
	%	**8.8%**	7.5%	*4.6%*	7.3%	6.7%	7.5%
	AsR	4.4	.0	-5.1	-.1	-.7	
Analytic/ Psychodynamic + Systemic	n	138	86	28	55	16	323
	%	3.2%	4.6%	*1.7%*	**9.8%**	2.8%	3.6%
	AsR	-1.8	2.6	-4.8	8.1	-1.0	
Cognitive-Behavioral + Humanistic	n	211	30	75	12	12	340
	%	**5.0%**	*1.6%*	4.4%	2.1%	2.1%	3.8%
	AsR	5.4	-5.6	1.5	-2.1	-2.2	
Broad Spectrum	n	953	227	474	164	125	1,943
	%	22.4%	*12.2%*	**28.1%**	**29.3%**	22.1%	21.7%
	AsR	1.4	-11.2	7.0	4.5	.2	
"Other" orientation	n	115	38	87	16	35	291
	%	2.7%	2.0%	**5.2%**	2.9%	**6.2%**	3.3%
	AsR	-2.8	-3.3	4.9	-.6	4.1	
No Salient Orientation	n	247	282	156	58	20	763
	%	*5.8%*	**15.2%**	9.2%	10.4%	*3.5%*	8.5%
	AsR	-8.8	11.5	1.1	1.6	-4.4	
Total	N	4,259	1,861	1,689	560	566	8,935
	%	100.0%	100.0%	100.0%	100.0%	100.0%	100.0%

χ^2 = 1369.5, df = 36, p = .000; AsR cut-off at p =.01 for 50 cells = ± 3.72 (at p = .05, ± 3.29)

Table 2.2 Psychotherapists' Gender and Generation (Birth Year Cohort)

		Birth Year Cohort					Total
		1907–1936	1937–1946	1947–1956	1957–1966	1967–1990	
Female	n	243	1,198	2,432	1,892	1,670	7,435
	%	*46.8%*	*59.7%*	*(61.3%)*	63.6%	73.3%	63.3%
	AsR	-8.0	-3.7	-3.2	.4	11.0	
Male	n	276	809	1,535	1,082	609	4,311
	%	**53.2%**	**40.3%**	*(38.7%)*	36.4%	*26.7%*	36.7%
	AsR	8.0	3.7	3.2	-.4	-11.0	
	N	519	2,007	3,967	2,974	2,279	11,746
	%	100.0%	100.0%	100.0%	100.0%	100.0%	100.0%

χ^2 = 176.5, df = 4, p = .000; AsR cut-off at p =.01 for 10 cells = ± 3.29 (at p = .05, ± 2.81)

Table 2.3 Psychotherapists' Gender and Generation by Profession

Psychology		1907–1936	1937–1946	1947–1956	1957–1966	1967–1990	Total
Female	n	116	477	1,043	924	893	3,453
	%	*42.2%*	*54.6%*	*58.8%*	**66.5%**	**74.6%**	62.7%
	AR	-7.2	-5.4	-4.1	3.4	9.6	
Male	n	159	396	731	465	304	2,055
	%	**57.8%**	**45.4%**	**41.2%**	*33.5%*	*25.4%*	37.3%
	AsR	7.2	5.4	4.1	-3.4	-9.6	
	N	275	873	1,774	1,389	1,197	5,508
	%	100.0%	100.0%	100.0%	100.0%	100.0%	100.0%

χ^2 = 166.5, df = 4, p = .000; AsR cut-off at p =.01 for 10 cells = 3.29 (at p = .05, ± 2.81)

Psychiatry		1907–1936	1937–1946	1947–1956	1957–1966	1967–1990	Total
Female	n	36	128	289	305	128	886
	%	30.5%	35.0%	38.0%	**(45.6%)**	47.9%	40.6%
	AsR	-2.3	-2.4	-1.8	3.1	2.6	
Male	n	82	238	472	364	139	1295
	%	69.5%	65.0%	62.0%	*(54.4%)*	52.1%	59.4%
	AsR	2.3	2.4	1.8	-3.1	-2.6	
	N	118	366	761	669	267	2181
	%	100.0%	100.0%	100.0%	100.0%	100.0%	100.0%

χ^2 = 24.8, df = 4, p = .000; AsR cut-off at p =.01 for 10 cells = ± 3.29 (at p = .05, ± 2.81)

(Continued)

Table 2.3 (Cont.)

Counseling		1907–1936	1937–1946	1947–1956	1957–1966	1967–1990	Total
Female	n	41	336	613	334	372	1696
	%	78.8%	79.4%	80.0%	75.6%	80.9%	79.1%
	AsR	-.1	.2	.8	-2.1	1.0	
Male	n	11	87	153	108	88	447
	%	21.2%	20.6%	20.0%	24.4%	19.1%	20.9%
	AsR	.1	-.2	-.8	2.1	-1.0	
	N	52	423	766	442	460	2143
	%	100.0%	100.0%	100.0%	100.0%	100.0%	100.0%

$\chi^2 = 4.6$, df = 4, p = ns

Table 2.4 Psychotherapists' Gender by Profession

Gender		Therapeutic Profession					Total
		Psychology	Psychiatry	Counseling	Social Work	Lay Therapist/Analyst	
Female	n	3,494	898	1,719	552	521	7,184
	%	62.7%	_40.7%_	**79.3%**	**77.0%**	**70.7%**	63.0%
	AR	-.6	-24.2	17.4	8.0	4.5	
Male	n	2,075	1,310	450	165	216	4,216
	%	37.3%	**59.3%**	_20.7%_	_23.0%_	_29.3%_	37.0%
	AR	.6	24.2	-17.4	-8.0	-4.5	
Total	N	5,569	2,208	2,169	717	737	11,400
	%	100.0%	100.0%	100.0%	100.0%	100.0%	100.0%

$c^2 = 797.3$, df = 4, p = .000; AsR cut-off at p = .001 for 10 cells = ± 3.29 (at p = .05, ± 2.81)

Table 2.5 Therapists' Ages in Years by Profession*

Profession	Current Age			Age at Start of Practice				
	N	1	2	N	1	2	3	4
Psychology	5,531	44.1		5386	31.0			
Medicine/Psychiatry	2,195	43.2		2018		32.4		
Social Work	712	43.9		665		33.3		
Lay Therapist/Analyst	728		49.2	709			36.7	
Counseling	2,156		48.9	2056				39.2

* 1-way ANOVA; Scheffe post-hoc test of subset differences (alpha = 0.01)

Table 2.6 Therapists' Genders by Theoretical Orientation (N ≥ 500)

Gender		Analytic/ Dynamic	Cogni- tive- Behavioral	Huma- nistic	Analytic/ Dynamic + Humanistic	Broad Spectrum	No Salient Orienta- tion	Total
Female	n	1,627	503	649	414	1,309	487	4,989
	%	61.9%	*56.7%*	**70.4%**	61.5%	**(65.9%)**	60.8%	63.2%
	AsR	-1.6	-4.2	4.8	-.9	2.9	-1.5	
Male	n	1,001	384	273	259	677	314	2,908
	%	38.1%	**43.3%**	*29.6%*	38.5%	*(34.1%)*	39.2%	36.8%
	AsR	1.6	4.2	-4.8	.9	-2.9	1.5	
Total	N	2,628	887	922	673	1,986	801	7,897
	%	100.0%	100.0%	100.0%	100.0%	100.0%	100.0%	100.0%

χ^2 = 47.5, df = 4, p = .000; AsR cut-off at p =.01 for 10 cells = ± 3.34 (at p = .05, ± 2.87)

Table 2.7 Therapists' Ages in Years by Theoretical Orientation*

Main Theoretical Orientations (n > 500)		Current Age		
	N	1	2	3
Humanistic	919	47.3		
Analytic/Dynamic	2,611	45.9	45.9	
Broad Spectrum	1,967	45.5	45.5	
Analytic/Dynamic + Humanistic	671		44.5	
Cognitive-Behavioral	878			41.9
No Salient Orientation	790			41.3

* 1-way ANOVA; Scheffé post-hoc test of subset differences (alpha = 0.01)

Table 2.8 Psychotherapists by Nation

Nation	N	Valid %
Norway	1,678	13.9
USA	1,207	10.0
UK	1,108	9.2
Germany	1,175	9.8
Australia	1,004	8.3
Canada	600	5.0
Denmark	540	4.5
S. Korea	539	4.5
China	509	4.2
Portugal	416	3.5
New Zealand	331	2.8
Switzerland	306	2.5
India	277	2.3
Austria	234	1.9
Israel	205	1.7
Others: Western Europe[a]	1,011	8.4
Others: Latin America[b]	346	2.9
Others: Eastern Europe[c]	205	1.7
Others: Asia[d]	121	1.0
Others: Middle East[e]	100	.8
Others: Africa[f]	41	.3
Missing	83	.7
Total	12,036	100.0

[a] Belgium, Finland, France, Greece, Ireland, Italy, Netherlands, Sweden
[b] Argentina, Brazil, Chile, Mexico, Panama
[c] Croatia, Czech Republic, Poland, Russia, Slovakia
[d] Hong Kong, Indonesia, Malaysia, Singapore
[e] Egypt, Lebanon, Saudi Arabia, Turkey, United Arab Emirates
[f] South Africa

Table 2.9 Cultural Marginality: Secularity vs. Religious Affiliation

Nation		No affiliation	Protestant Christian	Catholic/ Orthodox	Jewish	Muslim	Hindu	Buddhist	Mixed/ other	Total
New Zealand	n	201	35	26	2	0	1	4	27	296
	%	**67.9%**	*11.8%*	8.8%	*(0.7%)*	0.0%	0.3%	1.4%	9.1%	100.0%
	AR	6.7	-4.1	-.8	-3.7	-1.8	-.5	-2.8	1.0	
Denmark	n	233	109	6	1	0	0	10	13	372
	%	**62.6%**	*29.3%*	*1.6%*	*0.3%*	0.0%	0.0%	2.7%	3.5%	100.0%
	AR	5.4	3.9	-5.7	-4.6	-2.0	-1.5	-1.9	-3.1	
Canada	n	235	63	28	27	0	0	8	17	378
	%	**62.2%**	16.7%	7.4%	7.1%	0.0%	0.0%	2.1%	4.5%	100.0%
	AR	5.3	-2.3	-1.9	1.5	-2.1	-1.5	-2.5	-2.4	
UK	n	591	245	62	22	1	2	24	59	1,006
	%	**58.7%**	24.4%	*6.2%*	*2.2%*	0.1%	0.2%	*2.4%*	5.9%	100.0%
	AR	6.9	2.7	-4.8	-5.2	-3.3	-1.8	-3.9	-2.4	
Latin America, other	n	117	4	57	3	0	0	11	10	202
	%	57.9%	*2.0%*	**28.2%**	1.5%	0.0%	0.0%	5.4%	5.0%	100.0%
	AR	2.5	-6.9	8.7	-2.5	-1.5	-1.1	.5	-1.5	
Eastern Europe, other	n	43	3	28	1	0	0	2	2	79
	%	54.4%	*(3.8%)*	**35.4%**	1.3%	0.0%	0.0%	2.5%	2.5%	100.0%
	AR	.9	-3.8	7.5	-1.6	-.9	-.7	-.9	-1.7	
Western Europe, other	n	79	15	81	0	0	0	5	2	182
	%	43.4%	*8.2%*	**44.5%**	0.0%	0.0%	0.0%	2.7%	1.1%	100.0%
	AR	-1.6	-4.4	15.6	-3.3	-1.4	-1.0	-1.3	-3.4	
USA	n	254	111	49	146	3	1	20	41	625
	%	*40.6%*	17.8%	7.8%	**23.4%**	0.5%	0.2%	3.2%	6.6%	100.0%
	AR	-4.6	-2.4	-2.1	21.4	-1.4	-1.5	-1.9	-1.1	
Middle East, other	n	10	0	0	0	21	0	0	0	31
	%	32.3%	0.0%	0.0%	0.0%	**67.7%**	0.0%	0.0%	0.0%	100.0%
	AR	-1.9	-2.9	-1.9	-1.3	37.2	-.4	-1.2	-1.6	
Australia	n	299	289	92	27	1	9	101	150	968
	%	*30.9%*	**29.9%**	9.5%	*2.8%*	0.1%	0.9%	**10.4%**	**15.5%**	100.0%
	AR	-13.0	7.3	-.8	-4.1	-3.2	1.7	9.7	10.6	
Asia, other	n	23	32	4	0	17	11	13	1	101
	%	*22.8%*	31.7%	4.0%	0.0%	**16.8%**	**10.9%**	**12.9%**	1.0%	100.0%
	AR	-5.4	2.6	-2.1	-2.4	16.1	14.0	4.0	-2.5	
Total	N	2,087	906	433	230	43	24	198	322	4,243
	%	**49.2%**	21.4%	10.2%	5.4%	1.0%	0.6%	4.7%	7.6%	100.0%

$\chi^2 = 3241.8$, df = 84, p = .000; AsR cut-off at p =.01 for 88 cells = ± 3.86 (at p = .05, ±3.45)

Table 3.1 Personal Self Qualities: Item Statistics

Interpersonal Traits				Temperament Traits			
% High	Item Scale	$M^\dagger$	SD	% High	Item Scale	$M^\dagger$	SD
94.8	*Friendly*	2.46	.61	–	–	–	–
94.0	*Warm*	2.46	.63	83.6	*Intuitive*	2.24	.77
89.0	*Tolerant*	2.25	.67	83.6	*Optimistic*	2.17	.72
88.8	*Accepting*	2.28	.78	76.2	*Energetic*	2.04	.79
85.2	*Nurturant*	2.25	.75	71.6	*Pragmatic*	1.92	.82
83.0	*Receptive*	2.14	.77	71.3	*Determined*	1.92	.79
68.2	*Protective*	1.85	.79	66.9	*Organized*	1.88	.87
52.8	*Permissive*	1.41	1.04	59.1	*Intense*	1.69	.88
45.5	*Challenging*	1.42	.84	49.7	*Quiet*	1.51	.87
39.0	*Directive*	1.32	.78	48.5	*Demonstrative*	1.46	.99
37.5	*Demanding*	1.26	.86	47.3	*Private*	1.49	.91
37.0	*Authoritative*	1.25	.79	45.4	*Subtle*	1.39	.88
36.5	*Critical*	1.27	.83	–	–	–	–
31.7	*Reserved*	1.17	.81	24.8	*Skeptical*	1.03	.79
27.6	*Guarded*	1.06	.85	11.2	*Fatalistic*	0.53	.74
6.2	*Cold*	0.39	.63	–	–	–	–

† Ratings on a 0 to 3 scale (0 = Not at all, 3 = Very much)

Table 3.2 Personal Self Dimensions: Factor Structure

Interpersonal Dimensions[1]				Temperament Dimensions[1]			
Item Scales	Genial/ Caring	Forceful/ Exacting	Reclusive/ Remote[a]	Item Scales	Ardent/ Dramatic	Business- like[b]	Reclusive/ Remote[a]
Warm	**.71**			*Intense*	**.64**		
Friendly	**.67**			*Energetic*	**.60**		
Nurturant	**.67**			*Intuitive*	**.57**		
Tolerant	**.63**			*Demonstra- tive*	**.57**		
Receptive	**.60**			*Determined*	**.54**	.40	
Accepting	**.53**						
Protective	.48			Quiet	-.47	.40	
Permissive							
Directive		**.71**		Organized		**.74**	
Demanding		**.71**		Pragmatic		**.69**	
Author- itative		**.67**		Optimistic		**.48**	
Critical		**.64**					
Challenging		**.58**		Skeptical			**.80**
Reserved			**.80**	Private			**.76**
Guarded			**.76**	Subtle			**.58**
Cold	-.33		**.58**				
Standardized α =	.74	.71	.60/.71[a]	Standardized α =	.64	<.60	<.60/.71[a]

[1]Loadings in bold type included in computing dimension factors.
a – α = .71 for the combined dimension defined by the six item scales for reserved, guarded, cold, skeptical, subtle, and private.
b – *Businesslike* did not reach an acceptable level of reliability (α) as a dimension with 3 items.

Table 3.3 Personal Self Dimension Scales

Dimension	Scale Statistics					Intercorrelations[a]			
	n	M^b	Med	SD	α	Genial/ Caring	Forceful/ Exacting	Reclusive/ Remote	Ardent/ Dramatic
Genial/ Caring[c]	11,149	2.31	2.33	0.46	0.74	–	-.15	-.18	**.34**
Forceful/ Exacting[d]	11,136	1.30	1.20	0.56	0.71		–	**.27**	**.37**
Reclusive/ Remote[e]	11,108	1.10	1.17	0.52	0.71			–	.06
Ardent/ Dramatic[f]	11,143	1.87	1.80	0.54	0.64				–

[a] $n > 11,000$ in all cells; all $p < .000$ due to large Ns.

Table 3.4 Most and Least Common Personal Self Profiles of Psychotherapists

Personal Self Profile Pattern	Genial/ Caring	Forceful/ Exacting	Reclusive/ Remote	Ardent/ Dramatic	N	Valid %
	Most Common					
2222	Affectionate	Collaborative	Circumspect	Communicative	651	5.9
1222	Sympathetic	Collaborative	Circumspect	Communicative	557	5.0
3222	Devoted	Collaborative	Circumspect	Communicative	378	3.4
2212	Affectionate	Collaborative	Approachable	Communicative	336	3.0
1221	Sympathetic	Collaborative	Circumspect	Reserved	316	2.9
3212	Devoted	Collaborative	Approachable	Communicative	315	2.8
3112	Devoted	Accommodating	Approachable	Communicative	313	2.8
1322	Sympathetic	Assertive	Circumspect	Communicative	304	2.7
1121	Sympathetic	Accommodating	Circumspect	Reserved	301	2.7
2232	Affectionate	Collaborative	Wary	Communicative	291	2.6
	Least Common				3,762	33.8%
2133	Affectionate	Accommodating	Wary	Ardent	17	.2

Table 3.4 (Cont.)

1311	Sympathetic	Assertive	Approachable	Reserved	17	.2
1233	Sympathetic	Collabora-tive	Wary	Ardent	15	.1
2311	Affectionate	Assertive	Approachable	Reserved	13	.1
2331	Affectionate	Assertive	Wary	Reserved	13	.1
1133	Sympathetic	Accom-modating	Wary	Ardent	8	.1
1123	Sympathetic	Accom-modating	Circumspect	Ardent	8	.1
3321	Devoted	Assertive	Circumspect	Reserved	7	.1
3311	Devoted	Assertive	Approachable	Reserved	6	.1
3331	Devoted	Assertive	Wary	Reserved	6	.1
					110	1.2%

Table 3.5 Personal Self Dimensions by Therapist Gender*

Personal Self	Gender	N	M	SD	t	df	P
GENIAL/ CARING	Female	6,993	<u>2.35</u>	.44	11.82	8187.9	.000
	Male	4,058	2.25	.46			
FORCEFUL/ EXACTING	Female	6,976	1.41	.53	1.56	8777.6	ns
	Male	4,053	1.39	.51			
RECLUSIVE/ REMOTE	Female	6,957	1.14	.60	-10.24	8617.5	.000
	Male	4,050	<u>1.26</u>	.59			
ARDENT/ EXPRESSIVE	Female	6,986	<u>1.93</u>	.53	16.58	8539.5	.000
	Male	4,054	1.76	.52			

* Independent samples t-test; equal variances not assumed

Table 3.6 Personal Self Dimensions by Therapist Gender†

GENIAL	Indifferent	Sympathetic	Affectionate	Devoted	*n*	*m**	*sd*	χ^2 †
Female	0.3%	*15.8%*	49.3%	34.6%	6,993	2.35	.44	115.2
	-1.0	-9.4	0.0	7.9				
Male	0.4%	**22.9%**	49.3%	*27.3%*	4,058	2.25	.46	
	1.0	9.4	0.0	-7.9				
FORCEFUL	Retiring	Accommodating	Collaborative	Directive	*n*	*m*	*sd*	χ^2 †
Female	16.9%	(*34.6%*)	37.5%	**11.0%**	6,976	1.41	0.5	23.0
	1.3	-2.8	-.9	4.2				
Male	16.0%	(**37.2%**)	38.4%	*8.4%*	4,053	1.39	0.5	
	-1.3	2.8	.9	-4.2				
RECLUSIVE	Trusting	Approachable	Circumspect	Wary	*n*	*m*	*sd*	χ^2 †
Female	**33.3%**	31.8%	*29.6%*	*5.2%*	6,957	1.14	0.60	99.9
	9.2	-1.2	-5.6	-4.6				
Male	*25.0%*	32.9%	**34.7%**	**7.4%**	4,050	1.26	0.6	
	-9.2	1.2	5.6	4.6				
ARDENT	Reticent	Reserved	Communicative	Ardent	*n*	*m*	*sd*	χ^2 †
Female	*2.6%*	*17.7%*	42.0%	**37.8%**	6,986	1.93	0.5	261.2
	-5.3	-12.4	-.3	13.1				
Male	**4.4%**	**27.7%**	42.2%	*25.6%*	4,054	1.76	0.5	
	5.3	12.4	.3	-13.1				

† *df* = 3, p = .000; AsR cut-off at *p* =.01 for 8 cells = ± 3.23 (at *p* = .05, ± 2 .73)
* 1 way-ANOVA comparison of means showed P ≤ .000 for all except *Forceful* (p = ns)

Table 3.7 Correlations of Personal Self Dimensions and Therapist Age

	Total			Female			Male		
	n	*r*	*p*	*n*	*r*	*p*	*n*	*r*	*p*
GENIAL	10,977	.11	.000	6,910	.08	.000	4,022	.18	.000
FORCEFUL	10,955	-.12	.000	6,894	-.13	.000	4,016	-.09	.000
RECLUSIVE	10,933	-.12	.000	6,875	-.11	.000	4,013	-.15	.000
ARDENT	10,965	.04	.000	6,903	.02	.02	4,017	.09	.000

Table 3.8 Personal Self Qualities by Therapist Age Group*

		Younger 21 to 34	Midlife 35 to 54	Older 55 to 85
GENIAL	n	1	2	3
21–34 yrs	2471	2.27		
35–54 yrs	6314		2.30	
55–85 yrs	2182			2.40
FORCEFUL	n	1	2	
21–34 yrs	2469	1.43		
35–54 yrs	6297	1.45		
55–85 yrs	2179		1.26	
RECLUSIVE	n	1	2	3
21–34 yrs	2469	1.26		
35–54 yrs	6292		1.20	
55–85 yrs	2162			1.06
ARDENT	n	1	2	
21–34 yrs	2470	1.83		
35–54 yrs	6302	1.87	1.87	
55–85 yrs	2183		1.90	

* P = .000 for all comparisons; means in homogenous subsets differentiated at *p* = .01

Table 3.9 Personal Self Qualities by Therapist Gender and Age Group

GENIAL SELF[1]		Younger Women 21 to 34	Midlife Women 35 to 54	Older Women 55 to 85	Younger Men 21 to 34	Midlife Men 35 to 54	Older Men 55 to 85	Total
Devoted	n	552	1,304	532	169	616	307	3,480
	%	33.9%	33.3%	39.0%	20.2%	26.0%	38.1%	31.9%
	AR	2.0	2.4	6.1	-7.5	-7.0	3.9	
Affectionate	n	802	1,960	648	420	1,186	374	5,390
	%	49.3%	50.0%	47.5%	50.2%	50.0%	46.4%	49.3%
	AR	.0	1.1	-1.5	.5	.7	-1.7	
Sympathetic	n	263	643	183	237	563	125	2,014
	%	16.2%	16.4%	13.4%	28.3%	23.7%	15.5%	18.4%
	AR	-2.6	-4.1	-5.1	7.7	7.5	-2.2	
Indifferent	n	9	11	1	10	7	0	38
	%	0.6%	0.3%	0.1%	1.2%	0.3%	0.0%	0.3%
	AR	1.5	-.9	-1.8	4.3	-.5	-1.7	
Total	N	1,626	3,918	1,364	836	2,372	806	10,922
	%	100.0%	100.0%	100.0%	100.0%	100.0%	100.0%	100.0%

[1] $\chi^2 = 242.8$, df = 15, $p = .000$; AsR cut-off at $p \leq .01$ for 24 cells = ± 3.53 (at $p = .05$, ± 3.08)

Table 3.9 Personal Self Qualities (continued)

FORCEFUL SELF[2]		Younger Women 21 to 34	Midlife Women 35 to 54	Older Women 55 to 85	Younger Men 21 to 34	Midlife Men 35 to 54	Older Men 55 to 85	Total
Assertive	n	223	454	83	77	220	41	1,098
	%	**13.7%**	**11.6%**	*6.1%*	9.2%	9.3%	*5.1%*	10.1%
	AR	5.3	4.0	-5.2	-.9	-1.4	-4.9	
Collaborative	n	626	1,564	396	300	996	244	4,126
	%	38.5%	**40.0%**	*29.1%*	35.9%	**42.1%**	*30.2%*	37.9%
	AR	.6	3.5	-7.1	-1.2	4.8	-4.7	
Accommodating	n	514	1,338	539	306	837	348	3,882
	%	*31.6%*	34.2%	**(39.7%)**	36.6%	35.4%	**43.1%**	35.6%
	AR	-3.6	-2.2	3.3	.6	-.3	4.6	
Retiring	n	262	552	341	152	312	175	1,794
	%	16.1%	*14.1%*	**25.1%**	18.2%	*13.2%*	**21.7%**	16.5%
	AR	-.4	-4.9	9.2	1.4	-4.8	4.1	
Total	N	1,625	3,908	1,359	835	2,365	808	10,900
	%	100.0%	100.0%	100.0%	100.0%	100.0%	100.0%	100.0%

[2] χ^2 = 264.2, df = 15, p = .000; AsR cut-off at $p \leq .01$ for 24 cells = ± 3.53 (at p = .05, ± 3.08)

Table 3.9 Personal Self Qualities (continued)

RECLUSIVE SELF[3]		Younger Women 21 to 34	Midlife Women 35 to 54	Older Women 55 to 85	Younger Men 21 to 34	Midlife Men 35 to 54	Older Men 55 to 85	Total
Trusting	n	494	1,250	538	164	573	264	3,283
	%	30.4%	32.0%	**40.0%**	19.6%	24.2%	32.8%	30.2%
	AR	.2	3.1	8.4	-6.9	-7.1	1.7	
Approachable	n	491	1,223	479	257	782	275	3,507
	%	30.2%	31.3%	35.6%	30.7%	33.1%	34.2%	32.2%
	AR	-1.9	-1.5	2.8	-1.0	1.0	1.2	
Circumspect	n	538	1,211	291	344	825	224	3,433
	%	33.1%	31.0%	21.6%	**41.1%**	**34.9%**	27.8%	31.6%
	AR	1.5	-.9	-8.4	6.2	3.9	-2.4	
Wary	n	101	220	37	71	184	42	655
	%	6.2%	5.6%	2.8%	(**8.5%**)	**7.8%**	5.2%	6.0%
	AR	.4	-1.3	-5.4	3.1	4.1	-1.0	
Total	N	1,624	3,904	1,345	836	2,364	805	10,878
	%	100.0%	100.0%	100.0%	100.0%	100.0%	100.0%	100.0%

[3] χ^2 = 243.9, df = 15, p = .000; AsR cut-off at p ≤.01 for 24 cells = ± 3.53 (at p = .05, ± 3.08)

Table 3.9 Personal Self Qualities (continued)

ARDENT SELF[4]		Younger Women 21 to 34	Midlife Women 35 to 54	Older Women 55 to 85	Younger Men 21 to 34	Midlife Men 35 to 54	Older Men 55 to 85	Total
Ardent	n	594	1,507	508	179	605	241	3,634
	%	36.6%	**38.5%**	(**37.2%**)	21.4%	25.6%	29.9%	33.3%
	AR	3.0	8.6	3.3	-7.6	-9.0	-2.2	
Communicative	n	669	1,644	587	352	991	350	4,593
	%	41.2%	42.0%	43.0%	42.1%	41.9%	43.4%	42.1%
	AR	-.8	-.1	.7	.0	-.2	.8	
Reserved	n	306	664	245	247	679	188	2,329
	%	18.8%	17.0%	(18.0%)	**29.5%**	**28.7%**	23.3%	21.3%
	AR	-2.7	-8.3	-3.3	6.0	9.9	1.4	
Reticent	n	56	97	24	58	91	28	354
	%	3.4%	(2.5%)	(1.8%)	**6.9%**	3.8%	3.5%	3.2%
	AR	.5	-3.4	-3.3	6.3	1.9	.4	
Total	N	1,625	3,912	1,364	836	2,366	807	10,910
	%	100.0%	100.0%	100.0%	100.0%	100.0%	100.0%	100.0%

[4] χ^2 = 314.6, df = 15, p = .000; AsR cut-off at $p \leq .01$ for 24 cells = ± 3.53 (at p = .05, ± 3.08)

Table 3.10 Personal Self Qualities by Therapist Profession and Gender*

Women

	n	1	2	3	4
GENIAL					
Psychiatry	867	2.24			
Lay Therapist/Analyst	466	2.30	2.30		
Psychology	3,244		2.34	2.34	
Social Work	526			2.42	2.42
Counseling	1,556				2.43
FORCEFUL		1	2	3	
Counseling	1,552	1.28			
Social Work	524		1.38		
Psychiatry	863		1.38		
Lay Therapist/Analyst	464		1.39		
Psychology	3,238			1.49	
RECLUSIVE		1	2	3	
Social Work	523	1.03			
Counseling	1,541	1.07			
Psychology	3,235	1.13			
Lay Therapist/Analyst	461		1.20		
Psychiatry	862			1.32	

Men

	n	1	2
GENIAL			
Psychiatry	1,258	2.12	
Psychology	1,905		2.30
Social Work	162		2.30
Lay Therapist/Analyst	189		2.30
Counseling	411		2.33
FORCEFUL		1	2
Counseling	412	1.22	
Psychiatry	1,254		1.39
Social Work	162		1.40
Lay Therapist/Analyst	189		1.41
Psychology	1,904		1.44
RECLUSIVE		1	2
Counseling	409	1.20	
Psychology	1,903	1.21	
Social Work	162	1.22	
Lay Therapist/Analyst	189	1.25	
Psychiatry	1,254		1.38

(Continued)

Table 3.4 (Cont.)

Women

ARDENT	n	1	2	3
Psychiatry	863	1.76		
Psychology	3,241		1.92	
Social Work	524		1.98	1.98
Counseling	1,557		2.00	2.00
Lay Therapist/Analyst	466			2.03

Men

ARDENT	n	1	2
Psychiatry	1,255	1.66	
Psychology	1,904	1.78	1.78
Counseling	412		1.83
Social Work	162		1.89
Lay Therapist/Analyst	189		1.92

* $P = .000$ for all comparisons; means in homogenous subsets differentiated at $P = .01$

Table 3.11 Personal Self Correlates of Theoretical Approach

		AnalyticPsycho-dynamic	Cognitive-Behavioral	Huma-nistic	Systemic	Broad Spectrum[†]
Total Sample[1]						
GENIAL	r	-.04	.12	.10	.12	.17
	p	.000	.000	.000	.000	.000
FORCEFUL	r	.03	.00	-.02	.04	.02
	p	.004	ns	ns	.000	ns
RECLUSIVE	r	.04	-.05	-.02	-.04	-.05
	p	.000	.000	ns	.000	.000
ARDENT	r	-.01	-.00	.08	.09	.12
	p	ns	ns	.000	.000	.000
Women[2]						
GENIAL	r	-.04	.13	.10	.12	.16
	p	.000	.000	.000	.000	.000
FORCEFUL	r	.02	.00	-.02	.04	.02
	p	ns	ns	ns	ns	ns
RECLUSIVE	r	.03	-.05	-.00	-.03	-.03
	p	.000	.000	ns	.01	.007
ARDENT	r	-.02	.01	.07	.08	.11
	p	ns	ns	.000	.000	.000
Men[3]						
GENIAL	r	-.03	.12	.12	.10	.18
	p	.03	.000	.000	.000	.000
FORCEFUL	r	.04	.01	-.02	.08	.04
	p	.008	ns	ns	.000	.007
RECLUSIVE	r	.06	-.06	-.04	-.04	-.08
	p	.000	.000	.015	.019	.000
ARDENT	r	-.02	-.00	.09	.09	.14
	p	ns	ns	.000	.000	.000

[†] Broad Spectrum = ≥ 3 salient orientations (influence on practice rated 'great' or 'very great')
[1] N ≥ 10,750. [2] N ≥ 6,750. [3] N ≥ 3,940

Table 4.1 Sociological Perspective on Spheres of Individual Life in Modern Society†

Social Norms	Individual Spheres	Public Spheres
'Universalistic' investments: rule-based norms (value: *efficiency*)	**CAREER/WORK LIFE** Instrumental Skills & Cognitive Style ('Mentality')	**POLITICAL/ECONOMIC LIFE** 'Gesellschaft' (Society-at-Large)
'Particularistic' attachments: affect-based norms (value: *loyalty*)	**PRIVATE LIFE** Personal Relationships & Intimate Self ('Personality')	**ETHNIC/RELIGIOUS COMMUNAL LIFE** 'Gemeinschaft' (Personal Community)

† This conceptualization draws on classic sociological writings of Talcott Parsons, Ferdinand Tönnies, and Max Weber.

Table 4.2 Private Life Situations of Psychotherapists

Marital Status		Parental Status			
		Childless	Parent	Subtotal[1]	Total
Single	n	791	172	963	1,911
	%	13.9%	3.0%	16.9%	16.8%
Living w. partner	n	292	343	635	1,367
	%	5.1%	6.0%	11.2%	12.0%
Married/remarried	n	447	2,883	3,330	6,698
	%	7.9%	50.7%	58.5%	59.0%
Divorced or separated	n	121	480	601	1,114
	%	2.1%	8.4%	10.6%	9.8%
Widowed	n	10	84	94	148
	%	0.2%	1.5%	1.7%	1.3%
Other	n	34	31	65	123
	%	0.6%	0.5%	1.1%	1.1%
Total	N	1,695	3,993	5,688	11,361
	%	29.8%	70.2%	100.0%	100.0%

[1] Due to limited parental status data, the combination of marital and parental status are shown as a 'Subtotal' with the column Total showing only marital status.

Table 4.3 Therapists' Private Life Patterns by Age Group

Private Life Pattern		Younger Therapists (21 to 34)	Midlife Therapists (35 to 54)	Older Therapists (55 to 85)	Total
Single & childless	n	378	293	108	779
	%	**41.6%**	*10.1%*	*6.7%*	14.4%
	AsR	25.7	-9.7	-10.4	
Single parent	n	30	85	53	168
	%	3.3%	2.9%	3.3%	3.1%
	AsR	.4	-.8	.5	
Live-in partner & childless	n	112	140	38	290
	%	**12.3%**	4.8%	*2.4%*	5.3%
	AsR	10.3	-1.9	-6.3	
Live-in partner & parent	n	21	203	116	340
	%	*2.3%*	7.0%	7.2%	6.3%
	AsR	-5.4	2.3	1.9	
Married & childless	n	150	219	73	442
	%	**16.5%**	7.5%	*4.5%*	8.1%
	AsR	10.1	-1.8	-6.3	
Married & parent	n	193	1,653	973	2,819
	%	*21.3%*	**56.8%**	**60.5%**	52.0%
	AsR	-20.3	7.7	8.2	
Divorced/separated childless	n	17	75	24	116
	%	1.9%	2.6%	1.5%	2.1%
	AsR	-.6	2.4	-2.1	
Divorced/separated & parent	n	7	240	223	470
	%	*0.8%*	8.3%	**13.9%**	8.7%
	AsR	-9.3	-1.2	8.8	
Total	N	908	2,908	1,608	5,424
	%	100.0%	100.0%	100.0%	100.0%

χ^2 = 1139.9, df = 14, p = .000; AsR cut-off at p =.01 for 24cells = ± 3.53 (at p =.05, ± 3.08)

Table 4.4 Therapists' Private Life Patterns by Gender

Private Life Pattern		Gender		Total
		Female	Male	
Single & childless	n	570	215	785
	%	15.0%	12.9%	14.3%
	AsR	2.0	-2.0	
Single parent	n	136	33	169
	%	(3.6%)	(2.0%)	3.1%
	AsR	3.1	-3.1	
Live-in partner & childless	n	206	86	292
	%	5.4%	5.1%	5.3%
	AsR	.4	-.4	
Live-in partner & parent	n	248	93	341
	%	6.5%	5.6%	6.2%
	AsR	1.3	-1.3	
Married & childless	n	322	122	444
	%	8.5%	7.3%	8.1%
	AsR	1.4	-1.4	
Married & parent	n	1,857	993	2,850
	%	*48.8%*	**59.5%**	52.1%
	AsR	-7.3	7.3	
Divorced/separated childless	n	94	26	120
	%	2.5%	1.6%	2.2%
	AsR	2.1	-2.1	
Divorced/separated & parent	n	372	102	474
	%	**9.8%**	*6.1%*	8.7%
	AsR	4.4	-4.4	
Total	N	3,805	1,670	5,475
	%	100.0%	100.0%	100.0%

χ^2 = 64.7, df = 7, p = .000; AsR cut-off at p =.01 for 16 cells = ± 3.42 (at p =.05, ± 2.96)

Table 4.5 Therapists' Private Life Patterns by Age Group

Private Life Pattern		Younger Therapists (21 to 34)		Midlife Therapists (35 to 54)		Older Therapists (55 to 85)	
		Female	Male	Female	Male	Female	Male
Single & childless	n	283	94	203	88	79	29
	%	41.3%	42.9%	10.1%	10.0%	7.5%	5.3%
	AsR	-.4	.4	.1	-.1	1.6	-1.6
Single parent	n	23	7	69	15	42	11
	%	3.4%	3.2%	3.4%	1.7%	4.0%	2.0%
	AsR	.1	-.1	2.6	-2.6	2.1	-2.1
Live-in partner & childless	n	83	29	93	47	28	10
	%	12.1%	13.2%	4.6%	5.3%	2.6%	1.8%
	AsR	-.4	.4	-.8	.8	1.0	-1.0
Live-in partner & parent	n	16	5	155	47	74	41
	%	2.3%	2.3%	7.7%	5.3%	7.0%	7.6%
	AsR	.0	.0	2.3	-2.3	-.4	.4
Married & childless	n	122	27	150	67	47	26
	%	17.8%	12.3%	7.5%	7.6%	4.4%	4.8%
	AsR	1.9	-1.9	-.1	.1	-.3	.3
Married & parent	n	140	52	1,100	546	587	381
	%	20.4%	23.7%	_54.8%_	**61.8%**	_55.5%_	**70.2%**
	AsR	-1.1	1.1	-3.5	3.5	-5.7	5.7
Divorced/ separated childless	n	14	3	57	18	21	3
	%	2.0%	1.4%	2.8%	2.0%	2.0%	0.6%
	AsR	.6	-.6	1.2	-1.2	2.2	-2.2
Divorcedsepa- rated & parent	n	5	2	182	56	179	42
	%	0.7%	0.9%	9.1%	6.3%	**16.9%**	_7.7%_
	AsR	-.3	.3	2.5	-2.5	5.12	-5.1
Total	N	686	219	2,009	884	1,057	543
	%	100%	100%	100%	100%	100%	100%

[1] $\chi^2 = 4.64$, df = 7, p = ns.
[2] $\chi^2 = 24.4$, df = 7, p = .001; AsR cut-off at p =.01 for 16 cells = ± 3.42 (at p =.05, ± 2.96)
[3] $\chi^2 = 47.3$, df = 7, p = .000; AsR cut-off at p =.01 for 16 cells = ± 3.42 (at p =.05, ± 2.96)

Table 4.6 Marital and Parental Status by Profession, and Profession by Gender★

		Psychol-ogy	Psy-chiatry	Social Work	Counsel-ing	Lay Thera-pist/ Analyst	Total
Total Sample (χ^2 = 203.4, df = 12, P = .000) [†]							
Single	n	982	330	150	274	92	1,828
	%	**18.7%**	16.1%	**22.1%**	*14.0%*	13.9%	17.2%
	AsR	3.9	-1.5	3.5	-4.2	-2.3	
Living with partner	n	767	145	79	205	105	1,301
	%	**14.6%**	*7.1%*	11.7%	10.4%	15.9%	12.3%
	AsR	7.2	*-8.0*	-.5	-2.7	2.9	
Married/ remarried	n	3,015	1,425	364	1,260	366	6,430
	%	*57.3%*	**69.4%**	*53.7%*	**64.2%**	55.3%	60.6%
	AsR	*-6.8*	9.2	-3.8	3.6	-2.9	
Divorced or sepa-rated	n	497	152	85	225	99	1,058
	%	9.4%	*7.4%*	12.5%	11.5%	**15.0%**	10.0%
	AsR	-1.8	-4.3	2.3	2.4	4.4	
Total	N	5,261	2,052	678	1,964	662	10,617
	%	100.0%	100.0%	100.0%	100.0%	100.0%	100.0%
Female Therapists (χ^2 = 115.1, df = 12, P = .000)[†]							
Single	n	687	156	116	208	72	1,239
	%	**21.1%**	18.8%	22.4%	*13.6%*	15.5%	18.8%
	AsR	4.8	.0	2.2	-6.0	-1.9	
Living with partner	n	493	77	58	156	62	846
	%	**15.2%**	*(9.3%)*	11.2%	*10.2%*	13.3%	12.8%
	AsR	5.6	-3.2	-1.2	-3.6	.3	
Married/ remarried	n	1,692	517	272	971	255	3,707
	%	*52.0%*	**62.4%**	52.5%	**63.3%**	54.8%	56.2%
	AsR	-6.7	3.9	-1.8	6.4	-.6	
Divorced or sepa-rated	n	379	78	72	199	76	804
	%	11.7%	9.4%	13.9%	13.0%	16.3%	12.2%
	AsR	-1.3	-2.6	1.2	1.1	2.8	
Total	N	3,251	828	518	1,534	465	6,596
	%	100.0%	100.0%	100.0%	100.0%	100.0%	100.0%

(Continued)

Table 3.4 (Cont.)

Male Therapists (χ^2 = 96.4, df = 12, P = .000)

Single	n	291	171	33	63	19	577
	%	14.8%	14.3%	21.0%	15.3%	9.9%	14.7%
	AsR	.2	-.5	2.3	.4	-1.9	
Living with partner	n	272	67	21	47	42	449
	%	**13.8%**	*5.6%*	13.4%	11.4%	**21.9%**	11.4%
	AsR	4.7	-7.6	.8	.0	4.7	
Married/ remarried	n	1,292	888	90	280	109	2,659
	%	65.6%	**74.1%**	57.3%	67.8%	*(56.8%)*	67.6%
	AsR	-2.8	5.7	-2.8	.1	-3.3	
Divorced or separated	n	116	73	13	23	22	247
	%	5.9%	6.1%	8.3%	5.6%	11.5%	6.3%
	AsR	-1.0	-.3	1.1	-.6	3.0	
Total	N	1,971	1,199	157	413	192	3,932

† AsR cut-off for 20 cells at p = .01 = ± 3.48 (at p =.05, ± 3.02)

Table 4.7 Marital Status by Profession and Age Group★

		Psychology	Psychiatry	Social Work	Counseling	Lay Therapist/ Analyst	Total
Younger Therapists (χ^2 = 109.1, df = 12, P = .000) †							
Single	n	506	202	96	95	24	923
	%	38.8%	36.6%	**51.6%**	40.9%	34.8%	39.4%
	AsR	-.7	-1.5	3.6	.5	-.8	
Living with partner	n	279	39	27	19	15	379
	%	**21.4%**	*7.1%*	14.5%	*8.2%*	21.7%	16.2%
	AsR	7.7	-6.6	-.6	-3.5	1.3	
Married/ remarried	n	478	298	57	114	27	974
	%	*36.7%*	**54.0%**	*(30.6%)*	49.1%	39.1%	41.6%
	AsR	-5.4	6.8	-3.2	2.5	-.4	
Divorced or separated	n	41	13	6	4	3	67
	%	3.1%	2.4%	3.2%	1.7%	4.3%	2.9%
	AsR	.9	-.8	.3	-1.1	.8	
Total	N	1,304	552	186	232	69	2,343

(Continued)

Midlife Therapists (χ^2 = 82.2, df = 12, P = .000) [†]

Single	n	379	111	42	109	50	691
	%	12.5%	9.7%	11.8%	10.3%	12.5%	11.5%
	AsR	2.3	-2.2	.2	-1.4	.6	
Living with partner	n	409	85	40	123	69	726
	%	**(13.4%)**	*7.4%*	11.3%	11.6%	**(17.2%)**	12.1%
	AsR	3.3	-5.4	-.5	-.5	3.3	
Married/ remarried	n	1,927	854	217	715	226	3,939
	%	*63.3%*	**74.4%**	61.1%	67.6%	*56.4%*	65.6%
	AsR	-3.7	7.0	-1.8	1.5	-4.0	
Divorced or sepa- rated	n	327	98	56	111	56	648
	%	10.7%	8.5%	**(15.8%)**	10.5%	14.0%	10.8%
	AsR	-.1	-2.7	3.1	-.3	2.1	
Total	N	3,042	1,148	355	1,058	401	6,004

Older Therapists (χ^2 = 27.8, df = 12, P = .006) [†]

Single	n	85	12	10	66	17	190
	%	10.1%	*(3.9%)*	7.7%	10.2%	9.5%	9.0%
	AsR	1.4	-3.4	-.5	1.3	.2	
Living with partner	n	74	20	12	61	20	187
	%	8.8%	6.5%	9.2%	9.5%	11.2%	8.9%
	AsR	-.1	-1.6	.1	.6	1.1	
Married/ remarried	n	562	241	87	413	107	1,410
	%	66.7%	**77.7%**	66.9%	64.0%	59.8%	66.9%
	AsR	-.2	4.4	.0	-1.9	-2.1	
Divorced or sepa- rated	n	122	37	21	105	35	320
	%	14.5%	11.9%	16.2%	16.3%	19.6%	15.2%
	AsR	-.7	-1.7	.3	.9	1.7	
Total	N	843	310	130	645	179	2,107

[†] AsR cut-off for 20 cells at p = .01 = ± 3.48 (at p =.05, ± 3.02)

Table 4.8 Parental Status by Profession

Parental Status		Psychology	Psychiatry	Social Work	Counseling	Lay Therapist/ Analyst	Total
Non-parent	n	758	215	78	487	128	1,666
	%	**34.4%**	28.4%	28.9%	*24.3%*	29.2%	29.4%
	AsR	6.6	-.6	-.2	-6.2	-.1	
Parent	n	1,446	542	192	1,514	310	4,004
	%	*65.6%*	71.6%	71.1%	**75.7%**	70.8%	70.6%
	AsR	-6.6	.6	.2	6.2	.1	
Total	N	2,204	757	270	2,001	438	5,670
	%	100.0%	100.0%	100.0%	100.0%	100.0%	100.0%

χ^2 = 51.6; df = 4; P = .000; AsR cut-off at $p \leq$ .01 for 10 cells = ± 3.29 (at p =.05, ± 2.81)

Table 4.9a Parental Status by Profession and Gender

		Psychology	Psychiatry	Social Work	Counseling	Lay Therapist/ Analyst	Total
Female Therapists (χ^2 = 79.2, df = 4, P = .000) [†]							
Non-parent	n	544	124	51	375	99	1,193
	%	**38.2%**	34.6%	25.5%	*23.7%*	30.9%	30.7%
	AsR	7.7	1.7	-1.6	-7.9	.1	
Parent	n	880	234	149	1,207	221	,2691
	%	*61.8%*	65.4%	74.5%	**76.3%**	69.1%	69.3%
	AsR	-7.7	-1.7	1.6	7.9	-.1	
Total		1,424	358	200	1,582	320	3,884
Male Therapists (χ^2 = 5.50, df = 4, P = ns)[†]							
Non-parent	n	210	90	24	109	29	462
	%	27.5%	23.4%	35.8%	27.3%	25.0%	26.7%
	AsR	.7	-1.7	1.7	.3	-.4	
Parent	n	554	295	43	291	87	1,270
	%	72.5%	76.6%	64.2%	72.8%	75.0%	73.3%
	AsR	-.7	1.7	-1.7	-.3	.4	
Total		764	385	67	400	116	1,732

[†] AsR cut-off at p = .01 for 20 cells = ± 3.48 (at p =.05, ± 3.02).

Table 4.9b Parental Status by Profession and Age Group

		Psychology	Psychiatry	Social Work	Counseling	Lay Therapist/ Analyst	Total
Younger Therapists (χ^2 = 43.0, df = 4, P = .000)[†]							
Non-parent	n	370	89	27	138	28	652
	%	**78.6%**	(58.2%)	64.3%	58.0%	73.7%	69.2%
	AsR	6.2	-3.2	-.7	-4.3	.6	
Parent	n	101	64	15	100	10	290
	%	21.4%	(41.8%)	35.7%	**42.0%**	26.3%	30.8%
	AsR	-6.2	3.2	.7	4.3	-.6	
Total		471	153	42	238	38	942
Midlife Therapists (χ^2 = 4.84, df = 4, P = ns)							
Non-parent	n	281	112	35	243	69	740
	%	26.2%	24.9%	25.7%	23.0%	28.8%	25.1%
	AsR	1.1	-.1	.2	-1.9	1.4	
Parent	n	791	337	101	812	171	2,212
	%	73.8%	75.1%	74.3%	77.0%	71.3%	74.9%
	AsR	-1.1	.1	-.2	1.9	-1.4	
Total		1,072	449	136	1,055	240	2,952
Older Therapists (χ^2 = 6.65 df = 4, P = ns)							
Non-parent	n	97	12	15	99	29	252
	%	15.5%	8.9%	17.0%	14.6%	19.3%	15.1%
	AsR	.4	-2.1	.5	-.4	1.5	
Parent	n	527	123	73	578	121	1,422
	%	84.5%	91.1%	83.0%	85.4%	80.7%	84.9%
	AsR	-.4	2.1	-.5	.4	-1.5	
Total		624	135	88	677	150	1,674

[†] AsR cut-off at p = .01 for 20 cells = ± 3.48 (at p =.05, ± 3.02)

Table 4.10a Marital Status by Theoretical Orientation

Marital Status		Analytic/ Dynamic	Cognitive-Behavioral	Humanistic	Analytic/ Dynamic & Humanistic	Broad Spectrum	No Salient Orientation	Total
Single	n	400	162	143	120	296	159	1,280
	%	16.1%	18.8%	16.3%	19.0%	16.1%	21.1%	17.2%
	AsR	-1.8	1.3	-.7	1.3	-1.5	3.0	
Living with partner	n	283	90	106	96	208	82	865
	%	11.4%	10.4%	12.1%	15.2%	11.3%	10.9%	11.6%
	AsR	-.4	-1.1	.5	3.0	-.5	-.7	
Married/ remarried	n	1,530	556	518	354	1,151	455	4,564
	%	61.6%	64.5%	59.2%	56.2%	62.4%	60.3%	61.3%
	AsR	.4	2.1	-1.3	-2.7	1.2	-.5	
Divorced or separated	n	272	54	108	60	189	58	741
	%	10.9%	*6.3%*	12.3%	9.5%	10.2%	7.7%	9.9%
	AsR	2.0	-3.8	2.5	-.4	.5	-2.2	
Total	N%	2,485	862	875	630	1,844	754	7,450
		100.0%	100.0%	100.0%	100.0%	100.0%	100.0%	100.0%

χ^2 = 50.4; df = 15; P = .000; AsR cut-off at $p \le$ .01 for 24 cells = ± 3.53 (at p =.05, ± 3.08)

Table 4.10b Parental Status by Theoretical Orientation

Parental Status		Analytic/ Dynamic	Cognitive-Behavioral	Humanistic	Analytic/ Dynamic & Humanistic	Broad Spectrum	No Salient Orientation	Total
Non-parents	n	342	159	155	93	290	84	1,123
	%	29.4%	32.8%	27.6%	32.7%	27.3%	25.8%	28.9%
	AsR	.4	2.0	-.8	1.5	-1.4	-1.3	
Parents	n	821	326	407	191	771	241	2,757
	%	70.6%	67.2%	72.4%	67.3%	72.7%	74.2%	71.1%
	AsR	-.4	-2.0	.8	-1.5	1.4	1.3	
Total	N	1,163	485	562	284	1,061	325	3,880
	%	100.0%	100.0%	100.0%	100.0%	100.0%	100.0%	100.0%

χ^2 = 8.96; df = 5; P = ns.

Table 4.11 Personal Self Dimensions by Marital Status*

Women				Men			
GENIAL[1]	n	1	2	GENIAL[5]	n	1	2
Single	1,266	2.31		Single	581	2.18	
Living w. Partner	861	2.35	2.35	Living w. Partner	456	2.22	2.22
Married/ Remarried	3,753	2.36	2.36	Married/ Remarried	2,603	2.26	2.26
Divorced/ Separated	820		2.38	Divorced/ Separated	242		2.30
FORCEFUL[2]	n	1	2	FORCEFUL[6]	N	1	
Divorced/ Separated	820	1.34		Single	579	1.37	
Single	1,263	1.38	1.38	Living w. Partner	2,600	1.39	
Married/ Remarried	3,740		1.43	Married/ Remarried	457	1.43	
Living w. Partner	861		1.44	Divorced/ Separated	242	1.44	
RECLUSIVE[3]	n	1	2	RECLUSIVE[7]	N	1	2
Living w. Partner	859	1.07		Living w. Partner	456	1.22	
Married/ Remarried	3,730	1.10		Married/ Remarried	2,597	1.24	
Divorced/ Separated	817	1.13		Divorced/ Separated	242	1.27	
Single	1,260		1.29	Single	580		1.44
ARDENT[4]	n	1	2	ARDENT[8]	n	1	2
Single	1,264	1.90		Living w. Partner	457	1.72	
Living w. Partner	862	1.91		Single	579	1.75	
Married/ Remarried	3,748	1.94	1.94	Married/ Remarried	2,601	1.75	
Divorced/ Separated	819		1.98	Divorced/ Separated	242		1.89

* Post-hoc Scheffe test: means for homogenous subsets at $p = .01$ separation criterion.
[1] N 6700, F 4.74, Df 3, P.003   [5] N 3882, F 6.38, Df 3, P.000
[2] N 6684, F 9.37, Df 3, P.000   [6] N 3878, F 2.18, Df 3, PNs.
[3] N 6666, F 32.24, Df 3, P.000   [7] N 3875, F 19.39, Df 3, P.000
[4] N 6693, F 3.90, Df 3, P.009   [8] N 3879, F 6.45, Df 3, P.000

Table 4.12 Personal Self Dimensions by Parental Status*

	Women				Men		
GENIAL	n	*m*	*p*	**GENIAL**	n	*m*	*p*
Non-parents	1,185	2.35	.000	Non-parents	457	2.33	ns
Mothers	2,647	**2.41**		Fathers	1,244	2.33	
FORCEFUL	n	m	*p*	**FORCEFUL**	n	*m*	
Non-parents	1,181	1.35	ns	Non-parents	459	1.30	ns
Mothers	2,638	1.33		Fathers	1,242	1.32	
RECLUSIVE	n	m	*p*	**RECLUSIVE**	N	*m*	
Non-parents	1,178	**1.22**	.000	Non-parents	458	**1.33**	.000
Mothers	2,623	1.06		Fathers	1,240	1.21	
ARDENT	n	*m*	*p*	**ARDENT**	n	*m*	
Non-parents	1,183	1.97	ns	Non-parents	459	1.82	ns
Mothers	2,644	1.99		Fathers	1,243	1.87	

Table 4.13 Private Life Patterns by Levels of Reclusive/Remote Personal Self

Private Life Pattern		Trusting	Approac-hable	Circum-spect	Wary	Total
Single & childless	n	170	234	285	66	755
	%	_22.5%_	31.0%	**37.7%**	**8.7%**	100.0%
	AsR	-6.1	-1.8	5.9	4.6	
Single parent	n	63	49	42	11	165
	%	38.2%	29.7%	25.5%	6.7%	100.0%
	AsR	1.7	-1.1	-.9	.8	
Partner & childless	n	87	102	77	11	277
	%	31.4%	36.8%	27.8%	4.0%	100.0%
	AsR	-.3	1.1	-.3	-1.0	
Partner & parent	n	122	122	75	11	330
	%	37.0%	37.0%	22.7%	3.3%	100.0%
	AsR	1.9	1.2	-2.5	-1.6	
Married & childless	n	123	134	141	29	427
	%	28.8%	31.4%	33.0%	6.8%	100.0%
	AsR	-1.5	-1.1	2.1	1.5	
Married parent	n	944	933	734	120	2,731
	%	**34.6%**	34.2%	(*26.9%*)	4.4%	100.0%
	AsR	3.9	.5	-3.1	-2.9	
Divorced/ separated & childless	n	30	45	35	9	119
	%	25.2%	37.8%	29.4%	7.6%	100.0%
	AsR	-1.6	.9	.2	1.1	
Divorced/ separated parent	n	152	162	121	20	455
	%	33.4%	35.6%	26.6%	4.4%	100.0%
	AsR	.6	.8	-1.0	-.9	
Total	N	1,691	1,781	1,510	277	5,259
	%	32.2%	33.9%	28.7%	5.3%	100.0%

χ^2 = 50.4; df = 15; P = .000; AsR cut-off at p = .01 for 24 cells = ± 3.53 (at p = .05, ± 3.08)

Table 4.14 Marital Patterns and Levels of Reclusive/Remote by Gender

Marital Status		Reclusive/Remote				Total
		Trusting	Approach-able	Circum-spect	Wary	
Female Therapists (χ^2 = 99.9; df = 9; P = .000)[†]						
Single	n	321	379	449	111	1,260
	%	_25.5%_	30.1%	**35.6%**	**8.8%**	100.0%
	AsR	-6.7	-1.6	5.5	6.5	
Living with partner	n	313	280	230	36	859
	%	36.4%	32.6%	26.8%	4.2%	100.0%
	AsR	1.9	.4	-1.7	-1.4	
Married/ remarried	n	1,335	1,187	1,053	155	3,730
	%	**35.8%**	31.8%	28.2%	_4.2%_	100.0%
	AsR	4.4	-.3	-2.1	-4.2	
Separated or divorced	n	267	287	220	43	817
	%	32.7%	35.1%	26.9%	5.3%	100.0%
	AsR	-.6	2.0	-1.6	.1	
Total	N	2,236	2,133	1,952	345	6,666
	%	33.5%	32.0%	29.3%	5.2%	100.0%
Male Therapists (χ^2 = 58.5; df = 9; P = .000)[†]						
Single	n	95	161	268	56	580
	%	_16.4%_	27.8%	**46.2%**	9.7%	100.0%
	AsR	-5.1	-2.8	6.2	2.2	
Living with partner	n	124	167	136	29	456
	%	27.2%	36.6%	29.8%	6.4%	100.0%
	AsR	1.2	1.9	-2.4	-1.0	
Married/ remarried	n	685	863	863	186	2,597
	%	**(26.4%)**	33.2%	_(33.2%)_	7.2%	100.0%
	AsR	3.2	.8	-3.1	-1.0	
Separated or divorced	n	58	80	86	18	242
	%	24.0%	33.1%	35.5%	7.4%	100.0%
	AsR	-.3	.1	.2	.0	
Total	N	962	1,271	1,353	289	3,875
	%	24.8%	32.8%	34.9%	7.5%	100.0%

[†] AsR cut-off at p = .01 for 16 cells = ± 3.42 (at p = .05, ± 2.96)

Table 4.15 Parental Status and Levels of Reclusive/Remote by Gender

Parental Status		Reclusive/Remote				Total
		Trusting	*Approach-able*	*Circum-spect*	*Wary*	
Female Therapists (χ^2 = 67.0; df = 3; P = .000)[†]						
Non-parent	n	331	381	387	79	1,178
	%	*28.1%*	32.3%	**32.9%**	**6.7%**	100.0%
	AsR	-5.9	-1.4	5.9	4.3	
Parent	n	998	908	623	94	2,623
	%	**38.0%**	34.6%	*23.8%*	*3.6%*	100.0%
	AsR	5.9	1.4	-5.9	-4.3	
Total	N	1,329	1,289	1,010	173	,801
	%	35.0%	33.9%	26.6%	4.6%	100.0%
Male Therapists (χ^2 = 11.3; df = 3; P = .01)[†]						
Non-parent	n	96	152	172	38	458
	%	21.0%	33.2%	37.6%	8.3%	100.0%
	AsR	-2.8	-.4	2.0	1.7	
Parent	n	342	424	400	74	1,240
	%	27.6%	34.2%	32.3%	6.0%	100.0%
	AsR	2.8	.4	-2.0	-1.7	
Total	N	438	576	572	112	1,698
	%	25.8%	33.9%	33.7%	6.6%	100.0%

† AsR cut-off at p = .01 for 16 cells = ± 3.42 (at p = .05, ± 2.96)

Table 4.16 Private Life Patterns by Levels of Reclusive/Remote Personal Self by Age

Marital Status		Trusting	Approach-able	Circum-spect	Wary	Total
Younger Therapists (22-34) (χ^2 = 68.4; df = 9; P = .000)†						
Single	n	191	291	382	89	953
	%	_20.0%_	30.5%	**(40.1%)**	**9.3%**	100.0%
	AsR	-6.0	.1	3.3	4.0	
Living with partner	n	148	120	110	13	391
	%	**37.9%**	30.7%	_28.1%_	_(3.3%)_	100.0%
	AsR	5.4	.2	-3.6	-3.0	
Married/ remarried	n	284	305	346	56	991
	%	28.7%	30.8%	34.9%	5.7%	100.0%
	AsR	1.7	.4	-1.0	-1.9	
Separated or divorced	n	20	13	28	5	66
	%	30.3%	19.7%	42.4%	7.6%	100.0%
	AsR	.7	-1.9	1.1	.3	
Total	N	643	729	866	163	2401
	%	26.8%	30.4%	36.1%	6.8%	100.0%
Midlife Therapists (35- 54) (χ^2 = 45.0; df = 9; P = .000)†						
Single	n	162	191	277	71	701
	%	_23.1%_	27.2%	**39.5%**	**10.1%**	100.0%
	AsR	-3.8	-2.8	4.3	4.1	
Living with partner	n	221	246	226	46	739
	%	29.9%	33.3%	30.6%	6.2%	100.0%
	AsR	.4	.9	-1.1	-.4	
Married/ remarried	n	1185	1271	1248	235	3939
	%	30.1%	32.3%	31.7%	6.0%	100.0%
	AsR	2.0	.8	-1.5	-2.4	
Separated or divorced	n	197	219	201	42	659
	%	29.9%	33.2%	30.5%	6.4%	100.0%
	AsR	.4	.8	-1.1	-.2	
Total	N	1765	1927	1952	394	6038
	%	29.2%	31.9%	32.3%	6.5%	100.0%

(Continued)

Table 4.16 (Cont.)

Older Therapists (55–85) (χ^2 = 23.1; df = 9; P = .006)[†]

Single	n	56	51	56	7	170
	%	32.9%	30.0%	(**32.9%**)	4.1%	100.0%
	AsR	-1.2	-1.6	3.0	.3	
Living with partner	n	67	78	31	6	182
	%	36.8%	42.9%	17.0%	3.3%	100.0%
	AsR	-.1	2.2	-2.2	-.3	
Married/ remarried	n	530	462	312	49	1,353
	%	39.2%	34.1%	23.1%	3.6%	100.0%
	AsR	2.7	-1.9	-.7	-.5	
Separated or divorced	n	98	128	76	14	316
	%	31.0%	40.5%	24.1%	4.4%	100.0%
	AsR	-2.5	2.0	.2	.7	
Total	N	751	719	475	76	2,021
	%	37.2%	35.6%	23.5%	3.8%	100.0%

† AsR cut-off at p = .01 for 16 cells = ± 3.42 (at p = .05, ± 2.96)

Table 4.17 Adult Attachment Dimensions of Therapists*

Experiences in Close Relationships Scales[1] Short Form	Attachment Dimensions	
	Anxious	Avoidant
Others don't want to get as close as I'd like.	**.72**	.14
I need a lot of reassurance that I am loved.	**.70**	.19
My desire to be very close scares people away.	**.69**	.15
I worry that others won't care as much as I care.	**.65**	.36
I get frustrated if others are not available when I need them.	**.55**	.15
I don't often worry about abandonment.	-.43	.00
I get nervous when people get too close.	.16	**.87**
I try to avoid getting too close to others.	.15	**.80**
I want to get close, but keep pulling back.	.31	**.77**
It helps to turn to others in times of need.	-.09	-.08
I turn to others for comfort & reassurance.	.15	-.04
I usually discuss my problems with close others.	-.11	-.22
α =	.74	.81

[1] Loadings in bold type included in computing dimension factors.
* Principal components extraction; Varimax rotation (N = 1,223)

Table 4.18 Adult Attachment Dimensions by Marital and Parental Status by Gender*

Marital Status	Women			Marital Status	Men		
Anxious Attachment	n	1	2	**Anxious Attachment**	n	1	
Married/ Remarried	498	2.40		Married/ Remarried	189	2.60	
Living w. Partner	163	2.60	2.60	Living w. Partner	53	3.02	
Divorced/ Separated	125	2.73	2.73	Single	36	3.14	
Single	121		2.85	Divorced/ Separated	17	3.40	
$p = .000$				$p = .003$			
Avoidant Attachment	n	1	2	**Avoidant Attachment**	N	1	2
Married/ Remarried	504	2.13		Married/ Remarried	189	2.18	
Living w. Partner	166	2.38	2.38	Living w. Partner	18	2.74	2.74
Divorced/ Separated	128		2.73	Divorced/ Separated	53	3.08	3.08
Single	123		2.86	Single	37		3.38
$p = .000$				$p = .000$			
Parental Status	**Women**			**Parental Status**	**Men**		
Anxious Attachment	n	1	2	**Anxious Attachment**	n	1	
3+ children	279	2.82		3+ children	95	2.60	
2 children	279	2.53	2.53	No children	57	2.75	
1 child	118	2.60	2.60	2 children	96	2.88	
No children	184		2.69	1 child	42	3.04	
$p = .001$				$p = $ ns			
Avoidant Attachment	n	1	2	**Avoidant Attachment**	N	1	
2 children	283	2.14		3+ children	95	2.19	
3+ children	286	2.16	2.16	2 children	97	2.40	
1 child	118	2.35	2.35	No children	57	2.75	
No children	188		2.68	1 child	41	2.81	
$p = .000$				$p = .04$			

* Scales are scored from 1 (low) to 7 (high). Means for groups in homogenous subsets are displayed based on Scheffe test.

Table 4.19 Adult Attachment Dimensions by Marital and Parental Status by Age*

Marital Status	Midlife Therapists			Marital Status	Older Therapists		
Anxious Attachment	*n*	*1*		**Anxious Attachment**	*n*	*1*	
Married/ Remarried	324	2.55		Married/ Remarried	325	2.32	
Living w. Partner	121	2.76		Living w. Partner	72	2.58	
Single	73	3.03		Divorced/ Separated	78	2.61	
Divorced/ Separated	55	3.09		Single	65	2.67	
p = .001				*p* = .02			
Avoidant Attachment	n	1	2	**Avoidant Attachment**	n	1	2
Married/ Remarried	327	2.21		Married/ Remarried	327	2.07	
Living w. Partner	122	2.63	2.63	Living w. Partner	74	2.46	2.46
Divorced/ Separated	56	2.86	2.86	Divorced/ Separated	81	2.56	2.56
Single	75		3.16	Single	66		2.78
p = .000				*p* = .000			
Parental Status	**Midlife Therapists**			**Parental Status**	**Older Therapists**		
Anxious Attachment	n	1		**Anxious Attachment**	n	1	
3+ children	163	2.52		3+ children	206	2.24	
1 child	75	2.67		2 children	170	2.46	
2 children	193	2.74		No children	78	2.55	
No children	121	2.78		1 child	72	2.70	
p = ns				*p* =.01			
Avoidant Attachment	n	1	2	**Avoidant Attachment**	n	1	
3+ children	165	2.26		3+ children	208	2.09	
2 children	196	2.28	2.28	2 children	175	2.15	
1 child	75	2.44	2.44	No children	79	2.48	
No children	123		2.87	1 child	71	2.49	
p = .001				*p* = .03			

* Scales are scored from 1 (low) to 7 (high). Means for groups in homogenous subsets are displayed based on Scheffe test.

Table 4.20 Adult Attachment Dimension and Personal Self, and by Gender and Age*

Personal Self Dimension		Total (N=1,219–1,250)		Women (N=914–941)		Men (N=300–304)	
		Anxiety	Avoidance	Anxiety	Avoidance	Anxiety	Avoidance
Genial/Caring	r	-.19	-.34	-.17	-.31	-.20	-.41
	p	.000	.000	.000	.000	.001	.000
Forceful/ Exacting	r	.19	.07	.21	.10	.16	-.00
	p	.000	.02	.000	.003	.006	ns
Reclusive/ Remote	r	.21	.42	.19	.40	.24	.47
	p	.000	.000	.000	.000	.000	.000
Ardent/ Expressive	r	.09	-.13	.12	-.12	.07	-.16
	p	.001	.000	.000	.000	ns	.005
Personal Self Dimension		**Younger (N=71–72)**		**Midlife (N=578–588)**		**Older (N=548–567)**	
		Anxiety	Avoidance	Anxiety	Avoidance	Anxiety	Avoidance
Genial/Caring	r	-.12	-.39	-.22	-.33	-.16	-.36
	p	ns	.001	.000	.000	.000	.000
Forceful/ Exacting	r	.25	-.04	.16	.04	.17	.07
	p	.04	ns	.000	ns	.000	ns
Reclusive/ Remote	r	.14	.48	.26	.39	.16	.45
	p	ns	.000	.000	.000	.000	.000
Ardent/ Expressive	r	.24	-.12	.08	-.14	.08	-.15
	p	.04	ns	ns	.001	ns	.000

* Correlation of Anxiety and Avoidance scales: r = .48 (N = 1,233)

Table 5.1 Content Defining the Dimensions of Spirituality and Religion

How important is each the following in your life at present?[1]	M[2]	SD	Factors[3]	
			Spirituality	Religiosity
Personal moral and ethical standards.	8.58	1.87	**.70**	–
A sense of spiritual dimension in personal experience.	7.27	3.03	**.74**	–
Finding a source of discipline and purpose in living.	6.26	3.31	**.74**	–
Expressing personal devotion through service to others.	4.90	3.54	**.56**	.53
Seeking inner assurance and communion through prayer.	3.72	3.72	.41	**.70**
Celebrating the beauty and dignity of the worship service.	2.87	3.28	.–	**.86**
Participation in a religious fellowship or community.	3.12	3.44	–	**.84**
Observing traditional religious holy days.	2.71	3.06	–	**.82**
Upholding a personally valued historical tradition.	3.26	3.29	–	**.67**
A specific creed or set of beliefs.	3.97	3.53	–	**.59**
Cronbach's α =			.71	.87

[1] Ns = 2,462 to 2,479
[2] Rated on a 0–10 scale: 0 = Not at all important in my life; 10 = Most important part of my life
[3] Principal components extraction, Varimax rotation; items used for scales in bold type

Table 5.2 Therapists' Belief-Value Orientation by Religious Background

Family of Origin Religious Affiliation		Ethical Secular	Spiritual Secular	Spiritual Religious	Ceremonial Religious	Total
No religious affiliation	n	304	115	64	16	499
	%	**60.9%**	23.0%	*12.8%*	3.2%	100.0%
	AsR	11.4	-2.1	-8.6	-2.9	
Protestant Christian	n	688	504	615	78	1,885
	%	36.5%	26.7%	**32.6%**	*4.1%*	100.0%
	AsR	-1.4	-.4	4.4	-4.8	
Roman Catholicism/Eastern Orthodox	n	299	308	317	69	993
	%	*30.1%*	**(31.0%)**	31.9%	6.9%	100.0%
	AsR	-5.6	3.2	2.1	1.3	
Judaism	n	126	77	65	46	314
	%	40.1%	24.5%	*(20.7%)*	**14.6%**	100.0%
	AsR	.9	-1.0	-3.5	6.6	
Islam	n	27	7	20	6	60
	%	45.0%	11.7%	33.3%	10.0%	100.0%
	AsR	1.2	-2.7	.7	1.3	
Hinduism	n	50	48	43	26	167
	%	29.9%	28.7%	25.7%	**15.6%**	100.0%
	AsR	-2.1	.5	-1.0	5.2	
Buddhism	n	9	8	18	1	36
	%	25.0%	22.2%	50.0%	2.8%	100.0%
	AsR	-1.6	-.7	2.8	-.8	
Mixed/other affiliations	n	63	58	74	11	206
	%	30.6%	28.2%	35.9%	5.3%	100.0%
	AsR	-2.1	.4	2.2	-.5	
Total	N	1,566	1,125	1,216	253	4,160
	%	37.6%	27.0%	29.2%	6.1%	100.0%

χ^2 = 268.9, df = 21, p = .000; AsR cut-off at p =.01 for 32 cells = ± 3.60 (at p =.05, ± 3.16)

Table 5.3 Therapists' Belief-Value Orientation by Current Religious Affiliation

Current Religious Affiliation		Ethical Secular	Spiritual Secular	Spiritual Religious	Ceremonial Religious	Total
No religious	n	1,165	675	130	28	1,998
affiliation	%	**58.3%**	**33.8%**	*6.5%*	*1.4%*	100.0%
	AsR	24.8	8.8	-30.2	-10.9	
Protestant	n	181	149	497	65	892
Christian	%	*20.3%*	*16.7%*	**55.7%**	7.3%	100.0%
	AsR	-12.9	-8.2	20.6	3.0	
Roman Catholi-	n	73	73	194	49	389
cism/Eastern	%	*18.8%*	*18.8%*	**49.9%**	**12.6%**	100.0%
Orthodox	AsR	-8.6	-4.0	10.0	6.7	
Judaism	n	89	36	58	44	227
	%	39.2%	*15.9%*	25.6%	**19.4%**	100.0%
	AsR	0.1	-4.0	-0.9	9.7	
Islam	n	14	5	19	5	43
	%	32.6%	11.6%	44.2%	11.6%	100.0%
	AsR	-0.9	-2.3	2.3	1.9	
Hinduism[1]	n	2	6	14	1	23
	%	8.7%	26.1%	**(60.9%)**	4.3%	100.0%
	AsR	-3.0	-0.2	3.5	-0.2	
Buddhism	n	30	59	94	11	194
	%	*15.5%*	30.4%	**48.5%**	5.7%	100.0%
	AsR	-6.9	0.9	6.4	0.2	
Mixed/other	n	37	119	147	14	317
affiliations	%	*12.1%*	**37.5%**	**46.4%**	4.2%	100.0%
	AsR	-10.4	4.2	7.5	-0.7	
Total	N	1,591	1,122	1,153	217	4,083
	%	38.2%	27.3%	29.0%	5.5%	100.0%

χ^2 = 1417.6, df = 21, p = .000; AsR cut-off at p =.01 for 32 cells = ± 3.60 (at p =.05, ± 3.16)
1 –Missing data for 148 therapists of Hindu background (due to 'current affiliation' item omitted).

Table 5.4 Therapists' Religious Backgrounds and Current Religious Affiliations

Religious Faith	Religious Background		Current Affiliation	
	N	%	N	%
Protestant Christian	1,921	44.5%	910	21.4%
Roman Catholic/Eastern Orthodox	1,089[1]	25.2%	434[1]	10.2%
None/Atheist/Agnostic	512	11.9%	2,089	49.1%
Judaism	324	7.5%	232	5.5%
Hindu[2]	168	3.9%	24	0.6%
Islam	60	1.4%	43	1.0%
Buddhist	36	0.8%	199	4.7%
Mixed or other religion	208	4.8%	324	7.6%
Total	4,319	100.0%	4,258	100.0%

[1] Roman Catholic = 1065→427, Eastern Orthodox (Greek, Russian, Serbian, Syrian) = 22→7.
[2] Missing data for 148 therapists of Hindu background (due to 'current affiliation' item omitted).

Table 5.5 Degree and Direction of Change in Therapists' Religious Identities[1]

Religious Background		Current Religious Affiliation								Total
		Unaffiliated	Protestant Christian	Catholic/ Orthodox	Jewish	Muslim	Hindu	Buddhist	Mixed/ Other	
None	n	383	43	13	4	0	1	18	24	486
	%	**78.8%**	8.8%	2.7%	0.8%	0.0%	0.2%	3.7%	4.9%	100.0%
Protestant Christian	n	814	764	29	7	0	2	100	160	1,876
	%	43.4%	**40.7%**	1.5%	0.4%	0.0%	0.1%	5.3%	8.5%	100.0%
Catholic/Orthodox	n	478	58	385	5	2	5	46	66	1,045
	%	45.7%	5.6%	**36.8%**	0.5%	0.2%	0.5%	4.4%	6.3%	100.0%
Jewish	n	71	2	3	213	1	0	8	17	315
	%	22.5%	0.6%	1.0%	**67.6%**	0.3%	0.0%	2.5%	5.4%	100.0%
Muslim	n	18	0	0	1	36	0	0	1	56
	%	32.1%	0.0%	0.0%	1.8%	**64.3%**	0.0%	0.0%	1.8%	100.0%
Hindu	n	3	2	0	0	0	14	0	0	19[2]
	%	15.0%	10.0%	0.0%	0.0%	0.0%	**73.7%**	0.0%	0.0%	100.0%
Buddhist	n	8	8	0	0	0	0	17	0	33
	%	24.2%	24.2%	0.0%	0.0%	0.0%	0.0%	**51.5%**	0.0%	100.0%
Mixed/Other	n	90	25	3	1	1	2	7	53	182
	%	48.9%	13.7%	1.6%	0.5%	0.5%	1.1%	3.8%	**29.1%**	100.0%
Total	N	1,865	902	433	231	40	24	196	321	4,012
	%	46.5%	22.5%	10.8%	5.8%	1.0%	0.6%	4.9%	8.0%	100.0%

[1] Bold black type in main diagonal = % Adherence (retention of religion); plain black type = % Conversion (change to another religion); faded black type in left column = % Apostasy (loss of each religion).
[2] Missing data for 148 therapists of Hindu background ('current affiliation' question was omitted).

Table 5.6 Periods of Change in Therapist Religiosity

Childhood to Adolescence[1]

Childhood Religiosity		Adolescent Religiosity		
		Low importance	High importance	Total
Low importance	n	1,538	261	1,799
	%	**85.5%**	*14.5%*	100.0
	AsR	31.1	-31.1	
High importance	n	470	989	1,459
	%	*32.2%*	**67.8%**	100.0%
	AsR	-31.1	31.1	
Total	N	2,008	1,250	3,258
	%	61.6%	38.4%	100.0%

Adolescence to Adulthood[2]

Adolescent Religiosity		Adult Religiosity		
		Low importance	High importance	Total
Low importance	n	1,467	433	1,900
	%	**77.2%**	*22.8%*	100.0%
	AsR	18.3	-18.3	
High importance	n	512	638	1,150
	%	*44.5%*	**55.5%**	100.0%
	AsR	-18.3	18.3	
Total	N	1,979	638	3,050
	%	64.9%	35.1%	100.0%

Childhood to Adulthood[3]

Childhood Religiosity		Adult Religiosity		
		Low importance	High importance	Total
Low importance	n	1,279	426	1,705
	%	**75.0%**	*25.0%*	100.0%
	AsR	13.2	-13.2	
High importance	n	699	645	1,344
	%	*52.0%*	**48.0%**	100.0%
	AsR	-13.2	13.2	
Total	N	1,978	1,071	3,049
	%	64.9%	35.1%	100.0%

[1] χ^2 = 967.1, df = 1, p = .000; AsR cut-off at p =.01 for 4 cells = ± 3.02 (at p =.05, ± 2.50)
[2] χ^2 = 336.0, df = 1, p = .000; AsR cut-off at p =.01 for 4 cells = ± 3.02 (at p =.05, ± 2.50)
[3] χ^2 = 174.6, df = 1, p = .000; AsR cut-off at p =.01 for 4 cells = ± 3.02 (at p =.05, ± 2.50)

Table 5.7 Therapists' Personal Belief Patterns by Gender[1] and Age[2]

Gender		Ethical Secular	Spiritual Secular	Spiritual Religious	Ceremonial Religious	Total
Women	n	1,202	925	898	168	3,193
	%	37.6%	**29.0%**	28.1%	(5.3%)	100.0%
	AsR	-1.7	4.0	-0.6	-2.9	
Men	n	524	300	378	98	1,300
	%	40.3%	_23.1%_	29.1%	(7.5%)	100.0%
	AsR	1.7	-4.0	0.6	2.9	
Total		1,726	1,225	1,276	266	4,493
		38.4%	27.3%	28.4%	5.9%	100.0%
Age Group						
Younger 21 to 34	n	241	85	126	57	509
	%	**47.3%**	_16.7%_	24.8%	**11.2%**	100.0%
		4.4	-5.7	-1.9	5.4	
Midlife 35 to 54	n	921	631	648	138	2,338
	%	39.4%	27.0%	27.7%	5.9%	100.0%
		1.4	-0.5	-1.0	0.0	
Older 55 to 85	n	544	498	485	67	1,594
	%	_34.1%_	**31.2%**	30.4%	_4.2%_	100.0%
		-4.4	4.4	2.3	-3.6	
Total	N	1,706	1,214	1,259	262	4,441
	%	38.4%	27.3%	28.3%	5.9%	100.0%

[1] χ^2 =21.86, df =3, p = .000; AsR cut-off at p =.01 for 8 cells = ± 3.23 (at p =.05, ± 2.73)
[2] χ^2 =85.92, df =6, p = .000; AsR cut-off at p =.01 for 12 cells = ± 3.34 (at p =.05, ± 2.87)

Table 5.8 Therapists' Personal Belief Patterns by Marital[1] (and Parental[2]) Status

Current Marital Status		Ethical Secular	Spiritual Secular	Spiritual Religious	Ceremonial Religious	Total
Single	n	249	160	188	47	644
	%	38.7%	24.8%	29.2%	7.3%	100.0%
	AsR	0.1	-1.5	0.6	1.4	
Living with partner	n	295	166	78	16	555
	%	**53.2%**	29.9%	*14.1%*	*(2.9%)*	100.0%
	AsR	7.6	1.5	-7.9	-3.4	
Married/ remarried	n	977	682	832	185	2,676
	%	*(36.5%)*	*(25.5%)*	**31.1%**	**(6.9%)**	100.0%
	AsR	-3.4	-3.3	5.3	3.0	
Divorced/ separated	n	156	178	131	16	481
	%	32.4%	**37.0%**	27.2%	3.3%	100.0%
	AsR	-2.9	5.1	-0.5	-2.7	
Total	N	1,677	1,186	1,229	264	4,356
	%	38.5%	27.2%	28.2%	6.1%	100.0%

[1] χ^2 = 128.7, df = 9, p = .000; AsR cut-off at p =.01 for 16 cells = ± 3.42 (for p =.05 = ± 2.96)
[2] For parental status, χ^2 = 4.4, df = 3, p = ns

Table 5.9 Belief-Value Dimensions by Personal Self and Attachment Patterns

Personal Self		*Religiosity* Current importance of religion in life	*Spirituality* Current influence of spiritual values in life
Genial/Caring	r	.07	.12
	p	.000	.000
	N	4,409	3,502
Forceful/Exacting	r	.02	-.03
	p	ns	ns
	N	4,403	3,496
Reclusive/Remote	r	.02	-.01
	p	ns	ns
	N	4,384	3,478
Ardent/Expressive	r	.06	.13
	p	.000	.000
	N	4,410	3,503
Attachment Pattern			
Anxious Attachment	r	-.01	-.05
	p	ns	ns
	N	1,241	1,235
Avoidant Attachment	r	-.05	-.08
	p	ns	.006
	N	1,257	1,251

Table 5.10 Belief-Value Orientations by Personal Self

Belief-Value Pattern		Personal Self: *Genial/Caring*[1]			
	n	1	2	F	P
Ethical Secular	1,689	2.34		21.87	.000
Ceremonial Religious	256	2.42	2.42	df=3	N = 4,371
Spiritual Religious	1,244		2.45		
Spiritual Secular	,		2.46		
		Personal Self: *Ardent/Expressive*[1]			
	n	1	2	F	P
Ethical Secular	1,688	1.90		27.77	.000
Ceremonial Religious	254		2.03	df=3	N = 4,372
Spiritual Religious	1,242		2.04		
Spiritual Secular	1,188		2.06		

[1] Scheffe test (p = .01 criterion): Means for groups in homogenous subsets are displayed.

Table 5.11 Therapists' Personal Belief Patterns by Professional Background

Profession		Ethical Secular	Spiritual Secular	Spiritual Religious	Ceremonial Religious	Total
Psychology	n	856	412	446	148	1,862
	%	**46.0%**	*22.1%*	*24.0%*	**7.9%**	100.0%
	AsR	9.7	-7.0	-6.0	4.8	
Medicine/ Psychiatry	n	95	51	47	22	215
	%	44.2%	23.7%	21.9%	10.2%	100.0%
	AsR	2.0	-1.3	-2.3	2.7	
Counseling	n	481	518	561	55	1,615
	%	*29.8%*	**32.1%**	**34.7%**	*3.4%*	100.0%
	AsR	-8.4	5.2	6.8	-5.5	
Social Work	n	72	70	62	13	217
	%	33.2%	32.3%	28.6%	6.0%	100.0%
	AsR	-1.4	1.6	0.0	0.0	
Lay Therapist/ Aanalyst	n	112	128	112	18	370
	%	*(33.2%)*	**(32.3%)**	28.6%	6.0%	100.0%
	AsR	-3.1	3.2	0.7	-0.9	
Total	N	1,616	1,179	1,228	256	4,279
	%	37.8%	27.6%	28.7%	6.0%	100.0%

χ^2 = 187.1, df = 12, p = .000; AsR cut-off at p =.01 for 20 cells = ± 3.53 (for p =.05 = ± 3.02)

Table 5.12 Therapists' Personal Belief Patterns by Therapeutic Approach

Salient orientation		Personal Belief Patterns				
		Ethical Secular	Spiritual Secular	Spiritual Religious	Ceremonial Religious	Total
Analytic/ Psychodynamic	n	359	156	138	36	689
	%	**52.1%**	22.6%	_20.0%_	5.2%	100.0%
	AsR	7.7	-2.7	-5.4	-0.6	
Cognitive- Behavioral	n	249	62	79	36	426
	%	**58.5%**	_14.6%_	_18.5%_	8.5%	100.0%
	AsR	8.6	-6.1	-4.7	2.6	
Humanistic	n	169	154	145	15	483
	%	35.0%	31.9%	30.0%	3.1%	100.0%
	AsR	-2.3	2.9	1.1	-2.7	
Analytic/ Dynamic & Humanistic	n	46	59	48	9	162
	%	28.4%	36.4%	29.6%	5.6%	100.0%
	AsR	-3.0	2.9	0.5	-0.1	
Broad Spectrum	n	203	278	307	43	831
	%	_24.4%_	**33.5%**	**36.9%**	5.2%	100.0%
	AsR	-10.7	5.3	6.8	-0.8	
No Salient Orientation	n	96	46	76	23	241
	%	39.8%	19.1%	31.5%	9.5%	100.0%
	AsR	0.1	-2.8	1.3	2.7	
Total	N	1,122	755	793	162	2,832[1]
	%	39.6%	26.7%	28.0%	5.7%	100.0%

χ^2 = 252.4, df = 15, p = .000; AsR cut-off at p =.01 for 24 cell = ± 3.53 (for p =.05 = ± 3.08)

[1] Reduced N due to limiting orientation categories used to > 500 in the total sample; χ^2 test using 10 orientation categories having N>300 showed same results with a larger sample.

Table 6.1a Experiences Related to Current Life Quality: Total Sample and by Gender[1]

In your own life at present, how often do you feel …		Current Life Satisfaction			Current Life Stress		
		Total	Women	Men	Total	Women	Men
Positive Experiences							
A satisfying sense of intimacy and emotional rapport.	r	.54	.53	.50	-.14	-.13	-.12
	p	.000	.000	.000	.000	.000	.000
A sense of being genuinely cared for and supported.	r	.48	.48	.42	-.10	-.12	-.11
	p	.000	.000	.000	.000	.000	.000
Moments of unreserved enjoyment.	r	.47	.46	.46	-.12	-.13	-.13
	p	.000	.000	.000	.000	.000	.000
A sense of belonging to a personally meaningful community.	r	.37	.37	.39	-.17	-.15	-.19
	p	.000	.000	.000	.000	.000	.000
Being able to freely express your private thoughts and feelings.	r	.33	.31	.29	-.07	-.05	-.05
	p	.000	.000	.000	.000	.000	.03
Taking opportunities to relax and refresh yourself.	r	.33	.31	.32	-.27	-.26	-.19
	p	.000	.000	.000	.000	.000	.000
Negative Experiences							
Hassled by the pressures of everyday life.	r	-.25	-.24	-.24	.61	.62	.60
	p	.000	.000	.000	.000	.000	.000
A heavy burden of responsibility, worry or concern for others close to you.	r	-.25	-.25	-.20	.49	.49	.45
	p	.000	.000	.000	.000	.000	.000
A sense of significant personal conflict, disappointment or loss.	r	-.34	-.36	-.31	.35	.36	.36
	p	.000	.000	.000	.000	.000	.000
Worry about money or financial security.	r	-.19	-.20	-.21	.34	.32	.34
	p	.000	.000	.000	.000	.000	.000
Worry about your physical health.	r	-.17	-.18	-.21	.27	.26	.31
	p	.000	.000	.000	.000	.000	.000

[1] Rated on 0–5 scale: 0=Never, 1=Rarely, 2=Occasionally, 3=Moderately, 4=Often, 5=Very often.

Table 6.1b Experiences Related to Current Life Quality by Age Group[1]

In your own life at present, how often do you feel ...		Current Life Satisfaction			Current Life Stress		
		Young-er	Midlife	Older	Young-er	Midlife	Older
Positive Experiences							
A satisfying sense of intimacy and emotional rapport.	r	.56	.54	.50	-.11	-.14	-.12
	p	.000	.000	.000	.000	.000	.000
A sense of being genuinely cared for and supported.	r	.50	.48	.42	-.06	-.11	-.11
	p	.000	.000	.000	.003	.000	.000
Moments of unreserved enjoyment.	r	.47	.46	.46	-.06	-.12	-.13
	p	.000	.000	.000	.002	.000	.000
A sense of belonging to a personally meaningful community.	r	.34	.36	.39	-.04	-.18	-.19
	p	.000	.000	.000	ns	.000	.000
Being able to freely express your private thoughts and feelings.	r	.36	.32	.29	-.01	-.08	-.05
	p	.000	.000	.000	ns	.000	.03
Taking opportunities to relax and refresh yourself.	r	.34	.32	.32	-.31	-.30	-.19
	p	.000	.000	.000	.000	.000	.000
Negative Experiences							
Hassled by the pressures of everyday life.	r	-.30	-.24	-.24	.61	.60	.60
	p	.000	.000	.000	.000	.000	.000
A heavy burden of responsibility, worry or concern for others close to you.	r	-.19	-.26	-.20	.45	.50	.45
	p	.000	.000	.000	.000	.000	.000
A sense of significant personal conflict, disappointment or loss.	r	-.32	-.34	-.31	.30	.36	.36
	p	.000	.000	.000	.000	.000	.000
Worry about money or financial security.	r	-.15	-.18	-.21	.30	.33	.34
	p	.002	.000	.000	.000	.000	.000
Worry about your physical health.	r	-.08	-.17	-.21	.23	.26	.31
	p	ns	.000	.000	.000	.000	.000

[1] Rated on 0–5 scale: 0=Never, 1=Rarely, 2=Occasionally, 3=Moderately, 4=Often, 5=Very often.

Table 6.2 Dimensions of Life Quality Experience

In your own life at present, how often do you feel …	Item Scales[1]			Life Quality Dimensions[2]	
	% high (4–5)	M[3]	SD	Personal Satisfactions	Personal Burdens
A satisfying sense of intimacy and emotional rapport	59.2	3.62	1.2	**.79**	-.07
A sense of being genuinely cared for and supported	63.3	3.74	1.1	**.79**	-.03
Moments of unreserved enjoyment	54.4	3.50	1.1	**.75**	-.2
Current life satisfaction	67.4	3.75	0.9	**.69**	-.31
Able to freely express private thoughts and feelings	63.8	3.75	1.0	**.65**	.07
A sense of belonging to a personally meaningful community[4]	59.1	3.56	1.2	**.59**	-.12
Opportunities to relax and refresh yourself[5]	55.2	3.54	1.1	**.55**	-.20
Hassled by the pressures of everyday life[6]	22.8	2.64	1.1	-.07	**.78**
Current life stress	25.8	2.65	1.2	-.14	**.75**
A heavy burden of responsibility, worry or concern for others close to you	20.1	2.38	1.3	.06	**.74**
A sense of significant personal conflict, disappointment or loss	13.7	2.07	1.2	-.17	**.65**
Worry about money or financial security[7]	22.0	2.27	1.4	-.02	**.62**
Worry about your physical health[8]	11.5	1.90	1.2	-.03	**.57**
			α =	**.81**	**.78**

[1] Rated on a 0–5 scale: 0=never, 1=rarely, 2=occasionally, 3=moderately, 4=often, 5=very often
[2] Loadings in bold type included in computing dimension factors.
[3] N ≥ 11,475 except as noted.
[4] N=3,798
[5] N=4,831
[6] N=4,622
[7] N=4,456
[8] N=4,829

Table 6.3 Life Quality Pattern by Gender and Age Group

Life Quality Pattern		Gender[1]			Age Group[2]			
		Female	Male	Total	Younger 21 to 34	Midlife 35 to 54	Older 55 to 85	Total
Fulfilling hi sat/lo stress	n	2,364	1,311	3,675	623	2,004	1,008	3,635
	%	33.9%	32.0%	33.2%	25.7%	31.7%	45.1%	33.1%
	AsR	2.0	-2.0	-8.8	-3.6	13.5		
Satisfactory hi sat/mod stress	n	1,522	797	2,319	497	1,314	497	2,308
	%	(21.8%)	(19.5%)	21.0%	20.5%	20.8%	22.2%	21.0%
	AsR	3.0	-3.0	-.7	-.7	1.6		
Hectic hi sat/hi stress	n	938	531	1,469	339	909	214	1,462
	%	13.5%	13.0%	13.3%	14.0%	**14.4%**	9.6%	13.3%
	AsR	.7	-.7	1.1	3.8	-5.8		
Dull lo-mod sat/lo stress	n	584	451	1,035	289	564	174	1,027
	%	8.4%	**11.0%**	9.4%	**11.9%**	8.9%	7.8%	9.4%
	AsR	-4.6	4.6	4.9	-1.8	-2.9		
Strained lo-mod sat/mod stress	n	715	458	1,173	290	676	193	1,159
	%	10.3%	11.2%	10.6%	12.0%	10.7%	(8.6%)	10.6%
	AsR	-1.5	1.5	2.5	.6	-3.3		
Distressed lo-mod sat/hi stress	n	847	546	1,393	387	852	151	1,390
	%	12.2%	13.3%	12.6%	**16.0%**	(13.5%)	6.8%	12.7%
	AsR	-1.8	1.8	5.5	3.0	-9.4		
Total	N	6,970	4094	11,064	2,425	6,319	2,237	10,981
	%	100.0%	100.0%	100.0%	100.0%	100.0%	100.0%	100.0%

[1] $\chi^2 = 34.31$, df = 5, p = .000; AsR cut-off at p =.01 for 12 cells = ± 3.34 (for p =.05 = ± 2.87)

[2] $\chi^2 = 295.1$, df = 10, p = .000; AsR cut-off at p =.01 for18 cells = ± 3.45 (for p =.05 = ± 2.99)

Table 6.4 Personal Life Quality by Gender and Age Group

Personal Satisfactions[1]	N	1	2	3	4
Younger Men (21–34)	847	3.30			
Midlife Men (35–54)	2,467		3.52		
Younger Women (21–34)	1,649			3.67	
Midlife Women (35–54)	4,021			3.71	3.71
Older Men (55–85)	859			3.73	3.73
Older Women (55–85)	1,416				3.79
Personal Burdens[2]	N	1	2		
Older Women (55–85)	1,418	2.19			
Older Men (55–85)	858	2.20			
Midlife Men (35–54)	2,467		2.42		
Younger Men (21–34)	845		2.44		
Midlife Women (35–54)	3,960		2.44		
Younger Women (21–34)	1,631		2.53		

[1] $F = 63.7$; $df = 5, 11253$; $p = .000$; subgroups differentiated at $p=.01$ by Scheffe test
[2] $F = 29.9$; $df = 5. 11255$; $p = .000$; subgroups differentiated at $p=.01$ by Scheffe test

Table 6.5 Life Quality Pattern by Gender and Age Group

Life Quality Pattern		Younger Women 21 to 34	Younger Men 21 to 34	Midlife Women 35 to 54	Midlife Men 35 to 54	Older Women 55 to 85	Older Men 55 to 85	Total
Ful-filling hi sat/lo stress	n	414	208	1,270	722	642	363	3,619
	%	26.0%	25.2%	32.5%	(30.2%)	**46.3%**	**43.4%**	33.1%
	AsR	-6.5	-5.0	-1.0	-3.4	11.2	6.6	
Satisfac-tory hi sat/mod stress	n	362	133	833	479	315	176	2,298
	%	22.8%	(16.1%)	21.3%	20.1%	22.7%	21.1%	21.0%
	AsR	1.8	-3.6	.6	-1.3	1.7	.0	
Hectic hi sat/hi stress	n	244	92	564	342	119	93	1,454
	%	15.3%	11.1%	14.4%	14.3%	8.6%	11.1%	13.3%
	AsR	2.6	-1.9	2.6	1.7	-5.5	-1.9	
Dull lo-mod sat/lo stress	n	147	140	330	232	99	74	1,022
	%	9.2%	**16.9%**	8.4%	9.7%	7.1%	8.9%	9.3%
	AsR	-.2	7.8	-2.4	.7	-3.0	-.5	
Strained lo-mod sat/mod stress	n	172	118	405	268	127	65	1,155
	%	10.8%	(**14.3%**)	10.4%	11.2%	9.2%	7.8%	10.6%
	AsR	.4	3.6	-.5	1.2	-1.8	-2.7	
Dis-tressed lo-mod sat/hi stress	n	251	135	504	344	85	65	1,384
	%	**15.8%**	(**16.3%**)	12.9%	14.4%	6.1%	7.8%	12.7%
	AsR	4.1	3.3	.6	2.9	-7.8	-4.4	
Total	N	1,590	826	,	2,387	1,387	836	10,932
	%	100.0%	100.0%	100.0%	100.0%	100.0%	100.0%	100.0%

$\chi^2 = 373$, df = 25, p = .000; AsR cut-off at $p = .01$ for 36 cells = ± 3.64 (for $p = .05$ = ± 3.20)

Table 6.6 Personal Satisfactions by Marital Status and Combined with Gender

Marital Status[1]	N	1	2	3	
Single	1,900	3.36			
Divorced/separated	1,110		3.46		
Married	6,665			3.74	
Cohabiting (Living with partner)	1,352			3.77	
Marital Status by Gender[2]	N	1	2	3	4
Single men	593	3.20			
Divorced/separated men	258		3.39		
Single women	1,295		3.44	3.44	
Divorced/separated women	844		3.49	3.49	
Cohabiting men	464			3.57	
Married men	2,724			3.60	
Married women	3,869				3.84
Cohabiting women	879				3.87

[1] $F = 146.9$; $df = 3, 11023$; $p = .000$; subgroups different at $p=.01$ by Scheffe test
[2] $F = 101.5$; $df = 7, 10918$; $p = .000$; subgroups different at $p=.01$ by Scheffe test

278   *Statistical Appendix*

Table 6.7 Personal Burdens by Marital Status

Marital Status[1]	N	1	2
Married	6,667	2.36	
Cohabiting (Living with partner)	1,352	2.45	2.45
Single	1,900	2.45	2.45
Divorced/separated	1,110		2.51
Marital Status by Gender[2]	N	1	
Married men	2,725	2.34	
Married women	3,870	2.37	
Cohabiting men	464	2.43	
Single men	593	2.45	
Cohabiting women	879	2.45	
Single women	1,295	2.46	
Divorced/separated men	258	2.45	
Divorced/separated women	844	2.52	

[1] $F = 12.6$; $df = 3, 11025$; p $= .000$; subgroups different at $p=.01$ by Scheffe test
[2] $F = 5.63$; $df = 7, 10927$; p $= .000$

Table 6.8 Life Quality Patterns by Marital Status

Life Quality Pattern		Single	Living w. partner	Married	Divorced/ Separated	Total
Fulfilling	n	496	420	2,324	306	3,546
hi sat/lo stress	%	*26.9%*	31.2%	36.2%	*28.2%*	33.1%
	AsR	-6.2	-1.7	8.2	-3.6	
Satisfactory	n	285	316	1,471	191	2,263
hi sat/mod stress	%	*15.5%*	23.4%	**22.9%**	17.6%	21.1%
	AsR	-6.6	2.2	5.4	-3.0	
Hectic	n	190	205	906	127	1,428
hi sat/hi stress	%	*10.3%*	15.2%	14.1%	11.7%	13.3%
	AsR	-4.2	2.2	2.8	-1.7	
Dull	n	281	100	481	128	990
lo-mod sat/lo stress	%	**15.3%**	7.4%	*7.5%*	**(11.8%)**	9.3%
	AsR	9.8	-2.5	-7.7	3.1	
Strained	n	275	124	566	153	1,118
lo-mod sat/mod stress	%	**14.9%**	9.2%	*8.8%*	**14.1%**	10.4%
	AsR	6.9	-1.6	-6.8	4.2	
Distressed	n	315	183	678	179	,
lo-mod sat/hi stress	%	**17.1%**	13.6%	*10.6%*	**16.5%**	12.7%
	AsR	6.3	1.1	-8.1	4.0	
Total	N	1,842	1,348	6426	1,084	,
	%	100.0%	100.0%	100.0%	100.0%	100.0%

χ^2 = 355.5, df = 15, p = .000; AsR cut-off at p =.01 for 24 cells = ± 3.53 (for p =.05 = ± 3.08)

Table 6.9 Life Quality Patterns by Belief-Value Patterns

Life Quality Pattern		Belief-Value Patterns				Total
		Ethical Secular	Spiritual Secular	Spiritual Religious	Ceremonial Religious	
Fulfilling hi sat/lo stress	n	569	479	498	84	1,630
	%	_34.7%_	41.1%	41.2%	37.2%	38.4%
	AsR	-4.0	2.2	2.3	-.4	
Satisfactory hi sat/mod stress	n	370	298	306	66	1,040
	%	22.5%	25.6%	25.3%	29.2%	24.5%
	AsR	-2.4	1.0	.8	1.7	
Hectic hi sat/hi stress	n	190	126	162	25	503
	%	11.6%	10.8%	13.4%	11.1%	11.9%
	AsR	-.5	-1.3	2.0	-.4	
Dull lo-mod sat/lo stress	n	127	74	52	11	264
	%	(7.7%)	6.3%	(4.3%)	4.9%	6.2%
	AsR	3.2	.2	-3.3	-.9	
Strained lo-mod sat/mod stress	n	178	97	108	15	398
	%	10.8%	8.3%	8.9%	6.6%	9.4%
	AsR	2.6	-1.5	-.6	-1.5	
Distressed lo-mod sat/hi stress	n	208	92	83	25	408
	%	**12.7%**	7.9%	_6.9%_	11.1%	9.6%
	AsR	5.4	-2.3	-3.8	.8	
Total	N	1,642	1,166	1,209	226	4,243
	%	100.0%	100.0%	100.0%	100.0%	100.0%

χ^2 = 70.6, df = 15, p = .000; AsR cut-off at p =.01 for 24 cells = ± 3.53 (for p =.05 = ± 3.08)

Table 6.10 Personal Life Quality, Personal Self and Attachment Dimensions

		Personal Satisfactions	Personal Burdens
Personal Self[1]			
Genial/Caring	r	**.42**	-.07
	p	.000	.000
	n	11,108	11,111
Forceful/Exacting	r	.09	.16
	p	.000	.000
	n	11,086	1,209
Reclusive/Remote	r	**-.22**	.13
	p	.000	.000
	n	11,066	11,069
Ardent/Expressive	r	**.30**	.10
	p	.000	.000
	n	11,098	11,101
Attachment			
Anxious	r	**-.38**	**.37**
	p	.000	.000
	n	1,242	1,243
Avoidant	r	**-.41**	**.20**
	p	.000	.000
	n	1,258	1,259

[1] Also computed separately by gender and age group with nearly identical results.

Table 6.11 Personal Life Quality by Professional Background

Personal Life Satisfactions[1]	n	1	2	3
Psychiatry	2,184	3.42		
Social Work	698		3.69	
Psychology	5,414		3.69	
Counseling	2,031		3.71	
Lay Therapist/Analyst	689		3.77	
Personal Life Burdens[2]	n	1	2	3
Lay Therapist/Analyst	688	2.26		
Counseling	2,032	2.27		
Psychiatry	2,182	2.37	2.37	
Psychology	5,417		2.45	
Social Work	699			2.60

[1] $F = 59.5$; $df = 4, 11011$; $p = .000$; subgroups differentiated at $p=.01$ by Scheffe test
[2] $F = 23.8$; $df = 4, 11013$; $p = .000$; subgroups differentiated at $p=.01$ by Scheffe test

Table 6.12 Personal Life Quality by Theoretical Approach

Theoretical Approach		Personal Life Satisfactions	Personal Life Burdens
Analytic/	r	-.01	.05
Psychodynamic	p	ns	.000
	N	11,305	11,306
Cognitive-	r	.06	-.03
Behavioral	p	.000	.000
	N	11,107	11,109
Humanistic	r	.07	-.03
	p	.000	.001
	N	11,307	11,309
Systemic	r	.11	.01
	p	.000	ns
	N	11,298	11,300
Broad Spectrum	r	.13	-.02
(Number of Salient	p	.000	*ns*
Orientations)	N	11,281	11,283

Table 6.13 Predictors of Personal Satisfactions

Predictors	% Predicted Variance		
	1	2	3
Personal Self: Genial/Caring (+)	48.1%	48.1%	23.3%
Personal Self: Ardent/Expressive (+)	21.3%	17.3%	7.5%
Marital Status: Married, Partnered (+) vs. Single, Divorced (-)	14.4%	12.7%	10.7%
Personal Self: Reclusive/Remote (-)	10.9%	7.8%	4.4%
Age/Gender group: Women, Older Men (+)	5.2%	6.2%	8.5%
Individual Beliefs: Spirituality (+)	–	7.8%	4.7%
Adult Attachment: *Anxious* (-)	–	–	**23.9%**
Adult Attachment: *Avoidant* (-)	–	–	**17.0%**
Total	100.0%		

[1] 5 variables predict **26%** of the variance [R=.508, Adj. R^2 = .257; N = 10,392]
[2] 6 variables predict **27%** of the variance [R=.521, Adj. R^2 = .266; N = 3,285]
[3] 8 variables predict **32%** of the variance [R=.581, Adj. R^2 = .317; N = 1,143]

Table 6.14 Predictors of Personal Burdens

Predictors	% Predicted Variance			
	1	2	3	4
Personal Self: Reclusive/Remote (+)	30.0%	8.4%	4.4%	4.4%
Personal Self: Ardent/Expressive (+)	27.1%	7.8%	8.5%	7.2%
Age/Gender groups: Women, Older Men (+)	25.2%	13.0%	8.0%	8.7%
Personal Self: Genial/Caring (-)	12.3%	6.2%	2.5%	–
Marital Status: Divorced (+) vs. Single, Partnered, Married (-)	5.4%	–	–	–
Adult Attachment: *Anxious* (+)	–	**64.6%**	**36.0%**	**40.4%**
Life Quality: *Personal Satisfactions*	–	–	40.6%	43.6%
Total	100.0%			

[1] 5 variables predict 5% of the variance [R=.227, Adj. R^2 = .049; N = 10,393]
[2] 5 variables predict 14% of the variance [R=.405, Adj. R^2 = .148; N = 1,193]
[3] 6 variables predict 20% of the variance [R=.464, Adj. R^2 = .198; N = 1,192]
[4] 4 variables predict 20% of the variance [R=.456, Adj. R^2 = .196; N = 1,207]

Table 7.1 Birth Order and Family Size

Family Size	Birth Order	N	% in Family	% in Sample	Total
1 child	only child	503	100.0%	10.5%	503
2 children	older of 2	783	53.9%	16.3%	1,453
	younger of 2	670	46.1%	14.0%	
3 children	oldest of 3	499	40.0%	10.4%	
	middle of 3	374	29.9%	7.8%	1,249
	youngest of 3	376	30.1%	7.8%	
4–5 children	oldest of 4–5	315	27.5%	6.6%	
	middle or 4–5	585	51.1%	12.2%	1,144
	youngest of 4–5	244	21.3%	5.1%	
6–12 children	oldest of 6–12	90	20.0%	1.9%	
	middle or 6–12	288	64.0%	6.0%	450
	youngest of 6–12	72	16.0%	1.5%	
	Total	4,804		100.0	4,804

Table 7.2 Family Size by Generation (Birth Cohort)

Family Size		Generation			Total
		Great Depression & WW2	Post-WW2 'Baby Boom'	Western Prosperity	
		1927–1946	*1947–1966*	*1967–1990*	
1 child	n	147	190	151	488
	%	**14.1%**	*7.6%*	**13.5%**	10.5%
	AsR	4.3	-6.8	3.8	
2 children	n	349	644	410	1,403
	%	33.4%	*25.9%*	**36.6%**	30.1%
	AsR	2.6	-6.8	5.4	
3 children	n	247	661	300	1,208
	%	23.6%	26.6%	26.8%	25.9%
	AsR	-2.0	1.0	.7	
4–5 children	n	216	695	207	1,118
	%	20.7%	**28.0%**	*18.5%*	24.0%
	AsR	-2.9	6.7	-5.0	
6–12 children	n	88	300	53	441
	%	8.4%	**12.0%**	*4.7%*	9.5%
	AsR	-1.3	6.4	-6.2	
	N	1,047	2,490	1,119	4,658
	%	100.0%	100.0%	100.0%	100.0%

χ^2 = 159.2, df = 8, p = .000; AsR cut-off at p =.01 for 15 cells = ± 3.40 (for p =.05 = ± 2.94)

Table 7.3 Parental Mortality by Therapist Age Group

Parental Mortality		Therapist Age Group			Total
		Younger Adult 22 to 34	Midlife Adult 35 to 54	Older Adult 55 to 85	
Both parents alive	n	394	959	103	1,456
	%	**85.3%**	**42.2%**	*6.5%*	33.6%
	AsR	24.9	12.5	-28.9	
Father died, mother alive	n	42	639	356	1,037
	%	*9.1%*	**28.1%**	22.3%	23.9%
	AsR	-7.9	6.7	-1.9	
Mother died, father alive	n	18	221	93	332
	%	*(3.9%)*	**9.7%**	*5.8%*	7.7%
	AsR	-3.2	5.3	-3.5	
Both parents died	n	8	455	1,044	1,507
	%	*1.7%*	20.0%	**65.4%**	34.8%
	AsR	-15.8	-21.5	32.3	
	N	462	2,274	1,596	4,332
%		100.0%	100.0%	100.0%	100.0%

χ^2 = 1573.9, df = 6, p = .000; AsR cut-off at p =.01 for 12 cells = ± 3.34 (for p =.05 = ± 2.87)

Table 7.4 Therapist Age at Time First Parent Died[1]

Therapist Age at Time of Loss	N	Total Sample		Birth-Cohort Generation		
		Bereaved %	Sample %	1927–1946	1947–1966	1967–1990
Child (>0–12)	187	7.2%	4.6%	6.9%	6.7%	17.6%
Adolescent (13–19)	209	8.1%	5.1%	6.6%	8.3%	16.9%
Young adult (20–29)	507	19.6%	12.5%	14.6%	21.5%	31.6%
Midlife adult (30–70)	1,686	65.1%	41.4%	71.9%	63.5%	33.8%
Both parents alive	1,481	–	36.4%			
Total	4,070	100.0%	100.0%	N = 875	1,489	136

[1] Small discrepancies in totals are due to some therapists not having specified their own age when a parent died.

Table 7.5 Therapist Age at Time of Parental Divorce of Separation[1]

Therapist Age	N	Divorced %	Sample %
Child (>0–12)	321	46.5%	7.6%
Adolescent (13–19)	178	25.8%	4.2%
Young adult (20–29)	120	17.4%	2.8%
Adult (30–70)	72	10.4%	1.7%
Parents remained married	3,525	–	83.6%
Total	4,216	100.0%	100.0%

[1] Small discrepancies in totals are due to some therapists not having specified their own age when their parents divorced or separated.

Table 7.6 Family Size by Family Economic Status

Family Size		Family Economic Status			Total
		Affluent	Secure	Challenged	
1-child family	n	38	77	30	145
	%	10.4%	14.9%	14.8%	13.4%
	AsR	-2.0	1.4	.7	
2-child family	n	149	174	53	376
	%	(40.8%)	33.6%	26.1%	34.6%
	AsR	3.1	-.7	-2.8	
3-child family	n	102	131	56	289
	%	27.9%	25.3%	27.6%	26.6%
	AsR	.7	-.9	.3	
4-child family	n	46	69	24	139
	%	12.6%	13.3%	11.8%	12.8%
	AsR	-.1	.5	-.5	
5–12 child family	n	30	67	40	137
	%	(8.2%)	12.9%	**19.7%**	12.6%
	AsR	-3.1	.3	3.4	
Total	N	365	518	203	1,086
	%	100.0%	100.0%	100.0%	100.0%

$\chi^2 = 26.7$, df = 8, p = .001; AsR cut-off at p =.01 for 15 cells = $\pm$ 3.40 (for p =.05 = $\pm$ 2.94)

Table 7.7 Therapist Age by Family Religious Background and Gender[†]

Total Sample	N	%	1	2	3
Non-religious	512	12.6%	47.5		
R. Catholic/E. Orthodox	1,089	26.9%	47.8		
Mixed	209	5.2%		51.4	
Protestant Christian	1,921	47.4%		52.5	
Jewish	324	8.0%			55.2

$F = 58.8$; df = 4, 3975; $P = .000$; subset alpha = 0.01

Female[1]	N	%			
Non-religious	392	**13.8%**	47.1		
R. Catholic/E. Orthodox	749	26.5%	47.5		
Mixed	156	5.5%		51.1	
Protestant Christian	1,351	47.7%		52.1	
Jewish	183	*6.5%*		53.4	

$F = 37.5$; df = 4, 2782; $P = .000$; subset alpha = 0.01

Male[1]	N	%			
Non-religious	117	*9.8%*	48.5		
R. Catholic/E. Orthodox	332	27.8%	49.0		
Mixed	50	4.2%		51.7	
Protestant Christian	557	46.7%		53.2	53.2
Jewish	137	**11.5%**		57.7	

$F = 20.6$; df = 4, 1170; $P = .000$; subset alpha = 0.01

[†] Numbers indicate mean age in years for each group.
[1] For gender comparisons: $\chi^2 = 41.1$, df = 4, p = .000; AsR cut-off at $p = .01$ for 10 cells = ± 3.29 (for $p = .05 = \pm 2.81$)

Table 7.8 Family Religious Background by Therapist Age Cohort

Family Religious Background		Birth Year Cohort			Total
		1927–1946	1947–1966	1967–1990	
Non-religious	n	80	284	132	496
	%	7.9%	12.5%	20.9%	12.6%
	AsR	-5.3	-.4	6.8	
Protestant Christian	n	545	1,120	197	1,862
	%	53.7%	49.1%	31.2%	47.4%
	AsR	4.6	2.5	-8.9	
R.Catholic/ E.Orthodox	n	192	614	259	1,065
	%	18.9%	26.9%	41.0%	27.1%
	AsR	-6.8	-.3	8.6	
Jewish	n	131	147	18	296
	%	12.9%	(6.4%)	2.9%	7.5%
	AsR	7.5	-3.1	-4.9	
Mixed	n	67	115	25	207
	%	6.6%	5.0%	4.0%	5.3%
	AsR	2.2	-.8	-1.6	
Total	N	1,015	2,280	631	3,926
	%	100.0%	100.0%	100.0%	100.0%

$\chi^2 = 41.1$, df = 4, p = .000; AsR cut-off at p =.01 for 10 cells = ± 3.29 (for p =.05 = ± 2.81)

Table 7.9 Childhood and Adolescent Religiosity by Family Religious Background

Childhood Religiosity[1]	N	1	2	3
Non-religious	327	1.18		
Protestant Christian	1,298		4.80	
Jewish	287		4.95	
Mixed	117		5.12	
R. Catholic/E. Orthodox	772			6.57

[1] $F = 232.2$; df = 4, 2796; $p = .000$; subset alpha = 0.01; Means on 0–10 scale

Adolescent Religiosity[2]				
Non-religious	327	1.45		
Jewish	287		4.30	
Protestant Christian	1,299		4.51	
Mixed	117		4.52	
R. Catholic/E. Orthodox	772			5.45

[2] $F = 104.4$; df = 4, 2797; $p = .000$; subset alpha = 0.01; Means on 0–10 scale.

Table 7.10 Childhood Family Size by Family Religious Background

Family Religious Affiliation		Number of Children in Family[1]					Total
		1	2	3	4–5	6–12	
Non-religious	n	43	198	125	84	25	475
	%	9.1%	**41.7%**	26.3%	_17.7%_	_(5.3%)_	100.0%
	AsR	-.1	6.0	-.1	-3.9	-3.3	
Protestant Christian	n	200	550	502	464	114	1,830
	%	**10.9%**	30.1%	27.4%	25.4%	_6.2%_	100.0%
	AsR	3.6	.2	1.2	.5	-6.5	
Roman Catholic or Eastern Orthodox	n	72	207	236	331	196	1,042
	%	6.9%	_19.9%_	_(22.6%)_	**31.8%**	**18.8%**	100.0%
	AsR	-2.9	-8.3	-3.3	5.9	12.2	
Jewish	n	24	141	97	42	9	313
	%	7.7%	**45.0%**	31.0%	_13.4%_	_2.9%_	100.0%
	AsR	-1.0	6.1	1.9	-4.9	-4.1	
Mixed	n	12	49	57	38	17	173
	%	6.9%	28.3%	32.9%	22.0%	9.8%	100.0%
	AsR	-1.0	-.5	2.0	-.9	.2	
Total	N	351	1,145	1,017	959	361	3,833
	%	9.2%	29.9%	26.5%	25.0%	9.4%	100.0%

χ^2 = 293.7, df = 16, p = .000; AsR cut-off at p =.01 for 25 cells = ± 3.54 (for p =.05 = ± 3.09)

Table 7.11 Family Functioning by Age at Childhood Family Disruption

Age at Childhood Family Disruption (by death/divorce)	Family Emotional & Psychological Functioning				
	N	1	2	3	4
Disrupted when a child (ages >0–12)	482	2.02			
Disrupted when a teen (ages 13–19)	352	2.23	2.23		
Disrupted when a young adult (ages 20–29)	526		2.49	2.49	
Disrupted when a Midlife adult (ages 30–70)	1,440			2.65	2.65
No family disruption	1,133				2.87

F = 42.25; df = 4, 3928; P = .000; Scheffe test of subset differences for alpha = 0.01

Table 7.12 Childhood Family Functioning by Therapist Age and Gender

Therapist Age/Gender		Childhood Family Functioning			Total
		Poor (0–1)	Mediocre (2–3)	Good (4–5)	
Younger Women (21–34)	n	91	311	342	744
	%	*12.2%*	*41.8%*	**46.0%**	100.0%
	AsR	-5.3	-4.1	8.9	
Younger Men (21–34)	n	25	114	112	251
	%	*10.0%*	45.4%	**44.6%**	100.0%
	AsR	-3.9	-1.1	4.5	
Midlife Women (35–54)	n	502	1,107	660	2,269
	%	**22.1%**	48.8%	*(29.1%)*	100.0%
	AsR	4.0	-.1	-3.3	
Midlife Men (35–54)	n	188	557	333	1,078
	%	17.4%	51.7%	30.9%	100.0%
	AsR	-1.8	2.0	-.6	
Older Women (55–85)	n	269	618	317	1,204
	%	22.3%	51.3%	*26.3%*	100.0%
	AsR	2.8	1.9	-4.4	
Older Men (55–85)	n	133	326	203	662
	%	20.1%	49.2%	30.7%	100.0%
	AsR	.4	.2	-.6	
Total	N	1,208	3,033	1,967	6,208
	%	19.5%	48.9%	31.7%	100.0%

χ^2 = 136.2, df = 10, p = .000; AsR cut-off at p = .01 for 18 cells = ± 3.45 (for p =.05 = ± 2.99)

Table 7.13 Family Functioning by Therapist Generation (Birth Year Cohorts)

Generation (birth cohort)		Childhood Family Functioning[1]			Total
		Poor (0–2)	Moderate (3)	Good (4–5)	
Depression/ WW2 (1927–1946)	n	581	366	369	1,316
	%	**44.1%**	27.8%	*(28.0%)*	100.0%
	AsR	4.1	-1.1	-3.2	
Post-WW2/ Baby Boom (1947–1966)	n	1,443	962	962	3,367
	%	**42.9%**	28.6%	_28.6%_	100.0%
		6.4	-.9	-5.8	
Western Prosperity (1967–1990)	n	397	465	626	1,488
	%	_26.7%_	31.3%	**42.1%**	100.0%
	AsR	-11.4	2.1	9.9	
Total	N	2,421	1,793	1,957	6,171
	%	39.2%	29.1%	31.7%	100.0%

χ^2 = 150.0, df = 4, p = .000; AsR cut-off at p .01 for 9 cells = ± 3.26 (for p =.05 = ± 2.77)
[1] Note slightly different categorization of family functioning made to highlight differences.

Table 7.14 Family Psychological Functioning by Family Economic Background

Family Functioning		Family Economic Background			Total
		Affluent	Secure	Challenged	
Good (4–5)	n	101	210	91	402
	%	_26.5%_	37.6%	42.7%	34.9%
	AsR	-4.2	1.9	2.7	
Mediocre (2–3)	n	237	309	77	623
	%	**62.2%**	55.4%	_36.2%_	54.1%
	AsR	3.9	.9	-5.8	
Poor (0–1)	n	43	39	45	127
	%	11.3%	_7.0%_	**21.1%**	11.0%
	AsR	.2	-4.2	5.2	
Total	N	381	558	213	1,152
	%	100.0%	100.0%	100.0%	100.0%

χ^2 = 58.1, df = 4, p = .000; AsR cut-off at p=.01 for 9 cells = ± 3.26 (at p=.05, ± 2.77)

Table 7.15 Childhood Experience Patterns: Quality of Care by Trauma or Abuse

Emotional Trauma or Abuse		Genuine Care & Support			Total
		Disregarded (0–2)	Maintained (3)	Loved (4–5)	
Protected (0–1)	n	226	352	1,373	1,951
	%	*5.5%*	*8.5%*	33.2%	47.2%
	AsR	-19.3	-5.8	21.6	
Distressed (2–3)	n	345	359	553	1,257
	%	8.3%	**8.7%**	*13.4%*	30.4%
	AsR	2.0	6.8	-7.4	
Hurt (4–5)	n	478	197	250	925
	%	**11.6%**	4.8%	*6.0%*	22.4%
	AsR	20.9	-.6	-17.7	
Total	N	1,49	908	2,176	4,133
	%	25.4%	22.0%	52.6%	100.0%

χ^2 = 688.8, df = 4, p = .000; AsR cut-off at p =.01 for 9 cells = ± 3.26 (at p=.05, ± 2.91)

Table 7.16 Childhood Experience Patterns by Generation (Birth Cohorts)

Childhood Experience Pattern		Generation			Total
		1927–1946	1947–1966	1967–1990	
Nurtured	n	369	1097	765	2,231
	%	51.0%	*50.3%*	**66.6%**	55.1%
	AsR	-2.4	-6.5	9.3	
Survived	n	91	301	154	546
	%	12.6%	13.8%	13.4%	13.5%
	AsR	-.8	.7	-.1	
Neglected	n	99	341	115	555
	%	13.7%	**15.6%**	*10.0%*	13.7%
	AsR	.0	3.9	-4.3	
Wounded	n	108	301	63	472
	%	**(14.9%)**	**13.8%**	*5.5%*	11.6%
	AsR	3.0	4.6	-7.7	
Rescued	n	57	139	52	248
	%	7.9%	6.4%	4.5%	6.1%
	AsR	2.2	.7	-2.7	
Total	N	724	2,179	1,149	4,052
	%	100.0%	100.0%	100.0%	100.0%

χ^2 = 118.4, df = 8, p = .000; AsR cut-off at p = .01 for 15 cells = ± 3.40 (at p=.05, ± 2.94)

Table 7.17 Childhood Experience Patterns by Generation and Gender

Childhood Experience Pattern		Born 1927–1946		Born 1947–1966		Born 1967–1990		Total
		Female	Male	Female	Male	Female	Male	
Nur-tured	n	250	117	800	295	587	175	2,224
	%	(48.0%)	58.8%	49.3%	53.9%	**67.8%**	62.7%	55.1%
	AsrR	-3.5	1.1	-6.1	-.6	8.5	2.7	
Survived	n	76	14	207	92	109	44	542
	%	14.6%	7.0%	12.7%	16.8%	12.6%	15.8%	13.4%
	AsrR	.8	-2.7	-1.0	2.5	-.8	1.2	
Neglec-ted	n	75	24	260	79	78	37	553
	%	14.4%	12.1%	(16.0%)	14.4%	9.0%	13.3%	13.7%
	AsrR	.5	-.7	3.5	.5	-4.5	-.2	
Woun-ded	n	81	26	242	57	55	8	469
	%	15.5%	13.1%	**14.9%**	10.4%	6.4%	2.9%	11.6%
	AsrR	3.0	.7	5.3	-.9	-5.5	-4.7	
Rescued	n	39	18	115	24	37	15	248
	%	7.5%	9.0%	7.1%	4.4%	4.3%	5.4%	6.1%
	AsrR	1.4	1.7	2.0	-1.8	-2.6	-.6	
Total	N	521	199	1,624	547	866	279	4,036
	%	100.0%	100.0%	100.0%	100.0%	100.0%	100.0%	100.0%

χ^2 = 154.8, df = 20, p = .000; AsR cut-off at p = .01 for 15 cells = ± 3.59 (at p=.05, ± 3.14)

Table 7.18 Childhood Experience Pattern by Age at Parental Divorce or Separation

Childhood Experience Pattern		Age at Parental Divorce or Separation					Total
		Child (>0–12)	Adolescent (13–19)	Young adult (20–29)	Adult (30–70)	Parents together	
Nurtured	n	94	43	39	24	1,621	1,821
	%	_34.8%_	_27.6%_	39.8%	44.4%	**56.4%**	52.8%
	AsR	-6.1	-6.4	-2.6	-1.2	9.6	
Survived	n	49	23	18	7	362	459
	%	18.1%	14.7%	18.4%	13.0%	12.6%	13.3%
	AsR	2.4	.5	1.5	-.1	-2.7	
Neglected	n	49	41	26	8	388	512
	%	18.1%	**26.3%**	**26.5%**	14.8%	_13.5%_	14.8%
	AsR	1.6	4.1	3.3	.0	-4.9	
Wounded	n	63	34	10	15	323	445
	%	**23.3%**	**21.8%**	10.2%	(**27.8%**)	_11.2%_	12.9%
	AsR	5.3	3.4	-.8	3.3	-6.5	
Rescued	n	15	15	5	0	180	215
	%	5.6%	9.6%	5.1%	0.0%	6.3%	6.2%
	AsR	-.5	1.8	-.5	-1.9	.2	
Total	N	270	156	98	54	2,874	3,452
	%	100.0%	100.0%	100.0%	100.0%	100.0%	100.0%

$\chi^2 = 137.6$, df = 16, p = .000; AsR cut-off at $p = .01$ for 25 cells = ± 3.54 (at $p=.05$, ± 3.09)

Table 7.19 Childhood Experience by Family Economic Background

Childhood Experience		Family Economic Background			Total
		Affluent	Secure	Challenged	
Nurtured	n	226	355	119	700
	%	59.6%	63.6%	56.1%	60.9%
	AsR	-.6	1.8	-1.6	
Survived	n	52	97	27	176
	%	13.7%	17.4%	12.7%	15.3%
	AsR	-1.1	1.9	-1.2	
Neglected	n	73	73	25	171
	%	**(19.3%)**	13.1%	11.8%	14.9%
	AsR	2.9	-1.7	-1.4	
Wounded	n	18	18	29	65
	%	4.7%	*3.2%*	**13.7%**	5.7%
	AsR	-.9	-3.5	5.6	
Rescued	n	10	15	12	37
	%	2.6%	2.7%	5.7%	3.2%
	AsR	-.8	-1.0	2.2	
Total	N	379	558	212	1,149
	%	100.0%	100.0%	100.0%	100.0%

χ^2 = 47.4, df = 8, p = .000; AsR cut-off at p=.01 for 14 cells = ± 3.38 (at p=.05, ± 2.91)

Table 7.20 Childhood and Adolescent Religiosity by Childhood Experience Pattern

Childhood Religiosity[1]	N	1*	2*
Neglected	357	4.15	
Wounded	307	4.80	4.80
Nurtured	1,172	4.84	4.84
Rescued	117		5.29
Survived	283		5.32

[1] F = 6.66; df = 4, 2231; P = .000; subset α = 0.01

Adolescent Religiosity[2]	N	1*	2*
Neglected	357	3.71	
Wounded	306	4.02	4.02
Survived	283	4.35	4.35
Nurtured	1,173	4.36	4.36
Rescued	118		4.57

[2] F = 3.63; df = 4, 2232; P = .006; subset differences α = 0.05

* Means on 0–10 scale

Table 8.1 Adult Personal Self by Family Religious Background[1]

Genial/Caring	N	1	2	3
Non-religious	502	2.36		
Protestant Christian	1,880	2.40	2.40	
R. Catholic/E. Orthodox	998	2.43	2.43	
Mixed	208		2.49	2.49
Jewish	317			2.54

$F = 12.1$; df $= 4, 3900$; $P = .000$; subset $\alpha = 0.01$; Means on 0–5 scale.

Forceful/ Exacting				
Protestant Christian	1,879	1.27		
Non-religious	501	1.36	1.36	
R. Catholic/E. Orthodox	996	1.39	1.39	
Mixed	208		1.40	
Jewish	317		1.40	

$F = 13.6$; df $= 4, 3896$; $P = .000$; subset $\alpha = 0.01$; Means on 0–5 scale.

Ardent/ Expressive				
Non-religious	502	1.92		
Protestant Christian	1,884	1.93		
R. Catholic/E. Orthodox	996		2.07	
Mixed	208		2.09	
Jewish	317		2.17	

$F = 28.4$; $df = 4, 3902$; $P = .000$; subset $\alpha = 0.01$; Means on 0–5 scale.

[1] Results for Reclusive/Remote were significant overall but did not differentiate significantly between specific groups.

Table 8.2 Adult Personal Self by Childhood Experience Patterns

Genial/Caring	N	1*	2*	3*
Neglected	556	2.23		
Survived	538	2.33	2.33	
Wounded	462		2.36	
Nurtured	2,173		2.43	
Rescued	243			2.56

$F = 35.1$; df = 4, 3967; $P = .000$.

Forceful/Exacting				
Nurtured	2,162	1.25		
Wounded	463	1.28	1.28	
Neglected	554	1.28	1.28	
Survived	537	1.31	1.31	
Rescued	244		1.38	

$F = 4.9$; df = 4, 3959; $P = .001$.

Ardent/Expressive				
Neglected	556	1.86		
Nurtured	2,164	1.89	1.89	
Survived	537	1.93	1.93	
Wounded	465		2.01	
Rescued	245			2.16

$F = 19.6$; df = 4, 3962; $P = .000$.

* Subset $\alpha = 0.01$; Means on 0–5 scale

Table 8.3 Therapists' Birth Order and Parental Status

Birth Order		Non-parent	Parent	Total
Only child	n	183	319	502
	%	**36.5%**	*63.5%*	100.0%
	AsR	4.9	-4.9	
Oldest child	n	406	1,292	1,698
	%	*23.9%*	**76.1%**	100.0%
	AsR	-3.8	3.8	
Middle child	n	307	949	1,256
	%	24.4%	75.6%	100.0%
	AsR	-2.6	2.6	
Youngest child	n	419	956	1,375
	%	**(30.5%)**	*(69.5%)*	100.0%
	AsR	3.2	-3.2	
	N	1,315	3,516	4,831
	%	27.2%	72.8%	100.0%

$\chi^2 = 43.2$, df = 3, $p = .000$; AsR cut-off at $p = .01$ for 8 cells = ± 3.23 (at $p=.05$, ± 2.73)

Table 8.4 Therapists' Adult Marital Status by Age at Family Disruption

Adult Marital Status		Age at Childhood Family Disruption				Total
		Child (age >0–12)	Adolescent (age 13–19)	Young adult (age 20–29)	Adult (age 30–70)	
Single	n	89	48	57	130	324
	%	**18.7%**	14.0%	11.4%	_9.4%_	12.0%
	AsR	5.0	1.2	-.4	-4.3	
Living w. partner	n	59	51	73	161	344
	%	12.4%	14.8%	14.7%	11.6%	12.7%
	AsR	-.2	1.2	1.4	-1.7	
Married/ remarried	n	267	199	316	900	1682
	%	(56.2%)	57.8%	63.5%	**(65.1%)**	62.3%
	AsR	-3.0	-1.8	.6	3.1	
Divorced or separated	n	60	46	52	191	349
	%	12.6%	13.4%	10.4%	13.8%	12.9%
	AsR	-.2	.3	-1.8	1.4	
Total	N	475	344	498	1382	2699
	%	100.0%	100.0%	100.0%	100.0%	100.0%

χ^2 = 40.0, df =9, p = .000; AsR cut-off at p =.01 for 16 cells = ± 3.52 (at p=.05, ± 2.96)

Table 8.5 Therapist Marital Status by Childhood Family Economic Background

Family Economic Background		Therapist Marital Status				Total
		Single	Living w. partner	Married	Divorced/ Separated	
Affluent	n	71	71	197	35	374
	%	19.0%	**19.0%**	_52.7%_	9.4%	100.0%
	AsR	1.6	4.0	-4.6	.9	
Secure	n	75	51	380	42	548
	%	13.7%	_9.3%_	**69.3%**	7.7%	100.0%
	AsR	-2.4	-3.8	4.9	-.7	
Chal- lenged	n	39	27	122	16	204
	%	19.1%	13.2%	59.8%	7.8%	100.0%
	AsR	1.1	.0	-.7	-.2	
Total	N	185	149	699	93	1,126
	%	16.4%	13.2%	62.1%	8.3%	100.0%

χ^2 = 31.6, df = 6, p = .000; AsR cut-off at p =.01 for 12 cells = ± 3.34 (at p=.05, ± 2.87)

Table 8.6 Current Marital Status by Family Religious Background

Family Religious Background		Therapist Status				Total
		Single	Living w. partner	Married	Divorced/ Separated	
Non-religious	n	79	72	275	66	492
	%	16.1%	14.6%	55.9%	13.4%	100.0%
	AsR	1.3	1.6	-2.9	1.4	
Protestant Christian	n	199	227	1,201	228	1855
	%	_10.7%_	12.2%	**(64.7%)**	12.3%	100.0%
	AsR	-5.9	-.3	3.5	1.5	
R. Catholic/E. Orthodox	n	224	128	590	104	1046
	%	**21.4%**	12.2%	_56.4%_	9.9%	100.0%
	AsR	7.8	-.2	-4.3	-1.8	
Jewish	n	20	35	220	32	307
	%	_6.5%_	11.4%	**71.7%**	10.4%	100.0%
	AsR	-4.0	-.6	3.7	-.6	
Mixed	n	32	22	129	18	201
	%	15.9%	10.9%	64.2%	9.0%	100.0%
	AsR	.7	-.6	.7	-1.2	
Total	N	554	484	2,415	448	3,901
	%	14.2%	12.4%	61.9%	11.5%	100.0%

χ^2 = 92.6, df = 12, p = .000; AsR cut-off at p =.01 for 20 cells = ± 3.54 (at p=.05, ± 3.02)

Table 8.7 Therapists' Marital Status by Childhood Family Functioning

Childhood Family Functioning		Adult Marital/Status				Total
		Single	Living w. partner	Married/ Remarried	Divorced/ Separated	
Good (4–5)	n	291	223	1,293	138	1,945
	%	15.0%	_(11.5%)_	**66.5%**	_7.1%_	100.0%
	AsR	.9	-3.3	5.4	-5.9	
Mediocre (2–3)	n	429	407	1,819	333	2,988
	%	14.4%	13.6%	60.9%	11.1%	100.0%
	AsR	.0	.1	-1.1	1.6	
Poor (0–1)	n	160	202	664	172	1,198
	%	13.4%	**16.9%**	_55.4%_	**14.4%**	100.0%
	AsR	-1.1	3.7	-4.9	4.9	
Total	N	880	832	3,776	643	6,131
	%	14.4%	13.6%	61.6%	10.5%	100.0%

χ^2 = 72.1, df = 6, p = .000; AsR cut-off at p =.01 for 12 cells = ± 3.34 (at p = .05, ± 2.87)

Table 8.8 Therapists' Marital Status by Childhood Experience Pattern

Childhood Experience Pattern		Adult Marital/Marital Status				Total
		Single	Living w. partner	Married/ Remarried	Divorced/ Separated	
Neglected	n	70	78	332	75	555
	%	12.6%	14.1%	59.8%	13.5%	100.0%
	AsR	-2.5	1.1	-.6	2.7	
Wounded	n	76	72	250	71	469
	%	16.2%	15.4%	*53.3%*	**15.1%**	100.0%
	AsR	.0	1.9	-3.6	3.7	
Survived	n	84	72	313	59	528
	%	15.9%	13.6%	59.3%	11.2%	100.0%
	AsR	-.2	.8	-.8	.7	
Rescued	n	34	29	145	34	242
	%	14.0%	12.0%	59.9%	14.0%	100.0%
	AsR	-.9	-.3	-.3	2.0	
Nurtured	n	384	251	1,397	172	2,204
	%	17.4%	11.4%	**63.4%**	*7.8%*	100.0%
	AsR	2.3	-2.5	3.5	-5.7	
Total	N	648	502	2,437	411	3,998
	%	16.2%	12.6%	61.0%	10.3%	100.0%

χ^2 = 54.4, df = 12, p = .000; AsR cut-off at p =.01 for 12 cells = ± 3.34 (at p = .05, ± 2.87)

Table 8.9 Adult Attachment by Childhood Experience Patterns

Anxious Attachment	N	1*	2*	3*
Nurtured	569	2.40		
Rescued	55	2.62	2.62	
Survived	157	2.78	2.78	
Neglected	236	2.79	2.79	
Wounded	221		2.84	

F = 9.1; df = 4, 1233; p = .000

Avoidant Attachment				
Rescued	55	1.76		
Nurtured	577	2.20	2.20	
Survived	156		2.59	2.59
Neglected	240		2.60	2.60
Wounded	227			2.72

F = 11.4; df = 4, 1250; p = .000

* Subset α = 0.05; Means on 0–5 scale

Table 8.10 Adult Religiosity and Spirituality by Family Economic Background

Religiosity	N	1*	2*
Affluent	298	2.15	
Secure	239	2.17	
Challenged	110		2.52
$F = 10.4$; df = 4, 644; $P = .000$			
Spirituality			
Secure	239	2.82	
Affluent	298	2.84	
Challenged	110		3.69
$F = 14.0$; df = 4, 644; $P = .000$			

* Subset $\alpha = 0.01$; Means on 0–5 scale

Table 8.11 Adult Belief-Value Patterns by Family Religious Background

Adult Belief-Value Pattern		Family Religious Background					Total
		Non-religious	Protes-tant Christian	Catholic/ Ortho-dox	Jewish	Mixed	
Ethical Secular	n	304	688	299	126	63	1,480
	%	**60.9%**	36.5%	*30.1%*	40.1%	30.6%	38.0%
	AsR	11.3	-1.8	-5.9	.8	-2.2	
Spiritual Secular	n	115	504	308	77	58	1,062
	%	23.0%	26.7%	31.0%	24.5%	28.2%	27.3%
	AsR	-2.3	-.7	3.1	-1.1	.3	
Spiritual Religious	n	64	615	317	65	74	1,135
	%	*12.8%*	32.6%	31.9%		*(20.7%)*	35.9%
	29.1%						
AsR		-8.6	4.7	2.2	-3.4	2.2	
Ceremo-nial Religious	n	16	78	69	46	11	220
	%	3.2%	*4.1%*	6.9%	**14.6%**	5.3%	5.6%
	AsR	-2.5	-3.9	2.1	7.2	-.2	
Total	N	499	1,885	993	314	206	3,897
	%	100.0%	100.0%	100.0%	100.0%	100.0%	100.0%

$\chi^2 = 54.4$, df = 12, p = .000; AsR cut-off at $p = .01$ for 20 cells $= \pm 3.48$ (at $p=.05$, ± 3.02)

Table 8.12 Adult Belief-Value Patterns by Childhood Family Functioning

Adult Belief-Value Pattern		Childhood Family Functioning			Total
		Poor	Mediocre	Good	
Ethical Secular	n	363	848	439	1,650
	%	22.0%	51.4%	26.6%	100.0%
	AsR	-2.8	2.3	.1	
Spiritual Secular	n	357	566	244	1,167
	%	**30.6%**	48.5%	*20.9%*	100.0%
	AsR	5.9	-.6	-5.1	
Spiritual Religious	n	285	562	365	1,212
	%	23.5%	46.4%	**30.1%**	100.0%
	AsR	-.8	-2.3	3.4	
Ceremonial Religious	n	29	118	79	226
	%	*12.8%*	52.2%	**(35.0%)**	100.0%
	AsR	-4.1	.9	3.0	
Total	N	1,034	2,094	1,127	4,255
	%	24.3%	49.2%	26.5%	100.0%

χ^2 = 65.1, df = 6, p = .000; AsR cut-off at p =.01 for 12 cells = ±3.34 (at p = .05, ± 2.87)

Table 8.13 Adult Religiosity and Spirituality by Childhood Experience Pattern

Religiosity	N	1	2	
Neglected	531	1.50		
Wounded	466	1.77	1.77	
Survived	469	1.80	1.80	
Nurtured	1,842		1.92	
Rescued	221		2.00	

F = 6.0; df = 4, 3524; P = .000; Subset α = 0.01; Means on 0–5 scale

Spirituality		1	2	3
Nurtured	1,704	3.16		
Neglected	508	3.20	3.20	
Survived	438	3.32	3.32	3.32
Wounded	439		3.53	3.53
Rescued	203			3.60

F = 7.4; df = 4, 3287; P = .000; Subset α = 0.05; Means on 0–5 scale

Table 8.14 Adult Belief-Value Orientation by Childhood Experience Patterns

Childhood Experience Patterns		Adult Belief-Value Orientation				Total
		Ethical Secular	Spiritual Secular	Spiritual Religious	Ceremonial Religious	
Nurtured	n	766	423	532	107	1,828
	%	41.9%	*23.1%*	29.1%	**5.9%**	100.0%
	AsR	2.8	-5.9	1.2	3.6	
Survived	n	186	128	129	22	465
	%	40.0%	27.5%	27.7%	4.7%	100.0%
	AsR	.1	.1	-.3	.1	
Neglected	n	223	161	121	14	519
	%	43.0%	31.0%	23.3%	2.7%	100.0%
	AsR	1.6	2.0	-2.7	-2.3	
Wounded	n	151	170	127	13	461
	%	*(32.8%)*	**36.9%**	27.5%	2.8%	100.0%
	AsR	-3.3	4.9	-.4	-2.0	
Rescued	n	61	75	78	6	220
	%	*27.7%*	34.1%	35.5%	2.7%	100.0%
	AsR	-3.8	2.3	2.4	-1.4	
Total	N	1,387	957	987	162	3,493
	%	39.7%	27.4%	28.3%	4.6%	100.0%

χ^2 = 74.7, df = 12, p = .000; AsR cut-off at p =.01 for 12 cells = ±3.48 (at p = .05, ± 3.02)

Table 8.15 Adult Life Quality by Childhood Family Religious Background

Personal Satisfactions	N	*1**	*2**
Non-religious	507	3.69	
Protestant	1,913	3.70	3.70
Catholic/Orthodox	1,085	3.77	3.77
Mixed background	209	3.78	3.78
Jewish	323		3.90

F = 6.34; df = 4, 4032; P = .000

Personal Burdens			
Protestant	1,914	2.32	
Non-religious	508	2.36	
Catholic/Orthodox	1,086	2.36	
Mixed background	209	2.46	
Jewish	323		2.69

F = 11.60; df = 4, 4035; P = .000

* Subset α = 0.05; Means on 0–5 scale

Table 8.16 Adult Life Quality by Childhood Experience Pattern

Personal Satisfactions	N	1	2	3
Neglected	565	3.33		
Survived	478		3.56	
Wounded	555		3.60	
Nurtured	2,263			3.79
Rescued	250			3.93

F = 30.2; df = 4, 4106; P = .000; Subset alpha = 0.01; Means on 0–5 scale

Personal Burdens				
Nurtured	2,265	2.18		
Wounded	565		2.38	
Neglected	478		2.42	
Survived	555		2.43	
Rescued	250		2.50	

F = 15.1; df = 4, 4108; P = .000; Subset α = 0.05; Means on 0–5 scale

Table 8.17 Systemic Theoretical Orientation by Childhood Family Size

Systemic Orientation	N	1	2
Only child	497	1.71	
2-child family	1437	1.91	1.91
3-child family	1240		2.04
4–5 child family	1122		2.06
6–12 child family	437		2.19

F = 6.08; df = 4, 4728; P = .000; Subset α = 0.01; Means on 0–5 scale

Table 8.18 Therapist Professional Identity by Childhood Family Economic Background

Family Economic Background		Professional Identity					Total
		Psychology	Psychiatry	Counseling	Social Work	Lay Therapist/Analyst	
Affluent	n	260	41	45	16	16	378
	%	**68.8%**	10.8%	*11.9%*	4.2%	4.2%	100.0%
	AsR	9.1	-1.6	-7.5	-1.3	-1.8	
Secure	n	225	80	181	34	33	553
	%	*40.7%*	14.5%	**32.7%**	6.1%	6.0%	100.0%
	AsR	-5.9	1.2	5.4	1.0	-.1	
Challenged	n	80	29	65	12	20	206
	%	*38.8%*	14.1%	31.6%	5.8%	9.7%	100.0%
	AsR	-3.4	.4	2.2	.3	2.4	
Total	N	565	150	291	62	69	1,137
	%	49.7%	13.2%	25.6%	5.5%	6.1%	100.0%

$\chi^2 = 93.7$, df = 6, p = .000; AsR cut-off at $p = .01$ for 15 cells = ± 3.40 (at $p = .05$, ± 2.94)

Table 8.19 Therapist Professional Identity by Childhood Family Religious Background

Family Religious Background		Professional Identity					Total
		Psychology	Psychiatry	Counseling	Social Work	Lay Therapist/Analyst	
Non-religious	n	255	20	152	21	35	483
	%	**52.8%**	4.1%	*31.5%*	4.3%	7.2%	100.0%
	AsR	5.0	-.2	-4.0	-.3	-1.5	
Protestant	n	644	69	859	85	145	1,802
	%	*35.7%*	3.8%	**47.7%**	4.7%	8.0%	100.0%
	AsR	-7.7	-1.3	9.4	.3	-2.1	
R. Catholic/ E. Orthodox	n	464	48	358	37	114	1,021
	%	45.4%	4.7%	*35.1%*	3.6%	11.2%	100.0%
	AsR	2.4	.8	-3.6	-1.7	2.7	
Jewish	n	190	17	46	26	34	313
	%	**60.7%**	5.4%	*14.7%*		(**8.3%**)	10.9%
	100.0%						
AsR		6.9	1.0	-9.5	3.3	1.1	
Mixed	n	61	10	106	7	20	204
	%	*29.9%*	4.9%	**52.0%**	3.4%	9.8%	100.0%
	AsR	-3.7	.4	3.7	-.8	.4	
Total	N	1,614	164	1,521	176	348	3,823
	%	42.2%	4.3%	39.8%	4.6%	9.1%	100.0%

$\chi^2 = 189.9$, df = 16, p = .000; AsR cut-off at $p = .01$ for 25 cells = 3.54 (at $p = .05$ ± 3.09)

Table 8.20 Therapists' Professional Identity by Childhood Family Functioning

Childhood Family Functioning		Professional Identity					Total
		Psychology	Psychiatry	Counseling	Social Work	Lay Therapist/Analyst	
Good (4–5)	n	924	258	531	132	87	1,932
	%	32.7%	**44.6%**	*28.0%*	35.3%	*20.9%*	31.7%
	AsR	1.5	7.0	-4.2	1.5	-4.9	
Mediocre (2–3)	n	1,461	267	856	185	200	2,969
	%	**51.7%**	46.1%	*45.2%*	49.5%	48.1%	48.7%
	AsR	4.3	-1.3	-3.7	.3	-.3	
Poor (0–1)	n	443	54	508	57	129	1,191
	%	*15.7%*	*9.3%*	**26.8%**	15.2%	**31.0%**	19.6%
	AsR	-7.1	-6.5	9.6	-2.2	6.1	
Total	N	2,828	579	1,895	374	416	6,092
	%	100.0%	100.0%	100.0%	100.0%	100.0%	100.0%

χ^2 = 202.1, df = 8, p = .000; AsR cut-off at p =.01 for 15 cells = ± 3.40 (at p = .05, ± 2.94)

Table 8.21 Cognitive-Behavioral Orientation by Childhood Experience Pattern

Cognitive-Behavioral	N	1	2
Wounded	444	1.98	
Neglected	525	2.02	
Survived	498	2.02	
Rescued	242	2.22	2.22
Nurtured	2,144		2.38

F = 13.0; df = 4, 3848; P = .000; Subset alpha = 0.01; Means on 0–5 scale

Table 9.1 Personal Therapy by Career Level (Years of Practice)

Personal therapy: If and When		Career Level Cohorts				Total
		Novice >0 to <3 years	Graduate 3 to <10 years	Established 10 to <20 years	Senior 20 to 55 years	
No personal therapy	n	524	771	529	285	2,109
	%	**34.9%**	20.5%	_15.8%_	_13.2%_	19.6%
	AsR	16.2	1.8	-6.7	-8.4	
Personal therapy only now	n	158	261	120	49	588
	%	**10.5%**	**6.9%**	_3.6%_	_2.3%_	5.5%
	AsR	9.3	5.0	-5.8	-7.3	
Personal therapy now & past	n	313	937	706	298	2,254
	%	20.9%	**24.9%**	21.0%	_13.8%_	20.9%
	AsR	.0	7.5	.2	-9.1	
Personal therapy past only	n	506	1,795	2,001	1,533	5,835
	%	_33.7%_	_47.7%_	**59.6%**	**70.8%**	54.1%
	AsR	-17.1	-9.8	7.7	17.5	
Total	N	1,501	3,764	3,356	2,165	10,786
	%	100.0%	100.0%	100.0%	100.0%	100.0%

χ^2 = 756.79, df = 9, p = .000; AsR cut-off at p =.01 for 16 cells = ± 3.42 (at p = .05, ± 2.96)

Table 9.2 Current Personal Therapy by Level of Emotional/Psychological Wellbeing

Currently in Personal Therapy		Current Emotional/Psychological Wellbeing				Total
		Poor	Fairly good	Quite good	Very good	
No	n	212	1,065	1,608	1,145	4,030
	%	_61.1%_	_68.1%_	(**76.2%**)	**79.5%**	73.8%
	AsR	-5.6	-6.1	3.2	5.7	
Yes	n	135	498	501	295	1,429
	%	**38.9%**	**31.9%**	(23.8%)	_20.5%_	26.2%
	AsR	5.6	6.1	-3.2	-5.7	
Total	N	347	1,563	2,109	1,440	5,459
	%	100.0%	100.0%	100.0%	100.0%	100.0%

χ^2 = 85.8, df = 3, p = .000; AsR cut-off at p =.01 for 8 cells = ± 3.23 (at p = .05, ± 2.73)

Table 9.3 Personal Therapy Attitudes and Experience by Therapeutic Approach

Salient Theoretical Orientation		Personal therapy essential/desirable?[1]		Total	Ever had personal therapy?[2]		Total
		No	Yes		No	Yes	
Analytic/ Dynamic	n	74	1,827	1,901	236	2,329	2,563
	%	*3.9%*	**96.1%**	100.0%	*9.1%*	**90.9%**	100.0%
	AsR	-13.9	13.9		-16.3	16.3	
Analytic/ Dynamic & Humanistic	n	27	438	465	64	596	660
	%	*5.8%*	**94.2%**	100.0%	*9.5%*	**90.5%**	100.0%
	AsR	-4.3	4.3		-6.8	6.8	
Humanistic	n	38	346	384	109	805	914
	%	9.9%	90.1%	100.0%	*11.9%*	**88.0%**	100.0%
	AsR	-1.3	1.3		-6.2	6.2	
Cognitive-Behavioral	n	160	242	402	417	446	863
	%	**39.8%**	*60.2%*	100.0%	**48.3%**	*51.7%*	100.0%
	AsR	18.1	-18.1		22.7	-22.7	
Broad Spectrum Integrative	n	171	880	1,051	349	1,510	1,859
	%	**16.3%**	*83.7%*	100.0%	18.8%	81.2%	100.0%
	AsR	5.0	-5.0		-.9	.9	
No Salient Orientation	n	91	423	514	319	464	783
	%	**17.7%**	*82.3%*	100.0%	**40.7%**	*59.3%*	100.0%
	AsR	4.3	-5.0		15.8	-15.8	
Total	n	561	4,156	4,717	1,491	6,151	7,642
	%	11.9%	88.1%	100.0%	19.5%	80.5%	100.0%

[1] $\chi^2 = 468.6$, df = 5, p = .000; AsR cut-off at $p = .01$ for 12 cells = ± 3.34 (at $p = .05$, ± 2.87)
[2] $\chi^2 = 932.6$, df = 5, p = .000; AsR cut-off at $p = .01$ for 12 cells = ± 3.34 (at $p = .05$, ± 2.87)

Table 9.4 Reasons for Personal Therapy by Theoretical Approach

Theoretical Approach		Reasons for Personal Therapy			Total
		Training[1]	Growth[2]	Problems[3]	
Analytic/ Dynamic	n	1,547	1,636	1,366	2,040
	%	**75.8%**	**80.2%**	67.0%	100.0%
	AsR	12.8	3.8	-1.3	
Analytic/ Dynamic & Humanistic	n	385	443	364	514
	%	**74.9%**	**86.2%**	70.8%	100.0%
	AsR	4.9	5.0	1.4	
Humanistic	n	469	586	541	741
	%	63.3%	79.1%	**(73.0%)**	100.0%
	AsR	-1.1	1.2	3.1	
Cognitive- Behavioral	n	171	236	273	432
	%	*39.6%*	*54.6%*	63.2%	100.0%
	AsR	-11.6	-11.8	-2.3	
Broad Spectrum Integrative	n	811	1,086	944	1,389
	%	*58.4%*	78.2%	68.0%	68.0%
	AsR	-6.0	.8	-.1	
No Salient Orientation	n	222	302	282	423
	%	*52.5%*	*(71.4%)*	66.7%	100.0%
	AsR	-5.7	-3.1	-.6	
Total	N	3,605	4,289	3,770	5,539
	%	65.1%	77.4%	68.1%	100.0%

[1] $\chi^2 = 307.2$, df = 5, p = .000; AsR cut-off at $p = .01$ for 10 cells = ± 3.29 (p = .05, ± 2.81)
[2] $\chi^2 = 170.4$, df = 5, p = .000; AsR cut-off at $p = .01$ for 10 cells = ± 3.29 (p = .05, ± 2.81)
[3] $\chi^2 = 16.4$, df = 5, p = .006; AsR cut-off at $p = .01$ for 10 cells = ± 3.29 (p = .05, ± 2.81)

Table 9.5 Personal Therapy Attitudes and Experience by Professional Background

Professional Background		Personal therapy essential/desirable?[1]		Total	Ever had personal therapy?[2]		Total
		No	Yes		No	Yes	
Psychology	n	570	2,819	3,389	1,001	4,296	5,297
	%	**16.8%**	*83.2%*	100.0%	18.9%	81.1%	100.0%
	AsR	5.9	-5.9		-1.5	1.5	
Medicine/ Psychiatry	n	253	1,685	1,938	626	1,429	2,055
	%	13.1%	86.9%	100.0%	**30.5%**	*69.5%*	100.0%
	AsR	-1.9	1.9		14.0	-14.0	
Counseling	n	39	415	454	295	1,836	2,131
	%	*8.6%*	**91.4%**	100.0%	*13.8%*	**86.2%**	100.0%
	AsR	-3.6	3.6		-7.3	7.3	
Social Work	n	63	401	464	145	547	692
	%	13.6%	86.4%	100.0%	21.0%	79.0%	100.0%
	AsR	-.5	.5		1.0	-1.0	
Lay Therapist/ Analyst	n	13	286	299	48	641	689
	%	*4.3%*	**95.7%**	100.0%	*7.0%*	**93.0%**	100.0%
	AsR	-5.0	5.0		-8.6	8.6	
Total	N	938	5,606	6,544	2,125	8,739	10,864
	%	14.3%	85.7%	100.0%	19.6%	80.4%	100.0%

[1] $\chi^2 = 56.3$, $df = 4$, $p = .000$; AsR cut-off at $p = .01$ for 10 cells $= \pm 3.29$ ($p = .05$, ± 2.81)
[2] $\chi^2 = 272.2$, $df = 4$, $p = .000$; AsR cut-off at $p = .01$ for 10 cells $= \pm 3.29$ ($p = .05$, ± 2.81)

Table 9.6 Reasons for Personal Therapy by Professional Background

Professional Background		Reasons for Personal Therapy			Total
		Training[1]	Growth[2]	Problems[3]	
Psychology	n	2,460	3,051	2,767	4,000
	%	61.5%	76.3%	69.2%	100.0%
	AsR	-1.4	.4	2.1	
Medicine/ psychiatry	n	815	731	595	1,122
	%	**72.6%**	*65.2%*	*53.0%*	100.0%
	AsR	7.7	-9.3	-11.7	
Counseling	n	1,025	1,402	1,230	1,716
	%	59.7%	**81.7%**	**71.7%**	100.0%
	AsR	-2.5	6.2	3.6	
Social Work	n	243	382	390	513
	%	*47.4%*	74.5%	**76.0%**	100.0%
	AsR	-7.2	-.9	4.0	
Lay Thera- pist/Analyst	n	408	482	431	599
	%	**(68.1%)**	80.5%	72.0%	100.0%
	AsR	3.1	2.6	2.1	
Total	N	4,951	6,048	5,413	7,950
	%	62.3%	76.1%	68.1%	100.0%

[1] χ^2 = 114.3, df = 4, p = .000; AsR cut-off at p =.01 for 10 cells = ± 3.29 (at p =.05, ± 2.81)
[2] χ^2 = 110.6, df = 4, p = .000; AsR cut-off at p =.01 for 10 cells = ± 3.29 (at p =.05, ± 2.81)
[3] χ^2 = 148.4, df = 4, p = .000; AsR cut-off at p =.01 for 10 cells = ± 3.29 (at p =.05, ± 2.81)

Table 9.7 Personal Self Dimensions and Use of Personal Therapy within Age Group[1]

Younger Therapists	n	1	2	3		
Genial/Caring					F = 7.57	P = .001
No personal therapy	836	2.22			df = 2, 2279	
1 personal therapy	675		2.95			
2+ personal therapy	771		2.30			
Forceful/Exacting					F = 8.63	P = .000
No personal therapy	834	1.38			df = 2, 2277	
1 personal therapy	771		1.47			
2+ personal therapy	675		1.48			
Reclusive/Remote		1	2		F = 3.66	P = .03
No personal therapy	835	1.30			df = 2, 2277	
1 personal therapy	770	1.25	1.25			
2+ personal therapy	675		1.21			
Ardent/Expressive					F = 34.9	P = .000
No personal therapy	834	1.72			df = 2, 2277	
1 personal therapy	771		1.86			
2+ personal therapy	675			1.95		
Midlife Therapists	n	1	2	3		
Ardent/Expressive					F = 105.4	P = .000
No personal therapy	1,044	1.70			df = 2, 5883	
1 personal therapy	1,611		1.81			
2+ personal therapy	3231			1.95		
Older Therapists	n	1	2			
Ardent/Expressive					F = 15.10	P = .000
No personal therapy	216	1.74			df = 2, 2087	
1 personal therapy	481		1.85			
2+ personal therapy	1,393		1.93			

[1] Scheffe test (p = .05 criterion): Scale 0–3, Means for homogenous subsets are displayed.

Table 9.8 Use of Personal Therapy by Childhood Family Functioning and Age Group[1]

	n	Family Functioning 1	2	3		
Younger Therapists		1	2	3		
No personal therapy	836	3.60			$F = 37.4$	$P = .000$
1 personal therapy	675		3.19		$df = 2, 959$	
2+ personal therapy	771			2.77		
Midlife Therapists	n	1	2	3		
No personal therapy	1,044	3.31			$F = 18.31$	$P = .000$
1 personal therapy	1,611		2.85		$df = 2, 3254$	
2+ personal therapy	3,231			2.43		
Older Therapists	n	1	2	3		
No personal therapy	216	3.32			$F = 52.7$	$P = .000$
1 personal therapy	481		2.90		$df = 2, 1830$	
2+ personal therapy	1,393			2.42		

[1] Scheffe test ($p = .01$ criterion): scale 0–5; Means for homogenous subsets are displayed.

Table 9.9 Use of Personal Therapy by Childhood Experience Pattern

Childhood Experience Pattern		Times in Personal Therapy			Total
		0	1	2+	
Neglected	n	51	123	376	550
	%	9.3%	22.4%	68.4%	100.0%
	AsR	-4.4	-.8	4.0	
Wounded	n	14	59	392	465
	%	3.0%	12.7%	84.3%	100.0%
	AsR	-8.0	-5.9	11.1	
Survived	n	63	113	363	539
	%	11.7%	21.0%	67.3%	100.0%
	AsR	-2.7	-1.6	3.4	
Rescued	n	31	70	144	245
	%	12.7%	28.6%	58.8%	100.0%
	AsR	-1.3	1.9	-.6	
Nurtured	n	463	580	1,147	2,190
	%	21.1%	26.5%	52.4%	100.0%
	AsR	10.7	4.6	-11.9	
Total	N	622	945	2,422	3,989
	%	15.6%	23.7%	60.7%	100.0%

χ^2 = 223.8, df = 8, p = .000; AsR cut-off at p =.01 for 15 cells = ± 3.40 (at p =.05, ± 2.94)

Table 9.10 Reasons for Personal Therapy by Childhood Experience Pattern

Childhood Experience Pattern		Reasons for Therapy		
		Training[1]	Problems[2]	Growth[3]
Neglected	n	270	383	382
	%	55.4%	**78.6%**	78.4%
	AsR	-1.1	3.7	.1
Wounded	n	249	394	371
	%	56.3%	**89.1%**	(**83.9%**)
	AsR	-.7	8.8	3.1
Survived	n	279	354	391
	%	60.4%	76.6%	**84.6%**
	AsR	1.2	2.5	3.6
Rescued	n	113	155	151
	%	55.4%	76.0%	74.0%
	AsR	-.7	1.4	-1.5
Nurtured	n	973	1,053	1,260
	%	58.4%	_63.2%_	_75.6%_
	AsR	.7	-11.1	-3.9
Total	N	1,884	2,339	2,555
	Total N	3262	3262	3262
	Total %	57.8%	71.7%	78.3%

[1] $\chi^2 = 3.47$, df = 4, p = ns
[2] $\chi^2 = 145.0$, df = 4, p = .000; AsR cut-off at p =.01 for 10 cells = ± 3.29; at p = .05, ± 2.81)
[3] $\chi^2 = 28.6$, df = 4, p = .000; AsR cut-off at p =.01 for 10 cells = ± 3.29 (at p = .05, ± 2.81)

Table 9.11 Outcome of First-Listed Personal Therapy by Age Group and Gender

Therapist Age Group & Gender		'Value to you as a person'			Total
		Poor (little or none)	Middling (some or moderate)	Excellent (great or very great)	
Younger Women (21–34)	n	74	203	710	987
	%	**7.5%**	20.6%	71.9%	100.0%
	AsR	3.6	-1.3	-.6	
Younger Men (21–34)	n	27	124	270	421
	%	6.4%	**29.5%**	*64.1%*	100.0%
	AsR	1.2	3.7	-4.0	
Midlife Women (35–54)	n	153	630	2,315	3,098
	%	4.9%	*(20.3%)*	**(74.7%)**	100.0%
	AsR	-.5	-3.2	3.3	
Midlife Men (35–54)	n	90	430	1,140	1,660
	%	5.4%	**25.9%**	*68.7%*	100.0%
	AsR	.7	4.1	-4.1	
Older Women (55–85)	n	52	229	904	1,185
	%	4.4%	19.3%	**(76.3%)**	100.0%
	AsR	-1.2	-2.6	3.0	
Older Men (55–85)	n	13	162	481	656
	%	*2.0%*	24.7%	73.3%	100.0%
	AsR	-3.8	1.6	.4	
Total	N	409	1,778	5,820	8,007
	%	5.1%	22.2%	72.7%	100.0%

χ^2 = 71.1, df = 10, p = .000; AsR cut-off at p =.01 for 18 cells = ± 3.45 (at p = .05, ± 2.99)

Table 9.12 Outcome of First-Listed Personal Therapy by Theoretical Orientation

Theoretical Orientation		'Value to you as a person'			Total
		Poor (little or none)	Middling (some or moderate)	Excellent (great or very great)	
Analytic/	n	72	404	1,655	2,131
Dynamic	%	*3.4%*	*19.0%*	**77.7%**	100.0%
	AsR	-3.9	-3.5	5.1	
Analytic/	n	21	112	407	540
Dynamic &	%	3.9%	20.7%	75.4%	100.0%
Humanistic	AsR	-1.0	-.4	.9	
Humanistic	n	43	172	507	722
	%	6.0%	23.8%	70.2%	100.0%
	AsR	1.6	1.7	-2.4	
Cognitive-	n	42	110	240	392
Behavioral	%	**10.7%**	**(28.1%)**	*61.2%*	100.0%
	AsR	5.7	3.3	-5.9	
Broad	n	58	256	1,051	1,365
Spectrum	%	4.2%	18.8%	**(77.0%)**	100.0%
	AsR	-1.1	-2.7	3.1	
No Salient	n	29	130	230	389
Orientation	%	7.5%	**33.4%**	*59.1%*	100.0%
	AsR	2.6	6.0	-6.8	
Total	N	265	1,184	4,090	5,539
	%	4.8%	21.4%	73.8%	100.0%

$\chi^2 = 121.5$, df = 10, p = .000; AsR cut-off at $p = .01$ for 18 cells = ± 3.45 (at $p = .05$, ± 2.99)

Table 9.13 Cumulative Effects of Personal Therapy

Number of Personal Therapies		Cumulative Effect*			Total
		No excellent outcome	1 excellent outcome	2+ excellent outcomes	
1 personal	n	746	2,176	–	2,922
therapy	%	**25.5%**	**74.5%**	–	100.0%
	AsR	19.5	38.1	–	
2+ personal	n	508	1,651	3,200	5,359
therapies	%	*9.5%*	*30.8%*	**59.7%**	100.0%
	AsR	-19.5	-38.1	53.3	
Total	N	1,254	3,827	3,200	8,281
	%	15.1%	46.2%	38.6%	100.0%

$\chi^2 = 2846.5$, df = 2, p = .000; AsR cut-off at $p = .01$ for 6 cells = ± 3.14 (at $p = .05$, ± 2.64)
* 'Excellent' = therapy of 'Great' or 'Very great' personal value (4 or 5 on 0–5 scale)

Table 9.14 Cumulative Effects of Personal Therapy by Age Group and Gender

Therapist Age Group & Gender		'Value to you as a person'			At least 1 'excellent' outcome	Total
		No excellent outcome	1 excellent outcome	2+ excellent outcomes		
Younger Women 21 to 34	n	175	570	257		1,002
	%	17.5%	**56.9%**	*25.6%*	82.5%	100.0%
	AsR	2.2	7.2	-9.0		
Younger Men 21 to 34	n	105	226	94		425
	%	**24.7%**	53.2%	*22.1%*	75.3%	100.0%
	AsR	5.7	2.9	-7.2		
Midlife Women 35 to 54	n	396	1,403	1,337		3,136
	%	*12.6%*	44.7%	**42.6%**	87.3%	100.0%
	AsR	-4.9	-2.2	5.9		
Midlife Men 35 to 54	n	301	813	565		1,679
	%	**17.9%**	48.4%	*33.7%*	82.1%	100.0%
	AsR	3.6	2.0	-4.7		
Older Women 55 to 85	n	145	460	595		1,200
	%	(*12.1%*)	*38.3%*	**49.6%**	87.9%	100.0%
	AsR	-3.2	-6.0	8.4		
Older Men 55 to 85	n	102	279	286		667
	%	15.3%	41.8%	42.9%	84.7%	100.0%
	AsR	.1	-2.4	2.3		
Total	N	1,224	3,751	3,134	6,885	8,109
	%	15.1%	46.3%	38.6%	84.9%	100.0%

χ^2 = 247.6, df = 10, p = .000; AsR cut-off at p =.01 for 18 cells = ± 3.45 (at p = .05, ± 2.99)

Table 9.15 Cumulative Effects of Personal Therapy by Main Theoretical Orientations

Theoretical Orientation		'Value to you as a person'			At least 1 'excellent' outcome	Total
		No excellent outcome	1 excellent outcome	2+ excellent outcomes		
Analytic/ Dynamic	n	221	1,158	797		2,176
	%	*10.2%*	**53.2%**	36.6%	89.8%	100.0%
	AsR	-6.8	6.6	-1.9		
Analytic/ Dynamic & Humanistic	n	57	244	244		545
	%	10.5%	44.8%	**44.8%**	89.6%	100.0%
	AsR	-2.6	-1.4	3.3		
Humanistic	n	106	323	294		723
	%	14.7%	44.7%	40.7%	85.3%	100.0%
	AsR	.4	-1.7	1.5		
Cognitive-Behavioral	n	119	195	82		396
	%	**30.1%**	49.2%	*20.7%*	69.9%	100.0%
	AsR	9.4	.6	-7.4		
Broad Spectrum	n	180	577	620		1,377
	%	13.1%	*41.9%*	**45.0%**	86.9%	100.0%
	AsR	-1.3	-5.0	6.0		
No Salient Orientation	n	110	179	105		394
	%	**27.9%**	45.4%	*26.6%*	72.1%	100.0%
	AsR	8.1	-.9	-4.9		
Total	N	793	2,676	2,142	4,818	5,611
	%	14.1%	47.7%	38.2%	85.9%	100.0%

χ^2 = 252.4, df = 10, p = .000; AsR cut-off at p =.01 for 18 cells = ± 3.45 (at p = .05, ± 2.99)

Table 9.16 Cumulative Effects of Personal Therapy by Belief-Value Pattern

Belief-Value Pattern		'Value to you as a person'			At least 1 'excellent' outcome	Total
		No excellent outcome	1 excellent outcome	2+ excellent outcomes		
Ethical Secular	n	241	568	509		1,318
	%	**18.3%**	**43.1%**	_38.6%_	81.7%	100.0%
	AsR	3.5	5.0	-7.4		
Spiritual Secular	n	117	329	549		995
	%	_11.8%_	_33.1%_	**55.2%**	88.2%	100.0%
	AsR	-3.9	-3.7	6.4		
Spiritual Religious	n	148	349	500		997
	%	14.8%	35.0%	50.2%	85.2%	100.0%
	AsR	-.7	-2.2	2.7		
Ceremonial Religious	n	35	70	62		167
	%	21.0%	41.9%	37.1%	79.0%	100.0%
	AsR	2.0	1.1	-2.5		
Total	N	541	1,316	1,620	2,936	3,477
	%	15.6%	37.8%	46.6%	84.4%	100.0%

χ^2 = 252.4, df = 10, p = .000; AsR cut-off at p =.01 for 12 cells = ± 3.34 (at p = .05, ± 2.87)

Table 9.17 Cumulative Effects of Personal Therapy by Levels of Personal Self-Expression

Ardent/ Expressive		'Value to you as a person'			At least 1 'excellent' outcome	Total
		No excellent outcome	1 excellent outcome	2+ excellent outcomes		
Ardent	n	337	1,237	1,268		2,842
	%	*11.9%*	43.5%	**44.6%**	88.1%	100.0%
	AsR	-6.0	-2.8	7.3		
Commu-nicative	n	525	1,519	1,335		3,379
	%	15.5%	45.0%	39.5%	84.5%	100.0%
	AsR	.9	-1.0	.4		
Reserved	n	295	781	484		1,560
	%	**18.9%**	**50.1%**	*31.0%*	81.1%	100.0%
	AsR	4.7	3.9	-7.4		
Taciturn	n	50	105	50		205
	%	**24.4%**	51.2%	*24.4%*	75.6%	100.0%
	AsR	3.8	1.6	-4.4		
Total	N	1,207	3,642	3,137	6,779	7,986
	%	15.1%	45.6%	39.3%	84.9%	100.0%

χ^2 = 117.4, df = 6, p = .000; AsR cut-off at p =.01 for 12 cells = ± 3.34 (at p = .05, ± 2.87)

Table 9.18 Cumulative Effects of Personal Therapy by Levels of Genial/Caring Self

Genial/ Caring		'Value to you as a person'				Total
		No perso-nal therapy	0 excellent outcome	1 excellent outcome	2+ excellent outcomes	
Devoted	n	649	361	1,118	1,085	3,213
	%	20.2%	11.2%	34.8%	**33.8%**	100.0%
	AsR	-1.3	-1.5	-1.8	4.1	
Affec-tionate	n	723	441	1,358	1,173	3,695
	%	19.6%	11.9%	36.8%	31.7%	100.0%
	AsR	-2.6	.0	1.1	1.2	
Sympa-thetic	n	748	403	1,170	877	3,198
	%	**23.4%**	12.6%	36.6%	*27.4%*	100.0%
	AsR	4.1	1.4	.7	-5.3	
Total	N	,120	1,205	3,646	3,135	10,106
	%	21.0%	11.9%	36.1%	31.0%	100.0%

χ^2 = 39.8, df = 6, p = .000; AsR cut-off at p =.01 for 12 cells = ± 3.34 (at p = .05, ± 2.87)

Table 9.19 Cumulative Effects of Personal Therapy by Childhood Experience Pattern

Childhood Experience Pattern		'Value to you as a person'			At least 1 'excellent' outcome	Total
		No excellent outcome	1 excellent outcome	2+ excellent outcomes		
Neglected	n	75	192	210		477
	%	15.7%	40.3%	44.0%	84.3%	100.0%
	AsR	.5	.0	-.4		
Wounded	n	42	146	251		439
	%	*9.6%*	*(33.3%)*	**57.2%**	90.4%	100.0%
	AsR	-3.4	-3.2	5.6		
Survived	n	51	187	221		459
	%	11.1%	40.7%	48.1%	88.9%	100.0%
	AsR	-2.5	.3	1.5		
Rescued	n	27	84	91		202
	%	13.4%	41.6%	45.0%	86.6%	100.0%
	AsR	-.7	.4	.1		
Nurtured	n	285	681	668		1,634
	%	**17.4%**	41.7%	*40.9%*	82.6%	100.0%
	AsR	4.0	1.8	-4.6		477
Total	N	480	1,290	1,441	2,731	3,211
	%	14.9%	40.2%	44.9%	85.1%	100.0%

χ^2 = 48.4, df = 8, p = .000; AsR cut-off at *p* =.01 for 15 cells = ± 3.40 (at *p* = .05, ± 2.94)

Table 9.20 Mean Levels of Personal Life Satisfactions by Cumulative Therapy Outcome

Cumulative Outcome		Personal Life Satisfactions			
Younger Therapists	n	1	2		$F = 7.1\ P = .001$ $df = 2,\ 1402$
No excellent outcome	274	3.46			
1 excellent outcome	785		3.66		
2+ excellent outcomes	346		3.68		
Midlife Therapists	n	1	2	3	$F = 18.1$ $P = .000$
No excellent outcome	694	3.52			$df = 2,$ 4774
1 excellent outcome	2,204		3.65		
2+ excellent outcomes	1,879			3.72	
Older Therapists	n	1	2		$F = 8.9\ P = .000$ $df = 2,\ 1857$
No excellent outcome	243	3.61			
1 excellent outcome	737		3.78		
2+ excellent outcomes	880		3.84		

Scheffe test ($p = .01$ criterion): Scale 0–5, Means for homogenous subsets are displayed

Table 9.21 Percentages of Personal Life Satisfactions by Cumulative Therapy Outcome

Personal Life Satisfactions		'Value to you as a person'			Total
		No excellent outcome	1 excellent outcome	2+ excellent outcomes	
High (4–5)	n	760	2,549	2,246	5,555
	%	*61.5%*	67.6%	**71.2%**	68.1%
	AsR	-5.4	-.9	4.8	
Moderate (3)	n	354	955	744	2,053
	%	**(28.7%)**	25.3%	23.6%	25.2%
	AsR	3.1	.3	-2.6	
Less than moderate (< 3)	n	121	267	163	551
	%	**9.8%**	7.1%	*5.2%*	6.8%
	AsR	4.6	1.1	-4.5	
Total	N	1,235	3,771	3,153	8,159
	%	100.0%	100.0%	100.0%	100.0%

$\chi^2 = 50.9$, df = 4, p = .000; AsR cut-off at $p = .01$ for 9 cells = ± 3.26 (at $p = .05$, ± 2.77)

Table 10.1 Therapist Work Experience Dimensions: Basic Statistics

	Healing Involvement[1]	Stressful Involvement[1]
Standardized α =	.71	.82
N =	10,654	10,713
M =	7.50	3.85
Med =	7.56	3.75
SD =	1.15	1.59
Range =	2.16 – 10.56	0.14 – 11.06

[1] The number before each Level-2 dimension is the rotated loading in the Level-1 factor analysis through which they were empirically determined.

Table 10.2 Baseline Predictors of Healing Involvement

R = .460 Adjusted R² =.209 N = 9,442	Beta	% Predicted Variance	% Total Variance
Professional Characteristics			
Practice Duration (years)	.154	18.2	3.8
Professional Training Background	.157	18.9	4.0
Number of Salient Orientations	.155	20.1	4.2
Cognitive-Behavioral	.108	7.9	1.7
Humanistic	.089	8.1	1.7
Systemic	.081	7.0	1.5
Personal Characteristics			
Age (years)	.124	13.6	2.8
Gender	.103	6.2	1.3

Table 10.3 Levels of Healing Involvement by Career Level, Professional Background, Theoretical Orientation, Age and Gender

		HEALING INVOLVEMENT					
Career Level Cohort	n	1	2	3	4	$F = 231.2$	$P = .000$
Apprentice	1,394	6.92				$df = 3, 10288$	
Graduate	3,687		7.41				
Established	3,198			7.69			
Senior	2,013				7.83		
Professional Discipline		1	2				
Psychiatry	2,007	6.88				$F = 200.4$	$P = .000$
Psychology	4,910		7.60			$df = 4, 10217$	
Social Work	649		7.60				
Lay therapist/ analyst	634		7.73				
Counseling	2,022		7.74				
Orientation (N>500)		1	2	3	4		
No Salient Orientation	703	6.53				$F = 211.1$	$P = .000$
Analytic/ Dynamic	2,418		7.22			$df = 5, 7191$	
Cognitive– Behavioral	806			7.51			
Analytic/ Dynamic +Humanistic	603			7.53			
Humanistic	833			7.58			
Broad Spectrum	1,834				7.99		
Age Group x Gender		1	2	3	4		
Younger Men	777	6.65				$F = 162.8$	$P = .000$
Younger Women	1,546		7.28			$df = 5, 10426$	
Midlife Men	2,254		7.36				
Midlife Women	3,763			7.65			
Older Men	777			7.73	7.73		
Older Women	1,315				7.89		

Scheffe test (p = .01 criterion): Scale 0–15, Means for homogenous subsets are displayed.

Table 10.4 Baseline Predictors of Stressful Involvement

R = .265 Adjusted R^2 =.070 N = 9,654	Beta	% Predicted Variance	% Total Variance
Professional Characteristics			
Practice Duration (years)	-.058	11.7	0.8
Professional Training Background	.084	18.0	1.3
Number of Salient Orientations	-.054	4.7	0.3
Analytic/Psychodynamic Orientation	.109	17.0	1.2
Personal Characteristics			
Age (years)	-.156	43.9	3.1
Gender	.050	4.7	0.3

Table 10.5 Levels of Stressful Involvement by Career Level, Profession, Orientation, and Age/Gender[1]

		Stressful Involvement				
Career Level **Cohort**	n	1	2	3	$F = 83.5$	$P = .000$
Apprentice	1,390	4.36			$df = 3, 10331$	
Graduate	3,671		3.91			
Established	3,250			3.70		
Senior	2,024			3.57		
Profession		1	2	3		
Psychiatry	2,035	4.26			$F = 60.3$	$P = .000$
Social Work	662		4.01		$df = 4, 10273$	
Psychology	4,989		3.81			
Lay therapist/ analyst	660			3.57		
Counseling	1,932			3.55		
Theoretical **Orientation** (N>500)		1	2	3		
No Salient Orientation	716	4.20			$F = 20.2$	$P = .000$
Analytic/ Dynamic +Hum.	612	4.10			$df = 5, 7244$	
Analytic/ Dynamic	2,464	4.01	4.01			
Cognitive- Behavioral	805		3.76	3.76		
Broad Spectrum	1,800			3.69		
Humanistic	853			3.66		
Age Group x **Gender**		1	2	3	4	
Younger Men	789	4.38				$F = 88.1$ $P = .000$
Younger Women	1,528	4.27				$df = 5, 10484$
Midlife Men	2,268		4.00			
Midlife Women	3,779			3.75		
Older Men	771			3.57		
Older Women	1,355				3.28	

[1] Scheffe Test (P = .01 Criterion): Scale 0–15, Means for Homogenous Subsets Are Displayed.

Table 10.6 Personal Self as Predictors of Healing and Stressful Involvement

HEALING INVOLVEMENT

$R = .616$ Adjusted $R^2 = .377$ $N = 9,418$	Beta	% Predicted Variance	% Total Variance
Professional Characteristics			
Practice Duration (years)	.123	8.0	3.0
Professional Training Background	.120	7.6	2.9
Theoretical Breadth (number salient orientations)	.153	10.8	4.1
Personal Characteristics			
Age (years)	.103	6.3	2.4
Self: Genial/Caring	.361	46.2	17.4
Self: Ardent/Expressive	.211	21.1	8.0

STRESSFUL INVOLVEMENT

$R = .374$ Adjusted $R^2 = .137$ $N = 9,541$	Beta	% Predicted Variance	% Total Variance
Professional Characteristics			
Practice Duration (years)	-.063	6.1	.08
Professional Training Background	.074	7.3	1.0
Analytic/Psychodynamic orientation	.091	7.3	1.0
Personal Characteristics			
Age (years)	-.116	16.0	2.2
Self: Genial/Caring	-.108	13.8	1.9
Self: Forceful/Exacting	.083	8.7	12
Self: Reclusive/Remote	.211	40.8	5.6

Table 10.7 Main Personal Self Predictors and Work Practice Patterns

Genial/Caring[1]		Work Involvement Practice Patterns				
		Effective Practice	Challenging Practice	Disengaged Practice	Distressing Practice	Total
	n	2,238	756	169	120	3,283
Devoted (high)	%	**68.2%**	23.0%	*5.1%*	*3.7%*	100.0%
	AsR	22.7	.4	-18.4	-16.1	
Affectionate (medium)	n	1,999	920	514	338	3,771
	%	53.0%	**(24.4%)**	13.6%	*9.0%*	100.0%
	AsR	1.8	3.0	-1.9	-4.7	
Sympathetic (low)	n	1,092	666	806	660	3,224
	%	*33.9%*	*20.7%*	**25.0%**	**20.5%**	100.0%
	AsR	-24.7	-3.5	20.5	21.1	
Total	N	5,329	2,342	1,489	1,118	10,278
	%	51.8%	22.8%	14.5%	10.9%	100.0%
Reclusive/Remote[2]						
Wary (high)	n	924	750	288	421	2,383
	%	*38.8%*	**31.5%**	*12.1%*	**17.7%**	100.0%
	AsR	-14.6	11.5	-3.7	12.1	
Circumspect (medium)	n	2,378	1,109	743	540	4,770
	%	*49.9%*	23.2%	**15.6%**	11.3%	100.0%
	AsR	-3.8	1.0	3.1	1.3	
Approachable (low)	n	2,021	483	451	157	3,112
	%	**64.9%**	*15.5%*	14.5%	*5.0%*	100.0%
	AsR	17.5	-11.6	.1	-12.5	
Total	N	5,323	2,342	1,482	1,118	10,265
	%	51.9%	22.8%	14.4%	10.9%	100.0%

[1] $\chi^2 = 1269.9$, df = 6, p = .000; AsR cut-off at $p = .01$ for 12 cells = ± 3.34 (at $p = .05$, ± 2.87)
[2] $\chi^2 = 548.7$, df = 6, p = .000; AsR cut-off at $p = .01$ for 12 cells = ± 3.34 (at $p = .05$, ± 2.87)

Table 10.8 Attachment Dimensions as Predictors of Stressful Involvement

Stressful Involvement			
R = .501 Adjusted R^2 = .235 N = 1,149	Beta	% Predicted Variance	% Total Variance
Professional Characteristics			
Profession (Training Discipline)	.146	11.2	2.6
Personal Characteristics			
Self: Genial/Caring	-.128	13.0	3.1
Self: Forceful/Exacting	.126	8.8	2.1
Self: Reclusive/Remote	.182	22.3	5.2
Attachment: Anxious	.194	25.2	5.9
Attachment: Avoidant	.145	19.6	4.6

Table 10.9 Attachment Dimensions and Work Practice Patterns

Anxious Attachment[1]		Work Involvement Practice Patterns				
		Effective Practice	*Challenging Practice*	*Disengaged Practice*	*Distressing Practice*	*Total*
moderate to high	n	205	57	85	41	388
	%	*52.8%*	**14.7%**	21.9%	**10.6%**	100.0%
	AsR	-6.0	5.7	-.3	5.3	
low	n	580	42	175	26	823
	%	**70.5%**	*5.1%*	21.3%	*3.2%*	100.0%
	AsR	6.0	-5.7	-.3	-5.3	
Total	N	785	99	260	67	1,211
	%	64.8%	8.2%	21.5%	5.5%	100.0%

Avoidant Attachment[2]		Work Involvement Practice Patterns				
		Effective Practice	*Challenging Practice*	*Disengaged Practice*	*Distressing Practice*	*Total*
moderate to high	n	135	40	28	11	269
	%	*50.2%*	**14.9%**	24.5%	**10.4%**	100.0%
	AsR	-5.6	4.5	1.4	3.9	
low	n	657	61	198	41	957
	%	**68.7%**	*6.4%*	20.7%	*4.3%*	100.0%
	AsR	5.6	-4.5	-1.4	-3.9	
Total	N	792	101	264	69	1,226
	%	64.6%	8.2%	21.5%	5.6%	100.0%

[1] χ^2 = 68.5, df = 3, p = .000; AsR cut-off at p =.01 for 8 cells = ± 3.23 (at p =.05, ± 2.73)
[2] χ^2 = 44.9, df = 3, p = .000; AsR cut-off at p =.01 for 8 cells = ± 3.23 (at p =.05, ± 2.73)

Table 10.10 Belief-Value Patterns and Work Practice Patterns

Belief-Value Patterns		Work Involvement Practice Patterns				
		Effective Practice	Challenging Practice	Disengaged Practice	Distressing Practice	Total
Ethical Secular	n	979	307	246	129	1,661
	%	58.9%	18.5%	14.8%	7.8%	100.0%
	AsR	-4.9	-.4	3.8	5.6	
Spiritual Secular	n	808	219	104	34	1,165
	%	69.4%	18.8%	8.9%	2.9%	100.0%
	AsR	4.9	.0	-4.2	-4.3	
Spiritual Religious	n	794	231	137	46	1,208
	%	65.7%	19.1%	11.3%	3.8%	100.0%
	AsR	1.9	.3	-1.3	-2.8	
Ceremonial Religious	n	140	49	44	21	254
	%	55.1%	19.3%	17.3%	8.3%	100.0%
	AsR	-2.8	.2	2.5	2.1	
Total	N	2,721	806	531	230	4,288
	%	63.5%	18.8%	12.4%	5.4%	100.0%

χ^2 = 81.2, df = 9, p = .000; AsR at p =.01 for 16 cells, cut-off = ± 3.42 (p =.05, ± 2.96)

Table 10.11 Quality of Life as Predictors of Healing and Stressful Involvement

HEALING INVOLVEMENT $R = .629$ Adjusted $R^2 = .394$ $N = 9,392$	Beta	% Predicted Variance	% Total Variance
Professional Characteristics			
Practice Duration (years)	.102	5.9	2.3
Profession (Training Discipline)	.117	7.1	2.8
Theoretical Breadth (number of salient)	.148	10.0	3.9
Personal Characteristics			
Age (years)	.098	5.8	2.3
Self: Genial/Caring	.309	37.9	14.9
Self: Ardent/Expressive	.190	18.2	7.2
Life Quality: Personal Life Satisfaction	.158	15.0	5.9
STRESSFUL INVOLVEMENT $R = .443$ Adjusted $R^2 = .194$ $N = 9,801$	Beta	% Predicted Variance	% Total Variance
Professional Characteristics			
Profession (Training Discipline)	.091	6.9	13
Personal Characteristics			
Age (years)	-.119	12.0	23
Self: Genial/Caring	-.104	9.7	1.9
Self: Reclusive/Remote	.196	27.3	53
Life Quality: Personal Life Burdens	.272	44.1	8.6

Table 10.12 Quality of Life as Predictors of Stressful Involvement

$R = .524$ Adjusted $R^2 = .255$ $N = 1,149$	Beta	% Predicted Variance	% Total Variance
Professional Characteristics			
Profession (Training Discipline)	.149	10.5	2.7
Personal Characteristics			
Self: Genial/Caring	-.123	11.5	2.9
Self: Forceful/Exacting	.107	6.4	1.6
Self: Reclusive/Remote	.166	18.6	4.7
Attachment: Anxious	.149	17.6	4.5
Attachment: Avoidant	.140	17.4	4.4
Life Quality: Personal Life Burdens	.167	18.0	4.6

Table 10.13 Life Quality Patterns and Work Practice Patterns

Quality of Life Patterns		Work Involvement Practice Patterns				
		Effective Practice	*Challenging Practice*	*Disengaged Practice*	*Distressing Practice*	*Total*
Fulfilling	n	2,052	551	512	212	3,327
	%	**61.7%**	*16.6%*	15.4%	*6.4%*	100.0%
	AsR	14.0	-11.0	2.2	-10.1	
Satisfactory	n	1,228	539	238	151	2,156
	%	**57.0%**	25.0%	*11.0%*	*7.0%*	100.0%
	AsR	5.5	2.3	-4.8	-6.5	
Hectic	n	696	443	99	113	1,351
	%	51.5%	**32.8%**	*7.3%*	*(8.4%)*	100.0%
	AsR	-.1	9.0	-7.8	-3.2	
Dull	n	361	161	236	177	935
	%	*38.6%*	*17.2%*	**25.2%**	**18.9%**	100.0%
	AsR	-8.4	-4.5	10.1	8.3	
Strained	n	420	259	198	214	1,091
	%	*38.5%*	23.7%	**18.1%**	**19.6%**	100.0%
	AsR	-9.2	.5	3.9	9.8	
Distressed	n	495	401	167	236	1,299
	%	*38.1%*	**30.9%**	12.9%	**18.2%**	100.0%
	AsR	-10.5	7.0	-1.6	9.1	
Total	N	5,252	2,354	1,450	1,103	10,159
	%	100.0%	100.0%	100.0%	100.0%	100.0%

$\chi^2 = 809.7$, df = 15, p = .000; AsR cut-off at $p = .01$ for 24 cells = ± 3.53 (at $p = .05$, ± 3.08)

Table 10.14 Healing Involvement and Stressful Involvement by Childhood Experience Pattern

Healing Involvement	n	1	2	3	
Neglected	541	7.48			F = 21.46 P =.000
Survived	518	7.57			df = 4, 3841
Nurtured	2,100	7.65	7.65		
Wounded	453		7.90	7.90	
Rescued	234			8.14	
Stressful Involvement		1			
Rescued	237	3.47			F = 3.67 P =.005 df = 4, 3942
Neglected	553	3.49			
Wounded	466	3.51			
Nurtured	2,156	3.59			
Survived	535	3.79			

Scheffe test (p = .01 criterion): Scale 0–15, Means for homogenous subsets are displayed.

Table 10.15 Childhood Experience Patterns and Work Practice Patterns

Childhood Experience Patterns		Work Involvement Practice Patterns				
		Effective Practice	*Challenging Practice*	*Disengaged Practice*	*Distressing Practice*	*Total*
Nurtured	*n*	1,293	395	287	150	2,125
	%	60.8%	18.6%	13.5%	7.1%	100.0%
	AsR	-.3	-.2	.2	.6	
Survived	n	292	108	71	54	525
	%	55.6%	20.6%	13.5%	(10.3%)	100.0%
	AsR	-2.7	1.2	.1	3.4	
Neglected	n	326	82	95	42	545
	%	59.8%	15.0%	(17.4%)	7.7%	100.0%
	AsR	-.6	-2.4	3.0	.9	
Wounded	n	303	91	50	17	461
	%	65.7%	19.7%	10.8%	3.7%	100.0%
	AsR	2.2	.6	-1.7	-2.9	
Rescued	*n*	160	52	18	3	233
	%	68.7%	22.3%	7.7%	*1.3%*	100.0%
	AsR	2.5	1.5	-2.6	-3.5	
Total	N	2,374	728	521	266	3,889
	%	61.0%	18.7%	13.4%	6.8%	100.0%

χ^2 = 54.9, df = 12, p = .000; AsR cut-off at *p* =.01 for 20 cells = ± .3.48 (at *p* =.05, ± 3.02)

Table 10.16 Healing Involvement by Personal Therapy Utilization and Outcome

Utilization[1]	n	1	2	3	4	
No personal therapy	2,036	7.20				$F = 105.9$ $P = .000$
1 personal therapy	2,822		7.44			$df = 3, 10077$
2 personal therapy	2,687			7.62		
3 or 4 personal therapy	2,536				7.76	
Outcome (if therapy)[1]	n	1	2	3		
No excellent outcome	1,170	7.38				$F = 57.7$ $P =.000$
1 excellent outcome	3516		7.54			$df = 2, 7737$
2+ excellent outcomes	3,054			7.75		

[1] Scheffe test (p = .01 criterion): Scale 0–15, Means for homogenous subsets are displayed.

Table 10.17 Stressful Involvement by Personal Therapy Utilization and Outcome

Utilization[1]	n	1	2	
No personal therapy	1,997	4.04		F 13.26 $P =.000$
1 personal therapy	2,810		3.89	$df = 3, 10086$
2 personal therapy	2,702		3.79	
3 or 4 personal therapy	2,581		3.78	
Outcome (if therapy)[2]		1	2	
No excellent outcome	1,168	3.90		$F = 6.57$ $P = .001$
1 excellent outcome	3,522	3.87		$df = 2, 7751$
2+ excellent outcomes	3,064		3.75	

[1] Scheffe test (p = .01 criterion): Scale 0–15, Means for homogenous subsets are displayed.
[2] Scheffe test (p = .05 criterion): Scale 0–15, Means for homogenous subsets are displayed.

Table 10.18 Work Practice Patterns by Personal Therapy Outcome

Personal Therapy Occurrence		Work Involvement Practice Patterns				
		Effective Practice	*Challenging Practice*	*Disengaged Practice*	*Distressing Practice*	*Total*
2+ excellent outcomes	*n*	1,750	718	340	213	3,021
	%	**57.9%**	23.8%	_11.3%_	_7.1%_	100.0%
	AsR	7.7	.8	–5.0	–7.9	
1 excellent outcome	*n*	1,810	843	471	337	3,461
	%	52.3%	24.4%	13.6%	9.7%	100.0%
	AsR	.3	1.9	–.6	–2.4	
No excellent outcome	n	561	268	186	141	1,156
	%	48.5%	23.2%	16.1%	12.2%	100.0%
	AsR	–2.6	–.1	2.3	1.7	
No personal therapy	n	867	399	331	336	1,933
	%	_44.9%_	(_20.6%_)	**17.1%**	**17.4%**	100.0%
	AsR	–7.2	–3.1	4.6	10.6	
Total	N	4,988	2,228	1,328	1,027	9,571
	%	52.1%	23.3%	13.9%	10.7%	100.0%

χ^2 = 207.1, df = 9, p = .000; AsR cut-off at p =.01 for 16 cells = ± .3.42 (at p =.05, ± 2.96)

Table 10.19 Contextual Predictors of Therapeutic Work Involvement

HEALING INVOLVEMENT

$R = .694$ Adjusted $R^2 = .479$ $N = 7,586$	Beta	% Predicted Variance	% Total Variance
Professional Characteristics			
Professional Discipline	.097	5.6	2.7
Breadth/Depth of Treatment Cases x Modalities	.142	9.1	4.4
Theoretical Breadth (number of salient)	.111	6.8	3.3
Practice Setting			
Support in Main Treatment Setting	.088	5.9	2.8
Autonomy in Control of Treatment Parameters	.076	4.5	2.2
Work Morale: Currently Experienced Growth	.195	15.0	7.2
Personal Characteristics			
Therapist Age	.123	6.9	3.3
Self: Genial/Caring in	.269	27.7	13.3
Self: Ardent/Expressive	.142	11.0	5.3
Life Quality: Personal Life Satisfaction	.094	7.6	3.6
STRESSFUL INVOLVEMENT			
$R = .577$ Adjusted $R^2 = .331$ $N = 9,036$			
Practice Setting			
Autonomy in Control of Treatment Parameters	-.104	6.9	2.3
Healing Involvement	-.100	6.6	2.2
Work Morale: Currently Experienced Depletion	.369	52.5	17.4
Personal Characteristics			
Self: Reclusive/Remote	.153	12.1	4.0
Life Quality: Personal Life Burdens	.223	21.8	7.2

Analytical Table of Contents

Author Index

Subject Index

experience patterns 130, **302**; marital and parental status by age 63, **258**; personal life quality and 92–93, **281**; personal self 64, **259**; private life by gender 63, **257**; work practice experience 178–179, **333**

"Baby Boom" generation 119; childhood experience patterns by 116, **293–294**; family functioning by 112, **292**; family size by 102, **284**
belief-value orientation 70, 71; adult attachment 77, **268**; childhood experience patterns 133, **305**; cumulative effects of personal therapy 160, **322**; current affiliations 72–73, **262–263**; family religious background 132, **303**; life quality patterns by 90–91, **280**; personal demographics 76, **266**; personal self 77, **268, 269**; private life 76–77, **266**; professional discipline 77–78, **269**; religious affiliation 71–73; religious backgrounds 71–72, **261**; theoretical approach 78, **270**; therapists' characteristics 76–78; work practice experience and 179–180, **334**; *see also* Ceremonial Religious orientation; Ethical Secular orientation; Spiritual Religious orientation; Spiritual Secular orientation
birth order 100; and family size 101, 128, **283**; and parental status 128, **299**; among therapists 100, *101*
British studies: patient outcomes 210–211; therapist burnout 211
Broad-Spectrum orientation: ages in years 24, **224**; cumulative effects of personal therapy 160, **321**; first-listed personal therapy 158, **319**; genders 24, **224**; personal belief patterns 78, **270**; personal life quality 93–94, **282**; personal self correlates of **239**; personal therapy 152, **310**; professions 17–18, **221**
Buddhism: belief-value orientation by 71–72, **261–263**; change in identities 73–74, **264**

career levels 18–19; Healing Involvement by 174, **327**; personal therapy by 149, **309**; Stressful Involvement by 176, **330**
Ceremonial Religious orientation 70; childhood experience patterns 133, **305**; childhood family functioning 132,

304; cumulative effects of personal therapy 160, **322**; current religious affiliation 72–73, **262–263**; family religious background 132, **303**; gender and age 76, **266**; life quality patterns 90–91, **280**; marital and parental status 76, **267**; personal self 77, **269**; professional background 77–78, **269**; religious background 71–72, **261**; therapeutic approach 78, **270**; work practice patterns 179–180, **334**
Challenging Practice 171; attachment dimensions 179, **333**; belief-value patterns 179–180, **334**; childhood experience patterns 182, **338**; life quality patterns 181, **336**; personal self predictors 178, **332**; personal therapy outcome 183, **340**
childhood experience patterns: Neglected, Nurtured, Rescued, Survived, Wounded 115–118, *115*; age at parental divorce/separation **295**; cumulative effects of personal therapy 161, **324**; gender **293–294**; generation **293**; Healing Involvement and Stressful Involvement 182, **337**; individual beliefs 133, **304–305**; personal self 127, **298**; personal therapy 156, 161, **316–317**; private life 130, **302**; professional characteristics 138, **308**; quality of care by trauma or abuse **293**; quality of life 135, **306**; work practice patterns 182, **338**
childhood experiences: care and trauma 113–115, **293**; family economic background 117–118, **296**; family structure and family disruption 116; gender and generation 116, **293–294**; religious background and religiosity 118; variations in 116–118
childhood family background: influences on adult life 138, *139*; personal therapy 161
childhood family experience: personal therapy 156–157, **315**; work practice experience 181–182
childhood family functioning 109–111; age at time of loss 111, **290**; economic background 112–113, **292**; family disruptions 111; family structure 111; gender, age and generation 111–112, **291–292**; marital status 130, **301**; professional identity 137, **308**; religious background 113
childhood influence, sources of *139*, 145

354   *Subject Index*

Cognitive-Behavioral orientation: ages in years by 24, **224**; childhood experience pattern 138, **308**; cumulative effects of personal therapy 160, **321**; first-listed personal therapy 158, **319**; genders 24, **224**; personal belief patterns 78, **270**; personal life quality 93–94, **282**; personal self correlates of **239**; personal therapy 152, **310**; professions 17–18, **221**

Cognitive-Behavioral Theory (CBT) 209; childhood experience patterns 138; German study 213; Swedish study 212

Collaborative Research Network (CRN): database 214; Society for Psychotherapy Research 5, 216; *see* SPR Collaborative Research Network

coping strategies: dimensions of 208–209; Healing Involvement 194; Stressful Involvement 195–197

counseling profession: ages in years by **223**; gender **222–223**; generation **222**; marital status 59–60, **244–246**; parental status 60, **247–248**; personal belief patterns 77–78, **269**; personal life quality 93, **281**; personal therapy 153, **312**; psychotherapeutic profession 14, *15*; theoretical orientation 17–18, **221**

cultural marginality: secularity vs. religious affiliation **226**; social demographics 27

cumulative outcome, of personal therapy 159–162; age and gender 159, **320**; childhood experience 161, **324**; childhood family 161; individual beliefs 160, **322**; personal self 160–161, **323**; private life 161; profession and orientation 160, **321**

Currently Experienced Growth 189, 207

depression, outcome measures of 210–211

Development of Psychotherapists Common Core Questionnaire (DPCCQ) 5–6; application of 211; British study 210–211; Finland study 204–205, 207–208; German study 205–206, 209–210, 213–214; Norwegian study 203–204, 208–209; observational perspectives and levels of analysis 214–216; personal self 34; private life 55; psychotherapeutic practice, experiences of 168–169; research instrument 2, 5–6; Swedish study 212

Disengaged Practice 171; attachment dimensions 179, **333**; belief-value patterns 179–180, **334**; childhood experience patterns 182, **338**; life quality patterns 181, **336**; personal self predictors 178, **332**; personal therapy outcome 183, **340**

Distressing Practice 171; attachment dimensions 179, **333**; belief-value patterns 179–180, **334**; childhood experience patterns 182, **338**; life quality patterns 181, **336**; personal self predictors 178, **332**; personal therapy outcome 183, **340**

Development of Psychotherapists Common Core Questionnaire (DPCCQ as data source: analysis 6–7; collection 6; observational perspective 201–202, 215–216

economic status 104–105, *105*; childhood family functioning 112–113, **292**; and family situation 105–106, **286**; gender, age and generation 106; religion and 109; variations in childhood experience 117–118, **296**

Effective Practice 171; attachment dimensions 179, **333**; belief-value patterns 179–180, **334**; childhood experience patterns 182, **338**; life quality patterns 181, **336**; personal self predictors 178, **332**; personal therapy outcome 183, **340**

Ethical Secular orientation 70; childhood experience patterns 133, **305**; childhood family functioning 132, **304**; cumulative effects of personal therapy 160, **322**; current religious affiliation 72–73, **262–263**; family religious background 132, **303**; gender and age 76, **266**; life quality patterns 90–91, **280**; marital and parental status 76, **267**; personal self 77, **269**; professional background 77–78, **269**; religious background 71–72, **261**; therapeutic approach 78, **270**; work practice patterns 179–180, **334**

experienced/seasoned therapists 18

Experiences in Close Relationship Scale (ECRS) 62

family background: childhood experiences 113–118; childhood family functioning 109–113; economic 104–106; family